# THEMATIC TEST ANALYSIS

# THEMATIC TEST ANALYSIS

EDWIN S. SHNEIDMAN, Ph.D.

*Clinical Psychologist, Veterans Administration Neuropsychiatric Hospital, Los Angeles, California; Lecturer, University of Southern California*

With the Collaboration of

WALTHER JOEL, Ph.D.

*Assistant Chief Clinical Psychologist (Psychotherapy), V.A. Neuropsychiatric Hospital, Los Angeles, California; Lecturer, University of Southern California;* and

KENNETH B. LITTLE, Ph.D.

*Clinical Psychologist, V.A. Hospital, San Francisco, California; Research Associate, University of Southern California*

Foreword by

HENRY A. MURRAY, M.D.

Routledge
Taylor & Francis Group
New York London

Reviewed in the Veterans Administration and published with the approval of the Chief Medical Director. The statements and conclusions published by the authors are the result of their own study and do not necessarily reflect the opinion or policy of the Veterans Administration.


GRUNE & STRATTON, INC.
381 Fourth Avenue
New York City 16
First Printing, November 1951
Second Printing, April 1964

This edition by Routledge:

Routledge
Taylor and Francis Group
270 Madison Avenue
New York, NY 10016

Routledge
Taylor and Francis Group
2 Park Square, Milton Park
Abingdon, Oxon OX14 4RN

To

"JOHN DOE"

# CONTENTS

## PART V. SYNTHESIS AND SUMMARY

# Foreword

SURELY this book is an original, something unique in scientific literature, satisfying, in part, to curiosities which up to now psychologists have put aside as vain. Who believed that experts would be willing to make spectacles of their minds for the benefit of their fellows? More particularly, who anticipated that they would let their rivals watch them wend their way through the labyrinth of two projective protocols, groping for broken threads to lead them to a lucid formulation? Who but Dr. Shneidman and his collaborators?

Scientists are by conscience cautious, not disposed to speculate in public, more fearful of embracing error than of overlooking a new truth. Furthermore, experience has shown that *blind* analyses of stories from the MAPS test and the TAT are often no better than an astrologist's reading, and today most workers are agreed that interpreting in the dark is an extra-rational activity which should not, ordinarily, be attempted. Thus, the experts who declined the challenge offered them by Dr. Shneidman were in accord with cultural expectations; whereas those who unreservedly accepted it were deviants for the sake of experimental science.

The outcome of this exciting enterprise was statistically unreasonable. Those who laughed at probabilities and stretched inference to the limit succeeded in seizing the fruits of truth, which in this case were in the topmost branches of the protocols. In contrast, those who were more obedient, say, to their scientific superegos were uncriticizably less triumphant. They did not reach the best fruit of this tree of knowledge and so their eyes were not fully opened and they were not as gods.

Since the editors' own conclusions are not presented in this volume, but have been withheld for a sequel which is still in the making, the opinion I have just submitted has the status of a general impression and no more. If it is improperly premature or even presumptuous, I blame this very book, the lesson of which is boldness.

The fact, if it is a fact, that those who gave their intuitions freest play came closer to the mark can hardly be hailed as a prophetic sign. For some of the psychologists who in this experiment held most conscientiously to the ruts of a particular conceptual scheme may be contributing most, now and later, to the development of an instrument which will someday be unanimously accepted as the one which yields the highest percentage of valid diagnoses. Thus, in all likelihood, the more methodical tortoises will as usual be the first to arrive at the scientific goal—a reliable system instead of unreliable flashes of the imagination.

For those who have been wrestling with the giant problem of devising a comprehensive system for the interpretation of imaginal productions, this book is a cornucopia of riches. Although there was not sufficient space for a complete exposition of any one of the several modes of analysis, every contributor has thrown something different and necessary into the cauldron, and before long—as a consequence of this large collective effort—someone should present us with a brew which combines the indispensable ingredients of each of the sixteen schemes. The comparison, in this book, of their distinctive features is very helpful.

As for the relative merits of the two projective methods, the MAPS test seems to have revealed more unambiguous indications of schizophrenia than did the TAT. It is possible that the full efficiency of the latter was not exhibited, since the pictures were presented incompletely and irregularly and the stories were short of the standard length. But, anyhow, in the hands of these talented specialists, its utility seems to have been sufficiently demonstrated here, and I am prompted to suggest that if the testing period must be limited to two hours, a compound TA-MAPS test might be most efficient. Workers at the Harvard Psychological Clinic have recently noted the same special advantages of the MAPS test to which several of the participants in this experiment have called attention.

In short, Drs. Shneidman, Joel, and Little have given us a timely, even-handed book, unusually well constructed and edited. It is the report of a novel investigation which will interest all clinical psychologists. Teachers should welcome it with special cordiality, for it provides a fine parade of diagnostic intellections which students may oversee, as through a one-way mirror, without embarrassment and with much profit.

HENRY A. MURRAY, M.D., PH.D.

*Harvard Psychological Clinic*
*Cambridge, Massachusetts*
*May, 1951*

# Preface

THIS BOOK is the result of the attempt to work up a single clinical case in terms of all the published methods for thematic test analysis and of the realization that no one can present a system of interpretation better than the person who designed it; thus the several thematic methods, each presented by its own author. The primary purpose has always been to furnish the interested reader with a comprehensive manual showing the various methods of thematic test analysis in operation on the same case.

To me, the outstanding feature of this entire effort has been its cooperative aspect. It is in the spirit of personal humility that I wish to make a number of acknowledgments.

The primary debt—on the part of myself, my collaborators, and the readers —is to the twenty-five contributors. These include the seventeen thematic test contributors, the five supplementary test contributors, and the three clinical data contributors. The listing of their names in the table of contents indicates who they are. It is here that I wish to thank them all again for their graciousness and their cooperation.

While I must take responsiblity for the organization of the over-all project and the final form of its parts, the following specific credits should be given to my collaborators: Dr. Walther Joel wrote the synthesis of TAT and MAPS test comparisons, the synthesis of thematic approaches, and the Resumes which appear in Chapters 4 through 18; Dr. Kenneth B. Little did all the coding and tabulations and wrote the section on quantitative tabulations. Also, both have been extremely generous with their sound advice and constructive suggestions.

Separate thanks are due two of the contributors: Dr. Harry Grayson, who, in his capacity as Chief Clinical Psychologist at the Los Angeles Veterans Administration Neuropsychiatric Hospital, rendered me many kindnesses—I am very grateful, too, to the Veterans Administration generally for its policy of encouraging research activities—and Dr. Robert R. Holt, of the Menninger Foundation, who helped me by making many useful suggestions and by doing several special favors.

Appreciation is expressed to Mr. Herbert C. Goldenberg for his assistance in the preparation of the Index.

I want to make especial acknowledgment to Dr. Henry A. Murray, father of thematic apperception tests, for his generously providing this volume with his extremely valuable reactions, and for his kindness and encouragement, generally.

E.S.S.

*Los Angeles, California*
*June, 1951*

# Chapter 1

# INTRODUCTION

THIS BOOK is about thematic test analysis; that is, it is concerned with the various approaches to the interpretation of picture-thematic projective personality test data.

Picture-thematic tests are those psychological techniques which have "at least two elements: pictorial materials with human figures which are presented to a subject for his response; and the analysis of the content of the responses for thematic meaningfulness" [51].[1] Two such tests are the focus for this book: the Thematic Apperception Test (TAT) and the Make A Picture Story (MAPS) test. The major purpose of this volume is to present a bibliographic round table of several experts' interpretations of the same individual's test data, together with a set of historical and clinical data about this same individual—the latter not known to the test interpreters at the time they made their analyses.

## I. OVER-VIEW

The pattern of this study of the various approaches to the analysis of thematic tests may be described as follows:

Copies of the same TAT protocol (reproduced in Chapter 2) and MAPS test protocol (Chapter 3) for one person, "John Doe,"[2] were distributed to thematic test experts. The criterion for selecting the psychologists and psychiatrists chosen was that they had published a method or technique for interpreting or analyzing the TAT. The only data given to these experts, in addition to the test responses, was the subject's sex (male), his age (25), and his marital status (single).[3] Each potential contributor was requested to analyze the TAT and MAPS test by his own method and to give it the "full treatment." We indicated that we were interested primarily in the techniques and asked

[1] Numbers in brackets refer to references cited in the bibliography at the end of the book.

[2] The case was selected so that the following criteria were met: (a) that there be a number of psychological tests on the subject; (b) that the test materials be sufficiently "rich" to yield interpretations; (c) that there be adequate case history and clinical material about the subject; and (d) that all the material be so sufficiently diverse as to remove the case from any simple or obvious nosological category—and make it the diagnostic and psychodynamic problem which it is.

[3] The MAPS test *Figure Location Sheet* also indicated that John Doe had had 12th grade education.

that each contributor return his working procedures such as work notes, step-by-step notations, work sheets, and tabulations, as well as his final write-up. We also asked each interpreter to indicate the extent to which he believed that his TAT method was applicable to the MAPS test and to make any comparisons between the two tests that he wished.

Fifteen TAT methodologists wrote sixteen interpretations of John Doe's TAT and MAPS test protocols. These contributions were edited and appear as separate chapters in this book (Chapters 4 through 18; Chapter 16 contains two different methods: Helen Sargent's Insight Test scoring method and Beverly Cox's and Helen Sargent's Normative scoring method). These fifteen chapters have been organized so that they consist of the following six sections: (a) selected references for the method under discussion; (b) a resume of the contributor's method of analysis or interpretation; (c) the contributor's "working notes" or working procedures or tabulations or preliminary drafts to his interpretation—the aspects of his *modus operandi* which precede the preparation of the final report and which are usually not presented as part of the report; (d) the contributor's interpretation of John Doe's TAT; (e) the contributor's MAPS test working notes; and (f) the MAPS test interpretation.

The comments of the thematic test contributors relevant to their comparing the TAT and MAPS test were grouped together and organized and appear as a single chapter (Chapter 29).

The TAT interpretations, and the supplementary test interpretations and certain portions of the behavioral data (see below), were all reduced to discrete items of personality descriptions (e.g., the statement, "This individual is depressed, hostile, anxious, and fearful," became four separate items). Approximately 1200 statements resulted from this process. Some syntheses were made from the items of personality description. These resulted in the formulation of generic types of thematic test analysis.[4] It is proposed that all approaches to thematic test interpretation can be discussed in terms of their primary purposes, their essential elements which are analyzed, their working procedures, and their main emphases. These are discussed in Chapter 30.

In addition to the TAT and MAPS test, there were other test protocols available for this same subject. These tests are the Rorschach ink blots, the Wechsler-Bellevue intelligence scale, the Minnesota Multiphasic Personality Inventory, the Draw-A-Person, and the Bender-Gestalt figures. Each of these tests was interpreted by one expert in that particular test. These test protocols and interpretations are presented in Chapters 19 through 23.

We also had—unavailable to the contributors until publication in this

[4] The analysis of the interpretations into discrete items of personality description also served the purpose of providing data for statistical computations. The communication of the results of these statistical procedures is planned for separate publication.

volume—"behavioral data" for John Doe. These consist of some factual material about a real person whose test protocols are herein reproduced. This information consists of five segments: Chapter 24 is the abstract of John Doe's case history prepared by the psychiatrist who was in charge of John Doe's case when he was a patient in a Veterans Administration neuropsychiatric hospital; Chapter 25, "Course in Neuropsychiatric Hospital," consists of verbatim notations of the ward physicians and consulting psychiatrists in relation to diagnosis, treatment, testing and disposition, which had been entered in John Doe's hospital clinical folder; Chapter 26 presents excerpts from psychiatric interviews with John Doe while he was in the hospital, including some dream material; Chapter 27 presents (a) notes made by his psychiatric social worker therapist at the Veterans Administration mental hygiene clinic where John Doe went for out-patient treatment following his discharge from the hospital, and (b) a summary evaluation of John Doe's personality and therapeutic problems made by this same therapist; and Chapter 28 presents a report by the chief psychiatrist at the same mental hygiene clinic of a psychiatric follow-up interview with John Doe conducted approximately two and one-half years after the dates on which he was administered the psychological tests at the neuropsychiatric hospital. It should be indicated that these behavioral data are not presented as validating criteria for the psychological tests, but rather as another set of observations on the same person.

## II. Purposes

The purposes of this volume can now be stated. They are as follows:

1. To bring together, in relation to the same thematic test protocols, many of the published techniques for dealing with thematic tests. Thus the study aims to serve as a comprehensive manual or guide by describing each method of analysis and then presenting the originator's own working procedures and interpretations of the same thematic test materials.

2. To indicate some of the major principles and important dimensions of thematic test interpretation.

3. To permit comparisons among the various thematic test interpretations, between thematic test interpretations and other test interpretations, and between thematic test interpretations and actual case history and psychotherapy data.

4. To demonstrate what areas or topics are mentioned in thematic test reports and to present data which indicate to what extent areas of personality discussed in thematic test interpretations are dependent upon the particular method of analysis or interpretation.

5. To cite the comparisons between the TAT and the MAPS test made

by the thematic test experts and to indicate some of the implications of these comparisons.

6. To present a study in which the emphasis is on the prediction of behavior rather than the validation of a technique; i.e., to hold a "psychological autopsy" on one case.

7. To demonstrate the variety of possible approaches to the analysis of thematic test material and to illustrate the current and challenging nature of the entire area of projective testing and the great need for experimental researches with these promising techniques.

## III. Limitations and Delimitations

There are a number of obvious and important limitations to this study. It is best that these shortcomings of the product be stated at this time so that the reader will not be disappointed by expecting more than he will find, and so that the authors will not be embarrassed by being expected to do more than the situation would permit. These may be set down as follows:

1. The methodologic setting within which the entire study was done constitutes a limitation upon the possible conclusions; i.e., this investigation is a research but not an experiment; it employed systematic observation rather than controlled observation; it focused attention on certain variables of thematic test analysis, but it did not freeze or manipulate these variables as one does in a controlled experiment.

2. The entire research revolves around one case (John Doe). How any of the methods or procedures of test interpretation cited in relation to John Doe would have worked with other types of cases which might have been selected is not known. It may be that whatever conclusions are justified from the study of John Doe will have to be in terms of this one case. Another limitation within this sphere is the fact that there was no systematic inquiry into the reliabilities of the various scoring schemes. (Actually, we feel that the conclusions do have somewhat more general implications than those limited to this one case).

3. There are methodologic limitations to this research in terms of the relationships among the variables of the research. Two such can be cited. (a) A direct comparison between the results of the TAT and the results of the MAPS test is handicapped because of the lack of perfect experimental design in the administration of the two tests: they were administered by different examiners, they were given two months apart, and there were the intervening variables of unknown effect such as six insulin comas between the two administrations. However, inasmuch as this inter-test comparison was not central to this round-table study, this case was chosen because of its "typical" neuropsychiatric hospital nature and its potential clinical richness, and in spite of

the limitation cited above. (b) The same sort of limitation applies to the role of the psychiatric follow-up interview, where there were known intervening variables of unknown effect (such as psychotherapy) between the testing and the follow-up two years later, and any number of unknown variables. Thus, the predictions made by the test interpreters, where they disagree with the known "facts" of the behavioral data, might have agreed with these data if the intervening factors (such as the psychotherapy) had not taken place.

4. A different kind of limitation—one mentioned by several of the test contributors as being a limitation on their interpretative efforts—was the "blind analysis" task imposed upon the contributors. This refers to having the interpreters do their test analyses without any of John Doe's case history material or personal data (except his sex, age and marital status). The reason for this procedure was simply that it was necessitated by the research design, and is quite apart from the controversy of whether test interpretations should be done with a minimum or a maximum of supplementary data. This book does not include the problem of the proper role of "blind analysis" in thematic test interpretation, nor its supplementary methodologic problem of the explanation of failures of thematic test interpretation to be consistent with clearly demonstrable clinical data—even assuming that this latter phenomenon occurred among any of the test interpreters represented in this volume.

5. There are two limitations to the scope of this effort, and they are similar to one another. (a) This study on thematic projective techniques is limited to the TAT and the MAPS test, and is concerned primarily with the TAT. It does not pretend to discuss systematically the entire field of thematic testing, nor does it cover such similar and related tests as van Lennep's Four Picture Test, Rosenzweig's Picture Frustration Study, and the many modifications of the TAT principle for special groups. (b) Not all the existing systems for TAT analysis and interpretation are represented. Of the thirty different methods reported in the psychological and psychiatric literature, sixteen are to be found in this volume. The reader should be aware of this limitation in the scope of the book, although the systems not represented do not, on the whole, differ remarkably in type from those which are included. (The more remarkable fact is in terms of the cooperation and willingness that was exhibited by many members of the psychological and psychiatric professions).

6. A limitation in the scope of this volume, that of not including a statistical analysis of the interpretations, may be a disappointment for some readers. Statistical treatment of the data, as already stated, is being planned for separate publication. The nature of these statistical procedures is given in Chapter 30, footnote 4, page 303.

The statement of all these limitations and delimitations serves to reenforce the primary purpose of this volume, which is to present data — first the test records of an individual, then the several interpretations of that individual's test records, and finally some case history and psychotherapy information about that individual. The purpose is simply to present these data and let the reader do with them essentially what he will.

## IV. Rationale

This project was done within the framework of the desire to contribute to psychology and psychodiagnostics as *predictive* sciences. The point of view is propounded that interpretation of psychological test material usually includes or implies prediction of the subject's future behavior as well as description of the present personality of the subject. One can go so far as to say that prediction of overt behavior from test material responses (test productions are themselves a form of behavior at the fantasy level) is one of the primary purposes of test interpretation in the clinical setting. The interpretations included in this book made by the several experts of the same set of test protocols are implied predictions; e.g., the statement, "The subject is homicidal," is certainly a prediction that the subject may attempt murder. There are in this volume psychiatric follow-up data, which means that the predictions implied in the interpretations of the TAT and the MAPS test records can be compared in two ways: (1) with behavioral data contemporary with the test records which are also presented (such as clinical ward notes from the neuropsychiatric hospital where the subject was tested and psychotherapy records taken at approximately the same time), and (2) with data which did not occur until two and one-half years later — "future data," as it were.

Psychodiagnosis should predict what the patient—not the examiner or the therapist—is going to do. Personality-probing techniques cannot be validated on the basis of experts' opinions or against other techniques; the emphasis should be on the prediction of specific behavior of the subject. Apropos of this topic, Dr. James G. Miller has indicated rather succinctly that "Diagnosis is irrelevant and unproductive unless it is also prediction at the same time."[5] He has also, in the same context, pointed out the need for clinico-pathologic conferences in psychology similar in function to those held in medicine. This book, then, is a sort of "psychological autopsy," wherein the postmortem is performed not on the patient but on the test interpretations. This is made possible by the availability of the clinical and psychiatric data indicated above.

Another point of view implicit in this entire project is the belief that all thematic test methods can be thought of in terms of fulfilling one of two major

[5] These concepts were presented by Dr. Miller in his lecture series, "Design of Clinical Research in Psychology, Psychiatry and Social Work," February, 1950, at the University of California at Los Angeles.

functions: service or research. Psychology moves forward in terms of these two activities; the psychologist must answer the call to render psychodiagnostic service reports on patients, using his techniques as though they were valid and rendering his reports as though he believed in his techniques, but he must also respond to the challenge of investigating his techniques through experimental research, treating them as though they were not valid. Nowhere is this healthy bipartite division of activities seen more clearly than in the field of picture-thematic tests. The data in this book are presented as an example of the possibilities for development in both of these directions.

# Part I

# THEMATIC TEST DATA

# Chapter 2

# THEMATIC APPERCEPTION TEST

THIS CHAPTER consists of a brief description of the Thematic Apperception Test (TAT), some information about how this test was administered to John Doe, and the verbatim reproduction of John Doe's TAT protocol.

The TAT was first introduced in 1935 by Murray and Morgan. The set of TAT material used in this study (there have been three earlier sets) consists of thirty-one pictures printed achromatically on $9\frac{1}{2}$ by 11 inch cardboard cards. The various pictures usually depict one or two people; one card is blank. The subject's task is to look at each picture and make up a story about it. The pictures are divided among those suitable for young boys (13B), for young girls (13G), for males over fourteen years (12M), for females over fourteen years (12F), for both boys and girls (12BG), for males and females over fourteen (13MF), for boys and older males (3BM, 6BM, 7BM, 8BM, 9BM, 17BM, 18BM), for g rls and older females (3GF, 6GF, 7GF, 8GF, 9GF, 17GF, 18GF), and, the remaining eleven, for both sexes of all ages.[1]

The literature on the TAT is vast. A discussion of it will not be attempted here except to state that there are several excellent sources of information in this area.[2]

[1] Thematic Apperception Test materials are available from the Harvard University Press, Cambridge, Massachusetts.

[2] References to the literature on the TAT can be discussed as follows: (a) The ***primary references*** are: MURRAY, H. A., *Thematic Apperception Test Manual.* Cambridge: Harvard University Press, 1943, 20 pp.; and MURRAY, H. A., *Explorations in Personality.* New York: Oxford University Press, 1938, 761 pp. (b) The *theoretical background* of the TAT is discussed in: SARGENT, H., Projective Techniques: Their Origins, Theory and Application in Personality Research. *Psychological Bulletin,* 1945, *5,* 257–293; and WHITE, R. W., Interpretation of Imaginative Productions—in HUNT, J. McV. (Ed.), *Personality and the Behavior Disorders.* New York: Ronald Press Company, 1944 (Volume I, pp. 214–251). (c) Excellent discussions of the *history of the TAT, application to various groups, studies of validity and reliability, etc.,* appear in the following: BELL, JOHN E., *Projective Techniques.* New York: Longmans, Green and Company, 1948 (Chapters VIII and IX, "The Thematic Apperception Test" and "Direct Modifications of the Thematic Apperception Test," respectively); MAYMAN, M., Review of the Literature on the Thematic Apperception Test—in RAPAPORT, D. (Ed.), *Diagnostic Psychological Testing.* Chicago: The Year Book Publishers, Inc., 1946 (Appendix III, pp. 496–505); SYMONDS, P., *Adolescent Fantasy.* New York: Columbia University Press, 1949 (Chapter II, "History of the Thematic Apperception Test"); and TOMKINS, S. S., *The Thematic Apperception Test.* New York: Grune and Stratton, 1947 (Chapter I, "History and Development of the Thematic Apperception Test"); and (d) *current researches and comprehensive bibliographies* may be found in HOLT, R. R. (Ed.),

In administering the TAT to John Doe,[3] Murray's standard instructions, Form A (suitable for adolescents and for adults of average intelligence and sophistication) were employed.[4]

*"This is a test of imagination, one form of intelligence. I am going to show you some pictures, one at a time; and your task will be to make up as dramatic a story as you can for each. Tell what has led up to the event shown in the picture, describe what is happening at the moment, what the characters are feeling and thinking; and then give the outcome. Speak your thoughts as they come to your mind. Do you understand? . . .*[5] *Here is the first picture."*

For Card 16, the Blank, the examiner said, *"See what you can see on this blank card. Imagine some picture there and describe it to me in detail . . . Now tell me a story about it."*

The subject's responses were recorded verbatim. The questions asked by the examiner (inquiry) are indicated by italics in parentheses in the protocol.

Eleven TAT cards were administered to John Doe. They were all given in one session. The numbers of the cards, and Murray's description of them, as they were presented to the subject, are as follows[6]:

1 (A young man is contemplating a violin which rests on a table in front of him); 3BM (On the floor against a couch is the huddled figure of a boy with his head bowed on his right arm. Beside him on the floor is a revolver); 4 (A woman is clutching the shoulders of a man whose face and body are averted as if he were trying to pull away from her); 6BM (A short elderly woman stands with her back turned to a tall young man. The latter is looking downward with a perplexed expression); 7BM (A gray-haired man is looking at a younger man who is sullenly staring into space); 11 (A road skirting a deep chasm between high cliffs. On the road in the distance are obscure figures. Protruding from the rocky wall on one side is the long head and neck of a dragon); 12M (A young man is lying on a couch with his eyes closed. Leaning over him is the gaunt form of an elderly man, his hand stretched out above the face of the reclining figure); 13MF (A young man is standing with downcast head buried in his arm. Behind him is the figure of a woman lying in bed); 13B (A little boy is sitting on the doorstep of a log cabin); 14 (A silhouette of a man, or

---

*The TAT Newsletter.* Topeka: The Menninger Foundation, 1947 *et seq.* (*The TAT Newsletter* is also printed as part of the *Journal of Projective Techniques*). For a complete bibliography on the TAT up to 1950, see *The TAT Newsletter*, Spring, 1950, Volume III, Number 4 (also printed in the *Journal of Projective Techniques*, 1950, *14*, 80–100).

[3] It should be emphasized that the description of procedures which follows is meant to describe what was done in this study (to John Doe) and is offered in the interests of accurate reporting; it is not meant in any sense as a guide for TAT administration.

[4] Reprinted by permission of the Harvard University Press.

[5] The phrase, *"Since you have fifty minutes for ten pictures, you can devote about five minutes to each story,"* was omitted.

[6] Reprinted by permission of the publishers from MURRAY, HENRY A., *Thematic Apperception Test Manual.* Cambridge, Massachusetts: Harvard University Press, 1943.

woman, against a bright window. The rest of the picture is totally black); and 16 (Blank card).

It was felt that good rapport was established and maintained. The subject seemed interested in the task and had no difficulty verbalizing. The test was administered vis-a-vis. The testing was done in an office on the ward of the neuropsychiatric hospital. Testing conditions were good; the room was well lighted, quiet and private.

Following is the verbatim reproduction of the TAT protocol for John Doe, printed as it was distributed to the contributors in this study.[7]

## TAT RECORD

DOE, John Male Age 25 Single

1 This child is sick in bed. He has been given sheet music to study, but instead of the music, he has come across a novel that interests him more than the music. It is probably an adventure story. He evidently does not fear the chance that his parents will find him thusly occupied as he seems quite at ease. He seems to be quite a studious type and perhaps regrets missing school, but he seems quite occupied with the adventure in the story. Adventure has something to do with ocean or water. He is not too happy, though not too sad. His eyes are somewhat blank—coincidence of reading a book without any eyes or knowing what is in the book without reading it. He disregards the music and falls asleep reading the book.

3 BM This is a girl in a cell and she has been jailed because she was found guilty of prostitution. She is in this position in the picture because she is very ashamed, not because of being arrested, because she is quite familiar with the police, but because of the fact that her picture and a newspaper write-up was being sensationally spread across the country. She knew that her sister, who was a nun, would suffer from it, and it made her feel very badly because she, at one time, had a chance and an opportunity to follow her elder sister's example, but it was too late now. She grabs a concealed knife from under her blouse and stabs herself.

4 The girl in the picture is half-caste. She is in love with the man who is going to leave her and return to his wife. They have spent quite some time together in intimacy. She is pleading with him to stay with her or help figure some way to plan for the coming of the child she is going to bear. She is in poor circumstances financially, and he tells her she should make arrangements to conclude the birth and thus everything would iron out because he is definitely determined to leave as the affair in his mind is at an end. She is very broken up by it. She pleads for him to spend one more night which he agrees to, and in the middle of the night she sets fire to the house, thus solving the problem of all concerned.

[7] The TAT was administered to John Doe by Mr. Charles Cabeen, August 11, 1947. The chronology of all testing given to John Doe in the neuropsychiatric hospital as well as other entries in his clinical notes are presented in Chapter 25, "Course in Neuropsychiatric Hospital."

6 BM This is a scene in a play. The two characters are on the stage, one is a famous elderly actress, who has a son about the age of the young man appearing opposite her. The dialogue in the play has suddenly taken a new meaning for her. She sees now that the play which was written by her son, has an entirely different meaning, in this scene in the picture. The boy is telling the mother that he has just committed a murder. She understands now that this was her son's way of conveying to her the terrifying facts that that is actually what had happened. In the play, as her son had written it, the climax comes when the mother calls the police. But the famous actress decides to put her own climax into action after the play is over. She calls her son and says, The climax of your play will have to be changed. She says, I think the audience will prefer this one, so here she draws a revolver and shoots him. (*What kind of murder was it?*) Oh, a girl. Motive primarily to do with sexual. She had been unfaithful.

7 BM This would be a man and his son. The son is very depressed over his health. The father is telling him that as a young man he too had the same illness, and that it can be cured if the son has the will to cure it. The father tells the young man that he himself alone can cure it. The son believes that there is no hope, but replies that he will go away for a little while and think it over. The father replies, You are not doing a favor to me by saying that. I am thinking about your getting well for the simple reason that you have a wife and children to support, and in the event of your being bed-ridden, the responsibility for your family will be put entirely upon your mother and I. The young man finally concludes that he will take his wife and family with him and try to make things go better in a healthier climate. (*What kind of illness did he have?*) T.B. (*Did he get better?*) No, I don't think he does. After a few years he dies and the children are old enough to support mother or perhaps he left insurance. Never contacted father again. No correspondence. After not having heard from each other for a long time, the old man dies and leaves the children a large estate. This is his way of having repented.

11 This is a fantasy. This highway cuts over an arched bridge. The people on the road are black and wearing capes. There are perhaps two pack animals carrying supplies. About the middle of the picture there is a prehistoric animal with just his serpentine neck showing and a web foot. He has been waiting for these travelers until they came into sight and then, when he saw them, he started rolling huge boulders across their path. However, they must have been predestined to reach their goal, because the boulders have fallen short of the highway. They are evidently the first travelers to get this far because it is presumed that the black area to the right of the beast is a pitfull of lost human souls. However, the beast looks as though he will race ahead of them and in some future spot along the road send them to whatever fate has for them in the future. (*Fate?*) Looks like wicked people trying to escape or something, and this seems to be going deeper into more of a dark place than from where they came from.

12 M This is a young artist in Paris who is badly off financially; so badly in fact

that, because he hadn't sold a painting in over a month, he is prostrate from starvation. But the painting he had sold for a loaf of bread had somewhow gotten into the home of a wealthy patron of the arts who had seen great magnificence in it and had turned it over to the director of an art institute. The picture was sold for a large sum. The director, after great pains, had finally located the artist and was standing over him now trying to get some response, trying to tell him that he was to be commissioned to paint for the wealthy woman for a large retaining fee. But, however, it was too late. The picture that had brought the director to his bedside had had too great an effect on the artist. It was a picture of a loaf of bread.

13 MF These two people have come to a strange city and taken lodgings in a middle-class hotel. They both met while riding on a bus. The girl approached him first by saying she was a stranger and had no place to stay. The man too was a stranger and welcomed the opportunity because she did not appear to be just a common pick-up. They registered as man and wife and retired to their room, where the man in the glaring bright light of the room saw the girl for the first time. He saw in her the very thing he had come to this town to get away from. She was the same in proportion, in color and even in manner as the girl he could not have at home, because the girl at home had died. Overcoming this feeling by turning off the light, they had relations, and now with the lights on again, a feeling of shame has come over him and he leaves. This girl was morally a different girl from the one that had died. He could never get the other girl.

13 B This doesn't say much to me. This scene is of a very poor farmhouse in an isolated part of the country. The little boy has just been told that he is going to have a little brother. However he can't quite figure it out. He has been told to stay out of the way, and some other small children have told him that they have had little brothers too, and since they have arrived the mother has not had so much time for them. The little boy in the picture is thinking all this over, and since he cannot get much affection from his father who is too busy working in the fields to even be kind to him, the boy, in his small mind, comes to the conclusion that it's a hopeless case. He looks behind him into the black room which only accentuates the fact that his case looks black also. He decides to leave home and just then his mother calls him, the baby is going to arrive and he must rush over to get Mrs. Smith, the nearest neighbor. The mother tells him that she thanks God that she has a son like him to help her now, which makes him feel very elated and he decides he will never leave home. He had really done more than his father had in doing this.

14 This is a photograph that the man has taken while exploring a deserted house. Directly after taking this picture he had turned his flashlight to the floor and discovered a mutilated human body. This was the only possible suspect, the figure in the picture. He could, with imagination, almost put together characteristics of the figure shown in the picture. As this man lived in a small town not frequented often by visitors, he knew who this figure was seen leaving the window, but he being a minister, was not sure he should divulge the identity because between the time that

the murder was committed and the time that the police discovered it, the suspect had confided in the minister what had occurred. The man in the picture had told the minister that it was in self defense; that he had been startled by an intruder who had suddenly sprung upon him. However, the minister believed that it was the other way around and did notify the police who found out actually what had happened. The man in the picture was hiding because earlier he had robbed a jewelry store and been followed by the victim.

16 This is a great plain where there used to be a settlement not so long ago. It is very hot and dry on the plain and the people who had been inhabitants had suffered a great deal from the heat, lack of water, and even outside influences. They were entirely reliant upon themselves and no one was reliant upon them. Because of the reason that they were alone was also the reason that they came to their doom. If they had had one line of contact, one way of conversing, even a telepathic touch with the outside world, they could have perhaps been saved. Now nothing is left except ruins and destruction of something that had once been evident as at least having been here. We know that it must have been there because of the ruins, and yet no one is sure because no proof is offered in either having had contact or having seen. It could all be imagination.

# Chapter 3

# MAKE A PICTURE STORY TEST

This chapter consists of a brief description of the Make A Picture Story (MAPS) test, some information about how this test was administered to John Doe, and the verbatim reproduction of John Doe's MAPS test protocol.

The MAPS test, developed by Shneidman in 1947, has been called a "younger brother of the Thematic Apperception Test."[1] It varies the TAT material principally by separating the figures and the backgrounds, allowing the subject to populate (i.e., select and place) his own choice of figures on depopulated backgrounds, before he tells his story, TAT-wise. This means that the subject then responds to a stimulus-situation which he has partly created himself and that the subject has the opportunity—if not the necessity—for using motor expressive action in accomplishing the test task.

The materials for the MAPS test consist of the following parts[2]:

(A) *Backgrounds*. There are twenty-two background pictures, 8½ x 11 inches, printed achromatically on thin cardboard. With two exceptions, there are no figures in any of the pictures.[3] The set includes unstructured or ambiguous backgrounds such as the Stage, the Dream, the abstract Doorway, and the Blank card; semi-structured backgrounds such as the Forest, the grotto-like Cave, and the desert-like Landscape; and definitely structured backgrounds—the remaining fifteen pictures, which include the Livingroom, Street, Medical Scene, Bathroom, Bridge, Bedroom, Closet, Camp, Cellar, Raft, Attic, Shanty, Cemetery, Nursery, and Schoolroom. An attempt was made on an *a priori* basis to include background pictures which would allow for the possibility of obtaining information on most of the important specific

[1] Holt, Robert R., Book Review: Schizophrenia and the MAPS Test. *Journal of Personality*, 1950, *18*, 385.

[2] The MAPS test materials are available from The Psychological Corporation, 522 Fifth Avenue, New York 18, New York. The basic reference and manual for the MAPS test is "A Manual for the MAPS Test," *Projective Techniques Monographs*, 1951, *1*, No. 2. In addition a primary reference is "Schizophrenia and the MAPS Test," *Genetic Psychology Monographs*, 1948, *38*, 145–223. There are reviews of this monograph, and of the test, by Robert R. Holt (*Journal of Personality*, 1950, *18*, 385–387) and by John E. Bell (*Journal of Projective Techniques*, 1950, *14*, 196–198).

[3] There is an ambiguous human head in the bottom left of the *Dream* background picture and a human-like lump in the bed of the *Bedroom* background picture.

problem areas and specific problem conflicts encountered in clinical practice. Some empiric data are now available.[4]

(B) *Figures.* A distinguishing feature of the MAPS test is that it offers the subject the opportunity to *select* the figures as well as to enliven and interpret them. There are 67 figures. A 6-foot human figure is $5\frac{1}{2}$ inches tall and all others are scaled proportionately. With few exceptions, the figures are shown as standing. Any figure can be placed on any background without violating realistic proportions. The figures are depicted with various facial expressions, are in various poses, some are partially clothed, etc. The types of figures, their identification letters, and the number of figures within each type are as follows: male adult (M), 19; female adult (F), 11; children (C), 12; minority group figures, such as Negroes, Jews, Orientals, Mexicans (N), 10; animal figures (A), 2; figures of indeterminate sex (I), 2; legendary and fictitious characters (L), 6; and silhouettes and figures with blank faces (S), 5.

(C) *Figure Location Sheet.* This is a sheet on which there are lightly printed reduced reproductions of all the background pictures. This enables the examiner to record the subject's *choice* and *placement* of the figures, which are identified according to their type, for later recapitulation of the subject's performance. This recording is done by the drawing of an ellipse to represent the test figure in the *corresponding* place on the reproduction of the background picture and labeling it with the correct code symbol for that figure. Figures which are chosen and then rejected are also noted; movement of a figure is indicated by drawing an arrow to indicate the precise nature of the movement.

(D) *Figure Identification Card.* This card serves to group the figures and to identify each one by a code symbol so the examiner may label them properly on the *Figure Location Sheet* as they are used by the subject. The figures are numbered consecutively within each letter category, thus "F-4" is the fourth female figure, "A-2", the second animal figure, and so on. No identifying marks appear on the figures themselves—it is felt that the appearance of any marks

[4] Data on the "card-pull" of various MAPS test background pictures with different groups may be found in the following sources: (a) CONANT, JAMES, A Comparison of the Thematic Fantasy among Normals, Neurotics, and Schizophrenics. Unpublished Ph.D. Dissertation, University of Southern California, 1950 [10]; (b) FARBEROW, NORMAN, Personality Patterns of Suicidal Mental Hospital Patients. *Genetic Psychology Monographs*, 1950, *42*, 3–79 [18]; (c) FINE, REUBEN, The Personality of the Asthmatic Child. Unpublished Ph.D. Dissertation, University of Southern California, 1948 [19]; (d) JOEL, WALTHER, The Use of the Make-A-Picture-Story (MAPS) Test with Disturbed Adolescents. *Journal of Projective Techniques*, 1948, *12*, 1–10 [29]; and (e) WALKER, ROBERT G., A Comparison of Clinical Manifestations of Hostility with Rorschach and MAPS Test Performances. Unpublished Ph.D. Dissertation, University of Southern California, 1950 [57]. The results of all these studies are summarized in the following article: GOLDENBERG, HERBERT, A Resume of Some Make-A-Picture-Story (MAPS) Test Results. *Journal of Projective Techniques*, 1951, *15*, 79–86 [21].

on the figures might have varying meanings to different subjects and thus be undesirable. The *Figure Identification Card* has a verbal description of each figure on one side and a miniature picture of each figure on the other.

(E) *Theater-Carrying Case.* The miniature wooden theater also serves as a carrying case for the test materials. Its use makes it possible for the figures to be placed erect—on little wooden bases—at varying distances in front of the background picture. (Without the theater-carrying case, the background picture is simply laid flat on the table and the test figures laid on it by the subject). The theater-carrying case is employed when the MAPS test materials are used primarily for therapeutic (as opposed to primarily diagnostic) purposes.[5] It was not used in the administration of the test to John Doe. A picture of the MAPS test theater-carrying case, with one background picture and some sample test figures is presented in Figure 1.

The MAPS test was administered—after proper rapport had been established—with the following instructions:

"*What I am going to do is show you pictures like this, one at a time.*" At this point, the Livingroom background picture was placed directly in front of the subject, so that the bottom of the picture was along the edge of the table. "*You will have figures like this*"—at this point all the figures were poured out of their envelope onto the table top—"*and your task is simply to take one or more of any of these figures and put them on the background picture as they might be in real life. We might start by sorting the figures so that you can see each one. Spread them out on the table.*" At this point, the examiner took a few figures and laid them on the table with the feet of the figures toward the subject. He then permitted the subject to arrange the remainder of the figures. The subject placed all the figures on the table and asked no questions about the purpose of the test. There were no peculiarities of placement of the figures on the table by the subject or any evidence of "system" or of grouping of the figures noted.

After all of the figures had been placed on the table by the subject, the examiner stated: "*I would like to go over the instructions in a little more detail. As I said, all you are to do is take one or more of any of these figures, put them on the background as they might be in real life, and tell a story of the situation which you have created. In telling your story, tell, if you can, who the characters are, what they are doing and thinking and feeling, and how the whole thing turns out. Go ahead.*"

[5] Examples of the use of the MAPS test materials in psychotherapy are cited in the following: (a) Bach, George R., Dramatic Play Therapy with Adult Groups. *Journal of Psychology*, 1950, *29*, 225–246; (b) Fantel, Ernest, Report on Psychodramatic Therapy. *Group Psychotherapy*, 1950, *3*, 55–58; and (c) Fantel, Ernest, and Shneidman, E. S., Psychodrama and the MAPS Test. *Rorschach Research Exchange and Journal of Projective Techniques*, 1947, *11*, 42–67.

After the first story was completed and the examiner had finished writing the story and had indicated the choice and placement of the test figures by making appropriate markings on the *Figure Location Sheet*,[6] he stated the following: "*That was a very good story. You caught on perfectly. You took one or more of the figures and placed them on the background picture as they might be in real life and told a story of the situation you created. In the other stories you may use either the same or different figures. We are going to do about a dozen of these background pictures.*" The subject was then asked to take the figures he used for the Livingroom background and place them back anywhere on the table. The background picture was withdrawn and the second (Street) background picture was placed before him.

As each story was completed the examiner asked about any important aspect of the instructions omitted in the story, such as how it turned out; any part of the story not clear to the examiner; and the title of the story. The examiner's questions are indicated in the test protocol by italics in parentheses.

Ordinarily, eleven background pictures are used with each subject. In this case, largely because of the length of John Doe's stories, only the following seven were employed: Livingroom, Street, Bathroom, Dream, Bedroom, Blank, and the seventh background picture, the Stage, chosen by the subject himself from among the remaining sixteen background pictures.

During the testing session, rapport was good. The subject spoke freely, although he did appear to be under some strain. The testing, as in the case of the TAT, was done in an office on the neuropsychiatric hospital ward. The examiner sat to the right of the subject and a little behind him.

Following is the verbatim reproduction of the MAPS test protocol for John Doe, printed as it was distributed to the contributors to this study.[7]

## MAPS TEST RECORD

DOE, John    Male    Age 25    Single

1. Livingroom (Used L-6, F-8, M-11, A-2, M-5)

Well, let's see. (Selected L-6, F-8, M-11, A-2.) Just make up anything I feel like making up? I can add as I go along? (Pause.) Well, there's been a knock at the door. This housewife (F-8) goes to her door and sees this terrible looking woman

[6] Figure 2, showing the outline of some of the test backgrounds (and the ellipses made by the examiner to recapitulate the choice and placement of test figures by John Doe) is a reproduction of the *Figure Location Sheet*. Figure 3, which is a photographic reproduction of actual MAPS test materials, was specially prepared to give the thematic test contributors to this study (and the readers of this volume) a clearer picture of the background pictures and test figures used by John Doe. (The originals of Figures 2 and 3 have been reduced in size by about 40 per cent for reproduction in this book.)

[7] The MAPS test was administered to John Doe by Dr. Edwin S. Shneidman on June 19, 1947.

FIG. 1

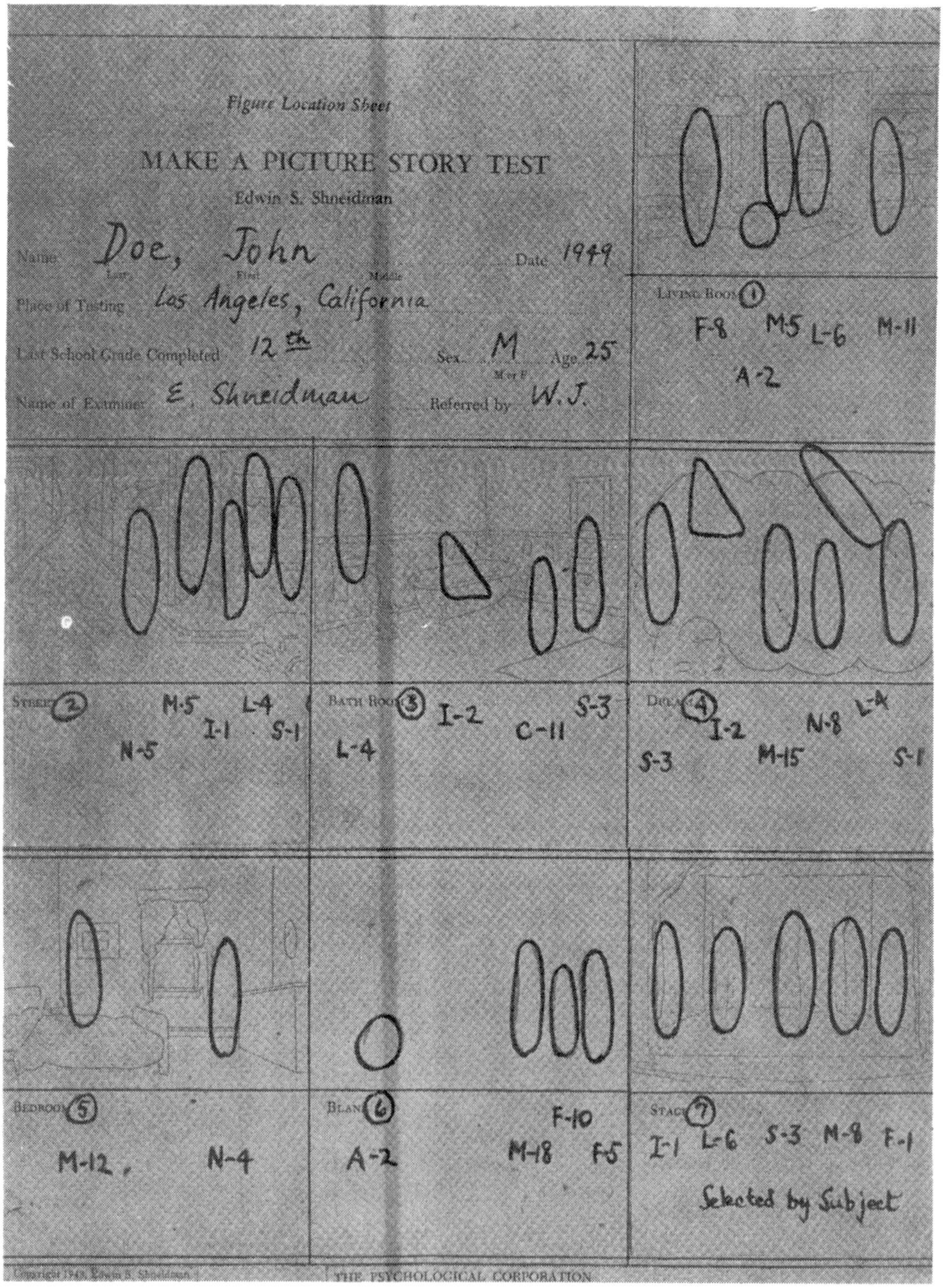
Figure Location Sheet
MAKE A PICTURE STORY TEST
Edwin S. Shneidman
Name Doe, John
Date 1949
Place of Testing Los Angeles, California
Last School Grade Completed 12th
Sex M
Age 25
Name of Examiner E. Shneidman
Referred by W. J.
Living Room 1
F-8 M-5 L-6 M-11 A-2
Street 2
M-5 L-4 I-1 S-1 N-5
Bath Room 3
I-2 S-3 C-11 L-4
Dream 4
I-2 N-8 L-4 S-3 M-15 S-1
Bedroom 5
M-12 N-4
Blank 6
F-10 A-2 M-18 F-5
Stage 7
I-1 L-6 S-3 M-8 F-1
Selected by Subject
THE PSYCHOLOGICAL CORPORATION

FIG. 2

*Figure Location Sheet*

MAKE A PICTURE STORY TEST

Edwin S. Shneidman

Name Doe, John (Last, First, Middle) Date 1949

Place of Testing Los Angeles, California

Last School Grade Completed 12th Sex M (M or F) Age 25

Name of Examiner E. Shneidman Referred by W. J.

(1) Living Room

F-8 M-5 L-6 M-11 A-2

(2) Street

M-5 I-1 L-4 S-1 N-5

(3) Bath Room

I-2 S-3 L-4 C-11

(4) Dream

L-4 S-3 I-2 N-8 M-15 S-1

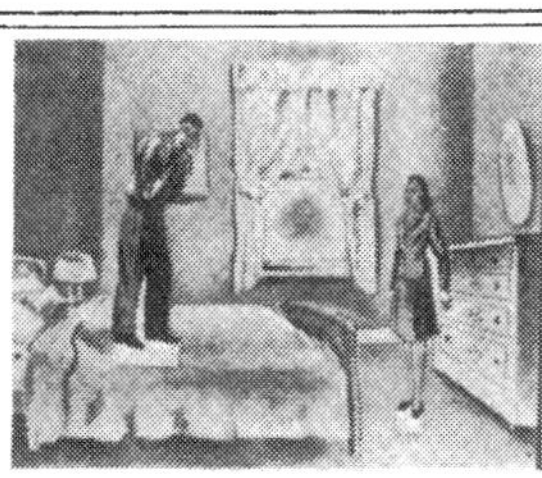

(5) Bedroom

M-12 N-4

(6) Blank

F-10 A-2 M-18 F-5

(7) Stage

I-1 L-6 S-3 M-8 F-1

Selected by Subject



THE PSYCHOLOGICAL CORPORATION

FIG. 3

(L-6) and recognizes it as her mother. The woman is being followed by a snake (A-2) which is the symbol of what she really is, I suppose. She calls her husband (M-11) who is very indignant at having the old woman come to the door and also the daughter is very indignant because she had told her mother never to come and let the neighbors see her. But the mother tells her that I had—she had come because she wants some money to help her son out of a jam. The daughter asked her why she insisted on having that awful looking snake following her. The mother said, He's the only one I can trust because all snakes don't wear clothes. Then the snake leaves to go out in the yard. (Removed A-2.) Meanwhile a cop appears. (Added M-5.) An officer appears at the door. He inquires into the identity of the old woman. The daughter turns on the officer and says, I have never seen this woman before. The mother, of course, is broken-hearted. She says, I can't help it if my face is this way. It all happened the day you were born. When they were taking me to the hospital there was an accident and I received both you and a terrible face. The daughter takes out her handbag and says, Here's five dollars, beggar. Now, officer, see that she goes. As the old lady leaves she turns and says, Before I am through you'll give me more than money. She exits.[8] (Removed L-6.) The officer enters the room and inquires if they are sure they do not know the old woman. The daughter replies, Perhaps I've seen her but I would not want to admit it. The officer says O.K. and leaves. (Removed M-5.) The husband comes over to the wife and says, I hope I don't have to look forward to the day when you'll get that old and look like that and quite an argument ensues. During all this time the door has been left open and the snake slithers in (Added A-2) and bites them both. As the wife is dying she says, At least you won't have to see me when I get old, and they both collapse. That's the end of the story. Is that the way? Short stories like that? (*What might you call this story?*) A title? The woman and the snake.

2. Street (Used I-1, L-4, S-1, N-5, M-5)

(Selected I-1.) Let me find a suitable character here. (Added L-4, S-1, N-5; added and removed L-2, N-7.) Ready? This girl is hiding in one of the corners in a street in Shanghai. She sees this man. She is a white girl, incidentally, and quite degraded in character, although still beautiful. She's been having an affair with a Chinaman, who suspects she's been playing around with someone else and he's out to kill her with a knife. The street is very dark and yet the other man she's been having an affair with is hiding in the shadows. While she's hiding there, the ghost of an old love back in America is hovering over her. The Chinaman turns every which way on the street to see if he can spy her. He goes from one bar to another. The man in the shadows does not know she is hiding a few steps away. He hears someone rustle a bit and is certain it is the Chinaman. As it is very dark and he cannot see who is around the corner, he blindly goes after his prey and stabs the supposed Chinaman in the heart. An officer (Added M-5) walking listlessly down the street shines his flashlight on the face of the dead woman. Then the man realizes what has

[8] In the mimeographed protocol which was distributed to the contributors, this word was incorrectly printed as "exists."

happened and turns the knife on himself. (*What title could you give this story?*) The man with the knife.

3. BATHROOM (Used S-3, C-11, I-2, L-4)

(Selected S-3, C-11.) I need one more character. (Added I-2.) A woman is looking in the mirror in her bathroom but she can see no reflection except her dark hair. Her son has come into the bathroom and has asked this thing if it has seen its mother. The mother tries to speak but cannot because she has no mouth. She tries to see her son but she has no eyes. All she has is ears. Her husband, taking a bath, recognizes her by her figure but turns away in agony. He remembers the night before she had said I wish I could get rid of this old face, and certainly she had. Her wish had come true. The son is compelled to run out of the room. (Removed C-11; added L-4.) A phantom appears, visible only to the woman's inner self. She cries to him, through her mind, and said, It was only an idle wish and I didn't believe in fairy tales. The phantom said, Your face is gone forever. Nobody will ever like or dislike your face any more, so you can be neither happy nor discontented. The husband looked up and said, At least I will have to listen no more to your complaining. I—at least—wait a minute—your complaining. And one thing you have to be thankful for is that while I grow old you will always be the same. (*Title?*) No reflection.

4. DREAM (Used L-4, N-7, M-15, I-2, F-7, S-1)

(Selected L-4, N-7, M-15, I-2, F-7.) This is the story of a middle-aged woman who is confused. She's thinking back over her life: the father she had poisoned because he didn't have hair like other fathers did (Removed N-7); her sister whom she had pushed off the boat because she had seduced this woman's husband; the husband who turned away in shame and disappeared (Removed F-7, I-2); and the spirit that heckled her life and was still hanging over her new marriage (Added S-1) by the fact that another man had appeared in the shadows and excited her so much with passion that she was tormented. She had to do something about her situation. She took out a large insurance policy on her husband and to smooth things over—no, change that—to make things look all right, she agreed to let him take one out on her also. Her intentions were to do away with him and follow the other man, but her husband had the same idea and another love. He killed her and things worked out beautifully. (*Title?*) Clouded mind.

5. BEDROOM (Used N-4, M-12)

(Selected N-4.) Well, let's see. Here's a suitable character. (Added M-12.) He's supposed to be behind the bed. The scene is a room in a large apartment house. The tenant in the next apartment has heard a scream. She rushes next door, finds all the doors unlocked, and enters the bedroom. She sees a man crying. Also—I mean, there's someone in bed. The sheet is pulled up and she can't see who's in the bed. She asks what has happened. The man replies, Nothing, my wife just saw a mouse. But the woman doesn't believe it for the reason that she can see blood trickling on the floor. The man is bruised too and can't look her in the face. The woman says if nothing is wrong, prove it. He makes a lunge for the window even though he knows they are thirty floors above the street. He shatters the glass and falls to the street. She approaches the bed, pulls down the sheet, and there she sees her daughter, the victim of this mad fiend, whom she recognizes on second thought as being an inmate of the state asylum. That's that. (*What would you call this?*) I don't know. (*What made you think of this?*) Every story I write I put myself in a part. Subconsciously I think I do that.

6. Blank (Used F-10, A-2, M-18, F-5)

Let's see, I'll have to — (Selected and put aside F-10, A-2, M-18, F-5.) None of them are on the scene yet. This is great plains, neither earth nor—just something with great distance to it. Neither a beginning nor an end to it. Just seems endless. (Added M-18.) This young man has been walking across it for years followed by something significant with age always close behind but not too close. (Added F-10.) This woman (F-5) has been walking across it too, always frightened. Ahead, if they look (Added A-2), there is something coming towards them, but it's like a mirage. Each time they come close, it vanishes. It is something evil. Some of them are searching for it. Some would rather not. As these three are walking along (Moved figures to the left), they are followed by innumerable more. The young man falls by the wayside (Removed M-18) because his crutches become too heavy. The old lady's shawl becomes a burden and she too drops out. (Removed F-10.) The girl alone comes within short distance of it. She sees what it is and is devoured so that even she is not left to tell the secret. That's all. (*Title?*) The secret. (*What was the secret?*) I don't know. Just what they couldn't see, but they knew it was there because they could almost see it.

7. Stage (Background selected by Subject from among the remaining sixteen) (Used F-1, M-8, L-6, S-3, I-1)

Are you ready? I'd better put my characters in. (Selected F-1, M-8, L-6, S-3, I-1.) Now I'll take them all off except this one (I-1.) (Removed F-1, M-8, L-6, S-3.) The scene is a small theater, old, dark, and musty. There is a lifelike statue of a girl (I-1) at the left of the stage. Spectators have often had their doubts as to the origin of this figure. The lights dim and from the parted curtains (Added F-1) a girl appears with nothing on. She looks defiant at the audience. They wonder if it's all real. She speaks as if from a dream and says, If you live to be as old as this statue you will never forget the show tonight, and laughs wildly. A scream is heard. It seems to come from the statue and the girl says, The show is on. An old lady (Added L-6), very grotesque, says, This is act one, and dismembers the girl and cackles. (Moved F-1 to horizontal position on floor of Stage.) She's down. She has been cut up. Wait till you see act three. The ushers come on stage and put the pieces into a box and also pounce on the old lady and throw her in the box too. (Removed L-6, F-1.) After a minute (Added M-8) a man in the robe of a priest comes on stage. Looks at the girl—he looks at the statue and says, I have waited fifty years to see this statue move and you people have only to wait ten minutes. With that a girl comes on stage (Added S-3) without a face. Her long dark hair she throws over the priest and he vanishes. She says to the audience, He will never have to wait any longer, and with that she walks over to the girl. The priest has vanished, naturally. (Removed M-8; moved S-3 to left next to I-1.) She says, Now the moment has arrived; move, statue, move. All at once there is a hush; the flicker of an eyelid; the movement of a finger. The statue moves out to the center of the stage. Slowly there is a great rumble like an earthquake. Three hundred souls smashed in twenty seconds. Today only the statue is standing in the room, for she had been supporting the building and no one knew except the girl in the last act. That's all. (*Title?*) Girl in the last act, I guess. (*Can you tell more about what the story might mean?*) It means—that the people who are on the same show with you will try to preserve their act and sometimes, like the statue who just stood watching, had the real power.

# Part II

# TECHNIQUES OF THEMATIC TEST ANALYSIS

# Chapter 4

# MAGDA ARNOLD

Dr. Arnold was born in 1903. She received her Ph.D. degree in Psychology from the University of Toronto in 1942. She taught at the University of Toronto, Wellesley College, Harvard University, and Bryn Mawr College. After World War II she was Director of Research and Training in the Psychological Services of the Department of Veterans Affairs in Canada, where she developed her method of TAT analysis. Since 1950 she has been at the Barat College of the Sacred Heart, Lake Forest, Illinois, where she is Professor of Psychology and Head of the Department. Her work is largely in the fields of emotion, personality and personality diagnosis. She is one of the contributors to the *Mooseheart Symposium on Feelings and Emotions* (Ed., M. L. Reymert) and is the author of articles on emotion, suggestion and hypnosis, and the TAT. For the past ten years, she has been doing clinical work with adults and children, using primarily a Jungian orientation.

## SELECTED REFERENCES

ARNOLD, MAGDA B., A Demonstration Analysis of the Thematic Apperception Test in a Clinical Setting. *Journal of Abnormal and Social Psychology*, 1949, *44*, 97–111.

## RESUME OF METHOD[1]

THE EMPHASIS in this approach is on the content of the stories. Situations involving mostly interpersonal relations, such as parent-child, heterosexual, etc., are examined "for the feelings and actions described." In this way, information is obtained about the subject's attitudes, conflicts, and dominant problems. In addition to this "situational" analysis, the stories are also subjected to a brief "sequential" analysis in order to see whether there is a consistent development of the central theme. The five steps in the procedure are: synopsis, situational analysis, analysis of attitudes (from the situational analysis), sequential analysis, and final integration.

## TAT WORKING NOTES

*Step 1. Synopsis.*

Card 1. Sick child prefers reading instead of studying sheet music. Mood neutral. Eyes blank—"coincidence of reading a book without any eyes and knowing what is in the book without reading it."

[1] Each chapter in Part II (Chapters 4 through 18) contains a resume of the contributor's method written by the editors of this volume.

Card 3BM. Arrested prostitute with a nun as sister; is ashamed because of publicity—both for herself and sister. Stabs herself.

Card 4. Half-caste girl, pregnant, persuades lover, who wants to leave her, to spend one more night with her. Sets fire to house in the middle of the night, solving all their problems.

Card 6BM. Scene in play, written by actress' son who chooses this way to inform his mother that he shot his mistress who was unfaithful. In the play, mother calls the police; actually, after the play, actress-mother changes ending, shoots son.

Card 7BM. Father telling son he had been ill with same illness as son; son can cure himself too, if he has the will. Father tells son he ought to get well; otherwise he will have to support son's family. Son takes his family to healthier climate, but dies of T.B. without seeing father again. Old man dies and repentantly leaves fortune to grandchildren.

Card 11. Two travellers (wicked people) trying to escape; prehistoric animal lies in wait for them. They get this far, while others, lost human souls, have fallen in the pit to the right; but in the end they "seem to be going deeper into more of a dark place than where they came from."

Card 12M. Starving artist killed by sight of his painting — a loaf of bread — which had made his fortune. Too late.

Card 13MF. Man picks up strange girl in strange town; he discovers in hotel room she is just like the girl he loved who died back home. Sleeps with her; then is filled with shame and leaves. This is morally a different girl.

Card 13B. Little boy feels neglected because of coming baby brother; wants to leave home, but mother asks him to call nearest neighbor; thanks God she has such a helpful son. Boy is elated, will not leave home. "He had really done more than his father had in doing this."

Card 14. Photograph taken by minister while exploring deserted house. Man has killed another, is about to escape, confesses to minister, insisted he had acted in self-defense. Minister does not believe this, notifies the police, minister was right.

Card 16. Great plain with ruins of settlement. People had suffered from heat, lack of water, and "even from many outside influences." Because they had no way of contact with outside, they came to their doom. "Even a telepathic touch with the outside" could have saved them. Because there was no contact, no proof of settlement, it could all be imagination.

*Step 2. Situational analysis.*

*a. Parent-Child Situations.*

*1. Father.*

Card 7BM. Father tells son he is responsible for his own illness; can cure himself if he will. Later repents after son dies.

*2. Mother.*

Card 6BM. Mother acts in son's play; realizes play is reality—son is informing her he has killed his mistress in passion. In play, mother calls police; in reality mother shoots son.

*3. Parent-substitutes.*

Card 12M. Director of art institute tells starving painter his picture has made his fortune. Too late, the sight of his picture (a loaf of bread) has killed the painter.

*b. Heterosexual situations.*

*1. Married.*

Card 7BM. Young man with T.B. takes wife and family to healthier climate. Dies.

*2. Unmarried.*

Card 4. Man wants to leave pregnant half-caste mistress; stays one more night; girl sets fire to house; solves all their problems.

Card 13MF. Man discovers the strange girl he picked up and brought to hotel room is just like his dead sweetheart. Sleeps with her, then is ashamed of it because morally this is a different girl.

*c. Same sex situations.*

Card 14. Photograph of a man trying to escape after killing and mutilating another, discovered by minister. Man claims he has acted in self-defense; minister does not believe it, calls police who discover that victim was killed because he had surprised the murderer in a robbery.

*d. Singles.*

*1. Male.*

Card 1. Sick child daydreaming over book of adventures—water and ocean—instead of studying music. Not too happy, not afraid of parents. Eyes blank, falls asleep over book.

Card 13B. Little boy feels neglected, but is consoled by his mother's asking him to help her. Had really done more than father.

*2. Female.*

Card 3BM. Arrested prostitute with a nun as sister, is ashamed because of publicity; sorry she hasn't followed sister's example. Stabs herself.

*e. Miscellaneous.*

Card 11. Wicked people almost escape, but in the end "seem to be going deeper into more of a dark place than from where they came from."

Card 16. People came to their doom because they had no outside contacts.

### *Step 3. Analysis of attitudes* (from situational analysis)

*Fathers* (older men, men in authority) hold that patient is responsible for his illness, could be cured if he wanted to; they will find out they are mistaken. (7BM)

They may have the best intentions, may recognize patient's efforts, but they don't see that their very effort is fatal, help is too late. (12M)

*Bad men* rob, kill the victim, lie when discovered, are handed over to police. (14)

*Good men* would be willing to help or at least not to interfere; but as soon as they discover patient is at fault, they have to let him take the consequences. (14)

*Mothers* are difficult to convince that son is at fault, so son has to demonstrate it. But once convinced, mothers, too, see that he has to take consequences, in fact, may punish son themselves. (6BM)

*Women* have to suffer if husband is sick. (7BM)

Once entangled with them, it is difficult to escape; they may "solve all problems" by taking revenge and destroying themselves and the man. (4)

*Self*. As a child, daydreams provide an escape from unpleasantness. One can cultivate indifference and shield oneself from fear and disappointment. (1)

Even as a child, "his case was black," "it's a hopeless case," for there is no affection, others get it all. If his mother had depended on him, if he could have helped her, he would have "done more than his father" and escape would be unnecessary.[2] (13B)

As a grownup, one has to take the consequence of wrongdoing, regret is not enough. A child can escape into imagination or indifference, a grownup only into death, so he can expiate as well as escape. (3BM)

Fate is inescapable, even though escape may seem possible for a time. (11)

If one is so alone that there is no possibility of contact with others, one will come to one's doom. Even one line of contact could have saved him—but now it's too late, everything is in ruins. In fact, now it is difficult to believe that once he was whole and could have been saved—it could be all imagination, there is no possible proof. (16)

[2] It is necessary here to check with life history. What was his position in the family? What were his relations to mother and father? And to his siblings — did he have any? . . . For my kind of analysis it really is necessary to have a check with life history facts . . . I think it very poor clinical practice to encourage people to think an interpretation could be done without having the most elementary facts about the patient at one's disposal. For a final write-up there are some questions I would like to have answered:

A. Was the TAT or the MAPS test given first? What was the time interval between them, i.e., could the two be treated as a continuous sequence and in what order?

B. Was there any difference in the patient's psychiatric condition between TAT and MAPS stories?

C. Factual checks required for an analysis: (a) What were the patient's relations with his father? TAT story 7BM sounds as if the patient really had had that particular experience with his father (father saying "it's all in your imagination, if you really wanted to, you could get well") which is something I would like to check on. For an interpretation it is important to know whether this is what really happened or whether this is what the patient feels about his father. Also, with mother and sibs? (b) Is there any actual basis for the patient's guilt feeling as expressed in TAT 3BM, 4, 6BM, i.e., what did he actually do? It makes a difference for interpretation as well as for prognosis, whether he felt guilty because of a heterosexual experience, or because of masturbation, or because he felt himself to be so different that he always disappointed people's expectations; my guess would be that it is the first of these three possibilities he referred to, but I would feel surer of that if there had been more TAT stories.

*Step 4. Sequential analysis.*

Card 1. As a child, one can avoid unpleasant work by escape into adventure, imagination, and finally sleep. Indifference will shield you from fear of parents and from disappointments.

Card 3BM. As one grows up, it is impossible to escape. There is too much publicity, everybody knows about you. People you love will suffer, and it's your own fault, for you could have gone straight. Once on the wrong path, death is the only way out.

Card 4. Of course, it doesn't have to be suicide. The person you have wronged may take the law into her own hands.

Card 6BM. Or someone who loves you, your mother, may do it for you—only she would have to be convinced of your guilt first. It will terrify her, but once she knows she would make it easy.

Card 7BM. The father (doctor?) is no help, but then he doesn't love you. His solution is that it's all a matter of will, that the cure is in oneself. One may make an effort to believe that and try to play the role others have mapped out. But the best that will happen is that it makes it easier for one's family that way, but otherwise there is no hope.

Card 11. It may look as if there were a possibility of escape, no matter how many may have perished in the attempt. But if you have done wrong, you are only going deeper into more of a dark place than where you came from. Your fate is bound to overtake you.

Card 12M. No matter how concerned people are, no matter whether one has achieved something that finds belated recognition, it's too late for our patient, the very effort he makes is killing him.

Card 13MF. It's no use thinking that what you once had can come again. It would only have an outward resemblance to what was once real. Eventually you would turn away in shame and disgust.

Card 13B. Yes, if he had been accepted and loved at the right time, long ago, he could have found his way back and life could have been sweet again.

Card 14. Even now, confessing (discussing with psychiatrist?) might help if there were some justification for one's action. But there wasn't, so the outcome is bound to be the same—retribution is bound to come.

Card 16. Now everything is in ruins, but not so long ago there was still life. One could still suffer inwardly, and even from others. But our patient was so alone, with no contact with others—if he had had even the most tenuous contact then, he could have been saved. Whatever he has done or suffered, there is no evidence to show for it, so people can say it was all in his imagination. Still, today, there are the ruins to show for it.

## TAT INTERPRETATION[3]

John Doe is a seriously disturbed young man, probably suffering from paranoid schizophrenia. That a break with reality has occurred is shown by:

[3] Dr. Arnold's TAT interpretation was written after she had seen the behavioral data for John Doe. This was not the case for any of the other interpretations, nor was it so for

1. His reference in the first picture to the child whose "eyes are somewhat blank—*coincidence of reading a book without any eyes* or knowing what is in the book without reading it."

   According to the life history, patient had been told at age seven that he had a rare eye disease and would go blind at 17, but that did not happen. This fact would account for his attention to the child's eyes in the story, but not for his peculiar way of phrasing it, which indicates abnormal thought processes.
2. In the blank card (16) he expresses thoughts rather typical for schizophrenics. "The people ... had suffered a great deal from the heat, lack of water, and *even from many outside influences.* ... if they had had one line of contact, one way of conversing, *even a telepathic touch with the outside world,* they could have perhaps been saved."

   Furthermore, he ends the story with the suggestion that there is no proof for anything having happened, it could all have been imagination. The wording here seems completely normal, yet the impression it conveys is odd, much more indicative of a schizophrenic preoccupation than a neurotic or obsessional attention to detailed proof.

However, as the stories are otherwise quite coherent in spite of their depicted violence, I would judge that the patient has not yet lost touch with reality, that he may still be able to get along, though he is liable to misinterpret people's motives and is bound to be suspicious and withdrawn.

There is a slight possibility that the above indications are the result of confusion connected with insulin coma therapy, for the TAT was given two days after ICT was terminated. However, that possibility must be ruled out, for the MAPS test, given before ICT started, gave even stronger indications of a schizophrenic break.

The central theme of John Doe's TAT is his conviction that he has done something terribly wrong (3BM, 6BM, 11, 14), that he must accept his present state of helpless, hopeless despair as a just retribution; in fact, worse may be to come (3BM, 4, 11, 16). Because of his conviction that help is too late, what once was cannot be brought back again (7BM, 12M, 13MF, 14), the prognosis seems to be unfavorable.

The life history of the patient does not give any indication what wrong he could have done. This leaves us with two possibilities: he may really have committed a serious crime, but in that case he would not accuse himself in such devious ways, nor would he seek help from a psychiatrist. Or, there may not have been any act of his to which he could trace his overpowering feeling of guilt and by this very fact this feeling would increase in intensity. His last

---

Dr. Arnold's TAT working notes or MAPS test working notes. Her TAT interpretation was thus the only exception to the experimental design of having the TAT and supplementary test contributors interpret the test materials knowing only the subject's sex, age, and marital status.

remark (card 16), "no one is sure because no proof is offered in either having had contact or having seen. It could all be imagination.", seems to favor the latter possibility rather than the former. In other words, we are dealing with a psychotic feeling of guilt which is completely disproportionate to any sin for which, as a Catholic, he would and could receive absolution.

Analyzing his attitudes towards the people around him, one is not surprised at his overwhelming sense of isolation: He knows that in spite of his own and other people's best efforts, he cannot be helped, for he is to be punished (7BM, 12M). Women are stronger than men (who try to be kind); women can be ruthless enough to punish him.

According to the life history, John Doe lives with his mother at the present time. In spite of the fact that he loves and admires her (6BM, 13B), such a close association may lead to conflict, considering his attitude to women. Patient says his mother gets drunk: if true, this would be bound to turn his love and admiration into resentment, make her similar to all the other women in his stories who are out for their pleasure, regardless of whether their actions are right or wrong (3BM, 4). It is conceivable that John Doe, who accepts his blighted life as just retribution, might feel justified to punish his mother himself, if her delinquency seems serious enough to him.

## MAPS TEST WORKING NOTES

*Step 1. Synopsis.*

1. LIVINGROOM. (*The woman and the snake.*) Woman denies (to police officer) her mother, who comes begging for her son. Mother followed by snake who is the only one that can be trusted because not wearing clothes. Woman blames mother for looking old, awful; mother says that's the looks she got when woman was born; woman reminded by husband that day will come when she looks old; they quarrel. Trusty snake bites both, they die.
2. STREET. (*The man with the knife.*) White girl hiding from Chinaman lover, ghost of old American love hovering over her; white man she is deceiving Chinaman with is hiding in shadows, too. He and girl don't know of each other's presence. White man hears noise, thinks it's Chinaman, stabs him; recognizes instead he stabbed girl. When police officer flashes light on dead person's face, white man stabs himself.
3. BATHROOM. (*No reflection.*) Woman wants to get rid of her old face, has wish come true, only ears left. Cannot see or speak to son, scares him. Complains to phantom, but phantom says now she can be neither happy nor discontented any more. Husband points out advantages of her changed state.
4. DREAM. (*Clouded mind.*) Confused middle-aged woman thinks back to past deeds: killing father, seducing sister's husband, pushing sister off boat, disappointing husband who left her; decides she must kill present husband because another man has aroused her passion. Husband has same idea, carries it out first, and things worked out beautifully.

5. BEDROOM. Woman hears scream; finds inmate of state asylum crying. Finds her daughter dead under bed clothes, killed by him. He lunges through windows, shatters glass, falls 30 stories to street.
6. BLANK. (*The secret.*) Young man has been walking across endless plains for years, followed by something significant. Old woman and young woman walking, too. Ahead something evil, mirage; innumerable people walking toward it. Young man and old woman falling by wayside, only girl meets and is devoured by it. (Snake is figure in front; therefore considered as evil.)
7. STAGE. (*Girl in last act.*) Life-like statue of girl at left; doubts about her origin. Young girl comes on stage, is dismembered, put in box; old woman thrown in after. Girl without face makes priest vanish, makes statue move. Statue had supported building, now moves, smashes everyone, itself remains.

*Step 2. Situational analysis.*

*a. Parent-Child situations.*

*1. Father.*

Dream. Father killed by daughter because he didn't have hair like other fathers.

*2. Mother*

Livingroom. Mother begs assistance for son; is rudely denied by daughter.

Bathroom. Mother distressed when disaster brought about by herself makes it impossible to see son, talk to him.

Bedroom. Mother is too late to save daughter who is killed by madman.

*3. Authoritarian figures.*

Livingroom. Policeman asks daughter to identify (acknowledge?) mother.

Street. Policeman by accident discloses to man fatal mistake.

*b. Heterosexual situations.*

*1. Married.*

Livingroom. Woman upbraided by husband after she refuses to help mother. Husband says she will soon be as ugly as mother. Both killed.

Bathroom. Husband recognizes wife who has lost her face by own wish. Is glad he won't have to listen any more to her complaining. Consoles her that now she won't grow old.

*2. Unmarried.*

Street. White girl hiding from Chinaman lover, haunted by American lover, deceiving Chinaman with white man. Gets killed by mistake by latest lover.

Bedroom. Girl gets killed by madman.

Blank. Girl is walking toward evil, mirage; meets and is devoured by it. Old woman walking, too; shawl gets burdensome, falls by wayside.

Stage. Girl without face makes priest vanish, makes statue move and building collapse and crush people.

*c. Miscellaneous.*

Stage. Life-like statue of girl supports building which crushes people when statue comes to life.

*Step 3. Analysis of attitudes* (from situational analysis)

*Father* is not like other fathers.

*Mother* tries to help, but is dogged by fate; denied by those who could help. May herself have brought about the disaster which makes it impossible for her to remain in contact with her son, or to help him.
Is too late to save her child from madness.

*Women* use men, deceive them; but sometimes men anticipate them and they get their just deserts—or men get revenge inadvertently. Men may have to become inmates of an insane ayslum to have the courage to punish women.
Women are strong, stronger than men, but their strength will avail them nothing; life is stronger than they are.
But during life, they have power over those who are the actors on life's stage. Even if they seem powerless, it is they that support the foundations of our world. At any time they can bring destruction and eventually will do so. Only other-worldly men are safe from destruction.
They are vain and thoughtless, which sometimes is their undoing. Then men get welcome relief.
They are hard; won't help their own mothers.

*Men*, as fathers, are disliked by children;
as husbands, find it difficult to bear with women, profit from women's discomfiture, but sometimes perish with them;
as representatives of law, disclose wrongs;
as lovers, are deceived and revenge themselves;
as priests, are deceived in women's purposes.

*Step 4. Sequential analysis.*

1. If a man is in need, his mother will try to help, even beg for assistance for him; but nobody listens; everybody turns away in disgust and won't see the need, even if they eventually succumb to the evil they deny.
2. Women and men are deceivers and deceived; trying to kill a threat to illicit pleasure, one unintentionally kills what one wants and notices it only when the Law stumbles on it.
3. One's wanton wishes sometimes come true; one loses the self that aggravated but also gave us pleasure. From now on there is nothing but indifference.
4. When one thinks back to the past, one sees how one deed breeds the next: if you take what you want and destroy what you don't want, there comes the time when you are in someone's way and are destroyed in turn.
5. At last one finds oneself as inmate of an asylum—having killed the thing one wants and grieving over the necessity—all that is left now is self-destruction.
6. But dropping out of the race is not the worst, especially if you have a handicap: who could run on crutches? Even woman who is stronger than man will find defeat in the end, for there is no meaning, no purpose to life; it devours even the valiant and none is left to tell the tale.
7. For we are no more than puppets acting on a stage, intent on our own purposes, but all the time at the mercy of a faceless fate whose whim will engineer total destruction of life. Only one who has watched for life in death—the priest—could escape destruction—but then he is removed from the stage before he can know the outcome.

# Chapter 5

# BETTY ARON

Miss Aron was born in 1922. She was trained at the University of California at Berkeley and spent four years as a member of the staff of the Berkeley Public Opinion Study. Psychoanalytically oriented, her work has been largely in the fields of personality theory and its clinical application. Her TAT manual describes the research methods and general findings of extensive investigation with this technique. She is a collaborative author of *The Authoritarian Personality.* Her present research is concerned with the analysis of TAT records of adolescents collected by the staff of the Guidance Study of the Institute of Child Welfare in Berkeley.

## SELECTED REFERENCES


ARON, BETTY, *A Manual for Analysis of the Thematic Apperception Test.* Berkeley, California: Willis E. Berg, 1949.

———, The Thematic Apperception Test in the Study of Prejudiced and Unprejudiced Individuals— in ADORNO, T., FRENKEL-BRUNSWIK, E., LEVINSON, D. J., AND SANFORD, R. N., *The Authoritarian Personality.* New York: Harpers, 1950.


## RESUME OF METHOD

THIS METHOD, originally designed as a research tool, works on the level of manifest story content, deliberately leaving aside, for the most part, formal aspects of the performance. It uses the Murray-Sanford scheme of variables—need and press—with numerous changes intended to bring the scheme "into closer harmony with clinical approaches and psychoanalytic theory." Each need or press is recorded together with the characters who are the subject and object of the behavior, so that a given variable can be examined "in relation to the context in which it is expressed." Also recorded are surface defenses, such as conflict, denial, rejection of behavior, fantasy, uncertainty, etc.; intensity of variables, which is expressed numerically; and outcomes. The results are analyzed in terms of main features in variable scorings and in variable sequences.

## TAT WORKING NOTES

*Example of scoring: TAT story No. 1*

| | |
|---|---|
| /This child is sick in bed./ | B: + p Affl 2<br>(B = Boy; + indicates that Affl is descriptive of a state of being; Affl = Affliction; 2 = rating of intensity on 1 to 5 scale) |

| | |
|---|---|
| (He has been given sheet music to study,)[1] | |
| /but instead of the music, he has come across a novel that interests him more than the music./ | B: n Auto 2<br>(n Auto = n Autonomy) |
| /It is probably an adventure story/ | B: f Ela 3<br>(f = fantasy about; Ela = emotional excitement) |
| /He evidently does not fear the chance that his parents will find him thusly occupied/ | B: B dfp Agg–P (Par) 2<br>(d = denial; p Agg–P = press of rejection; (Par) = from parents) |
| /as he seems quite at ease./ | B: d Ten 2<br>(Ten = Tension) |
| /He seems to be quite a studious type/ | B: S–Mt 3<br>(S–Mt = mental sentience) |
| (and he probably regrets missing school) | |
| /but he seems quite occupied with the adventure in the story/ | (more f Ela and S–Mt) |
| (Adventure has something to do with ocean or water.) | |
| /He is not too happy/ | B: d Calm 2<br>(Calm = pleasant emotions) |
| /though not too sad/ | B: d Dej 2<br>(Dej = dejection, unpleasant emotions) |
| /His eyes are somewhat blank—coincidence of reading a book without any eyes or knowing what is in the book without reading it. | B: Pass 3<br>(Pass = passivity) |
| He disregards the music and falls asleep reading the book./ | Outcome—<br>B: Cont S: Pass<br>(Cont S = continuation of behavior) |

The abbreviated forms of the primary variables, generally used for scoring, do not appear in the following scoring record. For purposes of clarity, either the variable name is written out in full, or—in a few cases where the name itself would need explanation—a more common term is used to describe the scored material.

Notations that remain in their abbreviated form are defined below:

*Description of characters:* Ch = child, B = boy, G = girl, Pers = person, M = man, W = woman, Fa = father, Mot = mother, Auth = authoritarian law-enforcement group, Fam = family group, Grp = social group, Myth = mythical character, Sym = symbolic figure, E = environmental force.

(Appearing before the colon, these notations refer to the subject to which the variable is attributed; appearing immediately after the colon, they refer to the object of the behavior; appearing after the variable, they refer to the instrument of the behavior with which the subject is identified.)

*Notations of surface defenses:* Cft = conflict; d = denial; R = rejection

[1] Story content appearing in parentheses is not scorable.

by the story-teller of the behavior described; r = rejection of the described behavior by the story character; F = uncertainty of the story teller about; f = fantasy about; o = the variable is expressed through a secondary story character (who is described by a notation following the variable); + = the variable is a descriptive term, or refers to a static state of being, rather than referring to active behavior; − = lack of state of being.

| | *Preceding picture* | *Happening in picture* | *Outcome* |
|---|---|---|---|
| 1. | | B:+Affliction 2<br>:n Autonomy 2<br>:f Elation 3<br>:Bdfp Rejection (Par) 2<br>:d Tension 2<br>:Mental Sentience 3<br>:d calm 2<br>:d Dejection 2<br>:Passivity 3 | B:ContS:Pass |
| 3BM. | G:R Sexual behav. 4<br>E:Gp Blamavoidance 3<br>:Gp Punishment 2 | G:n Abasement–(self-destructive) 4<br>:(G)fn Respect 3<br>:(G)fp Rejection Soc 2<br>:G p Rejection Soc 2<br>:n Infavoidance 2 | G:Suicide |
| 4. | M&G:Sexual behav. 3 | G:M n Sex 2<br>M:G p Rejection 4<br>:(W) fn Sex 2<br>G:M n Succorance 4<br>+Poverty 2<br>M:G p Compliance 2 | G:Mn Aggression (Murder)<br>G:Suicide |
| 6BM. | B:(G) n Sex 2<br>(G):B p Rejection 2<br>B:(G)n Aggression (Murder) | Mot:oRn Aggression B 3<br>:Mot on Blamavoidance B 2<br>:B Fp Blamavoidance 4<br>:B Fp Rejection 3<br>:n Recognition 3 | Mot :B n Aggression (Murder) |
| 7 BM. | | B:Dejection 3<br>:+Affliction 3<br>:n Abasement–(self-destructive) 3<br>Fa:Bn Nurturance 2<br>:Bn Dominance 3<br>:B dn Nurturance 4<br>:B n Rejection 2<br>:f on Construction B 2 | B:Death<br>Fa:n Abasement (for) Bn Rejection & B dn Nurturance |

| | *Preceding picture* | *Happening in picture* | *Outcome* |
|---|---|---|---|
| | | B:n Construction 2<br>:Fam Imposed<br>n Nurturance 2 | |
| 11. | Anim:Grp n Aggression 3<br>:Grp n Cognizance 2<br>Grp:Rn Seclusion 2 | Fate:Grp p Nurturance 2<br>E:Grp +p Physical Danger 4<br>Fate:Grp n Punishment 4 | Grp:Death |
| 12M. | M1:n Recognition 3<br>M1:+ Artistry 3<br>E:M1—p Respect 3<br>M:+ Poverty 2<br>E:M1 p Affliction 2 | M1:+p Death 3<br>M2:M1 p Nurturance<br>:M1 p Respect 3 | ⟶ |
| 13MF. | M&G:np Affiliation 2<br>:np Succorance 2<br>M:fdR+Sexuality G 3<br>M:(G)fo p Death 2<br>M:G r Sexual behavior 3 | M:n Abasement 3 | M:G n Rejection (for) R Sexual behavior |
| 13B. | | B:Bfp Rejection (Fam) 4<br>:Dejection 3<br>:fdp Nurturance (Fa) 3<br>:Fam fn Seclusion 3<br>Mot:B n Succorance 3<br>:B n Respect 3<br>:B n Nurturance 2 | B:Elation<br>:Fa fn Aggression<br>:Mot f n Affiliation |
| 14. | M:(M2) Rn Aggression (Murder) 3<br>M:(M2)Rn Acquisition 2<br>(M1):(M2)fRn Aggression (Murder) M 3 | (M1):n Cognizance 4<br>(M1):on Seclusion M3<br>:on Blamescape M 3<br>:oRp Aggression (M2) 3<br>(M1):M p Blamavoidance 4 | Auth:M p Punishment (for) Murder |

| | *Preceding picture* | *Happening in picture* | *Outcome* |
|---|---|---|---|
| 16. | Grp:p Physical Danger 3<br>:p Affliction 2<br>:p Lack 4<br>:p Isolation 5 | | Grp: Death |

## MAPS TEST WORKING NOTES

| | | | |
|---|---|---|---|
| 1. | Mot: +Ugliness 4<br>:+ n Aggression 2<br>:W n Succorance 3<br>W&M:Mot n Rejection 5<br>M, Auth:Mot p Dominance 2 | W&M:np Aggression 3<br>Snake:W&M p Aggression 3 | M&W:Death |
| 2. | G:R + Sexuality 4<br>:M1&M2 R sexual behavior 3<br>:+Beauty 2<br>M1:G fan Aggression (Murder) 3<br>:G f Sexual behav. 2<br>G p Cognizance 3 | Sym :G p Cognizance 3<br>M2:M1 fn Aggression (Murder) 3<br>M2:M1 p Cognizance 3<br>M2:G n Aggression 4 (Murder) | M2:n Abasement |
| 3. | Mot:Sym Rn Acquisition 3<br>Sym:Mot p Dominance 3<br>p Blamavoidance 3<br>p Punishment 3<br>p Affliction 5 | B&M :Mot p Rejection 4 | Cont:Mot p Affliction |
| 4. | W:Fa o+Rn Aggression W (Murder) 2<br>W:M1 ro Sexual behavior G 3<br>W:G Rn Aggression (Murder) 2<br>M1:n Abasement 3 | Myth :W p Dominance 2<br>W:n Abasement 2<br>W:M3 f Sexual behavior 3<br>W:M2 fRn Aggression (Murder) 3 ——→failed | M2:W Rn Aggression (Murder) |
| 5. | M:G n Aggression (Murder) 3<br>W:M n Cognizance 4 | | W:G op Death<br>M:Suicide |

| Preceding picture | Happening in picture | Outcome |
|---|---|---|
| M:n Succorance 2<br>:W n Rejection 2<br>W:M n Rejection 3 | | |
| 6. Grp:n Construction 2<br>:n Cognizance 4 | | Grp:p Death |
| 7. Sym, G:n Recognition 3<br>+ Sexuality 3<br>Soc n Rejection 2<br>Soc n Autonomy 3<br>OW:G n Aggression (Murder) 3<br>:+n Aggression 3<br>:+ Ugliness 2 | Priest :n Cognizance 2<br>G2:Priest n Aggression (Murder) 3<br>G2:Soc n Aggression (Murder) 5 | Soc:p Death |

## INTERPRETATION

Readily observable in the variable scorings are these main features:

(1) An extraordinary amount of primitive aggression (murder).

(2) Repeated reference to vague environmental forces—fate, spirits, or the elements — as agencies of disaster (E or Sym: p Phy Dgr, p Aggression, p Death)

(3) Numerous descriptions of interplay of personal hostilities (np Rejection)

(4) Lack of positive interpersonal relationships (of Affiliation, Sex, Respect, Nurturance)

(5) Rejection of sexuality in women (R Sexual behavior)

(6) Negative description of women in the role of mother figures by referring to them as ugly, manipulative, domineering, and greedy (Mot: + Physical Ugliness, n Cognizance, n Acquisition, n Dominance)

(7) Outcomes: of death by suicide, of murder, or of death by the destructive elements of fate or nature.

The following common themas expressed by this subject become apparent by observation of the variable sequence:

(1) n Aggression → Auth or Sym, Auth: p Cognizance (observed by an actual representative of authority or a symbol of authority) → punishment by guilt (n Abasement, suicide), murder, and/or by authorities: TAT stories 4, 6BM, 14; MAPS stories 1, 2, 4, 5)

(2) W:R Sexual behavior → punishment by death (MAPS 2, 4, 7) or rejection (TAT 13MF), by guilt and suicide (TAT 3BM, 4)

(3) E or Sym: Grp p Physical Danger, p Death (to less structured pictures; TAT 11, 16; MAPS 6, 7)

(4) B:Mot n Succorance, Passivity → Gratification of needs (TAT 1, 13B)

(5) M:Fa n Succorance, n Recognition → Frustration of needs ( – p Respect, dp Nurturance) or M:p Death→M p Nurturance (TAT 7BM, 12M)

In analyzing this case an attempt has been made to explain the notations used, and to show how the events in the story can be described in psychologically meaningful terms, with attention to the subject and object of behavior, the defenses used in describing the behavior, and the sequence of events described. The various ways in which the variables can be manipulated for purposes of research with a large number of records has not been demonstrated. This would demand too lengthy a discussion to be attempted here. It may be well, though, to mention the twelve main groupings into which the primary variables fall: Aggression (1) directed outward, (2) directed toward the self; Interpersonal relationships of (3) dependence, (4) independence, (5) superiority, (6) equality, (7) manipulation; (8) Environmental press; (9) Mood; (10) Sentience; (11) Superego and ego ideal; (12) Endogenous and Exogenous benefits and deprivations.

We wish to stress the importance of an objective, molar approach for validating hypotheses used in interpretation of fantasy material. In examining the case under consideration here, it is apparent that there are a number of consistent trends from one story to the other, and from one test to the other, that stand out clearly in the scoring record. Though there is little doubt about the meaningfulness of these trends, serious consideration must be given both to the extent of our ability to interpret with validity to other aspects of behavior, broader personality dynamics, overt symptomatology, or prognosis in therapy—and to the nature of the cues used for such prediction.

# Chapter 6

# LEOPOLD BELLAK

Dr. Bellak was born in 1916. He studied at the University of Vienna Medical School, received an M.A. degree in Psychology from Boston University in 1939 and an M.A. degree from Harvard University in 1942. He obtained the M.D. degree at New York Medical College in 1944. He took his postgraduate psychiatric training at St. Elizabeths Hospital in Washington, D.C. and at the New York Psychoanalytic Institute. He is lecturer in Psychology at New York University and at the New School for Social Research, and Associate in Psychiatry at New York Medical College and the Flower-Fifth Avenue Hospital. His work is divided among the private practice of psychiatry and psychoanalysis, research in psychiatry and psychology, and teaching—primarily the TAT. He is author of the books *Dementia Praecox*, *Manic-Depressive Psychosis*, the *Children's Apperception Test*, and co-editor of *Projective Psychology*.

## SELECTED REFERENCES


BELLAK, LEOPOLD, The Concept of Projection; an Experimental Investigation and Study of the Concept. *Psychiatry*, 1944, 7, 353–370.

———, *A Guide to the Interpretation of the Thematic Apperception Test*. New York: Psychological Corporation, 1947. Pp. 8.

———, *Bellak TAT Blank: for Recording and Analyzing Thematic Apperception Test Stories*. New York: Psychological Corporation, 1947.

———, The Clinical Use of the Thematic Apperception Test—in ABT, L., AND BELLAK, L. (Eds.), *Projective Psychology*. New York: Knopf and Company, 1950.


## RESUME OF METHOD

THIS IS a scoring system which notes, mostly in the form of a check list, the main theme, the hero, attitudes toward parental figures, the handling of blame, conflicts, punishment, need gratification, the outcome, and some formal aspects including the omission or introduction of objects and figures into the pictures. Importance of items is quantified by the use of from one to three check marks. Interpretation is made on several levels, such as descriptive, interpretative, diagnostic, symbolic, and elaborative.

## TAT WORKING NOTES

In the following, only the first story of each test is analyzed in detail. The main features of the other stories (with a bit more for the second and third stories of the TAT) are indicated.

In my manual for the TAT, I recommend stating a descriptive, an interpretative and a diagnostic level of the theme. I do not recommend that all three levels have to be written out except for training purposes. In a simple story such as TAT story 1, descriptive and interpretative levels are nearly identical, and for this reason, I am stating only the interpretative and diag-

Name__________________ Story No.________ (TAT Picture No.________)

1. **Main Theme:**

2. **Main hero (heroine):** age______ sex______ vocation______
interests______
traits______
abilities______
adequacy (✓, ✓✓, ✓✓✓)______

3. **Attitudes to superior (parental) figures, or to society: (✓, ✓✓, ✓✓✓)**

| | | | |
|---|---|---|---|
| autonomous____ | compliant____ | respectful____ | devoted____ |
| grateful____ | dependent____ | remorseful____ | competitive____ |
| resistant____ | aggressive____ | abasive____ | fearful____ |

4. **Figures introduced: (✓)**

| | | | |
|---|---|---|---|
| punisher____ | pursuer____ | benefactor____ | teacher____ |
| friend____ | reformer____ | lover____ | supporter____ |
| enemy____ | | | |

5. **Objects introduced (symbols?):**

6. **Objects omitted:**

7. **Attribution of blame: (✓, ✓✓, ✓✓✓)**

| | | |
|---|---|---|
| injustice____ | indifference____ | deception____ |
| severity____ | deprivation____ | unfortunate influence____ |

8. **Significant conflicts: (✓, ✓✓, ✓✓✓)**

| | |
|---|---|
| Super Ego-Id____ | passivity-counteraction____ |
| compliance-autonomy____ | achievement-pleasure____ |

9. **Punishment — for crime: (✓, ✓✓, ✓✓✓)**

| | | |
|---|---|---|
| just____ | too severe____ | lenient____ |
| immediate____ | delayed____ | none____ |

10. **Attitude to hero: (✓, ✓✓, ✓✓✓)**
detached and objective____
critical and abusive____
involved and empathic____

11. **Signs of inhibition at aggression, sex, etc.: (✓, ✓✓, ✓✓✓)**
pauses____ change of trend____ stammer____

12. **Outcome: (✓, ✓✓, ✓✓✓)**
happy____ unhappy____ realistic____ unrealistic____

13. **Pattern of need gratification: (✓)**
need-conflict____
need-fusion____
need-subsidiation____

14. **Plot: (✓, ✓✓, ✓✓✓)**

| | |
|---|---|
| structured____ | unstructured____ |
| realistic____ | bizarre____ |
| complete____ | incomplete____ |

**Analysis Sheet for use with the Bellak TAT Blank**

 47-226AS The Psychological Corporation

nostic theme. Ordinarily, I recommend that the interpretative theme be stated on the analysis sheet pertaining to each story, and that the diagnostic level be recorded on the summary sheet together with other pertinent data culled from the analysis sheet. I might add that TAT story 1 of John Doe is about as poor a story to restate in my form of theme as a story can be, because of the lack of dramatic movement and structure. The second story is already much more suitable.

The actual interpretation of the TAT record took me half an hour; the typing much longer. I mention this undocumented fact as a matter of conviction that economy must be considered for a clinically useful test. My report is not meant to be exhaustive; if done in complete detail, I believe that every TAT can be transformed into a basis for a small monograph.

My *scheme* of interpretation is meant as a frame of reference for *minimal* and more concrete data, and as a training device. For myself, I often elaborate on the basis of psychoanalytic knowledge.

I regret that card 2 (farm scene) was not included in the record; it is nearly always useful. Even though I usually use only 10 pictures, selected to fit the case, it is a "must" picture for me.

In my "Final Report" I wish to emphasize the insistence that specific references to pictures be given to the general statements made on the basis of the TAT. I believe that this practice tends to curb too free a flight of fancy, and that it makes the report more concrete for readers. I made the statement on consistency of the record with a schizophrenic disorder with reluctance: (a) I believe that the diagnosis of schizophrenia is made too carelessly at present—very much in vogue. (b) I do not believe that the TAT or MAPS tests lend themselves primarily for diagnosis—if this means identification of a nosologic entity. I believe that the Rorschach, as an expressive-form analytic procedure, can do this better, while the apperceptive tests are better suited for a clear presentation of psychic dynamics. (c) I believe that if diagnoses are offered at all—on the basis of test material alone—it should be phrased not stronger than: this record is *consistent with* . . .

A. *Analysis of Scoring Categories of Story 1.*
(See reproduction of Analysis Sheet on facing page.)

1. Main theme: Interpretative theme: (If one is) a sick child, told to study music (ignores the fiddle), prefers an adventure story concerning water, feels not happy not sad, unafraid of punishment, possibly reading without eyes or knowing book without reading it, falls asleep.
(See below for diagnostic analysis.)
2. Main hero (heroine): age: child; sex: male; vocation: student;
interests: reading adventure stories concerning water
traits: studious, "unafraid," "not happy, not sad"
abilities: reading a book without eyes, knowing what is in it without reading it.
adequacy: o ?

3. Attitudes to superior (parental) figures, or to society: autonomous, resistant
4. Figures introduced: Parents
5. Objects introduced: Book, water, ocean, school, illness
6. Objects omitted: violin, bow
7. Attribution of blame: coercion?
8. Significant conflicts: compliance-autonomy, achievement-pleasure
9. Punishment: not noted
10. Attitude to hero: Apparently self-involved but without production of real feeling
11. Signs of inhibition at aggression, sex, etc.: change of trend
12. Outcome: not noted
13. Pattern of need gratification: need-subsidiation withdrawal subsidiary to resistance
14. Plot: complete, unstructured, bizarre

B. *Diagnostic Level Interpretation of Story 1.*

*Diagnostic Theme of Story 1, TAT, John Doe:*

Feels sick: poor body image (self-image)

*Ignores fiddle altogether:* This is rare in adults, usually signifying disturbance re violin and playing as sexual symbols, particularly masturbatory.

*Instead of studying, prefers fantasy:* Resistant to parents; unable to study, or unwilling; prefers fantasy.

*Fantasy concerns water, ocean:* Since this is entirely personal introduction by subject, wonder if related to enuresis, urethral complex, and premature ejaculation as sexual disturbance, aside from actual urinary disturbances.

*Unafraid of punishment:* Negation probably means: I wish I were not afraid . . . actually quite afraid?

*Not happy, not sad:* Anhedonia, underlying depression.

*Reading without eyes:* Bizarre statement; being blind is often punishment for voyeurism (related to exhibitionism) and often consistent with very great masturbation guilt.

*Knows what is in book without reading it:* Bizarre statement; implies telepathic notions, superhuman power, possibly related to cosmic delusions.

*Falling asleep:* Resolves conflict situation (disobeying parents) by withdrawal.

Story is far removed from stimulus, poorly structured, bizarre, consistent with severe thought disturbance; and flat mood consistent with schizophrenia.

C. *Summary—recording the themes and summarizing other significant data for each story.*

| Interpretative Level | Diagnostic Level |
|---|---|
| 1. See B. above. | |
| 3BM. If a girl is guilty of prostitution she is jailed; is ashamed of the publicity and the | Has great guilt over sex; feminine identification; severe superego concerning also ex- |

| | |
|---|---|
| hurting of sister whom she should emulate in being a nun, and kills herself. | hibitionism and ambivalence to sibling seen as pure; intra-aggression. |
| 4. If one commits adultery, one is "half-caste" (inferior); will be rejected, poorly off, will kill oneself and lover by fire. | Sexual guilt; social prejudice; punishment is rejection, poverty; has intra- and extra-aggressivity; urethral complex (identifies with girl again); but may also say: women are bad, do this sort of thing; endanger one (in secondary identification). |

6BM. [1] Extreme guilt feelings over aggressive impulses fused with sexual impulses; fear of being hurt by mother (probably projection; thus impulses are probably related toward her originally).

7BM. Father seen as cold, speculating; aggression toward father who is also seen as debilitated-castrated. Hero (subject) feels depressed, ill. (tBc: full of holes; or is it syphilis he is concerned with?)

11. Feels inevitability of final disaster, of being caught for being wicked; despair, religious thoughts.

12M. Poor body image; feels prostrate, neglected, orally rejected. Inevitable ruin.

13MF. Guilt feelings over sex-image of girl being disturbed by image of mother (looks the same as girl at home) to whom he has great attachment; still sees her as immaculate but is at the same time very afraid of her and hostile, too.

13B. Again oedipal difficulties, competition with father who is seen as rejecting, incapable.

14. Symbolic oedipal struggle re symbolic "jewelry box" with terrific hostile impulses toward father and fear of hostility from father. Mutilation is consistent with great disturbance, probably schizophrenic, paranoid features.

16. Feeling of deadness consistent with schizophrenic (catatonic?) subjective experience. Outside influence and telepathic touch suggest ideas of reference, cosmic delusions.

## TAT INTERPRETATION

*General:*

This is an extremely disturbed man: he conceives of himself as ill, incapacitated, mutilated, feels depressed, fearful, and dead inside.

He is extremely ambivalent toward both father and mother figures; his oedipal problems are entirely unresolved: he has a tremendous attachment to the mother, whom he sees as dangerous at the same time. He sees the father as cold, hostile, and inadequate.

The patient has tremendous guilt feelings concerning both sexual and aggressive impulses (which appear fused). (He frequently identifies with a female figure.) He also has conflicts concerning exhibitionistic and voyeuristic tendencies, related to urethral difficulties, possibly.

His thought processes appear disturbed, tending toward the bizarre. There are data consistent with cosmic delusions and hallucinations.

The total picture is consistent with a schizophrenic disorder, with potential paranoid and hebephrenic coloring. Suicidal risk is considerable. Homicidal

[1] No systematic interpretation in stories 4 to 11.

risk should be considered. Sexual criminology, including overt homosexuality are possible.

*Specific:*

Illness and mutilation appear in stories 1, 7BM, 12M, 14 and 16.

Depression, fear and guilt is apparent in every single story, usually related to sex, such as prostitution in 7BM, adultery in 4, sex and murder in 6BM, sex and disgust in 13MF, murder and stealing in 14. Homosexuality suggested by female identifications.

Blindness occurs in story 1, great notoriety in 3BM, stage acting in 6BM, not looking in 13MF, photography in 14. These themes are consistent with voyeurism and exhibitionism.

Water occurs in story 1, fire in 4, slightly suggestive of urethral problems.

Conflict with parental figures appears in story 1, female figure is seen as dangerous and seductive in 4, mother seen as dangerous in 6BM, father as cold in 7BM, as inadequate in 7BM (was also sick) and in 13B, and is fought with symbolically in 14.

The thought processes most clearly appear to be disturbed and bizarre in stories 1 and 16.

## MAPS TEST WORKING NOTES

A. *Analysis of Scoring Categories for Livingroom Story.*

1. Main theme: Descriptive level—A housewife sees her mother, a terrible looking woman (disfigured by childbirth) at her door, followed by a snake; indignantly calls her husband; wants to shoo mother away; however, the mother wants money for another child. The daughter has a police officer send the mother away, giving her some money; housewife is thereupon rejected by the husband herself, and both are killed by the mother's revenge.
2. Main hero (heroine): sex: F , vocation: housewife
3. Attitudes to superior (parental) figures, or to society: resistant, aggressive, remorseful, abasive, fearful
4. Figures introduced: policeman, mother, snake
5. Objects introduced (symbols?): money
6. Objects omitted: not noted
7. Attribution of blame: not noted
8. Significant conflicts: superego-id, compliance-autonomy
9. Punishment—for crime: immediate, too severe
10. Attitude to hero: involved and empathic
11. Signs of inhibition at aggression, sex, etc.: not noted
12. Outcome: not noted

13. Pattern of need gratification: not noted
14. Plot: structured, complete, bizarre

B. *Diagnostic Level Interpretation for Livingroom Story.*

*Interpretative level:* If one mistreats one's mother (who is false, phallic, terribly traumatized by childbirth and who favors another sibling) one's mother threatens revenge, one's mate will reject one in turn and both mate and oneself will die by the mother's revenge (snake).

*Diagnostic statements: "If one mistreats one's mother":* feelings of hostility toward mother and guilt feelings about it. Mother is seen as *false, dangerous, phallic, demanding, favoring a sibling,* i.e., sibling rivalry, and what applies to mother probably applies to patient's concept of females generally. Patient has conception that a *woman is hurt terribly by childbirth* and probably by *sex activity.* Since he identifies with a woman in this story, it is reasonable to conclude that he expects such *harm to himself,* either *from men or women,* whom he sees as phallic. *"Threatened by mother's revenge"; "rejected by mate":* The patient has tremendous guilt feelings about his hostility; uses projection as the outstanding defense mechanism, and expects not to be loved by anyone. *"die by mother's revenge":* tremendous intra-aggression; probably masochistic; suicidal risk. Because of projection mechanisms, may well have to consider homicidal tendencies, as well.

C. *Summary—recording themes and summarizing other significant data for each story.*

| Interpretative Level | Diagnostic Level |
|---|---|
| 1. Livingroom. See B, above. | |
| 2. Street. If degraded, one has affairs with "inferiors," doublecrosses with other man, is in danger of being killed by both, is killed by one who kills himself in turn. | Guilt over sex; social bias; triangular (oedipal) conflict; fear of being hurt as result of projection of hostile impulses and severe superego. |

(First identification with woman, secondary one with man.)

3. Bathroom.[2] Nothing but hair: no penis? unclear sex differences; no mouth, no eyes; mutilation, hostile ideas toward women, as expressed by husband; magic thoughts, phantom, and bizarreness consistent with schizophrenic disorder.

4. Dream. Identification with woman; aggression against father seen as without hair, i.e., not masculine, castrated; aggression against sibling (might be mother figure) seen in triangular conflict; heckling spirit: hallucinations? hostile impulses.

5. Bedroom. Sex and aggressive-murderous impulses fused, lead to intra-aggression, suicidal thoughts; some awareness of abnormality: reference to mental disease; starkness of scene suggestive of extraordinary pathology; possibly sex criminal: reference to attraction to minor.

6. Blank. Endlessness suggests disorder of time-space relationship; with stark symbolism suggestive of schizophrenic disorder. Hopelessness, guilt over curiosity (voyeurism).

7. Stage. Concern figure origin: where do babies come from, especially how are girls

[2] Abbreviated interpretation in stories 3 to 7.

made? identification with female, and extreme aggression and mutilation of mother-figure. Grotesqueness, symbolism suggestive of psychosis, with strong sexual coloring. Gross bizarreness. Suggestive of catatonic rigidity or subjective experience.

## MAPS TEST INTERPRETATION

I did not do a separate final report on the MAPS test since I believe the conclusions to be identical with those in the final report on the TAT. It seems to me that the two tests in this case show clearly the comparability and the practically identical dynamic material derived from them.

# Chapter 7

# LEONARD ERON

Dr. Eron was born in 1920. He received the Ph.D. degree in Psychology from the University of Wisconsin in 1949. He is an Associate of the American Psychological Association. He participated in the Veterans Administration training program in clinical psychology at the University of Wisconsin. Since 1948 he has been on the faculty of Yale University, where he is now Assistant Professor of Psychiatry and Psychology. He is also Chief Clinical Psychologist at the Yale Psychiatric Clinic and is on the faculty of the Smith College School for Social Work. His work is primarily in the fields of experimental psychopathology, perception and projective techniques. He is currently engaged in research on the personality assessment of medical students and the relationship of fantasy to overt behavior.

## SELECTED REFERENCES


ERON, LEONARD D., Frequencies of Themes and Identifications in the Stories of Schizophrenic Patients and Non-hospitalized College Students. *Journal of Consulting Psychology*, 1948, *12*, 387–395.

———, AND HAKE, D. T., Psychometric Approach to the Evaluation of the Thematic Apperception Test—in ZUBIN, J., AND YOUNG, K. M., *Manual of Projective Techniques*. Madison: College Typing Company, 1948.

———, A Normative Study of the Thematic Apperception Test. *Psychological Monographs*, 1950, *64*, No. 9, 1–48.

———, TERRY, D., AND CALLAHAN, R., The Use of Rating Scales for Emotional Tone of Thematic Apperception Test Stories. *Journal of Consulting Psychology*, 1950, *14*, 473–478.

RITTER, A. M., AND ERON, LEONARD D., The Use of the Thematic Apperception Test to Differentiate Normal from Abnormal Groups. *Journal of Abnormal and Social Psychology* (in press).


## RESUME OF METHOD

THIS IS "a normative, statistical approach." Norms are based on all 20 TAT cards for adult males administered in prescribed order and according to Murray's instructions. Stories are rated for emotional tone (from very sad to very happy) and for outcome (from complete failure to great success). Themes are noted according to a check list of more than 100 themes classified as interpersonal, intrapersonal, and impersonal; disequilibrium (tension), and equilibrium. Any deviations from the task of making up a narrative and any distortions of the physical properties of the pictures, as well as certain other formal characteristics, are noted. The ratings are then compared with the norms. The basic data for this system are the frequency and unusualness of specific fantasy content. Interpretation of personality structure and content depends on the theoretic orientation of the interpreter and on the behavioral data from other sources.

## TAT WORKING NOTES

The method of analysis and interpretation which I use in an evaluation of a TAT record is based on two assumptions: (1) We cannot expect a fantasy technique to do any more than give us some information about the nature of an individual's imaginative productions in response to certain specific stimuli which are included in the technique. How the fantasy is related to the overt behavior of a given individual is impossible to ascertain without access to complete behavioral data obtained by other means. For some individuals the fantasy may be reproductive of the subject's overt behavior, for others it may be compensatory, and for still others it may have no relationship at all to overt behavior. To try to decide which is which for any given record on the basis of the fantasy protocol alone makes a good parlor game, perhaps, but is without scientific justification in a clinical setting. (2) We ascribe significance to a fantasy response only when it differs from the modal response elicited by the given fantasy stimulus, or when there is a consistent pattern of fantasy responses from one fantasy stimulus to another regardless of its stimulus quality. When an individual distorts a stimulus, omits something from it, or adds something to it, there may be some justification, on the basis of experimental work in selective perception, in assuming that he must change the stimulus so that he can give expression to his own needs rather than the ones modally elicited by the stimulus. Or else it is necessary for him to change the stimulus so he can avoid its implications and thus not be faced with needs which he denies.

A study recently completed in our laboratory demonstrates that an examination of specific content and formal characteristics of stories cannot as a rule be used for diagnostic purposes. However, a tabulation of the frequency with which each individual fails to give expected responses and/or a tabulation of the presence in each record of an excessive number of formal deviations of a specific variety(ies) may serve as a means of weeding out some proportion of individual records as abnormal. This would seem to support our contention that fantasy is significant only when it deviates from norms for the group.

In general, therefore, mine is a normative, statistical approach, in which I determine how the responses of the individual in question differ from the responses of a number of other individuals of similar age, sex and general cultural background. This of course entails the accumulation of norms for a variety of groups, which are now in the process of being organized. The particular subject in whose protocol we are here interested fits a group of 150 male veterans whose responses have been analyzed.

There are a number of limitations, however, on the usefulness of this kind of procedure with the protocol submitted. The norms which I use are based on complete records of responses to the 20 cards recommended by Murray for use with adult males (Harvard University Press, 3rd Edition) administered in the prescribed order and according to Murray's instructions. Since this is a normative approach, only protocols administered in the same manner are strictly comparable. It is my feeling, based on tentative results obtained in our laboratory, that the pictures have a cumulative effect, so that, for example, picture number 16 following picture number 15 is not the same stimulus as when it follows picture number 14. Also "John Doe's" protocol contains only 11 stories, one of which is not a part of the adult male series.

However, I gave to each of the stories the treatment generally ascribed in order to give an idea of how the method works. First of all the story was rated for its emotional tone and outcome according to empirically derived criteria. Then the themes in each story were noted according to the theme check list. Any deviations from the instructions to make up a narrative and any distortions of the physical properties of the pictures (using Murray's descriptions as the criterion) were noted, as were various formal characteristics.

Then these ratings were compared to tables of norms in the following manner. Characteristics of the stories which were also contributed by less than 5 per cent of the standardization population were checked; if contributed by 1 per cent or less they received two checks; if they were completely individual and were not contributed by any one in the standardization group for that particular picture they received three checks Themes were then listed and tabulated according to their deviations from the norm for that particular picture (from zero weight if contributed by more than 5 per cent of the standardization group to weight of three if it did not appear in the standardization group at all). Other variables were treated in the same manner. Since card 13B is not in the adult series, variables elicited by this picture were tabulated as zero deviations so their occurrence could be noted, although there are no indications of how they deviated from the norm.

In this way we are able to determine any consistent themes and how deviant they are for the particular stimulus in question. These are basic data—the frequency and unusualness of specific fantasy content—which must be determined before any interpretive significance can be placed on the thematic material obtained. How any TAT analyst will then use these data to interpret personality structure and content will depend on his own theoretic orientation and on the amount of behavioral data obtained from other sources which are available to him and in the light of which he can ascribe meaning to the fantasy material.

The abbreviations of the symbols used in rating thematic stories by this method, and their meanings, are listed as follows:

A. *General Rating Scale for Emotional Tone of Stories:*

–2: Complete failure, submission to fate, death, murder, suicide, illicit sex with violence, revenge, aggressive hostility, severe guilt, complete hopelessness.

–1: Conflict with attempt at adjustment, rebellion, fear, worry, departure, regret, illness, physical exhaustion, resignation toward death, loneliness.

0: Description, lack of affect, balance of positive and negative feelings, routine activities, impersonal reflection.

+1: Aspiration, desire for success and doubt about outcome, compensation for limited endowment. Description with cheerful feeling, reunion with friends, contentment with world, feeling of security.

+2: Justifiably high aspiration. Complete satisfaction and happiness. Reunion with loved ones.

?: Can't make up a story.

B. *General Rating Scale for Outcomes:*

–2: Complete failure, submission to fate, death, murder, suicide, extreme punishment, extreme remorse.

–1: Some frustration: incomplete success in attaining goal, goal attained at expense of happiness, disappointment to friends and family, acceptance of unsatisfactory situation or submission to authority.

0: Continuation of ordinary situation, balance of happy and unhappy situations.

+1: Moderate success, reunion with friends, recovery from temporary disability or depression, happiness in success of others.

+2: Great success, discovery, and/or happiness. Extreme contentment, marital bliss, unusual good fortune, reunion with loved ones.

?: Cannot give an outcome, even when explicitly asked for, conditional ("if") outcomes, alternative outcomes of different emotional value.

C. *Key for Themes:*

I *Disequilibrium.*
II *Equilibrium.*
III *Level of interpretation.*

IA or IIA Disequilibrium (or equilibrium); *interpersonal*
IB or IIB Disequilibrium (or equilibrium); *intrapersonal*
IC or IIC Disequilibrium (or equilibrium); *impersonal*
IA1 or IIA1 Disequilibrium (or equilibrium); interpersonal; *parent.*
IA2 or IIA2 Disequilibrium (or equilibrium); interpersonal; *partner.*
IA3 or IIA3 Disequilibrium (or equilibrium); interpersonal; *peer.*
IA4 or IIA4 Disequilibrium (or equilibrium); interpersonal; *sibling.*
IIIA Level of interpretation; *symbolic.*
IIID Level of interpretation; *unreal.*
IIIG Level of interpretation; *autobiographical.*
IIIM Level of interpretation; *peculiar verbalization.*

*The indications for all other letters and numbers are written out.*

D. *Key for Comparison with Norms:*

O: Characteristic of story indicated by *more than 5 per cent* of standardization population.
X: Characteristic of story indicated by *less than 5 per cent* of standardization population.

XX: Characteristic of story indicated by *1 per cent or less* of standardization population.
XXX: Characteristic of story *not indicated by anyone* in standardization group for that picture.

Below are reproduced, in tabular form, the pencilled marginal notes made on the TAT protocol. These notations indicate the emotional tone of the story (Key A); the outcome (Key B); shifts to a happier or sadder conclusion; perceptual inaccuracies; the various themes (Key C); and, for each theme, the comparison with the norms for that story derived from the standardization population (Key D).

| *Story* | *Emotional Tone* | *Outcome* | *Shift* | *Perceptual Inaccuracies* | *Themes* | *Comparisons with Norms* |
|---|---|---|---|---|---|---|
| 1 | 0 | 0 | | book—xx | IB—Illness or death of central character | xxx |
| | | | | music sheet | IB—occupational dissatisfaction | |
| | | | | eyes | IIA1—cooperation | xxx |
| | | | | | IIB—retirement | xxx |
| | | | | | IIIM— | xxx |
| 3BM | −1 | −2 | x | girl | IC—legal restriction | |
| | | | | | IA2—illicit sex | xxx |
| | | | | | IB—guilt | |
| | | | | | IA4—concern | xxx |
| | | | | | IB—religion | xxx |
| | | | | | IB—suicide | |
| 4 | −1 | −2 x | x | half-caste-x | IA2—illicit sex | |
| | | | | | IA2—departure from | |
| | | | | | IA2—pressure | |
| | | | | | IA2—childbirth | xxx |
| | | | | | IA2—nurturance | xxx |
| | | | | | IC—economic pressure | |
| | | | | | IA2—decision | |
| | | | | | IA2—aggression to | xxx |
| | | | | | IB—suicide | xxx |
| 6BM | −2 | −2 | | paranoid | IIID— | xxx |
| | | | | quality, | IA1—confession | |
| | | | | characters | IA1—aggression from | xxx |
| | | | | not | IA1—death or illness of child | xxx |
| | | | | related | IA2—aggression to | xxx |
| | | | | | IA2—death or illness of partner | xxx |
| | | | | | IA2—jealousy | xxx |
| | | | | | IA2—infidelity | xxx |
| 7BM | −2 x | +1 | | introduces | IB—illness or death | xxx |
| | | | | wife and | IA1—succorance | |
| | | | | children | IIIM— | xxx |
| | | | | | IA1—pressure | |
| | | | | | IC—economic pressure | xxx |
| | | | | | IA1—death or illness of child | xxx |
| | | | | | IA1—death or illness of parent | xxx |
| | | | | | IB—retribution | xxx |
| 11 | −2 | ? | | people | IC—aggression from impersonal source | |
| | | | | | IB—religion | |

| Story | Emotional Tone | Outcome | Shift | Perceptual Inaccuracies | Themes | Comparisons with Norms |
|---|---|---|---|---|---|---|
| | | | | | IC—escape from perilous environment | |
| 12M | −1 | −2 xx | | | IC—economic pressure | xxx |
| | | | | | IB—illness or death | |
| | | | | | IB—inadequacy | xxx |
| | | | | | IA3—succorance | |
| 13MF | −1 | −1 | | | IA2—seduction | xxx |
| | | | | | IA2—illicit sex | |
| | | | | | IC—escape from environment | xxx |
| | | | | | IA2—death or illness of partner | xxx |
| | | | | | IB—guilt | |
| | | | | | IA2—unrequited | xxx |
| 13B | +1 | +1 | | introduces characters | IC—economic pressure | |
| | | | | | IA1—pressure | |
| | | | | | IA1—departure | |
| | | | | | IA1—nurturance | |
| | | | | | IB—religion | |
| | | | | | IIA1—fulfillment | |
| 14 | −2 x | −2 x | | introduces murder, paranoid quality | IIID— | xxx |
| | | | | | IB—curiosity | |
| | | | | | IB—religion | x |
| | | | | | IA3—aggression to peer | xxx |
| | | | | | IA3—death or illness of friend | xxx |
| | | | | | IB—moral struggle | xxx |
| | | | | | IA1—confession | xxx |
| | | | | | IC—aggression towards environment | xxx |
| 16 | −2 | 0 | | | IC—generalized restriction | x |
| | | | | | IC—aggression from impersonal source | x |
| | | | | | IB—loneliness | xxx |
| | | | | | IA3—desertion | xxx |
| | | | | | IIID— | xxx |

A frequency distribution of the themes for John Doe's TAT, related to the standardization group norms, is presented in tabular form below.

| 0 | 1 | 2 | 3 | Themes | |
|---|---|---|---|---|---|
| 2 | | | | IA1a | (Disequilibrium; interpersonal; parent; pressure) |
| 1 | | | | IA1b | (Disequilibrium; interpersonal; parent; succorance) |
| 1 | | | | IA1c | (Disequilibrium; interpersonal; parent; nurturance) |
| | | | 1 | IA1d | (Disequilibrium; interpersonal; parent; aggression from) |
| 1 | | | | IA1f | (Disequilibrium; interpersonal; parent; departure) |
| | | | 1 | IA1i | (Disequilibrium; interpersonal; parent; death or illness) |
| | | | 2 | IA1j | (Disequilibrium; interpersonal; parent; death or illness of child) |
| 1 | | | 1 | IA1n | (Disequilibrium; interpersonal; parent; confession) |
| 1 | | | | IA2a | (Disequilibrium; interpersonal; partner; pressure) |
| | | | 1 | IA2c | (Disequilibrium; interpersonal; partner; nurturance) |
| | | | 2 | IA2e | (Disequilibrium; interpersonal; partner; aggression to) |
| 1 | | | | IA2f | (Disequilibrium; interpersonal; partner; departure from) |
| 2 | | | 1 | IA2h | (Disequilibrium; interpersonal; partner; illicit sex) |
| | | | 2 | IA2j | (Disequilibrium; interpersonal; partner; death or illness) |

| | | | | |
|---|---|---|---|---|
| | | 1 | IA2m | (Disequilibrium; interpersonal; partner; jealousy) |
| | | 1 | IA2o | (Disequilibrium; interpersonal; partner; infidelity) |
| 1 | | | IA2p | (Disequilibrium; interpersonal; partner; decision) |
| | | 1 | IA2r | (Disequilibrium; interpersonal; partner; seduction) |
| | | 1 | IA2s | (Disequilibrium; interpersonal; partner; unrequited) |
| | | 1 | IA2u | (Disequilibrium; interpersonal; partner; childbirth) |
| 1 | | | IA3b | (Disequilibrium; interpersonal; peer; succorance) |
| | | 1 | IA3e | (Disequilibrium; interpersonal; peer; aggression to) |
| | | 1 | IA3f | (Disequilibrium; interpersonal; peer; desertion) |
| | | 1 | IA3i | (Disequilibrium; interpersonal; peer; death or illness) |
| | | 1 | IA4g | (Disequilibrium; interpersonal; sibling; concern) |
| | | 1 | IB2 | (Disequilibrium; intrapersonal; inadequacy) |
| 1 | | | IB3 | (Disequilibrium; intrapersonal; curiosity) |
| 1 | | 1 | IB5 | (Disequilibrium; intrapersonal; suicide) |
| | | 1 | IB6 | (Disequilibrium; intrapersonal; moral struggle) |
| 2 | | | IB7 | (Disequilibrium; intrapersonal; guilt) |
| 1 | | | IB11 | (Disequilibrium; intrapersonal; occupational dissatisfaction) |
| 1 | | 2 | IB12 | (Disequilibrium; intrapersonal; illness or death of hero) |
| | | 1 | IB13 | (Disequilibrium; intrapersonal; retribution) |
| 2 | 1 | 1 | IB16 | (Disequilibrium; intrapersonal; religion) |
| | | 1 | IB17 | (Disequilibrium; intrapersonal; loneliness) |
| 2 | | 2 | IC1 | (Disequilibrium; impersonal; economic pressure) |
| 1 | | | IC2 | (Disequilibrium; impersonal; legal restriction) |
| 1 | | | IC3 | (Disequilibrium; impersonal; generalized restriction) |
| | | 1 | IC4 | (Disequilibrium; impersonal; aggression towards environment) |
| 1 | | 1 | IC5 | (Disequilibrium; impersonal; aggression from impersonal source) |
| 1 | | 1 | IC7 | (Disequilibrium; impersonal; escape from environment) |
| | | 1 | IIA1a | (Equilibrium; interpersonal; parent; cooperation) |
| 1 | | | IIA1e | (Equilibrium; interpersonal; parent; fulfillment) |
| | | 1 | IIB4 | (Equilibrium; intrapersonal; retirement) |
| 25 | 0 | | | |
| | 3 | 35 | TOTAL | |
| | | 3 | IIID | (Level of interpretation: unreal) |
| | | 2 | IIIM | (Level of interpretation: peculiar verbalization) |
| | | 5 | TOTAL | |
| 9 | 2 | | TONE | |
| 8 | 2 | 1 | OUTCOME | |
| 1 | 2 | | SHIFT | |
| 2 | 1 | 1 | MISIDENTIFICATION | |
| | | | INTRODUCES CHARACTERS—3 | |

## TAT INTERPRETATION

As for the specific TAT protocol under consideration, because of the limitations noted above in the use of this technique with non-standard protocols, there is little that we can validly say except that these are productions which are very deviant from those usually obtained in response to these pictures by individuals of comparable status to the subject. Over 55 per cent of his themes are individualistic—not one subject of the standardization group offered a similar theme for these pictures. His fantasy is especially deviant in the heterosexual area and is markedly aggressive in content. There is concern in fantasy with self-destructive wishes (unusual and/or persistent themes of suicide and physical illness or death of central character). There is some religious preoccupation; and concern, in fantasy, with economic pressures. Some of the formal characteristics—peculiar verbalizations, and unreality ascribed to some of the pictures—are also representative of deviant intellectual processes.

## MAPS TEST WORKING NOTES

The following are the marginal notes made on the MAPS test protocol. These notations indicate the themes of the stories only, inasmuch as norms analogous to those used in this method for the TAT, are not available for the MAPS test.

| *Story* | *Themes* | |
|---|---|---|
| 1. Livingroom | IA1a | (Disequilib.; interpersonal; parent; pressure) |
| | IA1c | (Disequilib.; interpersonal; parent; nurturance) |
| | IA1d | (Disequilib.; interpersonal; parent; aggression from) |
| | IA1j | (Disequilib.; interpersonal; parent; death or illness of child) |
| | IA1b | (Disequilib.; interpersonal; parent; succorance) |
| | IA1L | (Disequilib.; interpersonal; parent; disappointment in) |
| | IA2a | (Disequilib.; interpersonal; partner; pressure) |
| | IC5 | (Disequilib.; *im*personal; aggression from) |
| | IA2j | (Disequilib.; interpersonal; partner; death or illness) |
| | IB12 | (Disequilib.; in*tra*personal; death or illness of hero) |
| 2. Street | IA2h | (Disequilib.; interpersonal; partner; illicit sex) |
| | IA2m | (Disequilib.; interpersonal; partner; jealousy) |
| | IA2e | (Disequilib.; interpersonal; partner; aggression to) |
| | IB27 | (Disequilib.; in*tra*personal; resurrection) |
| | IA3e | (Disequilib.; interpersonal; peer; aggression to) |
| | IA3i | (Disequilib.; interpersonal; peer; death or illness) |
| | IA2j | (Disequilib.; interpersonal; partner; death or illness) |
| | IB5 | (Disequilib.; in*tra*personal; suicide) |
| 3. Bathroom | IA1s | (Disequilib.; interpersonal; parent; lost) |
| | IA2g | (Disequilib.; interpersonal; partner; concern) |
| | IB27 | (Disequilib.; in*tra*personal; resurrection) |
| 4. Dream | IB14 | (Disequilib.; in*tra*personal; reminiscence—sad) |
| | IA1e | (Disequilib.; interpersonal; parent; aggression to) |
| | IA1i | (Disequilib.; interpersonal; parent; death or illness) |
| | IA4e | (Disequilib.; interpersonal; sibling; aggression to) |
| | IA4i | (Disequilib.; interpersonal; sibling; death or illness) |
| | IA2r | (Disequilib.; interpersonal; partner; seduction) |
| | IA2h | (Disequilib.; interpersonal; partner; illicit sex) |
| | IA2e | (Disequilib.; interpersonal; partner; aggression to) |
| | IA2i | (Disequilib.; interpersonal; partner; illicit sex with violence) |
| 5. Bedroom | IB5 | (Disequilib.; in*tra*personal; suicide) |
| | IA2e | (Disequilib.; interpersonal; partner; aggression to) |

| | | | |
|---|---|---|---|
| | | IA2i | (Disequilib.; interpersonal; partner; illicit sex with violence) |
| | | IA1j | (Disequilib.; interpersonal; parent; death or illness of child) |
| | | IB4 | (Disequilib.; in*tra*personal; behavior disorder) |
| | IIIG | | (Level of interpretation: autobiographical) |
| 6. Blank | IIIA | | (Level of interpretation: symbolic) |
| | | IB12 | (Disequilib.; in*tra*personal; illness or death of central character) |
| | | IB21 | (Disequilib.; in*tra*personal; exhaustion) |
| | | IC5 | (Disequilib.; *im*personal; aggression from impersonal source) |
| | | IB3 | (Disequilib.; in*tra*personal; curiosity) |
| 7. Stage | | IA1e | (Disequilib.; interpersonal; parent; aggression to) |
| | | IA1i | (Disequilib.; interpersonal; parent; death or illness of parent) |
| | | IB16 | (Disequilib.; in*tra*personal; religion) |

Below is presented a frequency distribution of the themes used by John Doe in his MAPS test stories.

| *Frequency* | *Theme* | |
|---|---|---|
| 1 | IA1a | (Disequilib.; interpersonal; parent; pressure) |
| 1 | IA1b | (Disequilib.; interpersonal; parent; succorance) |
| 1 | IA1c | (Disequilib.; interpersonal; parent; nurturance) |
| 1 | IA1d | (Disequilib.; interpersonal; parent; aggression from) |
| 2 | IA1e | (Disequilib.; interpersonal; parent; aggression to) |
| 2 | IA1i | (Disequilib.; interpersonal; parent; death or illness) |
| 2 | IA1j | (Disequilib.; interpersonal; parent; death or illness of child) |
| 1 | IA1L | (Disequilib.; interpersonal; parent; disappointment in parent) |
| 1 | IA1s | (Disequilib.; interpersonal; parent; lost) |
| 1 | IA2a | (Disequilib.; interpersonal; partner; pressure) |
| 3 | IA2e | (Disequilib.; interpersonal; partner; aggression to) |
| 1 | IA2g | (Disequilib.; interpersonal; partner; concern) |
| 2 | IA2h | (Disequilib.; interpersonal; partner; illicit sex) |
| 2 | IA2i | (Disequilib.; interpersonal; partner; illicit sex with violence) |
| 2 | IA2j | (Disequilib.; interpersonal; partner; death or illness) |
| 1 | IA2m | (Disequilib.; interpersonal; partner; jealousy) |
| 1 | IA2n | (Disequilib.; interpersonal; partner; compeitition) |
| 1 | IA3e | (Disequilib.; interpersonal; peer; aggression to) |
| 1 | IA3i | (Disequilib.; interpersonal; peer; death or illness) |
| 1 | IA4e | (Disequilib.; interpersonal; sibling; aggression to) |
| 1 | IA4i | (Disequilib.; interpersonal; sibling; death or illness) |
| 1 | IB3 | (Disequilib.; intrapersonal; curiosity) |
| 1 | IB4 | (Disequilib.; intrapersonal; behavior disorder) |
| 2 | IB5 | (Disequilib.; intrapersonal; suicide) |
| 2 | IB12 | (Disequilib.; intrapersonal; illness or death of hero) |
| 1 | IB14 | (Disequilib.; intrapersonal; reminiscence—sad) |
| 1 | IB16 | (Disequilib.; intrapersonal; religion) |
| 1 | IB21 | (Disequilib.; intrapersonal; exhaustion) |
| 2 | IB27 | (Disequilib.; intrapersonal; resurrection) |
| 2 | IC5 | (Disequilib.; impersonal; aggression from impersonal source) |
| 1 | IIIA | (Level of interpretation: symbolic) |
| 1 | IIIG | (Level of interpretation: autobiographical) |

# Chapter 8

# REUBEN FINE

Dr. Fine was born in 1914. He received the Ph.D. degree in Psychology from the University of Southern California in 1948. He has taught at the University of Southern California, Brooklyn College and the College of the City of New York. He was formerly on the staff of the Veterans Administration Hospital, Bronx, New York. He is now on the staff of the New York Consultation Center and in private practice, using an eclectic orientation. His work is in the fields of projective techniques and psychotherapy.

## SELECTED REFERENCES

FINE, REUBEN, The Personality of the Asthmatic Child. University of Southern California, 1948. Unpublished Doctoral Dissertation.

———, *Manual for Scoring Scheme for Verbal Projective Techniques* (*TAT, MAPS, Stories and the Like*). Washington, D. C.: Veterans Administration, 1948. Pp. 12. Mimeographed.

## RESUME OF METHOD

THIS METHOD "stresses primarily feelings and interpersonal relationships." It uses a check list for scoring the presence or absence in each story of feelings (affection, anxiety, pain, etc.); interpersonal relations (moving toward, moving against, etc.) between specific types of persons (mother to child, man to woman, etc.); and the outcomes (favorable, unfavorable, or indeterminate). The interpretation is a sort of qualitative "summing-up" of the results.

## TAT WORKING NOTES

The writer will reproduce his analysis of the TAT and MAPS tests as it was carried out.

First we turn to the TAT, not with the implication that it is a better test, but because more is known about it at the present time.

The stories were scored according to the system devised by the writer. This scoring led to the "psychogram." (See table, pages 65–67.)

We begin by a systematic analysis of the psychogram.[1]

[1] The writer has made his treatment of the TAT parallel to Klopfer's approach to the Rorschach. The psychogram is regarded neither as wholly unessential nor as an end in itself from which one can get a "diagnosis," but as a schematized picture of the personality which forms the core for further interpretations.

PSYCHOGRAM: SCORING SHEET FOR VERBAL PROJECTIVE TECHNIQUES—TAT

| I. FEELINGS | 1 | 3BM | 4 | 6BM | 7BM | 11 | 12M | 13MF | 13B | 14 | 16 | TOTAL |
|---|---|---|---|---|---|---|---|---|---|---|---|---|
| 1. a. Affection, Verbal | | | x | | | | | | x | | | 2 |
| b. Affection, Physical | | | x | x | | | | x | | | | 3 |
| 2. Anger | | | | | | | | | | | | 0 |
| 3. Anxiety | | | | x | | | | | | | | 1 |
| 4. Compulsion | x | x | | x | x | x | | | x | | | 6 |
| 5. Conflict | | | | | | | | | x | x | | 2 |
| 6. Crime | | | | | | | | | | x | | 1 |
| 7. Depression | x | | | | x | | | | x | | | 3 |
| 8. Drink | | | | | | | | | | | | 0 |
| 9. Effort | | | | | | | | | x | | | 1 |
| 10. Escape | | | | | x | x | | x | x | x | | 5 |
| 11. Excitement | | | | | | | | | x | | | 1 |
| 12. Frustration | | x | x | | | | x | x | x | | | 5 |
| 13. Guilt | | x | | | | x | | x | | | | 3 |
| 14. Hostility | | x | x | x | x | x | x | x | | x | | 8 |
| a. Verbal | | | | | | | | | | | | 0 |
| b. Physical | | | | | | | | | | | | 0 |
| c. Death | | x | x | x | x | x | x | x | | x | | 8 |
| *Management of—* | | | | | | | | | | | | |
| a. Externalized | | | | x | | | | | | x | | 2 |
| b. Internalized | | x | x | | | | | | | | | 2 |
| c. Repressed | | | | | x | | x | x | | | | 3 |
| d. Displaced | | | x | | | x | | | | | | 2 |
| e. Punished | | | | | | | | | | | | 0 |
| f. Other | | | | | | | | | | | | 0 |
| 15. Inferiority | | | x | | | | x | | x | | | 3 |
| 16. Loneliness | | | | | | | | | x | x | x | 3 |
| 17. Orality | | | | | | | | | | | | 0 |
| 18. Pain | x | x | | | x | | x | | | | x | 5 |
| 19. Path. Indicators | | | | | | | | | | | | 4 |
| a. Tabooed Activity | | | | | | | | | | | | 0 |
| b. Bizarre Verbal. | x | | | | | | | x | | | x | 3 |
| c. Rejection of Card | | | | | | | | | | | | 0 |
| d. Other | | | | x | | | | | | | | 1 |
| 20. Pleasure | x | | | | | | | | | | | 1 |
| 21. Possessiveness | | | x | | x | | | | | | | 2 |
| 22. Sexuality | | x | x | x | | | | x | | | | 4 |
| 23. Special States | x[a] | | | | x[b] | | | | | | x[c] | 3 |
| 24. Suicide | | x | x | | | | | | | | | 2 |
| 25. Superiority | | | | x | x | | x | | | | | 3 |
| 26. Wishful Thinking | x | | | | x | x | | | | | x | 4 |
| TOTAL | | | | | | | | | | | | 75 |

[a] Regret [b] Repentance [c] Self-reliance

| II. OUTCOMES | 1 | 3BM | 4 | 6BM | 7BM | 11 | 12M | 13MF | 13B | 14 | 16 | TO-TAL |
|---|---|---|---|---|---|---|---|---|---|---|---|---|
| a. Favorable | | | | | | | | | x | | | 1 |
| b. Unfavorable | | x | x | x | x | x | x | x | | x | x | 9 |
| c. Indeterminate | x | | | | | | | | | | | 1 |

PSYCHOGRAM: SCORING SHEET FOR VERBAL PROJECTIVE TECHNIQUES—TAT (*Cont'd*)

| III. INTERPERSONAL RELATIONSHIPS | Mother-Child | Child-Mother | Father-Child | Child-Father | Mother-Father | Father-Mother | Sibling-Sibling | Man-Man | Man-Woman | Woman-Man | Woman-Woman | Acquaintance-Stranger | Stranger-Acquaintance | Friend-Friend | Stranger-Stranger | Other | Total |
|---|---|---|---|---|---|---|---|---|---|---|---|---|---|---|---|---|---|
| 1. MOVING TOWARDS | | | | | | | | | | | | | | | | | |
| a. Affection | | | | | | | | | | | | | | | | | |
| (1) Verbal | | | 13B | | | | | | | 4 | | | | | | | 2 |
| (2) Physical | | | | | | | | | 4<br>13MF | 4<br>13MF<br>6BM | | | | | | | 3 |
| b. Acceptance | 4<br>7BM<br>13B | 6BM<br>7BM<br>13B | 4<br>7BM | 7BM | | 4<br>7BM | 3BM<br>13B | 13B | 4<br>13B<br>13MF | 12M | | | 14 | 7 | 12M | | 8 |
| c. Dominance | | | | | | | | | | | | | | | | | 0 |
| d. Submission | | | | | | | | | | | | 6BM | 14 | | | | 2 |

| | | | | | | | | | | | | | | | | | |
|---|---|---|---|---|---|---|---|---|---|---|---|---|---|---|---|---|---|
| 2. MOVING AGAINST | | | | | | | | | | | | | | | | | |
| a. Verbal | | | | | | | | 14 | | | | | | | | | 1 |
| b. Physical | | | | | | | | 14 | | | | | | | | | 1 |
| c. Death | | | | | | | | 14 | | 4 | | | | | 6BM | | 3 |
| 3. MOVING AWAY FROM | | | | | | | | | | | | | | | | | |
| a. Separation | | | | 7BM | | | | | 4<br>13MF | | | | | | | | 3 |
| b. Indifference | | | | | | | | | | | | | | | | | 0 |
| c. Rejection | 1<br>13B | | 1 | | | | | 13MF | | | | | | | | | 3 |
| 4. NO RELATIONSHIP | | | | | | | | | | | | | | | | | 0 |
| TOTAL ...................... | 5 | 3 | 4 | 1 | 0 | 2 | 2 | 2 | 3 | 4 | 0 | 2 | 1 | 1 | 2 | 0 | |

I. *Feelings:*

First the dominant feelings are picked out, on the hypothesis that these are in some way significant to the individual. With the exception of certain categories which are always significant, a rather arbitrary line can be drawn to select the most important. Here four seems to be the most reasonable number; that is, the feelings which occur four or more times are to be accorded the most weight. Then the following stand out: compulsion, escape, frustration hostility, pain, sexuality, and wishful thinking. Further, pathologic indicators, guilt, loneliness and suicide are significant whenever they occur (because they are rare in the average record), so they are included as well.

The absolute number of feelings is rather high—75 in a total of 11 stories, or an average of 6.81 per story. This points to an individual with considerable emotion in his make up; but how he handles this emotion cannot be decided from the psychogram alone.

We know, then, that we are dealing with an emotional individual who is dominated by the feelings listed above. Various combinations of these lead to certain conclusions. The triad of compulsion-guilt-suicide points to a powerful superego which leads to much compulsive activity, guilt and depression. From the triad escape-loneliness-wishful thinking it can be inferred that he makes much use of withdrawal and fantasy defenses to handle his problems. The combination of frustration and sexuality may be interpreted as severe frustration in the sexual sphere. The inordinate amount of death hostility shows that there is an enormous quantity of aggression being lived out in fantasy. Finally the pathologic indicators suggest that the subject is probably in the psychotic range.

From the above a tentative picture of the patient is derived. He is basically a schizoid individual who has a severe superego problem. Because of this, and for unknown historical reasons, he has been subjected to great frustrations in the sexual sphere. To these frustrations he has reacted with depression, guilt and subdued hostility which have a fantasy outlet. The strain is so great that he is most likely psychotic. In short, we are dealing with a reactive depression caused by frustration in love in a compulsive guilt-ridden schizoid personality whose defenses have failed and who is now an overt schizophrenic.

It is of interest that this tentative diagnosis based on the feelings alone is the same as the one finally reached, although the analysis of the psychogram as such cannot as a rule be regarded as sufficiently reliable for an accurate evaluation.

It is possible to go through the feelings in detail, but it is most useful to confine oneself to the three which theory tells us are the most significant in personality: frustration, hostility and sexuality.

Frustration occurs in five stories (3BM, 4, 12M, 13MF, 13B). In three of these the cause is rejection by a loved one: in two cases by a lover, in a third by the parents. In all cases the reaction is a strong one: twice it is suicide, once death from shock, twice escape. Thus it may be concluded that his frustration tolerance to rejection is so low that it can induce any one of a number of violent reactions, including withdrawal and suicide.

Hostility appears in eight of the eleven stories, an extremely high proportion. The writer's tentative figures for all 20 cards of the TAT range from one-third to one-half of the stories normally involving hostility. Furthermore, the aggressive action takes unusual or gruesome forms: suicide, sudden death, mutilation and the like. Such a pattern is found ordinarily in individuals who are for the most part meek and mild, but who from time to time lose control, and have violent outbursts. In this particular case, the outbursts may conceivably take a catatonic form.

An analysis of the direction of hostility (aggressor and victim of aggression) reveals only one significant trend—that the person who dies is close to the hero or heroine (3BM, 4, 6BM, 7BM, 12M, 13MF). From this it may be inferred that he is terrorized by a strong fear of separation, and that his close relationships are characterized by a high degree of ambivalence.

Sexuality appears in four of the eleven stories, which is fairly high. In most cases this points to a background of some sex experience, though no reliable conclusions as such can be drawn from the mere presence of sex stories. More important is the manner in which it comes up. In every case it is either carried out under unpleasant circumstances or leads to unpleasant consequences (in three cases literally followed by death). In three cases the woman is inferior to the man (prostitute, half-caste, pick-up). From these findings it may be inferred first that he has had some heterosexual experience, second that it has been of a casual nature, third that he idealizes "good" girls, with one of whom he may have had relations which led to further idealization and guilt feelings, and fourth that sex is a source of preoccupation to him.

Finally, under the feelings the pathologic indicators remain to be considered. In Card 1 he sees a boy "sick in bed" and "without any eyes." In general, seeing this boy as blind or half-blind points to a severe sense of inferiority, frequently attached to some traumatic incident, and is found more often among schizophrenics than among other groups, though it may be found in almost anyone. To see the boy without any eyes at all is very rare. It may be interpreted as the disturbed schizophrenic's wish to punish himself for his guilt (it is not uncommon for schizophrenics literally to try to put out their eyes or to castrate themselves), and second to institute a further regression, as a result of which he need no longer maintain contacts with others on a mature level. Being sick in bed is also in line with this interpretation.

The next pathologic indicator occurs in Card 6BM, where the mother kills her son. Such a crime is so rare that the word for it (filicide) is almost unknown, unless it is carried out in infancy (infanticide). The interpretation of this filicide is obvious: an extreme sense of hostility on the part of the mother-figure, which most analytic authors now consider to be part of the essence of the genesis of schizophrenia.

Third, in Card 13MF, there is a line of reasoning which strikes one as rather odd, though it is not as bizarre as the others. The hero picks up a girl who is identical with the dead beloved, and, instead of rejoicing, he has intercourse with her and leaves. Such reasoning suggests that the patient is fixated on some dream girl whom he cannot get out of his mind and who spoils his relationships with other girls. In view of the maternal hostility displayed, such a dream girl is presumably a fantasy compensation for the harshness of reality.

Finally the entire story on Card 16 sounds bizarre. A number of the verbalizations are peculiar, but the most peculiar of all is the comment that "if they had had one line of contact, . . . even a telepathic touch with the outside world, they could have perhaps been saved." This desire for a "telepathic touch" may be interpreted as the type of longing that leads on the one hand to ideas of reference, and on the other to auditory hallucinations, both of which in all likelihood the patient has had or now has.

II. *Outcome:*

In the analysis of the outcomes the most obvious finding is that nine of the eleven stories end unfavorably. This points to an active type of depression (somewhat agitated) in contrast to the patient with largely indeterminate endings, whose depression is more passive. The main difference is that this kind of personality is not stabilized; his depression is so painful that he must do something about it.

III. *Interpersonal Relationships:*

Three of the eleven stories are devoid of real relationships, the remainder are full of people. From these numbers as such it can be inferred only that he has many fantasies about people, but that his fantasy life is not consistent.

Next, the structure of Section III of the psychogram leads to certain inferences. (The totals at the right and bottom here are in terms of the number of stories.) In terms of the categories of moving towards, against and away, relationships involving moving against and away from occur almost as frequently as moving towards. The presence of death hostility in three relationships is particularly striking. This may be interpreted as a relative absence of soothing fantasies about people; in other words, again we find an agitated personality.

About half of the relationships occur among family members. In a subject of his age, this is somewhat high, but not unduly so. It indicates that he has broken away from the family to a limited extent.

Most information is obtained from a detailed examination of the individual relationships.

1. *Mother-child:* This occurs in five stories, but of these five, three describe fantasy relationships. ("Fantasy" is used here in the sense of something that a character in the story imagines or fears or looks forward to or fantasizes in any other way.) In Card 1 he is afraid of rejection, in Card 4 the mother looks forward to taking care of her child, in Card 6BM the mother kills her son, in Card 7BM the mother again looks forward to taking care of her child, and in Card 13B rejection is followed by acceptance. Thus a good real relationship between mother and child is not described in a single story, which is unusual. This may be interpreted as a sense of rejection by the mother, with variable hopes for acceptance by her which are soon dissipated and hence offer no adequate comfort.

2. *Child-mother:* The relationships here are in striking contrast to mother-child. In the three stories in which they occur (6BM, 7BM, 13B) they are all real and all acceptant. It is as though the patient were saying: "I have to be a good boy, and I have been such a good boy, yet mother still does not love me." The prevalence of guilt indicates that this lack of love is internalized, and made his fault, which implies that his efforts to regain maternal affection by model behavior will be intensified.

3. *Father-child:* These occur in four stories, twice in fantasy and twice in reality. One is rejecting, the other three accepting. The father-figure thus does not appear to be as frightening to the patient as the mother. However, this finding may be a function of the test situation since the TAT seems to be somewhat more revealing about mother-child relationships than father-child.

4. *Child-father:* Occurs only once. This relative rarity may be a function of the stimulus material, and no particular significance is attached to it.

5. *Mother-father:* There are no relationships at all between wife and husband ("wife-husband" and "mother-father" are used synonymously). This is quite unusual, and points to a severe disturbance in two directions: first, the mother-figure is again seen as extremely unpleasant, and second, he has little faith in his fantasies about a dream girl who will come along and save him; or, we might say, the mother-figure is so bad in his eyes that he is unable to establish any real relationship with a woman because of it.

6. *Father-mother:* This occurs in two stories (4, 7BM); in both, the husband is a man who does right by his family. Taken in conjunction with the absence of mother-father relationships, this may be interpreted to mean that the patient feels that he would be a model husband, but no suitable woman can be found for him.

7. *Sibling-sibling:* Sibling relationships are rare in the TAT, and when they do appear usually point to some sibling rivalry situation in childhood of clinical significance. The two stories (3BM, 13B) in which siblings are men-

tioned both highlight a sibling rivalry conflict. In 3BM, the "bad" girl contrasts herself with the "good" sister, i.e., the guilt results in part from a comparison with a well-behaved sibling. The other, 13B, may be interpreted to mean that when the sibling did arrive, he reacted with an intensification of his efforts to be kind to the mother, and regain her love in that way, with a concomitant repression of hostility towards the sibling. It may be (3BM) that when the maternal love was not forthcoming he then resorted to deliberate wickedness to draw punishment on his head.

8. *Man-man:* This comes up twice (13B, 14). In one case it is an ordinary scene between boys, in the other it involves various kinds of hostility between men. There is thus an absence of satisfactory relationships with men, which is not too rare in the TAT, but still sufficiently so to permit the interpretation of an inability to make close friends of the same sex or even to get along with them casually on a social level.

9. *Man-woman:* These come up in three stories. In all three cases, the attitude of the male is a submissive one: in 4 and 13MF he yields to the entreaties of the woman, in 13B the boy summons help from a neighbor. But in the two adult cases, in spite of his submissiveness the relationship ends unfavorably because of some action of the woman or because the woman is inadequate. Thus again we are led to the unconscious formula which this patient is using: "I am good and kind and submissive, but women are malevolent, hostile and inferior and ruin all my plans."

10. *Woman-man:* Occurs in four stories. The general pattern has already been indicated under man-woman.

11. *Woman-woman:* The complete absence of relationships in this category leads first to the same inference that the man-man relationships led to, that he is incapable of establishing close relationships with a person of the same sex. A second plausible inference is that he lacks the capacity to project his difficulties to an outside situation, as, e.g., the average man does when he complains of how bad women drivers are, or how women are always fighting with one another.

IV. *Individual Stories:*

Next we turn to an analysis of the individual stories. To carry this out properly, norms are necessary; the writer will have to draw on his own experience in the absence of adequate published material. On the basis of this experience, various hypotheses have been formulated about the range of meanings of each card, which will be referred to below. In view of the fact that much has already been learned from what has gone before, in examining the stories only questions of a more general character will be considered.

*Card 16:* The most useful card to begin with is the blank. Here the subject's image of himself and his most important hopes, aspirations and fears are mirrored most clearly. Consequently this is by far the most significant of the TAT cards.

Certain obvious things stand out about this story. First of all it can scarcely be called a story; it is more like a simple fantasy. Second, it is incoherent: there was a settlement, it might have been there, it might not have been there. Third there are no real relationships between people described, and the "inhabitants" mentioned are vague. Fourth the central theme of the story is that of despair at being alone, and destruction because of the aloneness.

The story may thus be interpreted as a description of a schizophrenic break. Patient was alone, no one to help him, he suffered, was lost, ruined—all this adds up to the depressive reaction accompanying the sense of isolation from people. There is no sign of a fantasy compensation; rather, continued depression.

Further, it is to be noted that it is a story, or more precisely an attempt at a story, and that it is not entirely incoherent. Thus we seem to be dealing with a relatively early schizophrenic, in a state of depression, perhaps shortly after some severe rejection. As mentioned above, the "telepathic touch" makes one suspect a history of auditory hallucinations and/or ideas of reference.

*Card 1:* A reasonably long story, with a most unusual plot. This card seems to bear a fairly close relationship to the person's childhood, and especially to the nature of the mother-figure. The sickness and the novel point of a childhood full of isolation from other kids, and retreat to a world of wishful thinking. Seeing the boy in bed is a strange perceptual distortion which highlights his withdrawal and need for help. There is an obvious fear of the mother, for what she might do to him if she found him so disobedient. The story may then be interpreted as that of a man who in childhood reacted to a domineering mother by sickness, guilt, overt disobedience, and retreat to fantasy compensations which, however, offered little comfort (he does not read the book).

*Card 3BM:* Almost everybody sees this as a depressing picture, and the story may thus be expected to shed some light on the dynamics of the depression. The theme may be reworded as follows: he has been punished because of a sex offense; the punishment is especially horrible not as punishment, since that has happened before, but because of the accompanying exposure. Comparison with a "good" sibling makes it all the worse. The resulting hostility is internalized. One would expect, in fact, a strong masochistic streak in a person of this type.[2]

*Card 4:* This brings out the subject's attitudes towards sex and aggression; it portrays a man and a woman with a sexy picture in the background, and the

[2] To the fact that the character is seen as female the writer attaches no importance, because this seems to be the rule rather than the exception.

man is usually seen in an aggressive mood. The guilt attached to sex is again apparent; the theme is actually that it has led to ruin which must be atoned for. Most likely this refers to a conflict about masturbation and some illicit sex experiences (prostitutes). The fact that he does not notice the woman in the picture again points to poor contact with reality. The displacement of aggression from the man to the woman is noteworthy, and in keeping with interpretations offered before.

*Card 6BM:* Since this is almost invariably seen as a mother and son, it reveals much about that relationship. Much has already been said on this subject, but some new comments may be added here. First it is seen as a scene in a play, which is virtually unique. It represents a method of creating distance between the patient and the horrible events surrounding his childhood and his mother. Second the exhibitionistic trends are now brought out. And third the maternal hostility is now directly related to his sexual guilt.

*Card 7BM:* Usually seen as father and son. Nothing new need be added here.

*Card 11:* This card seems to bring out the subject's attitude towards his unconscious. Since there is a story here, it may be interpreted as some fairly constant unconscious motivation. The essentials of this unconscious motivation are that he is being pushed by forces beyond his control (predestined), that he is superior to others and different from them, in spite of which or perhaps because of which he is being pursued by dark malevolent creatures, i.e., the hostility of those about him, that he must run away to escape this danger, but that regardless of what he does he is doomed.

*Card 12M:* This is fairly closely related to the individual's hopes about therapy. Here he is obviously pessimistic.

*Card 13MF:* The sex card. There is nothing new to add.

*Card 13B:* Another card which brings out the subject's view of his childhood. Parental rejection and sibling rivalry have already been mentioned.

*Card 14:* On this card the subject usually projects the fantasies he has when alone; occasionally patients even mention that directly. The fantasies our patient has are obviously of a most sadistic character. Such sadism is found either in criminal individuals or in Milquetoasts who can find no outlet for it in real life; our patient belongs to the latter category.

V. *Other:*

There are four other variables not included in the formal scoring scheme which yield fruitful information: story length, story cohesiveness, story plot, and vocabulary.

(a) *Story length:* Again it is necessary to proceed on home-baked norms for the time being. These stories are fairly long. From this it may be inferred that intelligence is above average, and that he has access to his fantasy life.

(b) *Story cohesiveness:* In normal or neurotic individuals one can expect cohesive stories, i.e., those in which there is a plot unfolded in some reasonable manner. The subject's stories here are adequately cohesive, except for the blank card. The degree of cohesiveness is roughly parallel to the severity of disorganization seen in the clinical picture. Hence it may be inferred that this patient is not too badly disorganized.

(c) *Story plot:* The one point still to be considered is whether the plots are usual or unusual (corresponding to the populars in the Rorschach). All the stories are unusual, some very much so. This indicates that his fantasy is off the beaten track, often odd or bizarre.

(d) *Vocabulary:* From intelligence tests we know that vocabulary is the best single indicator of intelligence. The writer would estimate this subject's basic endowment to be in the superior range, somewhere between an IQ of 120 and 125. Because of his disorganization, however, it is to be anticipated that he will test much lower; a reasonable estimate would be somewhere between 105 and 115 (Wechsler-Bellevue).

Finally, a word can be said about the diagnosis. In the above analysis schizophrenic, paranoid, catatonic and depressive features have been pointed out. This is the pattern seen in the early paranoid schizophrenic. However, there is no evidence of systematized delusions, so that he is probably an early over-ideational schizophrenic, whose main symptoms are confusion, auditory hallucinations, ideas of reference and inappropriate affect. Since he does not seem to have an established paranoid system, it may be inferred that he is still in a state of flux, perhaps a patient with an occasional remission or relatively clear period.

## TAT INTERPRETATION

His basic conflict is one of severe loneliness. He feels out of touch with people and with the world. Unable to establish any close relationships with either sex, he has drifted, become disorganized and confused, knowing no way to handle his problems. Bodily anxieties and a strong sense of guilt, especially about sexual matters, reinforce his sense of isolation from people.

Etiologically, the main factor which appears is an extremely hostile domineering mother. His reaction to her in childhood was one of withdrawal perhaps sickness, and emphasis on a fantasy world, but these fantasy defenses were never satisfactory. Most likely he has been an anxious, submissive, withdrawn schizoid individual all his life. A sibling rivalry conflict may have made the feeling of rejection even worse. The father-figure, though not so frightening as the mother, offered no adequate compensation.

In this background some kind of disappointment in a love relationship threw him into a bad reactive depression. Perhaps there was a picture of a dream girl in his mind which he almost found in real life, and then, when he was turned down, this culminating frustration was too much for him. By now the dream girl fantasy is so firmly entrenched that he is unable to establish any kind of relationship with a real girl, which sets up a vicious circle, and makes his feelings of isolation and loneliness worse. The depression is so powerful that suicide is a possibility that must be considered.

His sex life has consisted largely of casual experiences and compulsive masturbation. On the one hand this pattern arose from his strong feelings of guilt about sex, which were inculcated by the family, and on the other hand it came from the nature of his sex experiences, which increased the guilt. Although there is no direct evidence on this point in the TAT, it is possible that he has had some homosexual contacts, more out of desperation than out of desire.

Hostility was handled originally by a reaction formation, so that he became a meek submissive individual, in the hope that he would thereby gain the mother's love which was otherwise denied him. Associated with this was a strong masochistic streak, which has led to the use of self-punishing mechanisms. Now, however, there is an enormous amount of hostility which can no longer be adequately handled by the previous defenses; the result is that he resorts to violent outbursts every once in a while. It is possible that these on occasion take a catatonic or near-catatonic form. Most of his aggression, however, is contained by his peculiar fantasy life.

The primary defenses to his conflicts have been withdrawal and fantasy, although it has included both; i.e., when with people he reacts to a fantasy picture he has in his mind rather than to the real individual. His fantasy is not well organized, and hence offers no comforting sanctuary; rather, he flits from one thought to another without being able to concentrate properly. Because of this disorganization his personality structure remains unstabilized. It is probable that the lessening of the ability to distinguish fantasy from reality has led to a history of auditory hallucinations and ideas of reference.

Intelligence is basically superior, IQ roughly 120–125, but because of his emotional disturbance he is functioning at a much lower level, IQ perhaps 105–115.

The diagnosis is an over-ideational confused paranoid schizophrenia, relatively early, with the total picture still in a state of flux.

## MAPS TEST WORKING NOTES

Except for figure choice, the MAPS test can be handled in exactly the same manner as the TAT, and the psychogram of the MAPS lends itself to some interesting comparisons. (See table, pages 77-79.)

The total number of feelings in the MAPS is 45, or a mean of 6.42 per story, which is very close to the mean of 6.81 for the TAT. The average num-

Psychogram: Scoring Sheet for Verbal Projective Techniques—MAPS

| I. FEELINGS | LIV | STR | BTH | DRM | BED | BLK | STG | TOTAL |
|---|---|---|---|---|---|---|---|---|
| 1. a. Affection, Verbal | | | | | | | | 0 |
| b. Affection, Physical | | | | | | | | 0 |
| 2. Anger | | | | | | | | 0 |
| 3. Anxiety | | | | | | x | | 1 |
| 4. Compulsion | x | | x | x | x | | | 4 |
| 5. Conflict | x | | | | | | x | 2 |
| 6. Crime | | | | | | | | 0 |
| 7. Depression | | | | | x | | | 1 |
| 8. Drink | | | | | | | | 0 |
| 9. Effort | | | | | | | | 0 |
| 10. Escape | x | x | | x | | | | 3 |
| 11. Excitement | | | | | | | | 0 |
| 12. Frustration | x | | | | | | | 1 |
| 13. Guilt | | | | x | | | | 1 |
| 14. Hostility | x | x | | x | x | x | x | 7 |
| a. Verbal | x | | | | | | | 1 |
| b. Physical | | | | | | | | 0 |
| c. Death | x | x | | x | x | x | x | 6 |
| *Management of—* | | | | | | | | |
| a. Externalized | x | x | | x | x | x | x | 6 |
| b. Internalized | | x | | | x | | | 2 |
| c. Repressed | | | | | | | | 0 |
| d. Displaced | x | | | | | | | 1 |
| e. Punished | | | | | | | | 0 |
| f. Other | | | | | | | | 0 |
| 15. Inferiority | x | x | x | | | | | 3 |
| 16. Loneliness | | | | | | | | 0 |
| 17. Orality | | | | | | | | 0 |
| 18. Pain | x | | x | x | | x | | 4 |
| 19. Path. Indicators | x | x | x | x | x | x | x | 7 |
| a. Tabooed Activity | | | | | | | | 0 |
| b. Bizarre Verbal. | x | | | x | | x | | 3 |
| c. Rejection of Card | | | | | | | | 0 |
| d. Other | | x | x | | x | | x | 4 |
| 20. Pleasure | | | | | | | | 0 |
| 21. Possessiveness | | | | | | | | 0 |
| 22. Sexuality | | x | | x | | | | 2 |
| 23. Special States | x[a] | x[b] | x[c] | x[d] | x[e] | | x[f] | 6 |
| 24. Suicide | | x | | | x | | | 2 |
| 25. Superiority | | | | | | | | 0 |
| 26. Wishful Thinking | | | x | | | | | 1 |
| TOTAL | | | | | | | | 45 |

[a] Symbolization [b] Listlessness; ghost [c] Ghost [d] Confusion; ghost [e] Mad [f] Defiance

| II. OUTCOMES | LIV | STR | BTH | DRM | BED | BLK | STG | TOTAL |
|---|---|---|---|---|---|---|---|---|
| a. Favorable | | | | | | | | 0 |
| b. Unfavorable | x | x | x | x | x | x | x | 7 |
| c. Indeterminate | | | | | | | | 0 |

PSYCHOGRAM: SCORING SHEET FOR VERBAL PROJECTIVE TECHNIQUES—MAPS (*Cont'd*)

| III. INTERPERSONAL RELATIONSHIPS | Mother-Child | Child-Mother | Father-Child | Child-Father | Mother-Father | Father-Mother | Sibling-Sibling | Man-Man | Man-Woman | Woman-Man | Woman-Woman | Acquaintance-Stranger | Stranger-Acquaintance | Friend-Friend | Stranger-Stranger | Other | Total |
|---|---|---|---|---|---|---|---|---|---|---|---|---|---|---|---|---|---|
| 1. MOVING TOWARDS | | | | | | | | | | | | | | | | | |
| a. Affection | | | | | | | | | | | | | | | | | |
| (1) Verbal | | | | | | | | | | | | | | | | | 0 |
| (2) Physical | | | | | | | | | Str Drm | Str Drm | | | | | | | 2 |
| b. Acceptance | Liv Bth | Liv Bth | | | Liv | | | | Str Bed | Drm Bed | | Liv Str | Liv | | Stg | | 6 |
| c. Dominance | | Liv | | | | | | | | | | Liv | | | | | 1 |
| d. Submission | | | | | | | | | | | | | | | | | 0 |

| | | | | | | | | | | | | | | | | | |
|---|---|---|---|---|---|---|---|---|---|---|---|---|---|---|---|---|---|
| 2. MOVING AGAINST | | | | | | | | | | | | | | | | | |
| a. Verbal | Liv | | | | Liv | Liv | | | | | | | | | | | 1 |
| b. Physical | | | | | | | | | | | | | | | | | 0 |
| c. Death | | | | Drm | Drm | Drm<br>Bth | Drm | Str | Str<br>Bed<br>Stg | Str<br>Stg | | | | | Bed | | 5 |
| 3. MOVING AWAY FROM | | | | | | | | | | | | | | | | | |
| a. Separation | Liv | Liv | | | | | | | Bed | | | | | | | | 2 |
| b. Indifference | | | | | | | | | | | | | | | | | 0 |
| c. Rejection | | | | | | Liv<br>Bth | | | | | | | | | | | 2 |
| 4. NO RELATIONSHIP | | | | | | | | | | | | | | | | | 0 |
| TOTAL | 2 | 2 | 0 | 1 | 2 | 3 | 1 | 1 | 4 | 5 | 0 | 2 | 1 | 0 | 2 | 0 | |

ber of interpersonal relationships, however, is 4.43 per story in the MAPS, as contrasted with 3.36 in the TAT.

In the individual categories, we find less affection, frustration, superiority and wishful thinking in the MAPS, but more externalized hostility and more pathologic indicators. One might say that there is an acting out of bizarre fantasy in the MAPS which is often only hinted at in the TAT. Every story in the MAPS is obviously bizarre, while only four of the eleven TAT stories were so labeled.

In the MAPS, hostility is externalized in every story where it occurs. Further, the direction of hostility now yields significant results: it is primarily women who are killed by others, while in the two cases where suicide occurs, the story relates to a man who has done harm to a woman, and then kills himself. The externalization of hostility is usually found in individuals who live out their aggression in fantasy, but who have so much near the surface that there are occasional violent outbursts; the same conclusion arose from the TAT.

Apart from the points mentioned above, which are supplementary rather than contradictory, there is a striking similarity between the psychograms for the MAPS and the TAT. In a previous study with asthmatic children the writer obtained an analogous result. It would be redundant, therefore, to analyze the MAPS psychogram in greater detail. However, the choice of figures and the story content may be expected to yield more information.

In analyzing the figure choice, we have some norms in Shneidman's monograph. A comparison of this test with Shneidman's signs shows that there are three schizophrenic signs and eight normal ones. But as with all sign approaches to the projective techniques, this one too must be treated with caution.

The schizophrenic signs are FN-5 (average number of figures four or more), FM-2 (using figure to represent self), and FM-5 (using a figure as a concept or for its meaning). The normal signs are FI-1-6 (interactions with animal, stranger, acquaintance, spouse, and parent), FA 1-2 (fatal accident, social violence) and FM-3 (using a character not represented by a figure). This gives the subject a score of +5, which, according to the table, means that 22 per cent of the schizophrenics in Shneidman's study were at or above this level, as contrasted with only 4 per cent of the normals.[3] Thus, purely on a sign basis, the patient would be classified as an early or perhaps mild schizophrenic. It is of interest that this is in general agreement with the diagnosis based on the TAT.

[3] The number of stories in the present test is smaller than in the original study, so that strictly speaking the norms are not really applicable unchanged. But this difficulty is in herent in the nature of the published norms because the exact number of stories told by the psychotic patients was variable.

An examination of the meaning of the signs is also revealing. The high average number of figures, or over-inclusion, points to the type of schizophrenic who loses himself in a crowd with whom he has no contacts. The self-reference (Bedroom story) may be interpreted as universal identification, or a lack of an adequate self-concept (or low self-esteem, in the more usual terminology), and extreme self-centeredness. Using a figure as a concept or for its meaning may be interpreted to mean that he sees people primarily as symbols, rather than as real persons, which again fits in with the dream girl and the constantly disturbing mother-figure mentioned in the TAT analysis.

The normal signs consist primarily of interaction. However, these interactions are so peculiar in character that the sign as such is of little value. The situation is comparable to that of a Rorschach with a number of FC's, which then turn out to be forced or entirely inappropriate. All this activity fits in with the previous description of the patient as an over-emotional person, whose fantasies are full of people; the high average number of figures leads to a similar conclusion. The presence of the FA 1-2 signs merely indicates that he is the type of schizophrenic who fantasies too much violence, rather than, as Shneidman's cases seem to have been for the most part, too little. Using a character not represented by a figure is again consonant with our view of the patient as over-ideational.

The stories proper can be analyzed like the TAT material; indeed, as stories, there is no essential difference. The themes of violence, infidelity and the like are again prominent. Three points remain, however, which are worthy of mention.

First, the use of the ghost. In one story (Street) it is the ghost of an old love (again the dream girl frustration). In two (Bathroom, Dream) it is a phantom visible only to her that heckles her life or criticizes her, which once more points to auditory hallucinations and ideas of reference.

Second, the main identification in every case except the blank seems to be feminine. This did not obtain in the TAT. The apparent contradiction is easily resolved, if we bear in mind that this is an individual with confused identifications, which he can adopt or drop in brief order. With such confused identification, again homosexual experience is a possibility, but again it would be a resultant of frustration rather than a powerful need in itself.

Third, a comparison of the two stories to the blank cards is revealing. As mentioned above, the writer considers the Blank to be by far the most important single card in these tests. In both stories, the scene is the same—great plains, an endless arid expanse. Since such vast bodies commonly symbolize the mother, we are again led to think of the hostile mother here. In the TAT the theme was that of an inability to extract himself from the hell of loneliness, from which all attempts to rescue him failed. Essentially the same theme appears in the MAPS, but this time the attempts to get out are described. The search for a "secret" brings to mind sexual curiosity, and curiosity in general; punishment for the girl after she "sees what it is" would fit in with his enormous guilt about sex. The young man falling because his crutches are too heavy could be the hero overcome by his guilt and depression. That the girl alone comes within short distance of it is in line with the feminine identification mentioned before; but even being a woman, the story tells us, will not help, and hence the confusion in identification.

Analysis of the other stories yields no essentially new material. There is the bad mother in the Livingroom card, again interestingly with a fantasy of assistance to the son; the sex guilt and violence in the Street card; punishment for the mother in the Bathroom card, confusion and sexual guilt in the Dream; insane violence in the Bedroom; loneliness and restitution attempts in the Blank; exhibitionism and mad violence in the Stage.

The differences and similarities between the subject's TAT and MAPS can be summarized as follows. In essence, the structure revealed is the same in both. In the MAPS the pathology comes out more clearly—every story is bizarre. Further, the MAPS seems to bring out primarily the fantasy defenses, especially the confused identification and the wish to take revenge on the mother, which were not so apparent in the TAT. It is as though in the TAT he were telling what had happened to him, while in the MAPS he is revelling in fantasies of what he would like to see happen.

# Chapter 9

# A. ARTHUR HARTMAN

Dr. Hartman received his training in psychology at the University of Chicago and is a Diplomate in Clinical Psychology of the American Board of Examiners in Professional Psychology. He has held positions as Clinical Psychologist with the Illinois Division of the Criminologist and the Institute of Juvenile Research, the Cook County Juvenile Court, and the Chicago Municipal Court Psychiatric Department. During World War II he served as Personnel Consultant at a medical training center and in a general hospital overseas. Since 1949 he has taught at Boston University, where he is Associate Professor of Clinical Psychology. He is also Consultant in Clinical Psychology to the Veterans Administration. He has worked mainly in the fields of clinical psychology and criminology, his chief interests being in personality diagnosis and theory and in psychopathology.

## SELECTED REFERENCES


HARTMAN, A. A., An Experimental Examination of the Thematic Apperception Technique in Clinical Diagnosis. *Psychological Monographs*, 1949, *63*, 1–48.


## RESUME OF METHOD

THIS "PSYCHOMETRIC" approach, which was originally designed for research and aims at establishing quantitative norms as a basis for interpretation, consists of the following steps: (1) Each story is rated on a five-point scale for sixty-five response categories covering thematic elements, feeling qualities, topics of reference, and formal response characteristics; (2) numerical ratings on each category are totaled for all stories, and consistency and trend of ratings are noted; (3) from a list of over forty personality variables which previous research proved significantly correlated with certain response items, those personality variables are selected which are associated with each response category found important in the protocol; and (4) data thus obtained are integrated with other findings, to obtain a clinically meaningful personality picture.

## TAT WORKING NOTES

The application of formal quantitative scoring methods to thematic test protocols is still a task at the research level rather than a procedure appropriate to individual clinical diagnosis. To apply such methods to the interpretation of a single projective protocol is premature, just as it would be to determine an individual's mental age from a series of objective test items which were still in process of standardization. The comparison between objective and projective tests is more than metaphoric. The point of view taken here is that relatively simple components of thematic test records significantly reflect personality, and that the quantitative determination of these personality correlates will lead to a more precise interpretation of thematic materials.

It may be anticipated that an effective psychometric approach to thematic test interpretation will follow the development of normative studies similar to those involved in the standardization of intelligence tests. A major requirement would be to determine the significance of given thematic test elements for specific personality traits. The quantitative scoring of an individual protocol might then proceed somewhat as follows:

1. Determine a comprehensive list of response categories pertinent to the particular kind of test record and group of subjects represented. These categories should be as direct and objective as is consistent with a comprehensive coverage of major thematic elements, feeling qualities, topics of reference, and formal response characteristics. It would be expected that the list of categories would vary somewhat from group to group; for example, the main topics of reference utilized by a group of farm boys would differ from that of a group of urban adults.
2. Rate each story in the test protocol independently on each of the categories of analysis. Murray's suggested 1 to 5 scale is probably applicable to most categories. In the analysis, inquiry should be limited as far as possible to the question, "What is said or done?" Attributes of the language, form, and content of responses can be rated with a minimum of interpretation. Themes may also be interpreted directly from the content of the story without reference to distinguishing between press and need or to determining the hero.
3. Total the numerical ratings for each category. Observe the consistency with which the category is rated over the entire series of responses. Note the trend of rating of each category, with special attention to those which are either high or low for the particular group which the subject represents.
4. Review and compare in detail the more important personality variables associated with each response category, selecting those variables which appear to be clearly affirmed and eliminating those upon which there is contradictory or inconsistent evidence.
5. The final step then would be to integrate the series of personality traits or variables with other clinical data or information on the subject, and to arrive at a clinically meaningful picture of his personality.

The foregoing procedure can be illustrated by applying it to the present TAT record. Utilizing a series of response categories which had been previously examined (see reference, pp. 44–47), each of the TAT stories was rated for all of the categories, as shown on the work sheet reproduced as follows:

## WORK SHEET FOR ANALYSIS OF JOHN DOE'S TAT RECORD

| *Response Category* | *Picture Number* 1 | 3 BM | 4 | 6 BM | 7 BM | 11 | 12 M | 13 MF | 13 B | 14 | 16 | *Trend of Ratings* |
|---|---|---|---|---|---|---|---|---|---|---|---|---|
| 1. Fluency | 4 | 4 | 3 | 3 | 3 | 3 | 3 | 4 | 4 | 4 | 3 | Moderately fluent |
| 2. Feeling-tone | 4 | 2 | 2 | 2 | 2 | 1 | 2 | 2 | 2–4 | 3 | 2 | Unpleasant feeling-tone |
| 3. Originality | 4 | 2 | 2 | 2 | 3 | 2 | 2 | 3 | 1 | 2 | 2 | Unusual responses |
| 4. Picture rejection | 1 | 1 | 1 | 1 | 1 | 1 | 1 | 1 | 1 | 1 | 1 | No picture rejection |
| 5. Compliance | 3 | 4 | 4 | 4 | 5 | 4 | 4 | 4 | 4 | 4 | 3 | High compliance |
| 6. Organization | 3 | 4 | 4 | 4 | 4 | 5 | 4 | 4 | 5 | 3 | 4 | High organization |
| 7. Interpersonal emphasis | 4 | 5 | 4 | 4 | 5 | 3 | 4 | 4 | 5 | 4 | 4 | Whole-emphasis |
| 8. Interpersonal emphasis | 2 | 3 | 2 | 2 | 1 | 3 | 2 | 2 | 2 | 2 | 1 | Concept dominated |
| 9. Interpersonal emphasis | 2 | 1 | 2 | 3 | 1 | 3 | 3 | 2 | 2 | 4 | 3 | Intraceptive |
| 10. Self reference | 1 | 1 | 1 | 1 | 1 | 1 | 1 | 1 | 1 | 1 | 1 | No self-reference |
| 11. Certainty feeling | 3 | 4 | 4 | 4 | 4 | 3 | 4 | 4 | 3 | 3 | 3 | High certainty |
| 12. Vocabulary level | 4 | 3 | 3 | 3 | 3 | 4 | 3 | 3 | 3 | 4 | 3 | Average to high vocabulary |
| 13. Stereotypy | 2 | 2 | 2 | 2 | 2 | 1 | 1 | 1 | 2 | 1 | 1 | Slight stereotypy |
| 14. Action or movement | 1 | 2 | 3 | 4 | 3 | 4 | 3 | 4 | 3 | 4 | 3 | Average action level |
| 15. Interpersonal relations | 3 | 2 | 1 | 2 | 2 | 1 | 3 | 4 | 3 | 2 | 3 | Conflictful interpersonal relations |
| 16. Interpersonal relations | 2 | 4 | 4 | 4 | 4 | 4 | 2 | 4 | 4 | 3 | 2 | Strong interpersonal relations |
| 17. Environmental stress | 4 | 2 | 2 | 2 | 3 | 5 | 2 | 3 | 3 | 2 | 1 | Malign environmental stress |
| 18. Outcome | 4 | ? | 5 | 5 | 4 | 1 | 2 | 2 | 4 | 3 | 1 | Varied outcomes |
| 19. Outcome | 1 | 4 | 2 | 2 | 3 | 2 | 2 | 4 | 2 | 2 | 1 | Unreal outcomes |
| 20. Conflict solution | 1 | 1 | 4 | ? | 2 | 4 | 2 | 4 | 4 | 3 | 2 | Varied conflict solutions |
| 21. Achievement | 2 | 1 | 1 | 2 | 2 | 2 | 3 | 1 | 4 | 2 | 1 | Weak acheivement theme emphasis |
| 22. Frustration | 2 | 3 | 2 | 1 | 2 | 2 | 2 | 4 | 4 | 1 | 3 | Slight frustration theme emphasis |
| 23. Aggression | 2 | 3 | 4 | 5 | 3 | 5 | 1 | 1 | 1 | 5 | 4 | Moderately high aggression theme emphasis |
| 24. Conflict | 2 | 1 | 3 | 1 | 3 | 1 | 1 | 2 | 3 | 4 | 1 | Slight conflict theme emphasis |
| 25. Anxiety | 1 | 2 | 4 | 2 | 3 | 3 | 3 | 1 | 3 | 1 | 3 | Moderate anxiety theme emphasis |
| 26. Punishment | 2 | 5 | 2 | 5 | 3 | 5 | 1 | 1 | 1 | 2 | 3 | High punishment theme emphasis |
| 27. Reward | 1 | 1 | 1 | 1 | 1 | 1 | 3 | 1 | 5 | 1 | 1 | Weak reward theme emphasis |
| 28. Giving aid | 1 | 1 | 1 | 1 | 1 | 2 | 3 | 1 | 4 | 3 | 1 | Weak giving aid theme emphasis |
| 29. Receiving aid | 1 | 1 | 4 | 3 | 4 | 1 | 5 | 1 | 1 | 3 | 5 | High receiving aid theme emphasis |
| 30. Escape | 4 | ? | 1 | 1 | 3 | 3 | 2 | 4 | 3 | 4 | 1 | Moderately high escape theme emphasis |
| 31. Sensory gratification | 3 | 1 | 1 | 1 | 3 | 1 | 3 | 5 | 1 | 1 | 5 | Some sensory gratification theme emphasis |
| 32. Passivity | 5 | 1 | 1 | 1 | 3 | 1 | 2 | 1 | 1 | 1 | 1 | Slight passivity theme emphasis |
| 33. Aesthetic feeling | 1 | 1 | 1 | 2 | 1 | 1 | 2 | 2 | 1 | 1 | 1 | Slight aesthetic feeling |
| 34. Paranoid feeling | 1 | 2 | 1 | 1 | 1 | 2 | 1 | 1 | 2 | 1 | 5 | Slight paranoid feeling |
| 35. Guilt feeling | 2 | 5 | 1 | 2 | 3 | 4 | 1 | 3 | 1 | 3 | 2 | Some guilt feeling |
| 36. Narcissistic feeling | 2 | 1 | 1 | 1 | 1 | 1 | 1 | 2 | 2 | 1 | 1 | Weak narcissistic feeling |
| 37. Sadistic feeling | 1 | 2 | 3 | 4 | 4 | 3 | 2 | 1 | 1 | 2 | 3 | High sadistic feeling |
| 38. Inferiority feeling | 1 | 1 | 2 | 1 | 2 | 1 | 2 | 1 | 3 | 1 | 1 | Slight inferiority feeling |

| Response Category | Picture Number 1 | 3 BM | 4 | 6 BM | 7 BM | 11 | 12 M | 13 MF | 13 B | 14 | 16 | Trend of Ratings |
|---|---|---|---|---|---|---|---|---|---|---|---|---|
| 39. Ambivalence | 2 | 1 | 1 | 2 | 1 | 1 | 1 | 2 | 3 | 2 | 1 | Slight ambivalence feeling |
| 40. Reference to age | 1 | 2 | 1 | 3 | 3 | 1 | 2 | 1 | 2 | 1 | 1 | Marked age reference |
| 41. Reference to new-old | 1 | 1 | 1 | 1 | 1 | 1 | 1 | 3 | 1 | 1 | 2 | Very slight new-old reference |
| 42. Reference to neat-orderly | 1 | 1 | 1 | 1 | 1 | 1 | 1 | 1 | 1 | 1 | 4 | Very slight neatness reference |
| 43. Reference to light-dark | 1 | 1 | 1 | 1 | 1 | 5 | 1 | 5 | 4 | 3 | 1 | Marked light-dark reference |
| 44. Reference to smoke-fire | 1 | 1 | 4 | 1 | 1 | 1 | 1 | 1 | 1 | 1 | 2 | Some smoke-fire reference |
| 45. Reference to book, etc., as source | 1 | 1 | 1 | 5 | 1 | 2 | 1 | 1 | 1 | 1 | 1 | No book reference |
| 46. Reference to suicide | 1 | 5 | 4 | 1 | 2 | 1 | 2 | 1 | 1 | 1 | 1 | High suicide reference |
| 47. Reference to sex activity | 1 | 4 | 5 | 3 | 1 | 1 | 1 | 5 | 1 | 1 | 1 | High sex activity reference |
| 48. Interest in male appearance | 2 | 1 | 1 | 1 | 1 | 1 | 1 | 1 | 1 | 1 | 1 | No interest in male appearance |
| 49. Feminine identification | 1 | 2 | 3 | 3 | 1 | 1 | 1 | 1 | 1 | 1 | 1 | Some feminine identification |
| 50. Peculiar content | 5 | 2 | 2 | 3 | 1 | 2 | 2 | 1 | 2 | 2 | 3 | Marked peculiar content |
| 51. Symbolic content | 4 | 2 | 4 | 5 | 5 | 5 | 4 | 4 | 5 | 5 | 5 | High symbolic content |
| 52. Unusual detail noted | 4 | 1 | 2 | 1 | 1 | 2 | 1 | 2 | 2 | 1 | 1 | Some unusual detail |
| 53. Perceptual distortion | 5 | 1 | 1 | 1 | 1 | 1 | 1 | 1 | 1 | 1 | 1 | Slight perceptual distortion |
| 54. Picture criticism | 1 | 1 | 1 | 1 | 1 | 1 | 1 | 1 | 1 | 1 | 1 | No picture criticism |
| 55. Moralizing | 1 | 2 | 1 | 3 | 4 | 3 | 2 | 3 | 1 | 3 | 3 | Marked moralizing |
| 56. Questions | 1 | 1 | 1 | 1 | 1 | 1 | 1 | 1 | 1 | 1 | 1 | No questions |
| 57. Interjections | 1 | 1 | 1 | 1 | 1 | 1 | 1 | 1 | 1 | 1 | 1 | No interjections |
| 58. Dramatizing | 1 | 2 | 2 | 5 | 2 | 2 | 4 | 1 | 1 | 2 | 1 | High dramatizing |
| 59. Artificiality | 2 | 1 | 1 | 3 | 2 | 1 | 4 | 2 | 1 | 1 | 1 | High artificiality |
| 60. Humor | 1 | 1 | 1 | 1 | 1 | 1 | 1 | 1 | 1 | 1 | 1 | No humor |
| 61. Disjointedness | 2 | 1 | 2 | 1 | 2 | 2 | 2 | 1 | 1 | 3 | 2 | Some disjointedness |
| 62. Outcome indeterminate | 3 | 1 | 1 | 1 | 2 | 2 | 1 | 1 | 1 | 2 | 2 | Clear outcome |
| 63. Time emphasis, past | 2 | 2 | 2 | 3 | 1 | 2 | 3 | 4 | 3 | 4 | 4 | Some past time emphasis |
| 64. Time emphasis, present | 4 | 4 | 4 | 4 | 4 | 4 | 2 | 2 | 4 | 2 | 2 | High present time emphasis |
| 65. Time emphasis, future | 2 | 2 | 2 | 2 | 3 | 2 | 2 | 2 | 2 | 1 | 1 | Slight future time emphasis |

The work sheet ratings were then totalled and evaluated as to direction and significance. Following are some of the trends in response which appear to be characteristic of our subject:

Unpleasant feeling tone
Unpleasant interpretations
Conflictful interpersonal relations
Malign environmental stress
Low achievement theme emphasis
High aggressive theme emphasis
High punishment theme emphasis
High sadistic (masochistic) reference
High reference to age of characters
High reference to light and dark
High suicide reference
High sex activity reference
Peculiar content
Clear outcomes
Emphasis on present time

In the research cited, the personality correlates of given response emphases were tentatively determined for a group of adolescent boys of average intelligence. The list of TAT categories and personality or behavior variables reproduced *below* indicates the more significant relationships between TAT categories and personality variables as originally determined. For example, the category "Emphasis upon light or dark features of a picture," #52, is found to be highly correlated with the following personality variables: easily frustrated, self-reliant, autistic thinking, and unstable emotionally.

The TAT categories (listed below in capitals) are derived from a detailed quantitative analysis of the TAT records of 35 psychiatric clinic cases. The personality and behavior variables (listed below in small letters) represent clinical ratings on the same subjects based upon full case-studies and special tests. All of the items listed correlate (bi-serial r) above .38 with the given TAT category (or above a ratio of 2.0 between the correlation and its standard error). Correlations above .50 are indicated by asterisks.

*TAT Category* *Correlated Personality or Behavior Variable*

A. *Form Elements:*

1. FLUENCY: Popular*, Prefers group recreations*, Many recreation interests*, Feels superior, Extroverted, Fluent, Mature personality, Prefers active recreation, Happy temperament, Good total adjustment, Good behavior prognosis, Strong attachment to mother.
2. SPEED OF RESPONSE: Feels secure.
3. COMPLIANCE WITH DIRECTIONS: Exaggerated sex activity*, Fluent*, Strong appearance, Mature personality.
4. NUMBER OF QUESTIONS ASKED: Self-conscious*, Strong attachment to father*.
5. INTERJECTIONS: Happy temperament, Conflicted sex adjustment, Compliant with adults.
6. PICTURE CRITICISM: Poor behavior prognosis*, Anti-social standards, Self-conscious, Untidy appearance.
7. DEGREE OF SELF-REFERENCE: Emotionally deprived, Self-conscious, Handsome appearance.
8. CERTAINTY OF RESPONSE: Poised.
9. NUMBER OF PICTURES LIKED: Mature personality, Feels superior, Good total adjustment.
10. DISJOINTEDNESS OF RESPONSE: Unconflicted sex adjustment.
11. STEREOTYPY: Dull intelligence, Good behavior prognosis, Unconflicted sex adjustment.
12. CLEAR STORY OUTCOME STATED: Good total adjustment, Fluent.
13. EMPHASIS ON PAST TIME: No nervous symptoms,* Good behavior prognosis, Perceives home as pleasant, Realistic, Stable emotionally, Close attachment to mother.
14. EMPHASIS ON PRESENT TIME: Rejects father*, Asthenic appearance*, Perceives home as unpleasant.
15. EMPHASIS ON FUTURE TIME: Feels superior*, Extroverted, Popular, Realistic, Prefers group recreation.
16. VOCABULARY LEVEL: Fluent*, Many recreation interests*, Prefers active recreation*, Mature personality*, Energetic*, Friendly*, Bright*, Feels superior*, Happy

temperament*, Ambitious*, Prefers group recreation*, Popular, Uninhibited, Self-reliant, Extroverted.

17. POPULAR (vs. Unusual) INTERPRETATIONS: Infantile personality*, Taciturn, Autistic.
18. PICTURE DOMINATED INTERPRETATIONS: Autistic, Effeminate.
19. WHOLE (vs. Detailed) INTERPRETATION: Perceives home as pleasant, Masculine, Feels superior.
20. EXTRACEPTIVE INTERPRETATION: Rejects mother, Perceives home as unpleasant, Many nervous symptoms, Prefers solitary recreation, Untidy appearance, Emotionally deprived.
21. HIGH ACTION LEVEL: Good behavior prognosis.
22. CONFLICT ISSUES ATTACKED: Prefers group recreation*, Many recreation interests*, Prefers active recreation*, Energetic*, Bright, Popular, Extroverted, Feels superior.
23. PECULIAR CONTENT: Ambitious*, Ugly appearance.
24. RARE DETAILS OBSERVED: Asthenic appearance, Autistic, Effeminate.
25. PERCEPTUAL DISTORTION: Asthenic appearance*, Weak appearance*, Unambitious, Many nervous symptoms, Autistic.

B. *Themes Emphasized:*

26. ACHIEVEMENT: Extroverted*, Prefers group recreation*, Popular*, Prefers active recreation*, Happy temperament*, Compliant with adults*, Close attachment to father*, Feels superior*, Many recreation interests, Energetic, Emotionally satisfied, No nervous symptoms, Conventional standards.
27. FRUSTRATION: Poor total adjustment*, Emotionally deprived, Unconflicted sex adjustment, Bright, Retarded sex activity.
28. AGGRESSION: Self-conscious*.
29. ANXIETY: Satisfied materially*, Lacks energy*, Passive, Neat appearance, Dull intelligence, Dependent.
30. CONFLICT: Neat appearance*, Energetic, Handsome appearance.
31. PUNISHMENT: Infantile personality*, Effeminate*, Asthenic.
32. GIVING AID: (No significant correlations)
33. RECEIVING AID: Prefers group recreation*, Extroverted* Popular*, Prefers active recreation*, Bright*, Uninhibited, Energetic, Self-reliant, Aggressive.
34. ESCAPE: (No significant correlations)
35. SENSORY GRATIFICATION: Unambitious.
36. PASSIVITY: Rejects father*, Lacks energy.

C. *Feeling Qualities Emphasized:*

37. PLEASANT FEELING TONE: Extroverted*, Popular*, Prefers group recreation*, No nervous symptoms*, Feels secure, Prefers active recreation, Strong appearance, Happy temperament, Passive, Emotionally satisfied, Feels superior, Good total adjustment, Poised.
38. AESTHETIC FEELING: Good prognosis*, Good total adjustment*, Conventional standards*, Reacts deliberately, Close attachment to mother, Satisfied emotionally.
39. PARANOID FEELING: Ambitious*, Unconflicted sex adjustment*, Many recreation interests*, Pyknic appearance.

40. GUILT FEELING: Fluent, Ambitious, Strong appearance, Frank, Friendly, Autistic.
41. NARCISSISTIC FEELING: Prefers active recreation*, Prefers group recreation*, Popular*, No nervous symptoms*, Many recreation interests*, Extroverted*, Good behavior prognosis*, Good total adjustment*, Energetic, Realistic.
42. SADISTIC FEELING: Conventional standards*, Weak appearance*, Anxious*, Prefers sedentary recreation, Close attachment to mother, Good behavior prognosis, Many nervous symptoms, Dull intelligence, Lacks energy.
43. INFERIORITY FEELING: Masculine, Handsome appearance, Fluent, Bright.
44. AMBIVALENCE: Self-conscious*, Energetic, Good total adjustment, Handsome appearance.
45. ENVIRONMENT DESCRIBED AS BENIGN: Extroverted, Good total adjustment, Stable emotionally, Realistic.
46. CONCORDANT INTERPERSONAL RELATIONSHIPS: Unambitious, Poised, Realistic.
47. STRONG INTERPERSONAL RELATIONSHIPS: Bright*, Fluent*, Energetic*, Masculine, Mature, Handsome appearance, Deprived materially, Prefers active recreation, Emotionally deprived.
48. HIGH FEMININE IDENTIFICATION: Impulsive, Asthenic appearance, Poor total adjustment, Many nervous symptoms, Feels inferior, Self-conscious.

D. *Topics Emphasized:*

49. AGE OF CHARACTERS: Exaggerated sex activity, Emotionally satisfied, Prefers group recreation, Close attachment to mother.
50. NEWNESS OR AGE OF OBJECTS: Uninhibited.
51. NEATNESS OR ORDER: Bright, Prefers active recreation, Fluent.
52. LIGHT OR DARK FEATURES OF PICTURE: Easily frustrated*, Self-reliant, Autistic, Unstable emotionally.
53. BOOK OR MOVIE AS STORY SOURCE: Feels superior, Many recreation interests.
54. SUICIDE: Self-conscious*, Strong appearance, Energetic.
55. SEX ACTIVITY: Friendly, Stable emotionally, Frank.
56. MALE DRESS OR APPEARANCE NOTED: Autistic*, Effeminate.

The next step was to examine the pattern of personality variables linked to those TAT categories which appeared significant in the present record. A consideration of each of the TAT categories with reference to these relationships permits a selection of those personality variables for which the evidence is most consistent.

On the following behavior rating scale an attempt was made to predict a wide number of characteristics assumed to be true of this individual on the basis of quantitative evaluation of his TAT record. The evidence for some of these judgments is of course quite tenuous. On the face-sheet of the rating scale a more general judgment is made as to the probable direction of a few of the personality variables which are more clearly substantiated. For example, it would appear that our subject falls definitely in the direction of bright rather than dull intelligence, of fluent rather than taciturn verbal output, and of autistic rather than realistic approach to reality.

## BEHAVIOR RATING FOR USE IN TAT STUDY

I. APPEARANCE
1. Asthenic—Pyknic
2. Weak—Strong
3. Handsome—Ugly
4. Untidy—Neat

II. RESPONSE DURING INTERVIEW
5. Friendly—Hostile
6. Evasive—Frank
7. Self-conscious—Poised

III. PERSONALITY TRAITS
8. Dull—*Bright*
9. *Fluent*—Taciturn
10. Feminine—Masculine
11. Energetic—Apathetic
12. Aggressive—Passive
13. Depressed—Happy
14. Mature—Infantile
15. Inhibited—Uninhibited
16. Stable—*Unstable*
17. Anxious—Secure
18. Introverted—Extroverted
19. Deliberate—*Impulsive*
20. Self-reliant—Dependent
21. Realistic—*Autistic*
22. Feels inferior—Feels superior
23. *Easily frustrated*—High threshold

IV. AREAS OF ADJUSTMENT
24. Home atmosphere.................. Pleasant—Unpleasant
25. Relationship to father.............. Attachment—*Rejection*
26. Relationship to mother............. Attachment—Rejection
27. Relationship to siblings............. Attachment—Rejection
28. Relationship to adults.............. Defiant—Compliant
29. Relationship to peers............... Popular—Disliked
30. School adjustment................. Good—Poor
31. Material needs.................... Satisfied—Deprived
32. Emotional needs.................. Satisfied—Deprived
33. Recreation........................ Sedentary—Active
34. Recreation........................ Solitary—Group
35. Recreation interests................ Many—Few
36. Moral standards................... Conventional—Anti-social
37. Sex adjustment.................... Conflicted—Unconflicted
38. Sex activity....................... Retarded—*Exaggerated*
39. Nervous symptoms................ *Many*—None
40. Goals and ambition................ Ambitious—Drifter
41. Total personality adjustment........ Good—Poor
42. Prognosis......................... Poor—Good

V. CERTAINTY OF RATINGS
43. Certainty.......................... Certain—Doubtful

VI. COMMENTS

## RATING SCALES

1. What is his general physical habitus—long limbs and short trunk (asthenic), or short limbs and relatively large trunk (pyknic)?

| | | | | |
|---|---|---|---|---|
| | X | | | |
| Asthenic | Tends to asthenic | Athletic | Tends to pyknic | Pyknic |

2. Does he appear outwardly strong and healthy or weak and sick?

| | | | | |
|---|---|---|---|---|
| | | X | | |
| Weak. Sickly | Rather weak & sick | Average physique & health | Rather strong & healthy | Robust & healthy |

3. Judge his appearance with reference to usual standards of male beauty.

| | | | | |
|---|---|---|---|---|
| | | X | | |
| Handsome | Rather attractive | Average looks | Unattractive | Ugly & repulsive |

4. Is he slovenly or neat in personal appearance and dress?

| | | | | |
|---|---|---|---|---|
| | | X | | |
| Unkempt. Slovenly | Rather untidy & negligent | Average tidiness | Neat. Shows care | Very neat. Fastidious |

5. How pleasant and friendly is he during interview?

| | | | | |
|---|---|---|---|---|
| | X | | | |
| Friendly. Pleasant | Fairly pleasant | Neutral | Rather hostile | Hostile. Unpleasant |

6. How frank is he during interview?

| | | | | |
|---|---|---|---|---|
| | | X | | |
| Evasive. Untruthful | Rather evasive. Defensive | Average frankness | Rather frank | Frank |

7. Is he self-conscious or poised during interview?

| | | | | |
|---|---|---|---|---|
| | X | | | |
| Self-conscious. Ill-at-ease | Rather self-conscious | Average manner | Fairly poised. Seldom flustered | Poised. At-ease. Self-possessed |

8. How intelligent is he? Evaluate the psychological findings clinically and estimate the most valid rating.

| | | | | |
|---|---|---|---|---|
| | | | | (IQ 120) X |
| 80– Dull | 90–95 Low average | 100–105 Average | 115 Superior | 130+ Very sup. |

9. How fluent is he verbally under ordinary circumstances?

|———x———|————————|————————|————————|

| Fluent. "Pours out" | Spontaneous. Talkative | Average fluency | Meagre. Must be prompted | Taciturn. Must be "pumped" |
|---|---|---|---|---|

10. How does he impress you with regard to masculinity or femininity?

|————————|————————|———x———|————————|

| Very effeminate | Somewhat effeminate | Average boy qualities | Rather strongly masculine | Very masculine. A "buck" |
|---|---|---|---|---|

11. What is his characteristic output of energy?

|————————|———x———|————————|————————|

| Hyperkinetic. Bursts with energy | Lively. Energetic | Average display of energy | Rather limited energy | Apathetic. Sluggish |
|---|---|---|---|---|

12. How aggressively does he usually react (overtly)?

|————————|———x———|————————|————————|

| Very aggressive. Dominates | Rather aggressive. Assertive | Average | Passive. Tends to yield | Very passive. Gives in easily |
|---|---|---|---|---|

13. Does he ordinarily tend to be depressed or happy in temperament?

|————————|———x———|————————|————————|

| Depressed. Melancholic. Pessimistic | Generally dispirited | Average. Acc. to circumstances | Cheerful. Animated | Happy. Hilarious. Optimistic |
|---|---|---|---|---|

14. Is his general personality development advanced or retarded for his age?

|————————|———x———|————————|————————|

| Mature adult | Fairly mature | Average maturity | Rather retarded | Infantile |
|---|---|---|---|---|

(But immature in psychosexual area)

15. How inhibited is his behavior in personal or social relationships?

|————————|————————|———x———|————————|

| Inhibited. Restricted responses | Rather inhibited | Average | Fairly uninhibited | Very uninhibited |
|---|---|---|---|---|

16. Does he tend to be stable or changeable emotionally?

|————————|————————|————————|———x———|

| Stable. Very even moods | Fairly even temperament | Average stability | Rather variable. Over-reacts | Unstable. Extreme mood shifts |
|---|---|---|---|---|

17. Is he generally anxious or free of anxiety?

| | | | | |
|---|---|---|---|---|
| | x | | | |
| Very anxious | Rather anxious | Average anxiety | Fairly secure | Secure. Little anxiety |

18. Do you judge him to be predominantly introverted or extroverted?

| | | | | |
|---|---|---|---|---|
| | | x | | |
| Introverted | Rather introverted | Average. Mixed | Rather extroverted | Extroverted |

19. Does he tend to act impulsively, or with caution and deliberation?

| | | | | |
|---|---|---|---|---|
| | | | x | |
| Cautious. Deliberate. Calculating | Considers rather carefully | Average forethought | Acts quickly. Unreflective | Impulsive. Bolts. Unthinking |

20. Does he think and act for himself, or is he inclined to follow and depend upon others?

| | | | | |
|---|---|---|---|---|
| | x | | | |
| Self-reliant. Initiates action | Fairly independent | Average | Rather dependent. Seldom acts on his own | Dependent. Follows lead entirely |

21. Is he realistic or autistic in his mental approach to problems?

| | | | | |
|---|---|---|---|---|
| | | | | x |
| Objective. Literal. Mirrors reality | Fairly objective. Little distortion | Average reality approach | Day-dreams. Wishful thinking | Very subjective. Distorts reality |

22. Does he feel generally inferior or superior to others?

| | | | | |
|---|---|---|---|---|
| | x | | | |
| Strong inferiority feelings | Feels rather inferior | Average | Feels rather superior | Feels genuinely superior |

23. How much self-control does he show under frustration?

| | | | | |
|---|---|---|---|---|
| | x | | | |
| Easily frustrated. Explosive | Rather irritable. Impatient | Average self-control | Tolerant. Seldom loses control | Good control High threshold |

24. Is his picture of the home atmosphere one of harmony or of discord?

| | | | | |
|---|---|---|---|---|
| | | x | | |
| Pleasant. Harmonious. Mutual affection | Fairly harmonious. Mutual acceptance | Average family adjustment | Rather discordant. Quarrelsome | Unpleasant. Constant discord. Antagonisms |

25, 26, 27. Consider the closeness of his relationships to the other members of his family (or foster family if roles are well-defined).

25. Father (or father substitute)

| | | | | |
|---|---|---|---|---|
| | | | | X |

26. Mother (or mother substitute)

| | | | | |
|---|---|---|---|---|
| | | | X | |
| | | | (Ambivalent) | |

27. Siblings, in general

| | | | | |
|---|---|---|---|---|
| | | | X | |
| Close attachment. Mutual affection. Identification | Attached. Sympathetic relationship | Average acceptance | Indifferent. Ambivalent | Rejection. Rivalry. Open dislike |

28. How accepting is he of adults in authority?

| | | | | |
|---|---|---|---|---|
| | | | X | |
| Defiant. Openly rebellious | Critical. Suspicious. Resenting | Average | Generally docile. Respectful | Compliant. Trustful. Accepting |

(Surface compliance but with considerable underlying resentment.)

29. How well does he adjust to others of his own age-group?

| | | | | |
|---|---|---|---|---|
| | X | | | |
| Very well adjusted. Very popular | Good adjustment. Well liked | Average adjustment | Rather poor adjustment. Tolerated | Poor adjustment. Disliked |

30. How well has he adjusted to school during the past year?

| | | | | |
|---|---|---|---|---|
| | | | | |
| Very well-adjusted. Likes. Very interested | Good adjustment | Average. Usual minor problems | Rather poor. Often in trouble | Very poor. Many problems |

(*Not rated*)

31. Does he feel deprived or satisfied as far as material want such as food, money, or clothes are concerned?

| | | | | |
|---|---|---|---|---|
| | | | X | |
| Satisfied. Secure | Fairly secure. Usually satisfied | Average satisfaction or deprivation | Feels somewhat deprived | Feels very deprived |

32. Does he feel deprived or satisfied in his needs for love and affection?

| | | | | |
|---|---|---|---|---|
| | | | x | |
| Satisfied. Secure | Fairly secure. Usually satisfied | Average satisfaction or deprivation | Feels somewhat deprived | Feels very deprived |

33. Does he prefer sedentary or physically active recreation?

| | | | | |
|---|---|---|---|---|
| | | | x | |
| Prefers sedentary play | Usually sedentary | Average. Mixed types of play | Usually prefers active play | Seeks active play entirely |

34. Are his recreational activities predominantly social or solitary?

| | | | | |
|---|---|---|---|---|
| | | x | | |
| Prefers solitary play | Usually solitary | Average. Mixed | Usually prefers group play | Seeks group play entirely |

35. Are his recreational interests varied or restricted in range?

| | | | | |
|---|---|---|---|---|
| | | x | | |
| Varied. Many interests | Fairly wide interests | Average number & range | Few interests | Narrow activity No interests |

36. Are his standards of morality and conduct conventional or anti-social on the whole?

| | | | | |
|---|---|---|---|---|
| | | | x | |
| Rigid conventional standards | Strict standards | Average. Mixed attitudes | Standards rather loose & unconventional | Anti-social. Rebellious |

37. Does he worry much about sex problems?

| | | | | |
|---|---|---|---|---|
| | | x | | |
| Very worried. Preoccupied | Conflicted | Normal. Usual conflicts | Few conflicts | No conflict. Unconcerned |

38. What degree of sex interest or activity does he display?

| | | | | |
|---|---|---|---|---|
| | | | | x |
| Very retarded development | Quiescent. Retarded development | Normal for age | Exaggerated interest & activity | Very exaggerated |

Indicate the main area of sex interest:

AUTO-EROTIC HOMO-SEXUAL <u>HETERO-SEXUAL</u> (overtly) OTHER (specify)

39. To what extent are his conflicts expressed in psychosomatic behavior?

| Many nervous symptoms | Some nervous symptoms | Average symptomatic behavior | Few nervous symptoms | No nervous symptoms |
|---|---|---|---|---|
| x | | | | |

40. Is he strongly motivated towards achievement?

| Strongly motivated. Very ambitious | Fairly ambitious. Definite goals | Average aspiration & effort | Little ambition. Routine effort | Drifter. No plans Unambitious |
|---|---|---|---|---|
| | x | | | |

41. Consider his total personal and social adjustment, avoiding if possible special reference to any of the factors above; how well integrated and adjusted is he on the whole?

| Very well adjusted | Well adjusted | Average adjustment | Poor adjustment | Very poor adjustment |
|---|---|---|---|---|
| | | | x | |

42. Assuming he is released into the community, what is the expectation that he will continue delinquent behavior?

| Poor prognosis | Doubtful. Likely to get in trouble again | Average outlook | Unlikely to be in trouble again | Good Prognosis |
|---|---|---|---|---|

(*Not rated*)

43. As compared with the usual case, did you find most of your judgments of this boy's personality clear or difficult to define? Indicate the degree of certainty you feel in your ratings of his personality and behavior.

| Especially certain | Average degree of certainty | Doubtful |
|---|---|---|
| | x | |

## TAT INTERPRETATION

A tentative personality description of the subject can be proposed along the following lines:

This is a schizophrenic (or clearly schizoid) individual. He is not acutely disturbed at the time of the examination (TAT), but is fundamentally withdrawn and preoccupied. There is considerable surface responsiveness and some degree of insight but his thinking is predominantly at a regressed fantasy level.

The intelligence classification is superior (approximately 120 I.Q.). Basic intellectual functions (memory, comprehension) are little affected; at more complex levels, however, his thinking is characterized by highly symbolic autistic processes. The vocabulary level and general fluency are high, with some "straining" for effect.

He appears to be a person of superior, but unrealized, potentialities, with aspirations considerably greater than the persistence and drive necessary to fulfill them. He is very much aware of economic and class difference; quite likely he is a member of some minority group (?Negro).

In many areas of behavior it may be predicted that he shows an average range of adjustment, e.g., personal and social relationships, recreational interests and activities. A number of factors may be noted which are indicative of ego strength; for example, he utilizes a variety of defenses and is emotionally labile rather than rigid. Behavior deviations are suggested in the following directions: emotional instability—a tendency to be variable in temperament, with extreme mood shifts; impulsivity—a tendency to lose self-control and to react with impatience, irritability or even explosive behavior.

One of our subject's main problems seems to center around the control of aggression. Very marked aggressive needs are expressed. From the evidence of the record, he suppresses these and may therefore not be notably aggressive in his overt behavior. The probability is that the aggression is largely directed inward, as is suggested by the striking masochistic trend in the TAT record. Associated with this is a self-pitying hypochondriacal concern which is possibly delusional in intensity; in any case it may be anticipated that many psychosomatic symptoms are presented.

Another important problem area here is the subject's own family. He rejects his father and is highly ambivalent towards his mother. Both parents are seen as punitive superego figures. There is no clear pattern of identification with either parent. Some unusual feature in the original family constellation is suggested, possibly a traumatic event centering on the mother.

In the sex area, a somewhat exaggerated heterosexual interest and activity is suggested at the overt level. A strong latent homosexual trend may, however, be inferred. Evidence for this may be seen in subject's strong identification with and empathy for feminine figures in the TAT. Some basic anxiety over sexuality is expressed; both male and female sexuality are interpreted as threatening and ultimately annihilating. Incest fantasies are prominent. A definite immaturity in psychosexual development is suggested, although in other spheres of behavior he is fairly adequate.

In summary, subject appears to be a schizophrenic whose principal problems center around: (1) the control of aggressive impulses, both externally and internally directed; (2) the desire to escape from reality demands and responsibility; (3) the resolution of persisting emotional ties to the parents, particularly the mother; (4) the handling of conflicts arising from failure to establish mature sexual goals.

The fact that he responds relatively adequately on this test despite the clearly autistic overlay suggests that the prognosis for therapy is good. Since his problems are deep-lying and are expressed in symbolic form, he would probably respond best to an analytically oriented psychotherapeutic approach.

## MAPS TEST WORKING NOTES

The MAPS test record was analyzed and rated quantitatively in exactly the same manner as the TAT. The work sheet, below, indicates the procedure.

### WORK SHEET FOR ANALYSIS OF MAPS TEST RECORD

| *Response Category* | *Picture Number* LIV | STR | BTH | DRM | BED | BLK | STG | *Trend of Ratings* |
|---|---|---|---|---|---|---|---|---|
| 1. Fluency | 4 | 4 | 3 | 3 | 3 | 2 | 4 | Fluent |
| 2. Feeling-tone | 1 | 1 | 2 | 2 | 1 | 2 | 1 | Unpleasant feeling-tone |
| 3. Originality | 1 | 2 | 1 | ? | 2 | 2 | 1 | Unusual responses |
| 4. Picture rejection | 1 | 1 | 1 | 1 | 1 | 1 | 1 | No picture rejection |
| 5. Compliance | 5 | 4 | 4 | 4 | 4 | 4 | 5 | High compliance |
| 6. Organization | 3 | 4 | 2 | 3 | 4 | 3 | 4 | Average organization |
| 7. Interpersonal emphasis | 4 | 4 | 2 | 3 | 3 | 3 | 4 | Moderate whole emphasis |
| 8. Interpersonal emphasis | 2 | 2 | 3 | 2 | 3 | 3 | 2 | Moderate concept dominance |
| 9. Interpersonal emphasis | 3 | 5 | 3 | 2 | 4 | 4 | 5 | Extraceptive |
| 10. Self-reference | 3 | 2 | 2 | 1 | 3 | 2 | 3 | Some self-reference |
| 11. Certainty feeling | 3 | 4 | 4 | 3 | 3 | 2 | 4 | Average certainty |
| 12. Vocabulary level | 3 | 4 | 3 | 3 | 4 | 3 | 4 | Average to high vocabulary |
| 13. Stereotypy | 2 | 1 | 1 | 1 | 1 | 1 | 1 | No stereotypy |
| 14. Action or movement | 4 | 5 | 3 | 3 | 5 | 4 | 5 | High action |
| 15. Interpersonal relations | 2 | 1 | 2 | 1 | 1 | 3 | 1 | Conflictful interpersonal relations |
| 16. Interpersonal relations | 4 | 5 | 4 | 5 | 4 | 2 | 5 | Strong interpersonal relations |
| 17. Environmental stress | 1 | 1 | 2 | 2 | 2 | 1 | 1 | Environment malign |
| 18. Outcome | 1 | 1 | ? | 1 | 1? | 1? | ? | Very unsuccessful outcome |
| 19. Outcome | 1 | 3 | 1 | 2 | 3 | 1 | 2 | Rather unreal outcome |
| 20. Conflict solution | 2? | 4 | ? | 5 | 1 | 4 | ? | Varied conflict solution |
| 21. Achievement | 1 | 1 | 1 | 3 | 1 | 3 | 1 | Weak achievement theme emphasis |
| 22. Frustration | 3 | 5 | 4 | 4 | 1 | 5 | 3 | High frustration theme emphasis |
| 23. Aggression | 5 | 5 | 3 | 5 | 5 | 4 | 5 | High aggression theme emphasis |
| 24. Conflict | 5 | 3 | 4 | 3 | 3 | 1 | 3 | Moderately high conflict theme emphasis |
| 25. Anxiety | 3 | 3 | 3 | 1 | 3 | 5 | 1 | Moderate anxiety theme emphasis |
| 26. Punishment | 3 | 5 | 2 | 2 | 3 | 2 | 2 | Moderate punishment theme emphasis |
| 27. Reward | 1 | 1 | 1 | 1 | 1 | 1 | 1 | No reward theme emphasis |
| 28. Giving aid | 2 | 1 | 1 | 1 | 3 | 1 | 1 | Weak giving aid theme emphasis |
| 29. Receiving aid | 4 | 1 | 3 | 1 | 1 | 1 | 1 | Weak receiving aid theme emphasis |
| 30. Escape | 2 | 3 | 3 | 2 | 4 | 1 | 1 | Some escape theme emphasis |
| 31. Sensory gratification | 1 | 2 | 2 | 3 | 1? | 1 | 3 | Weak sense gratification theme emphasis |
| 32. Passivity | 1 | 1 | 1 | 1 | 1 | 1 | 1 | No passivity theme emphasis |
| 33. Aesthetic feeling | 2 | 2 | 3 | 2 | 1 | 1 | 3 | Some aesthetic feeling |
| 34. Paranoid feeling | 2 | 2 | 4 | 1 | 1 | 2 | 1 | Some paranoid feeling |
| 35. Guilt feeling | 5 | 4 | 1 | 2 | 4 | 1 | 1 | Fairly strong guilt feeling |
| 36. Narcissistic feeling | 2 | 1 | 3 | 1 | 1 | 1 | 1 | Weak narcissistic feeling |

| *Response Category* | *Picture Number* LIV | STR | BTH | DRM | BED | BLK | STG | *Trend of Ratings* |
|---|---|---|---|---|---|---|---|---|
| 37. Sadistic feeling | 4 | 3 | 1 | 5 | 4 | 3 | 5 | Strong sadistic feeling |
| 38. Inferiority feeling | 3 | 2 | 4 | 3 | 1 | 1 | 2 | Some inferiority feeling |
| 39. Ambivalence | 2 | 4 | 1 | 2 | 1 | 1 | 2 | Slight ambivalence feeling |
| 40. Reference to age | 5 | 1 | 4 | 2 | 1 | 4 | 3 | Marked reference to age |
| 41. Reference to new-old | 1 | 2 | 3 | 1 | 1 | 3 | 4 | Moderately high new-old reference |
| 42. Reference to neat-orderly | 2 | 1 | 1 | 1 | 1 | 1 | 2 | Slight neat reference |
| 43. Reference to light-dark | 1 | 5 | 1+ | 3 | 1 | 1 | 3 | Marked light-dark reference |
| 44. Reference to smoke-fire | 1 | 1 | 1 | 1 | 1 | 1 | 1 | No smoke reference |
| 45. Reference to book, etc., as source | 2 | 1 | 1 | 1 | 1 | 1 | 1 | No book reference |
| 46. Reference to suicide | 1? | 4 | 2? | 1 | 5 | 2 | 1 | Marked suicide reference |
| 47. Reference to sex activity | 1 | 4 | 1 | 5 | 5 | 1 | 1 | Marked sex activity reference |
| 48. Interest in male appearance | 1 | 1 | 1 | 1 | 1 | 1 | 1 | No interest in male appearance |
| 49. Feminine identification | 2 | 2 | 2 | 3 | 2 | 1 | 3 | Marked feminine identification |
| 50. Peculiar content | 4 | 2 | 5 | 3 | 3 | 3 | 5 | Marked peculiar content |
| 51. Symbolic content | 5 | 5 | 5 | 5 | 5 | 5 | 5 | Very high symbolic content |
| 52. Unusual detail noted | 1 | 1 | 1 | 3 | 1 | 1 | 1 | No unusual detail |
| 53. Perceptual distortion | 1 | 1? | 2 | 1 | 2? | 1 | 2 | Some perceptual distortion |
| 54. Picture criticism | 1 | 1 | 1 | 1 | 1 | 1 | 1 | No picture criticism |
| 55. Moralizing | 4 | 2 | 1 | 1 | 1 | 1 | 1 | Slight moralizing |
| 56. Questions | 4 | 1 | 1 | 1 | 1 | 1 | 2 | Slight question |
| 57. Interjections | 1 | 1 | 1 | 1 | 1 | 1 | 1 | No interjections |
| 58. Dramatizing | 4 | 4 | 1 | 1 | 1 | 1 | 5 | Moderately high dramatizing |
| 59. Artificiality | ? | 1 | 1 | 1 | 1 | 1 | 1 | No artificiality |
| 60. Humor | 1 | 1 | 1 | 1 | 1 | 1 | 1 | No humor |
| 61. Disjointedness | 3 | 2 | 1 | 3 | 2 | 2 | 2 | Marked disjointedness |
| 62. Outcome indeterminate | 1 | 1 | 2 | 1 | 1 | 1 | 1 | Clear outcome |
| 63. Time emphasis, past | 2 | 2 | 2 | 4 | 2 | 1 | 2 | Some past emphasis |
| 64. Time emphasis, present | 4 | 4 | 4 | 2 | 4 | 4 | 4 | High present emphasis |
| 65. Time emphasis, future | 1 | 2 | 2 | 2 | 2 | 2 | 2 | Some future emphasis |

## MAPS TEST INTERPRETATION

Results of the analysis duplicated the TAT so closely that a separate descriptive interpretation of the MAPS record is unnecessary. Most of the main trends which characterized the subject's response to the TAT were also revealed in the MAPS test. For example: unpleasantness of feeling-tone, conflictful interpersonal relationships, malign environmental stress, and marked emphasis on such topics as age of characters, light or dark features in the pictures, sex activity, and suicide.

Thematic emphases yielded by the two tests were, in order of quantitative frequency, as follows:

| TAT | MAPS |
|---|---|
| Aggression | Aggression |
| Punishment | Frustration |
| Frustration | Punishment |
| Receiving aid | Conflict |
| Anxiety | Anxiety |

Although the MAPS test record gives a first impression of greater thematic richness, the actual quantitative scoring on the two tests yields practically identical averages per picture and also for the total responses.

Certain of the response categories are of course altered by the special procedure of the test. Thus, as to whether a response is "picture-dominated" or "concept-dominated" is affected by the fact that the stimulus is not as fixed in the MAPS test as it is in the TAT; in the former, the subject selects and revises his own picture elements in terms of the story. Such categories as originality are also on a different level of judgment. In both the TAT and the MAPS test the method of category analysis described here ignores a very important area of interpretation, the negative content of the test; that is, what is actually given considered in the light of what might be said or is usually said about a particular picture.

# Chapter 10

# ROBERT R. HOLT

Dr. Holt was born in 1917. He received the Ph.D. degree in Psychology from Harvard University in 1943. He is a Fellow in Clinical Psychology of the American Psychological Association. He has taught at Harvard, American, and Kansas Universities. During World War II he was a study director with the Division of Program Surveys, USDA. Since 1947 he has been at the Menninger Foundation, where he is now Director of Psychological Staff. His work is largely in the fields of ego psychology and projective techniques. For the past four years he has been engaged in a cooperative research project on the assessment and selection of psychiatrists. He is an associate member of the Topeka Psychoanalytic Society, Chairman of the APA Clinical Division's Committee on Publication Outlets in Clinical Psychology, Editor of the *TAT Newsletter*, and member of the editorial board of the *Journal of Projective Techniques*.

## SELECTED REFERENCES


HOLT, ROBERT R. (Ed.), *The TAT Newsletter*. Topeka, Kansas: Menninger Foundation. Vol. *1*, No. 1, October 1946, through Vol. *2*, No. 4, June 1949. Mimeographed.

——— (Ed.), The TAT Newsletter, in *Rorschach Research Exchange and Journal of Projective Techniques*, 1949, *13*, No. 2, et seq.

———, The Thematic Apperception Test—in ANDERSON, H., AND ANDERSON, G., *Introduction to Projective Techniques*. New York: Prentice Hall, 1951.

———, The Assessment of Psychiatric Aptitude from the Thematic Apperception Test. *American Psychologist*, 1948, *3*, 271.

LUBORSKY, LESTER B., HOLT, ROBERT R., AND MORROW, WILLIAM R., Interim Report of the Research Project on the Selection of Medical Men for Psychiatric Training. *Bulletin of the Menninger Clinic*, 1950, *14*, 92-101.


## RESUME OF METHOD

THE METHOD used in this study is a clinical approach in which the interpreter reads over the stories, jots down tentative hypotheses as he goes along, and integrates these notes into a final personality summary. There is not a formal scoring system and the method may be described as intuitive. The theoretical bases are those of psychoanalytic theory and Murray's need-press formulations. (It should be stated that Holt, with Luborsky, has developed a formalized technique for predicting success as a psychiatrist from the TAT. This method was not employed in this study.)

## TAT WORKING NOTES

The case of John Doe was not analyzed in strict accordance with the method set forth in my chapter on the TAT in the handbook on projective techniques edited by Harold and Gladys Anderson. Rather than being a scoring system or a method of interpretation, what I have set forth there is essentially a rationale. It is designed to aid in the understanding of TAT responses, and it serves as a general frame of reference that guides my interpretative method.

To the extent that I could be said to have a method, it consists in reading over the stories and making notes on aspects of form and content that strike my attention as being deviant or as fitting together with impressions from other stories or from other tests. (In clinical work I always use a battery of tests.) These notes, which are more or less copious, depending on the time pressure under which I am working and on the purpose for which the TAT is being used, are quite similar to the ones reproduced here. They consist mainly of three types of material: notations of significant formal aspects of the record (where I depend heavily on Rapaport), rather unsystematic skeletonizing of content in terms of need-press themas (where my debt to Murray is most clear), and speculations about the symbolic and dynamic significance of anything in the record. I try to be free and undisciplined in these speculations (which derive mainly from what knowledge of psychoanalysis I have) but keep a watch on the extent to which I am projecting myself, and treat them only as speculations until they are corroborated.

After these notes have been made, I read them through again, often making additions, and collate them with similar notes from any other material I have about the subject, in pretty much the usual way: looking for repeated themas, for congruences and overlaps between different stories and between different tests.

In diagnostic studies, I believe very strongly in the position argued most clearly by Roy Schafer, that tests allow us to make inferences about aspects of personality and the organization or disorganization of thought and affect, *not* directly about diagnostic categories. From the picture of personality that emerges from the interpenetrating mosaic of these immediately inferred features, it is usually possible to form a diagnostic impression, couched in the terms of whatever nosology one may be currently using.

So far as I know, no one has reported anything very helpful on the final process, the synthesis of all one's more or less scattered ideas and impressions into a unified, more or less self-consistent picture of a personality.[1] Here is

[1] To some extent this, as well as the earlier and simpler stages in the diagnostic process, are being subjected to systematic scrutiny in a research project on the selection of psychiatrists, in which Dr. Lester Luborsky and I (and other collaborators) are engaged. We have attempted to record as much as possible of the inductive, inferential and synthetic processes that went on in our minds as we analyzed batteries of tests (including the TAT) for 35 to 40 subjects, predicting their later behavior as psychiatric residents. After our predictions have been validated, we hope to learn a good deal about the relative validity of different ways of interpreting clinical data.

where experience and knowledge of psychopathology are usually invoked, to help explain the more or less creative process that goes on, but I do not think that it contributes much to an understanding of thematic analysis to fall back on such truisms. Trying to introspect, I am inclined to think that it is a kind of hierarchic structuring of the material, really concept formation, in which implications of the raw data are grouped into first-order abstractions, and these in turn are related to each other leading to synthetic emergents, and so on. But this may well be an intellectualized rationalization of an essentially unconscious process. When we learn someday to study, understand, improve, and teach this aspect of TAT analysis, I think we shall be getting at the heart of the matter.

The following notes refer specifically to the TAT of John Doe.

Single man, 25 years (an age at which it's still OK to be single).

1. *Sick in bed*—unusual (never saw it before). Perceptual distortion, *self as sick*—(p Affliction→p Gratuity). Also some of the usual p Imposed task, but with an almost perverse twist: Question of *malingering?* Sees score as such—not very usual, and violin as a novel—very unusual perceptual distortion.

General *ease and freedom* in telling story—spontaneously gives quite a lot. Therefore, not a simple uneducated sort—especially with his vocabulary (coincidence, thusly), but probably college level. See also references to being "quite a studious type," regrets missing school.

Impression on first reading—intelligent, rather intellectual schizophrenic, probably paranoid, not very long duration (because of productivity, and freedom, lack of flatness).

Inappropriate flavor, complete *arbitrariness* of—"something to do with ocean or water" (break through of own preoccupation), *peculiar* statement beginning with "coincidence"—also *delusional-like idea*, "knowing what is in the book before reading it"—*delusions of being able to read minds*, or of having own mind read? Paranoid is supported by inferential tone, especially in second sentence.

Has to bring up *fear of parents* only to deny it. Flavor of masturbation conflict: (a) no violin: denial of phallus? (b) alone in bed doing something he should fear being caught at by parents—adventure?—water?

Suggestions of *bland front* in "not too happy, not too sad"—especially in "His eyes are somewhat blank."

Stays fairly picture-focused—doesn't stray far into an independent story—*obsessive-compulsive* structure, also supported by evidence for studiousness, and especially the ambivalent statement, "not too happy, though not too sad," and similar *balance between statement and denial throughout* story.

Idea of coming across a novel while confined to bed is loose and thoughtless—not very reality-oriented. I'm still puzzled by distortion of violin into novel. Speculation: violin = penis = books, intellectuality as phallic superiority ruse, compensation?

Adventure theme also very unusual here—a personal preoccupation (escape fantasies?). Cf. heightened dramatic tone throughout.

*Conception of parents:* rather harsh, unloving, inconsiderate; sick boy is given music to study, which he apparently doesn't want—(his disregard is an indirect and passive-resistance counter-aggression) and they would be angry at finding him reading something pleasurable *even* when he's sick, instead of "work." Severe discipline is suggested, against which he probably reacts passively. An elaborate tissue of indirect hostilities between parents and child is suggested.

"Coincidence of reading book *without any eyes*": last phrase a strikingly peculiar way of saying without looking, or with eyes shut or the like. Strongly suggests castration: not just anxiety, *feeling of being castrated* (cf. no violin).

Negative content: lack of any interpersonal relations—not too unusual, though hero-centered to a degree that is characteristic of quite narcissistic people.

*Facade:* based on slightly pretentious tone of verbalization—use of "thusly," not idiomatic, and stilted (see also next to last sentence). Ability to communicate with others beginning to break down (schizoid peculiarities).

On basis of this story alone, feel certain that there is a schizophrenic process present, even though not necessarily a pure schizophrenia. Slightly pretentious, façade tone, helped along with basic fact of perverse refusal to acknowledge presence of violin, strongly suggests that he *does* see violin but consciously thinks that he's being "clever" or "original," or is out-tricking the examiner (whom he might see as trying to trick him) by ignoring it or seeing it as a book. That he is aware of it on some level is suggested by the fact that the basic theme, p Parental Imposed Task → n Auto Resis, passive Aggression, comes through. Consistent also is statement at the end: he *disregards* the music. Not a psychopathic trying to act smart—too schizzy.

*Sick in bed as a child* may be an autobiographical theme. He's almost certainly "sick" (that is, psychotic) now, and so that may be enough explanation for it. But most psychotics don't; therefore it becomes plausible that he may have had long illnesses as a child, cutting him off from other kids, and→to fantasy escape—dreams of travel and adventure.

Sentence 3 may also describe his overt behavior: nonchalant, seemingly "at ease," really frightened underneath.

Above are almost all hypotheses, to be confirmed or excluded by later stories.

*Strong passivity* throughout—especially in outcome. Also suggestion of *flight* and *avoidance* of very passive sort—drastic enough to include denial of threatening aspects of reality.

*Nothing holds his interest long*—not even adventure novel. He soon withdraws into *own* fantasy, to conviction of knowing what's in book without reading it even though "took a chance" to read it, and finally withdraws into sleep.

3BM. Girl in a cell—ordinary apperception.

"Girl" only slight evidence for feminine identification; enough empathy with girl in thoughts and feelings to strengthen it, though.

"Jailed because guilty of prostitution.": *sex is something very criminal* for him, more than in reality. Implies intense sex-guilt.

Note that she feels *ashamed*, not guilty, and that it's not so much because of well-internalized values but because of external consequences. Implies *poorly internalized superego.*

Shame about tremendous p Cog suggests *unconscious need, against which there are reaction formations, to exhibit and look* (cf. implied fear of p Cog in 1, concern with eyes). Suggest possibility of *delusions of reference.*

Knew sister would suffer—confirmation of *passive aggression.* This time, through dragging self down, family members can be hurt; supported by other *intragression* (suicide carried through). So his techniques of aggression are *passive resistance plus self-destruction,* destroying poorly internalized family members (unconscious of it: "made her feel badly").

Sister—an unusual introduced figure. *Sibling rivalry?* And/or just a classic *sacred-profane split* (nun and prostitute). Latter split confirms externalization tendencies, consistent with paranoid developments. Moralism, superficial religiosity, suggested by *nun,* lost opportunity to identify with her.

Knife, not gun, a slight distortion, though not very unusual.

Note no real regret for the hurt to the sister: heroine feels badly because it was too late for *herself* to be saved the same way. Narcissism supported, *basic isolation, lack of true self-love.*

Story has a fair (better than average) degree of coherence and smooth dramatic development. Sounds as if told fairly easily and smoothly. (Would help to have times, also indication of technique of administration: how story was recorded.) (In story 1, inquiry would have helped.)

Suicide theme not unusual, though going through with it a little more indicative of something personal. Still not at all depressive.

4. Half-caste—suggests *ethnic prejudice, projection* of lust onto outgroup members. More *sexual preoccupation,* but probably seems somewhat ego-alien (because of above). Abortion is unusual theme—(even though brought in in stilted words; "conclude the birth")—suggests *raw, unsublimated nature* of his sexual fantasies.

Man is *callous,* shows no regard for woman with whom he has lived for some time "in intimacy": *no capacity for real love,* a genital object relationship. Same sacred-profane (wife vs. mistress) split as before. Lust, enjoyment of sex, is something unworthy, indulged in by morally bad people who must be harshly punished for it. So far, it's women who are crassly lustful, and they must destroy themselves for it (projective again).

Notable feminine identification here: almost all is from the woman's viewpoint, the one he naturally seems to adopt. But since women are so *bad,* his feminine side is probably ego-alien, repressed and projected. (Was his mother self-destructive too?)

Note concern with *pregnancy* (cf. water in story 1).

Sex is dangerous to the man: he spends the night and gets burnt up.

Final comment is too *bland or flip*—seems content with this very sudden, violent outburst of destructive aggression. This kind of sudden inappropriate aggressive ending (in no way suggested by the picture, as suicide in story 3BM was), especially when so blandly passed off, is another schizophrenic indicator. Something especially infantile and unmodulated about this aggression; setting fire to the house—destroying *everything*—self, lover and house too. Suggests hatred of whole family, whole world; possibly world destruction fantasies.

6BM. Traumatic relationship with mother is "too hot" to be approached directly—he must avoid, make it irreal. (All the avoidance and callousness suggest some *character disorder features. Also glibness of verbalization—may have catatonic features*—cf. "blank eyes" of story 1. *Acting out?* Possibly denial, through acting out, of own ego-alien femininity.)

*Stage—famous*—note repetition of exhibitionistic-voyeuristic theme. Some ***pre-occupation with external rewards (money, fame) as a substitute for love?***

Theme basically same as in last two: indulgence in sex→death. Now mother is definitely the punisher. Again, the "shocking" ending: sudden murder of a socially particularly unacceptable kind: mother shoots son in cold blood, and quite unnecessarily. And what a cold, inexorably moralistic mother!

Note that the defense isn't successful: the fear and hatred of the mother breaks through anyway.

Paranoid note in the second and third sentences. Some hint of contamination or confusion in the last spontaneous sentence: "so *here* (i.e., in the pictured scene?) she draws a revolver and shoots *him*"—whom? the young actor or the son?

External superego: "the *audience* will prefer this." Mother, not father, is the punisher. Cf. in story 3BM, not much concerned about police (father-figures)—it's a woman who administers the final punishment in each case so far.

Dramatic quality in rather *phony*, trumped up, shocker endings (facade). Nevertheless, the imaginal flow is remarkable, as is the originality (even though latter is primarily pathologic in origin). Suggests a person of some real talent and creativeness, at least potentially, before illness (though probably never enough inner resources ever to produce much).

7BM. Concern over health again (cf. story 1). *Hypochondriacal* features to be expected, especially before the break (if any). (This so far sounds like a rather acute phase of paranoid schizophrenia.)

NB.: hero is *more nearly adequate in relationship to father than in relationship to mother.*

Moralistic advice from father—probably the kind of talk he got himself about his complaints when without organic basis. Yet, implication that father was doing something wrong in applying coercion to son, because he "repented"—perhaps for having been concerned with the son's health only because it bade fair to force him to support daughter-in-law and grandchildren. *No love between father and son, no nurturance from father* stimulated by son's illness: *conception of parents as moralistic pressures, not loving and supporting persons.*

Note *sustained pessimism* (no hope . . . doesn't get better)—not a happy ending yet, only neutral retreat of story 1. This man lacks capacity either to break away from either parent or to enjoy himself at all.

Father had same illness: unclear significance as yet.

Still somewhat *preoccupied with money and material support.*

Son's reaction to father's pressure: *submit, go away, passive rejection* and *aggression* in never contacting father again: repeated, no "correspondence."

11. Note beginning: this is a fantasy. Still *can* recognize the difference between reality and fantasy, wants it clearly understood that he recognizes it when he goes off the deep end.

Extremely good perceptual sharpness here—in striking contrast to story 1!

Strongly *fatalistic* tone: the outcome is never in the hands of the people themselves, but is a matter of "predestination" or "fate"; implies *low self-reliance* (later on denied, see story 16), projection of responsibility.

Note obsessive paranoid "reasoning" quality appearing again: "must have been . . . because" (sentence 5); "evidently . . . because it is presumed that . . ." (sentence 6). Note verbal usage—on a consistently high intellectual level—with some of the slight formalism and stiltedness of the obsessive. Also, rather *excessive balance and counterpoise of ideas:* attack, but escape; fated to get to goal, but beast will run ahead and get them; they are fated to be (destroyed?). (Note vocabulary: serpentine; predestined; it is presumed.)

*Moralistic flavor:* wicked going into darkness—pit full of lost souls, no escape for the wicked. Unusual ending: particularly strong self-destructiveness, can't let self escape.

Beast is a superego force, aggression directed against the evil self.

Note escape theme—slight addition to previous.

12M. Note financial preoccupation again. Starvation—loaf of bread. *Deep oral cravings*—fear of starvation underlies the superficially anal-sounding concern with money.

Something of the previous fantasy of acclaim, fame, etc., here. Continued tragedy and failure, self-defeat is even nearly explicit. *Fantasy of the good parents* (mother and father) who will appreciate him, feed him, support him. But it's only a fantasy: would come too late.

Slick O. Henry quality again—supports the character disorder flavor of *glibness*.

13MF. Same sacred-profane split, sexual preoccupation, moralism. Voyeurism—denied in turning off light so he *can't* see her. Only a girl who doesn't permit any sex is really any good.

Note that girl is *initiator sexually*—man is passive and compliant. Note that he leaves—sex is something kept isolated from love—forcibly (sentence 8). He leaves this girl, and the other one died. *No stable sexual relationship*. (In 7BM, hero had a wife, but only as an attribute for purposes of the story—no relationship was described.)

13B. First half is keyed by statement, "this doesn't say much to me." Not much involved. *Theme of pregnancy* again. (Schizophrenic fantasy of rebirth?)

Only happy ending to date, and after a usually pessimistic view: "it's a hopeless case." Elation. Oedipal fulfillment—note final statement.

Repeated theme of flight, rejection of parents as a counter to feeling of being unloved, rejected.

The ending is probably a wish for what never was, and should have been. Of course, he never *has* left home really.

*Sibling rivalry* theme again (cf. 3BM)—seems like something real.

"Black room—case looks black"; schizophrenic flavor, physiognomic thinking, fluid.

14. More sudden uncalled-for crude aggression: "*mutilated* human body." Really sadistic aggressions, but quite ego-alien. Has the sound of a frequent fantasy.

Opening statement, an attempt to make a slick mystery out of it.

Note minister (cf. prayer in last)—suggests a good deal of religious content (probably derived from mother, through identification).

Robbery→pursuit→kills, mutilates (note: mutilation never satisfactorily explained—a sadistic flourish)→discover, confession, retribution.

Note that a *moralistic father-figure can't be trusted*—confidence isn't respected so that he may be punished. Superego is inexorable, implacable.

16. (Cf. Earnst.) Barren environment thema—*oral deprivation*. Cf. story 12M, starvation. Really fierce oral cravings from a loveless (= milkless = waterless) infancy. A really schizophrenic utterance: paranoid ideas of "outside influences," narcissistic withdrawal ("entirely reliant on themselves"), utter loneliness and sense of death, yearning for human contact while convinced it's unattainable. World destruction fantasies more clearly hinted at; their nature as a projection of inner deadness and emptiness clear. Note growing tone of slight confusion, breakdown of verbalization into near-peculiarity. Line between reality and fantasy very thin and easily lost (last sentences).

## TAT INTERPRETATION

*Diagnosis*. The young man who tells these stories appears to be suffering from a paranoid schizophrenia of relatively brief duration, which is probably not now in an acute efflorescence, although an acute break has probably occurred. This diagnosis is based upon evidence in the TAT of: (a) distortion of perceptual contact with reality (especially story 1); (b) pathologic loosening of orderly thought processes (seen most clearly in stories 1, 6BM—where there is a suggestion of contaminated thinking—and 16); (c) delusional ideas (e.g., telepathy); (d) occasional breaking down of the ability to communicate with lapses into autistic use of language; (e) extreme narcissistic withdrawal from interpersonal relationships; (f) preoccupation with raw sexual and sadistic fantasies, suggesting that primitive instinct-derivatives are breaking through pre-psychotic defenses; (g) paranoid ideas of reference and malign influence; (h) desperate but hopeless yearning for love conceived in very infantile, oral terms; (i) moralism and religiosity; and (j) emotional inappropriateness and blandness. These aspects of personality taken together are consistent only with the presence of a schizophrenic process, and make the diagnosis of a full-blown psychosis quite likely.

It is very likely that almost any test given this patient would yield evidence of schizophrenia; establishing the degree to which the illness has progressed, however, is more difficult and uncertain. To begin with, a long-standing, deteriorated condition is virtually ruled out by the substantial degree of coherence, liveliness and realism of most of the stories, indicating that many areas of ego-functioning are relatively intact. None of the grosser and more obvious hallmarks of schizophrenia is to be seen. The fact that verbal peculiarities are few and not particularly striking argues that the disease is not of long duration, or at least that there is considerable retention of a "social front." (This line of reasoning, incidentally, also supports the diagnosis of *paranoid* schizophrenia.) The liveliness and productivity of fantasy of which the subject is capable are hardly consistent with the flatness and stereotypy to be looked for in chronic schizophrenia; they suggest rather the "diseased fancy" of a mind that is suffering an acute or near-acute psychosis. Some emotional inappropriateness is present both in the flavor of the verbalizations and in inappropriate, arbitrary story events; nevertheless it is not rampant. Delusional thinking seems to be present, likewise, but it does not crop out a great deal. This is not to deny that the patient may be very much deluded, even hallucinatory; but in acute paranoid schizophrenia these secondary symptoms of the condition are very often in the background in a TAT. The words with which he begins story 11, and the cautious inferential approach adopted in several of the stories, show some of the suspicious self-control with which the paranoid often is able to conceal his psychosis in testing and other brief, relatively impersonal encounters. Further, the fluctuating nature of ego-controls, now letting through pathologic ideas, now maintaining an appearance of rational coherence, is characteristic of the acute phase. This phenomenon may be seen most strikingly in the contrast between the gross perceptual distortion of story 1 (violin = book) and the unusual perceptual sensitivity and accuracy of story 11. It would be rare indeed for a chronic schizophrenic to turn in such a brilliant performance as his description of the figures on the rocky path.

If the psychosis seems not to be chronic, could it then be in a very early stage, say a very schizoid personality on the verge of a break? The strong indications of world destruction fantasies in stories 4 and 16, along with all the evidence of a process that has "broken through," furnish evidence that things have gone much further: that the world of the pre-psychotic adjustment has been destroyed, and that the restitutive efforts of the psychotic ego are what we see now principally.

*Personality structure.* What *was* the pre-psychotic adjustment? Signs of intellectualization, ambivalent balancing of possibilities, and the somewhat stilted choice of words from a wide vocabulary suggest some obsessive elements; the occasional tendency to "prove" the story from observational details does not go far enough to support the conclusion of an ingrained paranoid personality structure. Rather, this inferential approach is further evidence for obsessive defenses. At the same time, aspects of character disorder are suggested in the many manifestations of avoidant defenses, the pretentious facade, and some callousness (as of the man in stories 4 and 13 MF) that does not sound like simply blandness, but an attempt to shock.

Consistent with this personality structure, we might expect that the illness has at times been complicated by hypochondriacal complaints and perhaps by catatonic-like features. Acting out (perhaps sexual promiscuity, in an attempt to deny his femininity) may have been prominent. I would expect to see him going around with an air of nonchalant sophistication, talking rather glibly and with pseudo self-assurance that hides a devastating sense of inner emptiness, longing and even deadness. Self-centered and aloof, he is incapable of giving any kind of love to another and of expecting any love from anyone else. He probably is insufferably narcissistic and exhibitionistic, affecting poses designed to attract shocked (and, he hopes, admiring) attention. For all of his intellectualization, he has very little insight.

These personality traits just described may in the past have raised a differential diagnostic problem involving psychopathic personality or severe narcissistic character disorder, but the schizophrenic quality must have shown itself nevertheless in clinical observation.

*Intellection.* The vocabulary, verbal usage and general imaginal productivity show the patient to be a man of at least bright normal, probably superior intelligence. He has a kind of originality that is distinctly pathologic, arising partly from perversity, but suggesting that he can with some justification consider himself talented, though he lacks the drive, the capacity for sustained interests and the self-confidence to have produced anything much. Probably he has had some college training but no degree. What ability he has is held back by a deep self-destructiveness that cannot tolerate success.

His thinking, which can be very sharp and clear, is at times broken by arbitrariness and physiognomic associations, as his over-valent preoccupations break through the smooth flow of thought. Raw, unsublimated sexual preoccupations, ideas about pregnancy, and sadistic fantasies probably make up a good deal of his thought content. His pretentious use of a somewhat intellectual way of talking may obscure the clinical observer's perception of these defects in thought organization a good deal of the time.

*Motivation.* Although the patient may have had a number of transitory sexual affairs, he has undoubtedly never had a stable heterosexual relationship.

He longs desperately for a human contact, yet feels unable to establish one. There are clear indications of a strong feminine identification, implying latent homosexuality, but whether or not there has ever been any overt homosexual experience is impossible to say; at any rate, continued accepted homosexuality is very unlikely. Despite his sophisticated front, he has intense feelings of guilt about masturbation and other manifestations of sexuality, even a conviction that he must die because of his sexual sins.

In the face of his overpoweringly destructive aggressive impulses, the patient feels helpless and struggles to keep them (like his sexual urges) ego-alien. Feeling rejected and unloved, he rejects the world, but apparently can rarely be directly hostile. Passive-resistive techniques, and striking at others through self-destructive behavior seem to be his preferred modes of aggression. His poorly internalized superego is savage and infantile, directing much of his aggressive energies against himself. One manifestation is in his ingrained, hopeless pessimism. He feels that his battles are lost: he may in a sense feel already castrated, already dead (though these are speculative conclusions from slight evidence). Another form the pessimism takes is fatalism, the feeling that he is unable to guide his own destinies, that everything is in the hands of the fates.

As is often true of persons who have not been able to form (through identification) a personally meaningful, integrated set of values, the patient is quite moralistic, with a good deal of superficial religiosity. The projective mechanism is used a good deal, probably expressing itself in ethnic prejudices as well as in more patently paranoid forms. Another manifestation of his moralism is his classically dichotomous conception of women as either good or bad (nun vs. prostitute, sacred vs. profane love). Women seem to be seen as the lustful, morally bad ones, while men are passively involved with them or righteously reject them. Shame, fear of external consequences and what people will think are more than usually important to this man. Consistent with this emphasis on externals is the repeated concern in the TAT stories with money, fame, other external rewards—as substitutes for the love he cannot get, one feels.

Underlying much of the patient's behavior are ragingly intense oral and passive cravings. He feels starved, deprived of the oral gratifications of infancy that were rightly his. There are some superficial reaction formations against these hungers, probably some show of pseudo-independence and self-reliance in an attempt to embrace the necessary, but his passivity and dependence on others easily show through.

A minor theme already mentioned is a voyeuristic-exhibitionistic need, which is again probably ego-alien and projected. It may be manifested in the content of some of the patient's delusional ideas, as well as in exhibitionistic behavior.

*Historical reconstruction.* There are a number of leads in the TAT stories which tempt one to make some genetic hypotheses. First of all, the parents are clearly depicted as moralistic, punitive, cold, and demanding persons, from whom the patient feels he never received love and support. The mother seems to have been the more frustrating and the more feared (consistent with his having identified himself with her more than the father). She was probably a harsh, religious, rejective person, from whom he vainly longed to hear loving words. The hatred of her that developed is so strong that he may be aware of it; his fear of her is so great that he may not be able to go against her will openly. At the same time, guilt-laden incestuous fantasies do not seem to be far from the surface of consciousness. His father he sees as weaker; in relationship to him he feels more adequate, though the patient very probably resists him passively rather than overtly. In fantasy he longs for good, kind, loving parents, but knows that it is impossible to find them.

A few indications of sibling rivalry conflict suggest that an added difficulty imposed on the patient as a child may have been the necessity to share the tiny amount of affection available to his family with one or more other children. More then this it is difficult to say. The unusual theme of illness in story 1 raises the possibility that his dependence, escape into fantasy, and isolation from companionship may have been exacerbated by protracted childhood illnesses.

*Prognosis.* This patient would probably be very difficult to deal with psychotherapeutically if one were not ready and able to give him great quantities of undemanding love for the long time that it would take to convince him that it was not a trap. Only then would it be possible to begin building the capacity to love others and the basic self-respect that he so totally lacks underneath his narcissistic lacquer. Despite the many defenses against the close interpersonal relationship of psychotherapy that exist, there are assets in this man (intelligence, an active and original mind) which might make one hopeful for a fair prognosis, if a sensitive and talented therapist wanted to devote himself to the difficult task of salvaging a potentially creative and useful human being. Without therapy, the outlook is dark indeed: the best one could hope for would be some uneasy remissions, which would bring the patient little happiness, followed by final relapses into chronic psychosis.

## MAPS TEST WORKING NOTES

(I read through the stories twice on different occasions and then set down the following notes on the third, more leisurely time, through.)

Story 1. Note he starts with a feminine identification—F-8; whole story told with her as the heroine. Sentence 5: L-6 for mother! What a monstrous mother I had, he is saying—as horrible in her unlovingness as this one is in looks.

Sentence 6: Snake is "symbol of what she really is." (a) Phallic mother? (b) A snake: poisonous (cf. Rosen: typical schizophrenic fantasy of poisoned milk), treacherous, sly, caused the downfall of man?—check against later material. (c) Note bland unconcern with which a symbolic and highly unrealistic conception is tossed off. Not only schizophrenic, debonairly so. Of course, use of legendary figure in naturalistic setting sounds pretty well divorced from reality too. This and the tone of the rest of the story suggest that when a situation is conventionally structured (like a TAT card) he can put up a good front of "normality," but when he's on his own and can structure things as he wishes, plenty of really schizophrenic material comes out. The question that remains unresolved is, to what extent can he control the appearance of his schizophrenic thinking at will?

Sentence 7: Now back into a naturalistic framework. Note need rejection towards the mother. Note fear of "what the neighbors will think"—externalized superego.

Sentence 8: Slip: suggests that he identifies himself with the monster. He is to his family just such a frightening and hideous thing they're ashamed for people to know about. Strengthens mother-identification; own conviction of being bad and frightening, which he probably has had when most psychotic. Wants money, not love—material preoccupations. "To get son out of a jam"; repetition of an old pattern, referring to self?

Sentences 9–10: More blandly given schizophrenic thinking. Behind the paranoid concern with whom one can trust (only an animal), an echo of an idea in Fritz Peters: it's hypocrisy to wear clothes; the only honest thing to do is to take them off. Clothes equal shame, covering of one's true identity, deceit—therefore, those who wear clothes aren't to be trusted. (Also when clothes come off one sees the old snake —the penis.) (So what?) Anyway—a hint, with other exhibitionistic stuff in the TAT, that this man may have exhibited himself with the delusion-rationalization that it was the only way to be honest—like Peters in "The World Next Door."

Sentence 11: Following woman's implied criticism, snake leaves. Submissive compliance?

Sentences 12–13: The authority figure appears—one might think, in some relation to the son's being in a jam. But no, it's mother who is the target of aggression today. (Sentence 14.)

Sentence 15: Note slip: "turns *on* the officer"—a condensation? She turns *on* her mother, and turns *to* the cop at the same time. Note heartlessness of hostility to mother—really cold. Rejection of mother even more strongly than before.

Sentence 16: The desired result: Mother is broken-hearted. An echo of his own reaction to the rejection he felt from mother?

Sentences 17–19: Note readiness of invention, how easily his mind goes back to infancy and basic childhood situations. Fantasy of being *responsible* for mother's (psychological?) deformity—perhaps an echo of something she has told him. Note mother's counter-weapon is *guilt*.

Sentence 20: More heartlessness—bitingly rejective while insulting mother with money (note how he returns to this theme).

Sentence 22: Note fairy-tale like sound of the witch's curse—adds to the general schizophrenic flavor. Also dramatic, even melodramatic quality, noted in TAT.

Sentence 23: "She exists"—a faithful transcription?[2] Did he say *exits* or this? If the slip is the patient's, it's an unusual and rather malign sounding one—a condensed statement that the mother can't be gotten rid of—she keeps on existing even though she exits?

Sentence 24: A rather unnecessary part of story, though apparently consistent with what's gone before.

Sentences 25–26: But he is very easily put off—too easily. This is an easily bribed superego; content with the protestations and external appearances, on one level, but deadly and inescapable on a much more primitive one (see end of story).

Sentence 27: Note complete lack of warmth or even friendliness in any and all interpersonal relationships—they're either hostile, rejective, inquisitive or formal. Here a rather unnecessary quarrel: he just can't see a man and wife getting along.

Sentences 28–29: The final retribution—the mother has her revenge. Is this concern with being like mother when she gets old a fear of growing more like mother as he ages? Poison is really involved. Note also a hint of the devouring mother in the death through biting.

An extraordinary story—for length, complexity, richness of symbolism and wealth of latent content. Despite its bizarre elements, it has a kind of specious form and coherence. He is able to hold together to a surprising extent despite the far advance of the schizophrenic process. The freedom of invention is in a way only apparent: the originality (which this undoubtedly has, norms or not) is a function of disordered thinking in large part. Arbitrary sudden turns of the story suggest emotional inappropriateness, but not too obviously. Of course, the bland way in which the most outrageous turns of events are told suggests a great deal of emotional inappropriateness on the patient's part.

Only 12 grades of school, yet this vocabulary and sophistication in story construction. He is really an intellectualizer, and can probably produce reams of such material, which is hardly felt at all, yet which contains so much unconscious material. Even a title springs glibly to his lips. And he's impressed with his own productiveness, too.

Story 2. Sentence 2: He is in contact—he is aware of the examiner and his need to get down everything. Probably this man dictates at times to be sure the examiner gets everything. Probably has superficially good rapport—keeps up appearances.

Sentence 3: Another feminine identification—and with a sort of inter-sex, too. Shanghai—exotic, to suit his flair for the dramatic, and probably to help make it more personally remote. Note *hiding* theme.

Sentence 5: Note repetition of theme: woman is sexual, morally bad. Moralistic tone of "quite degraded in character."

Sentence 6: N-5 a Chinaman!—either some perceptual distortion or willful

[2] A misprint. See footnote 8, Chapter 3.

arbitrariness here—probably some of both. Suspicion of infidelity leads to death. Again, sexual immorality calls for the supreme penalty.

Sentence 7: Story starts to get a little confused here. "dark *and yet*"—a non sequitur. S-1 as the other man; all these figures lurking in the shadows: real paranoid anxiety and apprehensiveness despite the surface unconcern.

Sentence 8: She really is a prostitute—still another "love"? Note the concreteness of schizophrenic symbolism: "the ghost of an old love" is expressed as an actual ghost, really above her in space. Only a schizophrenic would put it just like that.

Sentence 9: Note continued concern with *looking*, spying, seeing how people look. Intense voyeurism behind all this, probably projected in delusions of reference, etc. Not very much of a hint so far of grandiosity, but there may be occasional signs of it, clinically.

Sentence 10: Bar—an alchoholic note. Will it be repeated? Possibly one form his acting out has taken at times.

Sentence 11: Cf. TAT 16. The distance that separates people even though ostensibly very close together. Everyone in this story is alone in his own world, having the most tangential relationships with each other, despite the conventional framework of love affairs.

Sentences 12–13: The usual tragic ending—murders get monotonous. Same old theme: sex leads to death. Though not through ordinary channels of civilized morality—the police. The punishments are all direct personal revenges or attempts at it; further evidence for the infantile, primitive state of his superego, and for the supposition that he may show superficial "emancipation" from conventional morality despite his strong conventionality and moralism. It may also indicate his contempt and disregard for father-figures; the police and other figures of former authority are not really very threatening in these stories, they stroll aimlessly about, don't really frighten anyone very much, and never seem to punish anyone; this may be a reflection of his contemptuous disregard for a rather feckless father.

Sentence 14: Note: "listlessly." Cf. last remarks about father; lack of zest is made quite explicit also. Suicide, but again not at all depressive, and doesn't give me the feeling that he's a real suicidal risk. There is of course tremendous self-destructiveness in this man, the evidence for which keeps cropping up all the time, but his preferred mode seems to be the more chronic one of schizophrenia. Nevertheless, I imagine that there is a danger of his histrionic qualities getting the better of him. He might make a suicidal gesture really in order to make a splash and not with the serious intention of carrying it through, and succeed in spite of himself, as hysterics sometimes do.

Story 3. Intense concern with looking and with *appearance*. The latter could have been deduced from other indirect evidence, but very plain now. Cf. story 1: repeated theme of husband-wife conflict over changes in appearance with age. Story is less well organized, more filled with internal inconsistencies than others: in sentence 2 she can see her hair, though in sentence 5 she can't see the son because she has no eyes.

Note concreteness of his use of the blank face: uses it very literally. His conceptual thinking is probably quite concrete, though somewhat intellectualized overgeneralization, probably some symbolic concepts on Sorting test if given. He is fascinated by this figure: see her use in stories 4 and 7. Perhaps because this figure has two important aspects of his own self concept: femininity, and inner *emptiness.*

Phantom visible only to her inner self hints very directly at visual hallucinations.

Magical thinking very clear throughout this and story 1; despite his glib tossing these off, they represent real fears—that his destructive (self-destructive?) wishes will come true. All this concern with faces suggests that he may have delusions about his own face (based on fear that it doesn't look like a man's?)—people are looking at it, there's something wrong with it, no one can like him because of the way he looks—something like that.

For this patient, the next to last sentence shows unusual loss of coherence. But not really very bad.

Story 4. Note *consistent* feminine identification, here involving the slight perceptual distortion (though I'd need norms on how this part-face is usually perceived, in the dream card itself).

Sentence 1: Confused—begins to sound so himself.

Sentence 2: The outrageousness of this trivial motive to kill the father sounds as if it's a deliberate "shocker," put in for perversity's sake. Yet hair is important to this man—it's mentioned a couple of times, more frequently than one might expect, and has magic power in story 7 (last story). Confusion: on second thought, confusion apparently was in myself; I didn't notice that after the husband turned away in shame and disappeared that she got herself another one. The aggression is getting wilder, more infantile and arbitrary; it's clear that no motive is needed for a death-wish, though sex keeps being brought in as a motive and a form of evil.

The hovering spirit and the man in the shadows are getting to be old friends: pretty strongly suggest hallucinations and delusions. A man so much excites the subject's passion that he must kill a man: pretty classic paranoid fantasy.

Large insurance policy: more preoccupation with money.

Plot and counter-plot—more paranoid evidence.

Note callousness of end—he killed her and everything worked out beautifully.

Story 5. Selection of Negro girl, ignoring her color, as "a suitable character." Is this a subtle derogation of a mother-figure, again? Or is this another problem of perceptual distortion and arbitrariness?

Many of the previous elements are here again: the drama, the economically and vividly told murder story, sex leads to death, raw crude aggression. More about *seeing*, can't look in her face. Another shocker.

"Mad fiend . . . inmate of the state asylum"—he really thinks he is dreadful; because he has such violent and sexual fantasies, he must be as bad as people seem to think.

Final comment shows his superficial intellectualizing and phony psychologizing —phony in that it's without any feeling. Also suggests that he does some writing.

Story 6. Reminiscent of TAT 16. The endless emptiness of his inner feeling of yearning for milk and love in a motherless desert.

Note that this male hero, the first one, is crippled—a leg gone (castrated—so really a woman after all again). "Followed by something significant" etc.; now he gets a trifle incoherent, really disregards the conventions of communication. He's talking his own schizophrenic language. Note continued concern with age; literal-concrete symbolic use of figures (age is close behind, an old woman follows him). Overt anxiety now enters for the first time, but it's attributed to a woman.

The triviality of the reasons for the people's dropping out—the crutch or the shawl gets too heavy—is rather striking.

Mirage—vanishes, etc.—suggests visual hallucinations.

The lure of evil that must be sought. Gets rather pretentious.

Speculation: the fascinating evil, the secret, is the mother—she was the snake before, she is what's missing in his personal desert. But she's very ambivalently regarded: it's a desert *because* she's the way she is, castrating and phallic. So, the search for mother leads to death: projected overpoweringly strong oral carnivorous wishes make her a devouring monster. He probably *doesn't* know what this means.

His tragedy is in the fact that all good and all evil are for him contained in the same unattainable, sexually alluring, frightening and threatening figure: mother. She's the source of life-giving food and love; but she is a poison-secreting snake instead, her milk withers. So it's a vicious, self-destructive cycle for him: coming close, seeking love, only to be hurt and stung.

Story 7. Selection of *stage* significant of the same voyeuristic-exhibitionistic needs so often seen before. Also here seen is the nude girl, appearing before the audience, in a provocative and defiant way.

A real world-destruction fantasy, just right for the last act of this test, too. Under the very thin guise of a mystery or symbolic play, he lets his most violent and unmodified voyeuristic, sadistic, and masochistic fantasies come boiling out.

Projection of the psychotic world's atmosphere: "they wonder if it's all real. She speaks as if from a dream . . ." Wild laughter, screams: more emotional inappropriateness, as well as indicative of his histrionics.

The statue, a central figure of the story, and the real hero in a way—the one with all the real power, as he said—again suggests that there may have been catatonic episodes. Catatonics often remain statue-like because of the fantasy that if they move, the world will be destroyed. This statue who has the real power is what he'd like to be in a way; he is also the faceless girl who is the only one to know how it will end—the Cassandra.

"Wait till you see act 3"—makes clear his intent to shock or daze the observer: "See how crazy I am; you can't possibly understand me." Fearing aggression so much himself, he has to put on a big swagger and bravado, act tough and callous, to hide his own intense castration anxiety. In all these stories, very little sign of overt anxiety appears; rather, blandness and callousness as these primitive sadistic orgies are described. Underneath the slick front he is very anxious, but this defense, which robs him of all true feeling as well as protecting him from the painful sensations of anxiety, lets him express such fantasies.

## SUMMARY

Question of schizophrenic character is raised by the consistent exhibitionistic flourish of such rampantly schizophrenic material, in a person who apparently has a fair amount of social "front." He is a lot like some schizophrenic characters (or ambulatory schizophrenics) I have seen, but for two reasons I doubt that he's best diagnosed that way: (1) All the evidence for *ideational* symptoms (not just acting out): delusions and hallucinations. (2) General feeling that this is a relatively recent onset with an acute break, not a long drawn out insidiously developing chronic business. The latter feeling grows weaker, however, as the character disorder flavor grows stronger and particularly the free productivity, the free playing around with wild and bizarre ideas, makes me inclined somewhat to the diagnosis of schizophrenic character. I can't decide just on the basis of evidence in these tests; a Bellevue might help. If he is a schizophrenic character, I would expect much more freely and blandly given schizophrenic thinking than otherwise; or rather, if such were found, it would increase the chances for this diagnosis, though I have seen schizophrenic characters with very clean Wechsler-Bellevues. If the Rorschach were relatively brief and coarctated, it would clinch the diagnosis against schizophrenic character, but if it were long, dilated, full of bizarre confabulations, I would favor the schizophrenic character diagnosis. The real clincher of course is the *history*. How has he *acted* and for how long? Did he have an acute onset? I suspect that he did, that it had a catatonic as well as paranoid form (excitement, stupor, or both in succession) and that he has stabilized at this kind of adjustment, closely resembling a schizophrenic character, instead of the usual chronic schizophrenic.

# Chapter 11

# WALTHER JOEL and DAVID SHAPIRO

Dr. Joel was born in 1899. He received the Ph.D. degree in Psychology from the University of Southern California in 1934. He is a Fellow in the American Psychological Association and has received Diplomate status from the American Board of Examiners in Professional Psychology. He has taught at the Los Angeles City College and is at present a Lecturer at the University of Southern California. He has been Senior Clinical Psychologist at the Napa (California) State Hospital. Since 1948 he has been at the Veterans Administration Neuropsychiatric Hospital, Los Angeles, where he is Assistant Chief Clinical Psychologist in charge of psychotherapy. He has been Secretary-Treasurer of the Southern California chapter of the Society for Projective Techniques and is an Associate Editor of the *Journal of Projective Techniques*. At present, he and Dr. Shapiro are working on a book on group psychotherapy, using a psychoanalytic approach with emphasis on the relationships within the group.

Dr. Shapiro received the Ph.D. degree in Psychology from the University of Southern California in 1950. His clinical internship, 1947–1950, was at the Veterans Administration Neuropsychiatric Hospital, Los Angeles. He began his personal psychoanalysis in 1948. He is interested in and has worked in the field of the dynamics of interpersonal relationship. At present, he is in the private practice of psychoanalytically oriented psychotherapy, and conducts similarly oriented therapy-groups at the Community Medical Center, Los Angeles.

## SELECTED REFERENCES


JOEL, WALTHER, AND SHAPIRO, DAVID, A Genotypical Approach to the Analysis of Personal Interaction. *Journal of Psychology*, 1949, *28*, 9–17.

———, The Interpersonal Equation in Projective Methods. *Rorschach Research Exchange and Journal of Projective Techniques*, 1949, *13*, 479–482.

SHAPIRO, DAVID, A Study of the Influence of the Social Field on Individual Behavior. *Genetic Psychology Monographs*, 1950, *42*, 161–230.


## RESUME OF METHOD

THIS METHOD of "ego-function analysis" is "concerned with the manner in which the ego integrates the subject's internal needs, impulses, etc., with the demands of . . . particularly the social environment." First, interpersonal warmth and hostility and flight from such interpersonal feelings are translated into scoring symbols. Then, the sequence of these interactions is analyzed; and finally, the interpretation provides "a picture of the process of coping with the social environment."

## TAT WORKING NOTES

The method presented here deals primarily with the functioning of the ego. This important aspect of personality deserves more emphasis in the analysis of thematic test material than it has so far received. Rapaport is aware of this need when he states in the *Diagnostic Psychological Testing, II*, p. 414, "... understanding the TAT stories necessitates some familiarity with the recent development of concepts in psychoanalysis, whose emphasis has shifted in the last decade from the sole exploration of the content and demands of the unconscious to the defense mechanisms the Ego erects to cope with the danger implicit in these demands." Without proposing to neglect the content of intrapsychic conflicts, we are more concerned with the *manner* in which the ego integrates the subject's internal needs, impulses, etc., with the demands and opportunities of the environment, particularly the social environment. We wish to know *how* the subject uses the environment to satisfy his internal needs and *how* he protects himself against the threats of the environment, more than *what* are his needs, anxieties, etc. We believe that the most significant part of the environment is the social environment or "social field," and that the most definitive examination of ego-functioning must come by way of examining the personality in social interaction.

In relation to thematic test material we originally suggested a simple scheme designed to facilitate the analysis of the interaction among the characters of the story (see article in *Journal of Psychology*). Since that time we have realized that in order to get an adequate picture of ego-function it is necessary to go farther and to consider the subject's functioning in the entire social field, including: (1) His relationship with the examiner, both in terms of direct interaction and as it is revealed through the thematic production (this is not available in the material analyzed here). (See article in *Journal of Projective Techniques.*) (2) His reaction to the test materials as such and his direct relationship to the characters and situations in the stories. (3) The interaction of the characters within the stories.

Thus we lay particular stress on the *manner* in which the personality functions within the realistic social field of the test situation, within the social field of fantasy through the subject's identification with the story characters, and on the type of relationship established between these two modes of social interaction.

In order to understand *how* the subject's ego functions, it would help us little if we were to classify and tally the subject's reactions removed from the context in which they occurred. Rather what we need in ego-function analysis of thematic material is a careful examination of sequence. By making use of sequence interpretation we attempt to get a picture of the *process* of coping with the social environment. Thus in the analysis of a given story it is at times possible to predict in terms of ego-function what will happen in the next sentence.

The first TAT story and the first MAPS story are analyzed below. The *first* column lists brief references to all statements in the story which express directed feelings. The *second* column symbolizes these feelings. We have used symbols for the following three types of reaction: expression of *warmth*, expression of *hostility*, and *flight* or "leaving the field." These three reactions vary as to intensity and may be either direct or indirect. The method of symbolizing the reactions and their modifiers is shown in the Figure. The three symbolized categories are not meant as explanatory concepts; they serve rather to facilitate a careful sequence analysis of ego process by drawing attention to each detail of the interpersonal dynamics in the story process. The *third* column contains interpretive comments derived essentially from the symbolization in the second column.

THE SYMBOLS

| BASIC INTERPERSONAL REACTIONS | MODIFIERS | | | |
|---|---|---|---|---|
| | Direct | Indirect | Intense | |
| | | | Direct | Indirect |
| Warmth |  |  |  | 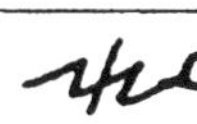 |
| Hostility |  |  |  |  |
| Flight |  |  |  | 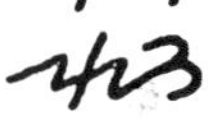 |

TAT First story

| | | |
|---|---|---|
| He has been given sheet music to study, but instead a novel interests him more than the music | child  music<br>child  novel | Preference is expressed for acceptable avenue of escape from reality task (music) |
| Does not fear parents | child  parents | Hostility to parents expressed by child using this avenue of escape from reality |
| He seems to be quite a studious type | Subject  child | Subject here begins to lose distance from character. Relationship of subject to test fantasy as such begins to break down |
| He is not happy—not sad—blank | child  | Beginning of real ego-function disruption and withdrawal from reality—first emotional and then perceptual—through the medium of the story character |
| He disregards the music and falls asleep reading the book | child  | Direct and complete rejection of reality task (music) and withdrawal from reality (falls asleep) |

## TAT INTERPRETATION

The patient's view of reality in general and of the immediate reality task in particular as unpleasant is readily apparent. Since he feels unable to cope with reality he seeks at first a method of escaping from its harshness through fantasy. This tendency in itself, though it might in other circumstances be an adequate ego-adaptive device, is for this subject the crack in ego-function, after which the whole brittle structure collapses. Through the mild and acceptable retreat from reality, hostile impulses toward parental figures emerge, causing apparently a greater and much more serious ego failure. The final result is distortion of and complete withdrawal from reality.

MAPS test. Livingroom.

| | | |
|---|---|---|
| Housewife sees terrible looking woman and recognizes her as her mother | Subject → mother | Failure of subject to utilize character of housewife to express hostility may indicate inability to use available reality factors as buffers and ego defenses |
| Woman is being followed by a snake which is the symbol of what she really is, I suppose | Subject → mother | Continuation of above |
| Husband very indignant at old woman | Husband → mother | Begins to make use of characters as appropriate channels of expression. This may indicate some recovery of ego-functioning |
| Daughter also very indignant because she had told mother never to come | Daughter → mother | Fact that subject can now use same character as channel for hostility which he could not use before confirms recuperation hypothesis |
| Mother tells that I had—she had come to help her son out of a jam | Mother, Subj. —C son | Reaction of warmth toward self (son) may be real break-through of wishful thinking along with indications of breakdown of previously established defensive channels, as apparent in slip |
| Daughter asks why she insists on having that awful looking snake following her | Daughter ⇝ mother<br>Daughter → snake | Again some recuperation in capacity to use characters. Also further defense achieved by displacing character's hostility from mother to snake. Thus previous direct expression of hostility now transformed into indirect expression of hostility |

| | | |
|---|---|---|
| Mother says he's the only one I can trust because all snakes don't wear clothes | Mother —C snake | Still uses the character—but draws close to and identifies with the despised snake and away from people. This may warn us of imminent regression in story material |
| Snake leaves<br>Officer inquires | Snake —⊃ | Through snake a withdrawal of cathexis from the situation at hand. Resignation to failure of ego-functioning. Immediate reentrance in delusional form (Omnipotent cop) |
| Daughter says I have never seen this woman before | Daughter ⇝ mother<br>↘ | Identifies apparently in part with cop, in part with daughter. Sexual confusion in this state of disrupted ego. Continuation of flight from reality (denial of existence of mother) and expression of hostility toward mother on this delusional level |
| Mother is broken-hearted; says I can't help it if my face is this way | Subject ⇝ mother<br>Mother ↻ | Draws closer to mother, and here a flowering of empathy and identification with her appears within delusional context |
| The day you were born I received both you and a terrible face | Mother → daughter | Continues feminine identification, both giving and receiving intense hostility as female |
| Here's five dollars, beggar—now, officer, see that she goes | Daughter ⇸ mother | Clear continuation on delusional level of feminine identification—ego failure |
| Before I'm through you'll give me more than money | Mother ⇝ daughter | |
| Mother exits<br>Officer enters | Mother —⊃ | After directing intense hostility toward himself in feminine role, subject flees from it and reenters the field in role of authority (cop). Conflict here remains on delusional level (between feminine role and authority role)—no room here for normal identification and expression of feelings |
| Daughter replies: perhaps I've seen her but I would not want to admit it | Daughter ⇸ mother | Still feminine identification but begins now to accept reality again (perhaps I've seen her before) |
| Cop leaves | Cop —⊃ | Here the delusional level is left— |

| | | |
|---|---|---|
| | | ego begins again to function on reality level |
| I hope I don't have to look forward to the day when you'll get that old and look like that | Husband → daughter | Subject identifies with reality male figure and expresses through him hostility toward the woman. (This is first time that figures on stage are entirely on reality level—man and woman.) Ego functioning well now but instability indicated by the phrase—"the door has been left open"—and already the realistic environment is unpleasant (argument) |
| Quite an argument ensues. During all this time the door has been left open | Husband ↔ daughter | |
| Snake slithers in and bites them both | Snake ⇸ husband<br>Snake ⇸ daughter | Finally psychotic self (snake) re-enters and destroys realistic self |
| As the wife is dying she says: at least you won't have to see me when I get old | Daughter ⇝ husband | Continuation of unbearable quality of reality and particularly future reality and ultimate flight from it in the death of the reality figures |

## MAPS TEST INTERPRETATION

Although, as in the TAT, the weakness of ego-functioning is apparent at the beginning, the subject does make certain adaptations to the reality situation which are, temporarily at least, successful. He is for a time able to make fairly good use of the defenses which the test material offers while expressing his feelings through the dramatic situation—although even at this point there are indications of the instability of this adjustment. At the point of best functioning not only does the subject make good use of the defense of speaking through the characters, but also he further protects himself by introducing a non-human object onto whom hostile feelings can be safely displaced. As in the TAT, however, these adaptations which might, for others, be successful, seem to permit for this subject an expression of hostility which is too great for the defense structure to bear, and it begins to crumble. There is then a rapid disintegration and withdrawal from the human characters and the realistic situation in the drama. This culminates in the complete withdrawal and the establishment of delusion about halfway through the story. The dynamic conflict within the subject becomes more open within the delusional context—the vacillating identification between the male authority figure and the maternal female figure appears together with the expression of great hostility, in large part directed toward himself in the feminine role.

Interestingly, the subject is able, once more, to reestablish some degree of effective ego-functioning at this point. The figures which were the basis for the delusional material are removed; the subject identifies with a male figure.

It is clear that this adjustment cannot be maintained, and the expression of hostility through the male character to the female apparently becomes too threatening. Ego-functioning is again disrupted and the final solution is complete withdrawal from reality.

## SUMMARY

The essence of the dynamics of the subject's ego-functioning appears in both the first MAPS test and the first TAT story. In each case he makes at first what might be a fairly adequate defensive adjustment to the difficult reality situation within the drama. Through this defensive system he is able to permit the expression of a certain amount of hostility. The hostility, however, very rapidly becomes beyond control and overwhelms the defenses themselves. The final result is complete disruption of ego-function and withdrawal from reality.

# Chapter 12

# SEYMOUR KLEBANOFF

Dr. Klebanoff was born in 1916. He received the M.S. degree in Psychology from Yale University in 1939 and the Ph.D. degree in Psychology from Northwestern University in 1947. He has Diplomate status in Clinical Psychology from the American Board of Examiners in Professional Psychology. He has taught at Northwestern University. After two years at the Worcester State Hospital, he served as Chief Psychologist at the Clarinda (Iowa) State Hospital. During World War II he was a Clinical Psychologist with the Army Air Forces. After the war he served as Chief Psychologist at the Downey (Illinois) Veterans Administration Hospital and Chief Psychologist at the North Shore Health Resort in Winetka, Illinois. At present he is Chief Psychologist at the Franklin Delano Roosevelt Veterans Administration Hospital in Montrose, New York, and Assistant Professor of Psychology in the Department of Psychiatry, Cornell University Medical College. His work has been largely in the fields of psychological testing in organic brain disease and in studies of projective techniques.

## SELECTED REFERENCES

KLEBANOFF, SEYMOUR G., Personality Factors in Symptomatic Chronic Alcoholism as Indicated by the Thematic Apperception Test. *Journal of Consulting Psychology*, 1947, *11*, 111–119.

## RESUME OF METHOD

IN THIS METHOD, intended primarily for research, the content of the stories is tallied on a check list according to overtly stated themas grouped under such categories as loss of life, aggression, internal stress, and positive themes. Profiles of absolute and percentage frequencies for each thema and each category are then analyzed. Interpretation is based upon that analysis.

## TAT WORKING NOTES

This schema is primarily for research, rather than clinical purposes. The use of such a schema in the routine psychological work-up of a case in a clinical situation would not be recommended. In our TAT work in a hospital setting, members of the Psychology Department interpret the content in terms of a preferred personality theory without the use of any formal scoring system. Thus, some persons will utilize a psychoanalytic framework, others will use Adlerian concepts, others will employ frustration-aggression theory, etc. In dealing with the individual case clinically, I feel that any formal or quantitative scoring technique will result in some loss of richness and will also tend to portray the dynamics as relatively isolated and segmental factors rather than point up the integrated and holistic aspect of the personality findings.

However, research demands do make it necessary to employ some sort of quantifiable technique, particularly when two or more groups are to be compared with respect to projected material. Dr. E. H. Rodnick and I thus selected these themas on the basis of our experience with the TAT and we found that they fell into five basic categories. These include: (1) loss of life; (2) physical aggression; (3) non-physical aggression; (4) internal emotional stress; and (5) positive themas. By tabulating the percentage of the total number of scored themas which fell into each of these categories, it was possible to construct individual and group profiles and the profiles of groups could then be compared. Since the study in which this schema was first used involved a study of reactions to frustration, the heavy emphasis upon the handling of aggressivity becomes understandable.

In the use of this schema, reliability is maintained by checking only those themas which appear explicitly in the projected content. The result, of course, is a surface kind of analysis. Effort is made to avoid inference of an underlying thema. The thema simply must be overtly stated to be scored or checked. Reliability checks have shown greater agreement among scorers when this set is maintained.

Following is reproduced the completed TAT scoring blank.

| | | 1 | 3BM | 4 | 6BM | 7BM | 11 | 12M | 13MF | 13B | 14 | 16 | Summary | | |
|---|---|---|---|---|---|---|---|---|---|---|---|---|---|---|---|
| *A. Thema* | | | | | | | | | | | | | | | |
| Loss of Life | Murder | | | x | xx | | | | | | x | | 4 | | |
| | Death | | | | | x | | x | x | | | x | 4 | | |
| | Suicide | | x | x | | | | | | | | | 2 | | |
| | *Total* | | | | | | | | | | | | | 10 | 19% |
| Physical Aggression | Phys. viol. | | | | | | x | | | | x | | 2 | | |
| | Injury-acc. | | | | | | | | | | | | 0 | | |
| | Illness | x | | | | x | | | | | | | 2 | | |
| | Crime | | x | | | | | | | | x | | 2 | | |
| | Punish | | x | | | | | | | | | | 1 | | |
| | Arrest-capt. | | | | | | | | | | x | | 1 | | |
| | Escape | | | | | | x | | | | | | 1 | | |
| | Thr.-rep-bul. | | | | | | | | | | | | 0 | | |
| | *Total* | | | | | | | | | | | | | 9 | 17% |
| Non-Physical Aggression | Quarrel | | | | | | | | | | | | 0 | | |
| | Domina. | | | | | | | | | | | | 0 | | |
| | Antag. | | | | | | | | | x | | | 1 | | |
| | Dishon.-cheat. | x | | | | | | | | | | | 1 | | |
| | Disloyalty | | | | x | | | | | | | | 1 | | |
| | Ext.-confl. | | | | | | | | | | x | | 1 | | |
| | Hate-revenge | | | | | | | | | | | | 0 | | |
| | Anger-rage | | | | | | | | | | | | 0 | | |
| | *Total* | | | | | | | | | | | | | 4 | 7% |

| | | 1 | 3BM | 4 | 6BM | 7BM | 11 | 12M | 13MF | 13B | 14 | 16 | Summary | | |
|---|---|---|---|---|---|---|---|---|---|---|---|---|---|---|---|
| Internal Emotional Stress | Deprivation | | | x | | | | x | | x | | | 3 | | |
| | Int. confl. | | | x | | | | | x | | x | | 3 | | |
| | Emot.-stress | | | x | | | | | | | | | 1 | | |
| | Misfortune | | x | | | | | | | | | x | 2 | | |
| | Disappoint. | | | | | | | | | x | | | 1 | | |
| | Separ. | | | | | | | | x | | | | 1 | | |
| | Despondency | | | | | x | | | | x | | | 2 | | |
| | Jealousy | | | | | | | | | | | | 0 | | |
| | Fear | | | | | | | | | | | | 0 | | |
| | Anxiety | | | | | | | | | | | | 0 | | |
| | Rejection | x | | x | | x | | | | x | | | 4 | | |
| | Guilt | | x | | | | | | x | | | | 2 | | |
| | *Total* | | | | | | | | | | | | | 19 | 36% |
| Positive Themes | Reassurance | | | | | | | x | | | | | 1 | | |
| | Sex | | x | x | | | | | x | | | | 3 | | |
| | Pity-forgive. | | | | | | | | | | | | 0 | | |
| | Grat.-friend. | | | | | | | | | | | | 0 | | |
| | Love | | | | | | | | | | | | 0 | | |
| | Happiness | | | | | | | | | x | | | 1 | | |
| | Obligation | | | x | x | x | | | | x | | | 3 | | |
| | Affection | | | | | | | | | | | | 0 | | |
| | Repentance | | x | | | x | | | | | | | 2 | | |
| | Goal | | | | | x | | | | | | | 1 | | |
| | *Total* | | | | | | | | | | | | | 11 | 21% |
| | *Grand Total* | | | | | | | | | | | | | 53 | 100% |
| *B. Solutions* | | | | | | | | | | | | | | | |
| Failure Central | Economic | | | x | | | | x | | | | | 2 | | |
| | Social | | x | | | | | | | | x | x | 3 | | |
| | Power | | | | | x | x | | | | x | x | 4 | | |
| | Love | | | x | | | | | x | | | | 2 | | |
| | *Total* | | | | | | | | | | | | | 11 | |
| Failure Minor | E | | | | | | | | | | | | 0 | | |
| | S | | | | | | | | x | | | | 1 | | |
| | P | x | | x | x | | | x | | | | | 4 | | |
| | L | | | x | x | | | | | | | | 2 | | |
| | *Total* | | | | | | | | | | | | | 7 | |
| Success Central | E | | | | | | | | | | | | 0 | | |
| | S | | | | | | | | | | | | 0 | | |
| | P | x | | | x | | | x | | | | | 3 | | |
| | L | | | | | | | | | x | | | 1 | | |
| | *Total* | | | | | | | | | | | | | 4 | |
| Success Minor | E | | | | | x | | x | | | | | 2 | | |
| | S | | x | | | | | | | | x | | 2 | | |
| | P | | | | | | x | | | | x | | 2 | | |
| | L | | | | | | | | | x | | | 1 | | |
| | *Total* | | | | | | | | | | | | | 7 | |

## TAT INTERPRETATION

The use of this schema with the submitted test material seems to reveal the following from the TAT. There is relatively heavy concentration upon themas of inner affective stress. This appears to transcend healthy expectation. Within this category, themes of economic deprivation, inner conflict, and themes of rejection are dominant. At the same time there is an unusually high frequency of loss of life themas which largely include death and murder. This appears to occur at the expense of themas of non-physical aggression, which seem to fall below normal expectancy. A general evaluation of the profile would suggest that this individual is expressing marked aggression in the destruction of so many of his fantasy characters. At the same time, this hostility provokes so much guilt which becomes directed toward the self in the nature of themas of deprivation, conflict and rejection by others. If this individual were able to utilize themas of non-physical aggression more frequently as a substitute for loss of life themas, one might hypothecate that there would be less need for themas of internal stress, which would place the total profile closer to healthy expectancy.

## MAPS TEST WORKING NOTES

The scoring blank for John Doe's MAPS test appears below.

| | | Livingroom | Street | Bathroom | Dream | Bedroom | Blank | Stage | Summary | | |
|---|---|---|---|---|---|---|---|---|---|---|---|
| | *A. Thema* | | | | | | | | | | |
| Loss of Life | Murder | | x | | xxx | x | | | 5 | | |
| | Death | xx | | | | x | x | x | 5 | | |
| | Suicide | | x | | | | | | 1 | | |
| | *Total* | | | | | | | | | 11 | 23% |
| Physical Aggression | Phys. viol. | x | | | | x | | xx | 4 | | |
| | Injury-acc. | x | | | | | x | | 2 | | |
| | Illness | | | | | | | | 0 | | |
| | Crime | | | | | | | | 0 | | |
| | Punish. | | x | x | | | | | 2 | | |
| | Arrest-capt. | | | | | | | | 0 | | |
| | Escape | | | | | x | | | 1 | | |
| | Thr.-rep-bul. | | x | | | | | | 1 | | |
| | *Total* | | | | | | | | | 10 | 21% |
| Non-Physical Aggression | Quarrel | x | | | | | | | 1 | | |
| | Domina. | | | | | | | | 0 | | |
| | Antag. | | | x | | | | | 1 | | |
| | Dishon.-cheat | x | | | xx | | | | 3 | | |
| | Disloyalty | | | | | | | | 0 | | |
| | Ext.-conflict | x | | | | | | | 1 | | |
| | Hate-revenge | x | | | | | | | 1 | | |
| | Anger-rage | x | | | | | | | 1 | | |
| | *Total* | | | | | | | | | 8 | 17% |

| | | Living-room | Street | Bathroom | Dream | Bedroom | Blank | Stage | Summary | | |
|---|---|---|---|---|---|---|---|---|---|---|---|
| Internal Emotional Stress | Deprivation | x | x | | | | | | 2 | | |
| | Int. confl. | | | | x | | | | 1 | | |
| | Emot. stress | | | x | | x | | | 2 | | |
| | Misfortune | | | | | | | | 0 | | |
| | Disappoint. | | | | | | | | 0 | | |
| | Separ.-reject. | x | | | x | | | | 2 | | |
| | Despondency | x | | | | | | | 1 | | |
| | Jealousy | | | | | | | | 0 | | |
| | Fear | | | | | | x | | 1 | | |
| | Anxiety | | | | | | | | 0 | | |
| | Rejection | x | | x | | | | | 2 | | |
| | Guilt | | | | xx | | | | 2 | | |
| | *Total* | | | | | | | | | 13 | 28% |
| Positive Themes | Reassurance | | | | | | | | 0 | | |
| | Sex | | x | | x | | | | 2 | | |
| | Pity-forgive. | | | | | | | | 0 | | |
| | Grat.-friend | | | | | | | | 0 | | |
| | Love | | | | | | | | 0 | | |
| | Happiness | | | | | | | | 0 | | |
| | Obligation | x | | | | | | | 1 | | |
| | Affection | | | | | | | | 0 | | |
| | Repentance | | | x | | | | | 1 | | |
| | Goal | | | x | | | | | 1 | | |
| | *Total* | | | | | | | | | 5 | 11% |
| | *Grand Total* | | | | | | | | | 47 | 100% |
| *B. Solutions* | | | | | | | | | | | |
| Failure Central | Economic | | | | | | | | 0 | | |
| | Social | | | x | | x | | | 2 | | |
| | Power | x | | | x | x | x | | 4 | | |
| | Love | x | x | x | x | | | | 4 | | |
| | *Total* | | | | | | | | | 10 | |
| Failure Minor | E | x | | | | | | | 1 | | |
| | S | x | | | | | | | 1 | | |
| | P | | | | | x | x | xx | 4 | | |
| | L | | x | | x | | | | 2 | | |
| | *Total* | | | | | | | | | 8 | |
| Success Central | E | | | | | | | | 0 | | |
| | S | | | | | | | | 0 | | |
| | P | | | | | | | x | 1 | | |
| | L | | | | | | | | 0 | | |
| | *Total* | | | | | | | | | 1 | |
| Success Minor | E | | | | | | | | 0 | | |
| | S | | | | | | | | 0 | | |
| | P | x | | | x | | | | 2 | | |
| | L | | | | | | | | 0 | | |
| | *Total* | | | | | | | | | 2 | |

## MAPS TEST INTERPRETATION

The profile obtained from the MAPS test again reveals the very marked emphasis upon the loss of life themas of death and murder. However, the profile upon this test falls closer to that of our normal group by virtue of greater use of non-physical aggression resulting in decreased expression of inner emotional stress. Although the themas of guilt, rejection by others, and economic deprivation are expressed on this test, the emphasis or frequency is not as strong. It appears that the non-physical aggression themas utilized, such as expression of anger, revenge, and dishonesty, detract from the need to punish the self. Thus there is this discrepancy between the TAT and MAPS test in this one case.

# Chapter 13

# SHELDON KORCHIN

Dr. Korchin was born in 1921. He received the Ph.D. degree in Psychology from Harvard University in 1946. He has taught at Harvard University and Princeton University. At different times he has been consultant to the Research Center for Group Dynamics, then at Massachusetts Institute of Technology, and to the Institute for Research in Human Relations, Philadelphia. For three years he was at the Veterans Administration Mental Hygiene Clinic in Philadelphia as Assistant Chief Clinical Psychologist. Since October, 1950, he has been Director of the Psychological Laboratory, Michael Reese Hospital, Chicago, and Lecturer in Psychology at the University of Chicago. His present research interests are in the areas of perception and personality and in projective techniques.

## SELECTED REFERENCES

TOMKINS, SILVAN S., *The Thematic Apperception Test; The Theory and Technique of Interpretation.* New York: Grune and Stratton, 1947, Pp. xi, 297.

## RESUME OF METHOD

TOMKINS' METHOD, which is primarily for training and research, comprises both scoring and interpretation.

*Scoring*: Each story is scored according to four main categories: ten vectors (from, toward, with, against, etc.); seventeen *levels* (behavior, thought, wish, memory, etc.); twelve *conditions* (lack, abundance, danger, etc.); and six *qualifiers* (intensity, negation, causality, etc.).

*Interpretation*: The interpretation utilizes three main approaches: *Canons of inference*, such as Mill's methods (of agreement, of difference, of concomitant variation, etc.) and additional methods (for the study of cause and effect involving two or more factors); *level analysis* (degree of variance, relative frequency, cause-effect relationships, and sequence analysis of levels) to study the relationship between overt and covert needs, the degree to which the subject is aware of his own wishes and behavior, and the nature of conflict between repressed wish and repressing force; and *diagnosis of personality* which includes relative importance of the family, love and sex, social relationships, and work.

Korchin's use of Tomkins' method is a variant of the above approach. It is less formalized and therefore better adapted to clinical use. It examines the characteristics of the heroes, the more generalized meanings of the main themes, the outcome, and the levels. It also analyzes the areas of family, social relationships, work, etc. "The greater part of analyzing the record consists of cerebral activity: trying to organize the material into some consistent picture, testing and discarding hypotheses, comparing the findings of one story with those of another, and so on."

## TAT WORKING NOTES

1: hero—male child—characterized as: sick, likes adventure, studious, emotionally "not happy, not sad," eyes blank
    work required of hero
    fear of parents—but no interiorization of parents' demands
    escape into sleep
        no parental pressure—no work
  outcome—neutral
  levels—events, object description, behavior, mood

3BM: hero—female adult—characterized as: prostitute
    hero jailed
    shame
    because sister (nun) suffers
    suicide
        intrapsychic conflict between good and bad wishes (nun and prostitute). Guilt because hero *could have* become good (asexual) but instead was bad (sexual).
  outcome—unhappy
  levels—object description, thought, mood, behavior

4: hero—female adult—characterized as: half-caste, mistress, poor
    woman and lover
    woman deserted—pregnant
    "very broken up about it"
    sets fire to house
    settles problem
        theme: illicit sex—death
        sexual object rejected
        note lack of love in sexual relation
  outcome—unhappy
  levels—behavior events

6BM: hero—young male adult
    son tells mother that he murdered
    through medium of play
    son suggests punishment
    mother kills son
    motive of son's murdering is sexual
        (1) theme of sex—death
        (2) lack of communication between mother and son
        (3) mother unnecessarily punitive

(4) (audience?)—depersonalization?
outcome—unhappy
levels—object description, events, behavior, intention

7BM: hero—young male adult—characterized as: son, depressed over health
son depressed
turns to father for help
will help only for own gain
leaves, never contacts father again
dies
father repents
(1) father cannot be counted on, will help son only for selfish gain
(2) father will give only too late
(3) fantasy of repentance?
outcome—both unhappy and happy
levels—events, behavior, mood, expectation

11: hero—a group of people, characterized as: wicked, travellers
travellers attacked by animal
attacked again
sent to their fate
(1) wicked trying to escape are inexorably destroyed
outcome—unhappy
levels—object description, events, behavior

12M: hero—young male adult, characterized as: artist, poor, starving, genius
starving artist
sells painting for loaf of bread
genius recognized
too late
artist dies after looking at his picture of bread
(1) harsh environment—genius unrecognized
(2) expectation of rejecting world
(3) rewards come too late
outcome—unhappy
levels—events, behavior, object description

13MF: hero—young male adult
strangers meet
man inhibited in sex because
woman looks like dead love
turns out light
has relations
shame, he leaves
first love was different, moral
(1) only time love is (a) sexless, (b) dead
(2) cannot have sexual relations with woman who looks like first love [ (1), (2) could represent mother]

(3) condition for having relations is turning off lights
outcome—unhappy
levels—object description, events, behavior, feeling (memory), thought

13B: hero—boy, characterized as: poor, depressed
boy rejected
birth of sibling
decides to leave home
approached by mother who
requests help
boy elated
done more than father
–sibling rivalry
(1) unloving parents neglect and reject
(2) depression
(3) condition for happiness is love of mother
(4) condition for happiness is besting father [(3), (4)—oedipal situation?]
outcome—happy
levels—object description, behavior, events, day-dream and thought, intention, mood

14: hero—male adult—? minister or murderer—probably latter
minister discovers
murder
knows murderer
who has confided in him
and claimed self-defense
but minister turns him over to police
(1) parental figure is not helpful when hero is in need
(2) parental figure does not respect confidence
(3) punishes excessively for aggression
(NB: similarity to story 6BM)
outcome—unhappy
levels—object description, behavior, perception, thought

16: hero—people, a community, characterized as: deprived, suffering, *isolated*
a community
located in desolate region
completely isolated, no communication
is destroyed
could have been prevented
if any communication
even telepathic, existed
(1) characterization of own status
(2) environment characterized by lack
(3) need for communication (social interaction)
(4) meaning of "it could be imagination"?
outcome—unhappy
levels—object description, events

### *Analysis of Areas—(Regions)*

*Family*—Relationships distant at least, more likely, hostile.

Only positive relation with either parent is when mother instigates (13B) and father is bested in competition (13B).

Mother excessively punitive (6BM), same true of father (14).

Father rejects S as boy (13B); as adult helps son only for own gain (7BM), help is only partial (14).

Lack of communication between S and mother—can reach only through fantasy medium (play, 6BM).

As child indication that parental demands not adequately interiorized (1).

No change in family constellation discoverable by comparison of stories at different age levels.

*Social Relationships*

No indication that S is capable of adequate relationships with anyone—no mention of friendships, etc.

Aggression—motivated by (a) desertion by loved object (4) (b) sex, unfaithfulness (6BM) (c) acquisition (14); always punished (excessively).

intragression motivated by sexuality (not reaching goal of being sexless) (3BM).

*Work*

No mention of work, achievement, etc., anywhere in record.

*Sex and Love*

Sex is evil.

Constant recurrence of sex—death theme.

Intrapsychic conflict between sexual impulse and its complete rejection (3BM).

Women are immoral—prostitute (3BM), half-caste (4), unfaithful (6BM), generally immoral (13MF).

Love is almost absent—only loved object is dead (13MF).

Implied that condition for heterosexual love is lack of sex (13MF).

*Personality structures and defenses*

Lack of insight, no ascription of motivation to heroes.

Concrete, held to present (lack of time perspective in records).

Impulsive--lack of critical thought between instigation and response.

Depressive trends—but little apparent anxiety.

Low ego strength

*Defense*

Withdrawal; sleep, avoidance (e.g., turning off lights, 13MF).

## TAT INTERPRETATION

This is the TAT of a profoundly sick individual who is severely withdrawn from the world of reality, in whom we see a schizophrenic blending of wish, fantasy and reality. S perceives a world about him which is consistently cold, unloving, hostile, friendless and which can cause him pain and suffering, but which he, in turn, is incapable of changing or mastering. Pressed by the outside world and disturbed by intrapsychic conflict, the only solution is withdrawal. S lacks insight almost completely, although at one point he describes the crux of the problem by stating that people who "were reliant upon themselves and no one was reliant on them" and have no communication with others are doomed (story 16). This single story, told to the blank card (which we believe because of its ultimate lack of structure is likely to release the most distinctly personal material), gives the best description of S's current problem. So he tells us that withdrawn in the midst of lack and desolation there is no hope unless some communication with the outside can be found.

The history of the individual, as we can infer from this protocol, reveals consistent schizoid trends. As a child, S is continuously rejected by harsh and unloving parents. Early in life he discovers an escape in fantasy and sleep (story 1). There is indication that both ego-ideal and superego were delayed in development and only incompletely formed because of a lack of adequate identification with either parent. Thus, the child is at ease only when there is no fear of parental discovery. Here and elsewhere in the stories there is little indication of the interiorization of parental or cultural values which would direct S toward positive goals.

The relationships with parental figures are curiously loveless both in childhood and young adulthood. The mother is pictured as distant, preferring other children to S. He can communicate with the mother only indirectly, in story 6BM through the medium of a play. The mother in turn is harsh and unnecessarily punitive. Thus, again in 6BM, she neither forgives the criminal son nor gives him the punishment he expects, but kills him instead. It might be interesting, but not too fruitful here, to speculate as to what is meant by the "audience" that would prefer the "climax" of the son's death. But, it is clear that the mother is pictured as being motivated by the most unmaternal of motives. Under only one condition can the child love the mother fully; that is when the mother approaches the child with love (13B). But even this does not imply acceptance into a wholesome, integrated family, but rather an incident in the oedipus drama. To be loved by the mother means besting the father and then the child is "elated." There is the implication here, too, that there exists or existed the fantasy of possessing the mother, fathering the child, and that in this there is happiness.

The father, too, rejects the son. He is "too busy to even be kind to him" as a child (13B). When the young man is ill, the father is willing to help only out of selfish motives and though he repents does so too late (7BM). Similarly, a minister betrays his criminal "son" (14). This last story repeats essentially the same theme already noted in connection with the mother. In both cases the son has been aggressive, committed a crime, and in both is betrayed by the parent figure. We may infer from this that S feels the strength of his own hostility, his tendency toward anti-social acts, but sees at the same time no sympathy or guidance from the parents.

There is no evidence that S is any better able to establish adequate interpersonal relations with age equals or other persons than he had with the parents. Throughout the stories there are no references to friendships, either transient or enduring. In the heterosexual region, as well, there are no healthy relationships. The only female object who is loved is now dead (13MF). Moreover, a condition for this love is that the girl is moral, i.e., the relationship is sexless. The dead female in this story might also be interpreted as meaning the mother (note, e.g., references to "at home"). In this case, the story might mean that the boy is incapable of loving, sexually, any female who might remind him of the mother, his only real, though asexual love. Sexual possession of a woman is tantamount to incest and, hence, gives rise to guilt. We have already noted the possibility of an incestuous wish in the discussion of story 13B.

Considering now the more specifically sexual area, we are confronted with material which indicates a central and important sexual problem. A repeating theme is that sex invariably leads to death and destruction. Woman are pictured as evil and degraded and the sexual relationships consistently end in disaster. Sexuality is shameful, but for an interesting reason. It seems that the problem for S is not between the sexual impulse and superego restraints but rather between sex and ego-ideal. This is illustrated best in story 3BM, which we interpret as reflecting an intrapsychic conflict. Here the antagonists are prostitute and nun—what better personification of sexual excess and sexual renunciation! The important aspect of this story is that the prostitute when arrested suffers guilt, not because of the arrest or even because of society's rejection, but rather because she will shame the nun and more particularly because she too could have been a nun. We interpret this to mean that the deep conflict in the sexual area is between the sexual impulse and the preferred image of the self as sexless. In this story, then, the heroine is guilty not because she is a prostitute, but because she is not what she could have been, a nun. Again, in story 13MF, we find support for this hypothesis. Guilt is not caused directly by sexuality, here it is aroused by having sexual relations with a woman who resembles an asexual loved object. Parenthetically, it may be remarked that in this story S again reveals his only defense against such conflicts; the hero can "overcome these feelings by turning off the light." Again, the schizoid withdrawal we noted earlier.

There is some evidence that S has difficulty in identifying his own sexual role. The choice of feminine heros in stories 3BM and 4, particularly 3BM which we consider in this case to be unusually revealing of intrapsychic conflict, might indicate latent and repressed homosexual trends. It is possible that the reason sexuality is so strongly rejected is because the threat is really of homosexual rather than heterosexual nature.

Although the principal conflict is conceived to be in the sexual area, there is strong evidence that the aggressive strivings in this individual are strong, enduring and barely if at all repressed. In one or another section of the protocol, aggression, particularly anti-social aggression, is expressed in many forms. Aggression is aroused by a variety of conditions: illicit sexuality, unfaithfulness, retribution, and so on. Of equal importance are the instances of intropunitive aggression and self-destruction. The evidence is strong that S may now be considerably depressed and possibly suicidal. The conflict over sexuality is "solved" in two cases, stories 3BM and 4, by the death of the hero, in the first of these by his own hand. In other cases the hero is destroyed because of a "sex crime" (6BM) or unspecified wickedness (11). Strong depressive trends are further revealed in the over-all hopelessness of the stories and the uniformly pessimistic outcomes. S seems fatalistically resigned to a bleak, rejecting and dangerous world which if it gives at all, gives only too late (note, e.g., stories 12M and 7BM).

The psychological conflicts of this S are so intense and consume so much of S's energy that there is little left for more positive and healthy strivings. Thus, there is no reference at all in the record to work, achievement, acquisition, recognition, etc. The entire work region is conspicuously absent. We may infer that S's intrapsychic problems are so pressing that he cannot be concerned with the ordinary problems of working, earning a living or making a career. Here again we see him withdrawing.

## MAPS TEST WORKING NOTES

1. Livingroom: hero—female adult—characterized as: housewife
   ugly mother comes to daughter's house
   with snake as companion
   snake symbolizes mother
   daughter indignant
   turns mother away—denies knowing her
   mother heart-broken
   husband argues with wife
   because he doesn't want her old and ugly
   snake returns
   and kills husband and wife
   (1) lack of relationship between husband and wife
   (2) characterization of mother as snake—evil, male symbol?
   (3) harsh rejection of mother by daughter
   (4) relative innocence of mother
   (5) snake is agency of death
   (6) concern with beauty and age
   outcome—unhappy
   levels—events, behavior

2. Street: hero—female adult—characterized as: degraded, beautiful
   woman hiding
   had affair with Chinaman

who seeks to kill her
because she's unfaithful
ghost of old lover
present lover hiding in shadow
kills her
thinking her Chinaman
kills self
(1) sex—death
(2) theme of the degraded woman
(3) violent anti-social aggression
outcome—unhappy
levels—object description, behavior, events

3. Bathroom: hero—woman—characterized as mute and blind
mute, blind, but can hear
husband in agony
son "compelled" to leave
with no face can neither be happy or unhappy
can communicate only with phantom
husband rejects
won't grow ugly with age
(1) theme of isolation—picture of schizophrenic state?
(2) rejection by members of family when S is in need—lack of relationship in family
(3) can communicate only with creatures of own imagination—hallucination?
(4) concern with aging
outcome—unhappy
levels—object description, events, behavior, perception, wish, feeling

4. Dream: hero—middle-aged woman
confused, thinking back over life
killed father, killed sister, seduced husband
husband turned away in shame
spirit heckled her life
tormented by sexual passion
decides to kill husband for insurance
gets killed first
(1) sex—death theme
(2) hostile acts against family members
(3) sex degrades
(4) no guilt
(5) ironic fate
(6) implication of hallucinatory experience
outcome—unhappy
levels—thought, behavior, intention, events

5. Bedroom: hero—adult woman?
woman hears scream
finds man crying

man denies
finds blood
man jumps through window
woman finds daughter dead in bed
man mad fiend
"I put myself in part"
(1) sex?—death theme
(2) violent anti-social aggression
(3) aggression—guilt (crying)?
(4) condition for suicide is insanity
(5) S identifies self as insane
outcome—unhappy
levels—events, behavior, feeling, perception

6. Blank: hero—young man
great plains, endless distance
young man walking for years
with something"significant with age" behind
woman, frightened
keep approaching, but not reaching something evil
man, old lady fall out
girl gets close is devoured by it
nearly reach it, but never quite
(1) desolation, lack
(2) endlessly searching, but never reaching goal
(3) discovery of secret—death
(4) secret—sexuality? (symbol of snake?)
outcome—happy
levels—object descriptions, behavior, events, feeling

7. Stage: hero—?
statue of girl
nude appears, speaks as in dream
old lady, grotesque, dismembers girl
priest wants to see statue move
faceless girl makes priest vanish
statue starts to move
theater collapses and kills 300
means that people in act with you will try to preserve their act and sometimes, like statue who stood watching, have real power
(1) statue may represent latent sexuality which when aroused destroys entire structure, i.e., personality (?)
(2) old woman killing girl—repression (?)
(3) priest ?
(4) distrust of people—delusion of power in schizoid detachment
outcome—unhappy
levels—object description, events, behavior, interest, expectation

## MAPS TEST INTERPRETATION

The material revealed by MAPS makes a fascinating basis for the continued interpretation of S's fantasy productions. In most important respects the data of this technique are completely consistent with the TAT material. In one major respect, however, the two protocols differ. The MAPS productions are more fantastic, less realistic, and, we may suppose, more closely related to S's schizophrenic ideation than are the stories told to the TAT pictures.

Much of the thematic material already discussed in connection with the TAT reappears here. The theme of sex and death appears directly in two stories (2 and 3) and inferentially in at least one other (5). The relationship between child and mother follows essentially the same lines already described. As before, the heroes of the stories live in a threatening and destructive world, and are destroyed by it.

The S reveals himself in these stories as suspicious, hostile, isolated from adequate interpersonal relationships. The schizophrenic trends noted in the TAT are even more clearly seen in this protocol. In one story (3), for example, S repeats the theme of isolation and lack of communication which was noted in the TAT. There are two interesting elements in this theme which illustrate S's expectation of rejection and his autism: The family of the mute woman desert and reject her when she can no longer talk with them; and, she can communicate only "through her mind" with a phantom "visible only to the woman's inner self." We are told, too, what is the consequence of withdrawal. S will neither be liked nor disliked and will be neither happy nor discontented. There is the specific suggestion of delusional content in his thinking. S's energies are consumed by profound intrapsychic conflicts which threaten the entire personality structure. He lacks control of his impulses, including antisocial strivings, and lacks sufficient ego strength to make any adequate adjustment. Apparently S lacks any insight into his own behavior, largely because of his weak ego structure which does not permit him to gain any distance from which to view himself and his problems.

The MAPS stories again show the central role of the sexual problem. In story 4, S describes eloquently the dangers of sexuality. Tormented by sexual impulses, the heroine is resolved to kill but is herself destroyed by a husband motivated as she was. Thus, sex and aggression are linked in S's fantasy. Similarly in story 2, sexuality, again pictured as degrading, leads to violent death. In both stories it is interesting to note that death occurs through the twist of a sardonic fate. It is clear from these stories that sexuality is conceived as an evil but nonetheless imperative need. It is likely that S is struggling with just such an impulse.

Even more striking than in the TAT we note S's tendency to use female heroines. When allowed the choice, S makes women the control figures in five of the seven stories. This may again be considered as indicating possible homosexual trends.

The strength and to some extent the direction of S's aggressive strivings are shown in this record. The hero kills (story 5) a woman and then himself. From the context—the fact that S is responding to a bedroom scene and that the woman is in bed—it seems likely that the object of aggression was first a sexual object. Whether or not S has ever committed such a crime cannot, of course, be known from this protocol, but it seems certain that S is fully capable of aggression against himself as well as others, particularly when these actions are sexually motivated. The amount of violence and self-destruction in these stories is evidence of the strength of S's aggressive strivings, a large part of which seem turned against the self and probably accompanied by depressive trends.

Again, as in the TAT, S tells to the blank card (6), a story which seems to reflect directly his current status. Here is described the desolation and loneliness of his life, the pointless wandering, the feeling of endlessly approaching but never reaching a goal. In addition, we get some further insight into the nature of his disease. The evil secret pursued by the characters of this story is represented by a snake, which we may interpret as representing sexuality. In the story the sex secret is discovered by only one character and she is destroyed by it.

The same theme is, we believe, repeated in the last story. Although it is very difficult to unravel the threads of this dream-like plot, we assume that the "statue" represents S's sexual impulses, perhaps, even more broadly, all of his primitive and asocial impulses, which, although deeply repressed, can lead to catastrophic destruction when awakened. The conscious, sexless self is probably depicted by the priest in this story.

A theme which appears in MAPS but not in the TAT seems to show S's concern with growing old and losing physical beauty. In two stories (1 and 3) a character is either killed or loses her face and hence will not grow old or ugly.

# Chapter 14

# JOSE I. LASAGA

Dr. Lasaga (full name: José Ignacio Lasaga y Travieso) was born in 1913. He received the degree of Doctor en Filosofía from the Universidad de la Habana in 1940. Postgraduate work in Psychology was done at Harvard University and Laval University (Canada). He has taught at the Universidad de la Habana as Instructor of Aesthetics and at the Universidad Católica de Santo Tomás de Villanueva (Havana) as Professor of General Psychology. He is now the Director of the Escuela Profesional de Psicología of the Universidad de Villanueva. He has been working in Clinical Psychology for several years in his private office and in the Sanatorio San Juan de Dios. His work is largely in the field of personality and he is interested in projective techniques. He is a member of the American Psychological Association and of the International Committee of the International Congress of Psychology.

## SELECTED REFERENCES

LASAGA Y TRAVIESO, JOSE I., AND MARTINEZ-ARANGO, CARLOS, Some Suggestions Concerning the Administration and Interpretation of the Thematic Apperception Test. *Journal of Psychology*, 1946, *22*, 117–163.

———, AND ———, Four Detailed Examples of How Mental Conflicts of Psychoneurotic and Psychotic Patients May be Discovered by Means of the Thematic Apperception Test. *Journal of Psychology*, 1948, *26*, 299–345.

MARTINEZ-ARANGO, CARLOS, AND LASAGA Y TRAVIESO, JOSE I., Psychotherapy Based on the TAT. *Quarterly Review of Psychiatry and Neurology*, 1947, *2*, 271–287.

## RESUME OF METHOD

THIS IS a clinical method, intended to discover the psychodynamic causes of neurotic and psychotic disturbances and to be an aid in psychotherapy. It focuses attention on the patient's main conflicts and emphasizes the fact that conflicts may be disguised by a process of symbolic substitution. The actual procedure consists of the following: reading the record for general impression; underlining phrases which express the main idea or important aspects of the main idea; summarizing each story in terms of the main idea; finding clues for discovering the key conflicts; studying anomalies among the ideas or among reaction times; taking into consideration "basic data" about the patient and knitting all these impressions together into a summary evaluation.

## TAT WORKING NOTES

For reasons which we shall explain more thoroughly at the end of this chapter, we recognize the MAPS test as a much more useful *diagnostic* tool than the TAT. We shall therefore employ it as the central point in the diagnosis of the case studied by us and shall use the TAT as a source of complementary information.

For studying the *dynamics* of the patient's conflicts, however, we prefer the TAT to the MAPS test and shall detail the reasons for our preference when we compare the two tests. Accordingly, we shall make first a minute analysis of the TAT, following the techniques suggested by Lasaga and Martinez-Arango. Then we shall try to show how a confirmation of the principal conclusions deduced from the TAT can be found in the MAPS test.

A. *The Basic Postulates of the Method*

The fundamental principles of our method of interpretation of the TAT are two:

1. The principle of primacy of conflicts.

If a person has extremely intense worries or conflicts, these worries or conflicts will show up again and again in a large number of the stories of the test, possibly in most of them. This means that every TAT certainly reflects several aspects of the whole personality of the subject being tested, but, when one or more intense conflicts exist in the subject's life at the moment the test is made, what will appear first of all in the TAT will be those conflicts.

Yet this does not mean that this will happen in every TAT, but only in those tests made with persons, either well or ill, who are experiencing internal conflicts. As a matter of fact in the cases of many psychotics no traces of such conflicts will be found.

The conflicts revealed by the TAT may be: (a) wholly conscious, partially unconscious, or wholly unconscious at the moment of making the test; (b) present conflicts or past conflicts which have not yet been emotionally settled and so continue to disturb the patient's mind.

2. The principle of symbolic substitution.

A person's conflicts may appear in the TAT either in literal form or in symbolic form. When a test presents stories other than those totally objective or completely trivial, which cannot be explained literally by conflicts or facts of the patient's life, then it is to be supposed that such stories express in a symbolic or metaphoric form worries and happenings in his real life.

B. *Procedures*

In analyzing a series of TAT stories we are accustomed to employ the following procedures:

1. We read all the stories one after another, trying to form a general impression from the whole series;

2. We then reread them, one at a time, marking or underlining in each: (a) the phrase or phrases which express the main idea of the plot; (b) those

phrases which show us secondary but still important aspects of the main idea; (c) those phrases or words which may give some clues for discovering a patient's conflict, either because they are charged with intense feeling or because they reveal failures in the patient's thinking which may be sometimes attributed to an emotional cause, such as: internal contradictions, slips of the tongue, distorted perception and the like;

3. In many cases we write on a sheet of paper a short abstract of each story, trying to summarize the main idea, but sometimes adding a few of the secondary ideas. This summary serves to show up more clearly the resemblances which may exist between some stories and others. (In an article published in *The Journal of Psychology*, in 1946—see references—we suggested the use of certain letters to designate the characters appearing in the stories, but that suggestion is absolutely secondary and no special importance need be attached to it. The sole important matter at this stage of the analysis of the test is to reduce to some few phrases the main ideas of each story.)

Example: In the story 3BM of the series being considered, the key phrase of the story is: "guilty of prostitution." Additionally, the following may be marked or underlined: "very ashamed" (this denotes the presence of intense remorse in the patient); "spread across the country" (this exhibits fear of publicity); "her sister... would suffer" (this shows fear that the family may know); "too late" (this involves the idea that the heroine can no longer change). The gist of this story would be entered later on the summary sheet in the following, or similar words: "N (the heroine), found guilty of prostitution. Fears her sister would know it. Thinks it is too late to change. Stabs herself."

This procedure is directed towards suggesting to the investigator one or more hypotheses which will be able to explain the greater part, perhaps even the whole of the stories of the test.

Our usual technique also comprises two additional steps which were not available in the present case: (a) the study of rejected ideas, those which the patient had on being shown each picture but which he did not include in his stories, and also of the new ideas which came into his mind on again being shown the pictures when asked to remember the ideas he had previously discarded; (b) the study of possible anomalies in his reaction times.

Furthermore it is very useful and sometimes absolutely necessary to take into consideration the patient's "basic data"; what his occupation is; whether he is bachelor, married, divorced or widower; whether he is engaged to be married; whether he lives with relatives and, if he does, which; whether his parents are dead, and so on. In the present case the sole particulars furnished about the patient whose stories have been submitted to us were these: (a) he is a male; (b) 25 years old; and (c) single.

## C. *Summaries of the TAT Stories*

1. N is sick. More interested in a story book than in music. N is reading the book "without any eyes. . . ."

3BM. N found guilty of prostitution. Very ashamed. Fears her sister knowing it. Thinks it is too late to change. Stabs herself.

4. N and X have had sexual relations. X is determined to leave. (X is married.) N prays him to stay or help her financially. They spend one night more. N sets fire to the house.

6BM. N has committed a murder. Trys to tell it to M by means of a play. M understands and shoots N. (Crime had a sexual motive.)

7BM. N depressed over his health. P tells him he himself alone can cure it. N has a family to support. N goes to a healthier climate. Does not get better. Dies. His family never contacts P. P repents. Leaves them estate.

11. A prehistoric animal rolls boulders across Ns' path. N's predestined to reach their goal. A pit of lost human souls. The animal will race ahead of N's and send them to their fate. N's are wicked people.

12M. N is badly off financially. Sells a magnificent painting. The director of an art museum visits him to offer him a good position, brings him a picture of a loaf of bread. The picture "has too great an effect. . . ." N dies.

13MF. N and X meet in the street. Have sexual intercourse. N is ashamed. N thinks about a girl he could not have at home. (A morally different girl who resembled X).

13B. N will have a brother. N is afraid of losing M's affection. N cannot get much affection from his P. M calls him. N is happy to help M. Has done more than P.

14. A mutilated human body. N (the murderer) tells Z it was in self-defense. Z does not believe it. The police find what had happened. N had robbed a jewelry store and killed his victim.

16. N's suffer from heat, lack of water, and many outside influences. N's were alone. N's came to their doom. Now nothing is left except ruins. (But it could all be imagination.)

## D. *Rough Draft Sheet for the Investigation of TAT Conflicts*

1. Do conflicts exist?

3BM —N very ashamed of prostitution. Stabs herself.
4 —N very broken up. (X leaving her.) Sets fire to the house.
6BM —Murder. Terrifying facts. M shoots N.
7BM —N very depressed over health.
11 —"lost human souls. . ."
12M —picture had too great effect on N.
13MF—Intercourse. Shame.
13B —N cannot get affection from P. "It's a hopeless case. . ."
14 —a highly dramatic story.
16 —Loneliness. Abandonment.

2. Guilt stories: 3BM, 6BM, 11 (wicked people), 13MF, 14.
3. Overt sexual stories: 3BM, 4, 6BM, 13MF, 14 (?)
4. Homosexual conflict:
   3BM —Prostitution.
   4 —Identification with woman. Immoral sexual relations.
   6BM —Murder (M kills son). "Terrifying facts."
   7BM —"He himself alone. . ."
   11 —Lost human souls. Wicked people. Danger. Fate.
   13MF—Sexual intercourse. Shame.
   14 —Mutilated body. Robbery.
   16 —Ruins(?)
5. Love: 13MF (?)
6. Vocational difficulties: 4 (?), 12M, 16 (?)
7. Home conflicts: 7BM, 13B

E. *The First Question in the Interpretation of the Stories:*

*Do mental conflicts exist in the patient who has been examined?*

On reviewing all the stories of a patient, in most cases no difficulty arises in forming a more or less vague impression as to whether the stories told by him suggest the presence of mental conflicts.

Such conflicts may be presumed to exist: (a) if a certain number of his stories seem to point in the same direction; (b) if those stories deal with emotional conflicts of the characters appearing in them.

Therefore, the existence of a conflict need not necessarily be supposed if the various stories of the test reflect several different aspects of the life and ideals of the narrator, pointing in very different directions; or if the stories appear to be completely lacking in any reference to possible situations of conflict in human life.[1]

In the case actually under review, no doubt exists about the affirmative character of the answer which has to be given:

1. Because the people in the stories are persons in whose lives problems of a sentimental sort exist, such as those of shame, thwarted desire, remorse, lack of affection and the like. Moreover, in the present test, feelings such as these have often been described, using words strongly charged with emotion: "very ashamed" (3BM); "very broken up" (4); "the terrifying facts" (6BM); "very depressed" (7BM); "it's a hopeless case" (13B), and so on. Besides, these persons react passionately when faced with problems: committing suicide, murdering, and so on.

[1] It must be remarked that though objective or superficial stories do not suggest the existence of intrapsychic conflicts, they do not necessarily prove that there are no conflicts at all. Under sodium amytal, very inhibited patients, whose stories were originally lacking in emotional intensity, may produce TAT stories where the trace of conflicts is clearly detectable.

2. Because, as we shall explain further on, almost all the patient's stories seem to point in one direction, towards one selfsame conflict.

F. *The Second Question: What kind of conflicts are they?*

Without attempting to present an exhaustive list of the conflicts which a young bachelor may experience, we shall enumerate a few of those commonly met with in tests made by young unmarried men. Such a list will serve as a useful guide to us in the case being considered.

1. Home conflicts: deaths, lack of home, having to leave home, parents' lack of understanding, domineering parents, lack of affection in the home, quarrels between parents, divorce, immoral conduct of the father or mother. . . .
2. Vocational and economic conflicts: unrealized vocational ideals, opposition of parents, fear of failure, dislike for actual work, empty life without any vocational ideals, worry about actual or future economic condition. . . .
3. Love conflicts (with a fiancee, a mistress, or simply a woman love): loss of the woman loved either by death or by quarrels, jealousy, misunderstanding with a woman loved, lack of interest in a fiancee, love affairs that must be broken off, love affairs opposed by family, unrequited love, life without love. . . .
4. Sexual conflicts: impotence, homosexual tendencies. . . .
5. Sexual guilt conflicts: masturbation, heterosexual relations violating the patient's ethical standards, abnormal sexual practices, homosexual acts. . . .
6. Nonsexual guilt conflicts: incorrect business practices, serious offenses or injury to others. . . .

What kind of conflict has the subject whose stories we are examining here?

1. A conflict of guilt exists.

This can be clearly seen when we recall that five of the eleven stories of the test turn on a criminal or immoral act which gives rise to feelings of remorse or shame:

(a) 3BM: prostitution, sense of shame;
(b) 6BM: "a murder," "terrifying facts," fear of telling the mother;
(c) 11: the heroes are "wicked people";
(d) 13MF: heterosexual relations with an unknown person, "a feeling of shame";
(e) 14: robbery in a jeweler's shop which leads to a murder.

2. It is guilt in sexual matters.

Among the stories dealing with wrong acts there are three which actually refer to a sexual motive:

(a) 3BM: prostitution;
(b) 6BM: "motive primarily to do with sexual";
(c) 13MF: sexual relations with an unknown woman.

Though in story 14 there is no literal reference to sexual acts, yet the description of the "murder" has a strong sexual tone. It must be noticed that the patient does not speak of an ordinary murder but of the mutilation of a human body.

We must add to these particulars that in story 4, although the idea of guilt or remorse does not appear, yet the incident is an illicit sexual relation, since it occurs between a woman and a married man. It is interesting to observe that the patient has specially emphasized the sexual, not the sentimental aspect of the relations between the pair. "They have spent quite some time together in intimacy . . . She pleads for him to spend one more night. . . ."

3. We have here a patient whose principal trouble is a homosexual conflict.

(a) In picture 3BM the patient sees a woman where it is more usual for men to see a man. Yet this would lack importance were it not for the fact that in the story the patient identifies himself with a woman ashamed because she is known to be a prostitute. This indicates that the patient feels shame for something that must be for a man a condition similar to that of being a prostitute for a woman. And what else can that be except leading the life of a homosexual, in which there are, as in prostitution: (a) sexual contacts with men; (b) open repulsion by society?

(b) In story 4 the patient identifies himself with the woman not with the man. This also would lack importance if the story did not treat of a heroine anxious to possess her lover for one more night. The immoral relations between the heroine and the married man may perhaps be a symbol of homosexual contact.

(c) In story 6BM the hero has committed a murder, "terrifying facts" have happened and he does not dare tell his mother. It is a crime based on a sexual motive. And the mother's reaction is not that of taking her son's part, but of seizing a revolver and killing him. What on earth can a man have done in order to imagine that his mother would be capable of killing him if she knew about it? A simple crime of passion because of an unfaithful woman? You cannot expect that a mother may kill her son for a motive like that. It must be something more "terrifying." Could it not very well be a homosexual act?

(d) In story 7BM the hero is "very depressed over his health." And his father tells him that: (1) "it can be cured if the son has the will to cure it"; (2) "he himself alone can cure it." On being asked what disease it was, the patient mentioned T. B. But the previous description does not appear to suit a physical disease so well as a mental or moral disease. Does it not appear, then, that the patient has got a vice and has thought that he alone can cure it, and what he needs to cure himself is to have the will to do so?

(e) In story 11 the patient has unnecessarily described his heroes as "wicked people." Besides the idea of trying to flee from one abyss or physical danger perhaps only to fall later on into another still deeper is an idea which frequently appears in the tests of homosexuals. The "pit full of lost human souls" and the "dark place," to where the people in the story seem to be going, are symbols of the complete moral perdition into which homosexuals dread to fall.

(f) In story 13MF the following interesting elements appear: (1) the hero has sexual relations with an unknown woman he has met in the street; (2) the relations take place in the dark, and, when the light is turned on again, the hero is aware of "a feeling of shame." This story by itself proves nothing more than the existence of feelings of shame for sexual acts. But the patient does not look like a man of delicate conscience, a person who feels remorse for a heterosexual adventure with an unknown woman. Could all this not be, therefore, a symbol of remorse for homosexual acts?

(g) Finally the idea of the "mutilated body" in story 14 does not constitute proof of homosexuality, yet it does suit the hypothesis of a person who has done things with another human body as contrary to nature as the carrying out of an act of mutilation.

G. *Techniques of elucidating the dubious points in the test conclusions and of making the patient indicate his conflicts*

1. The usual procedure consists in a careful evaluation of the data contained in the clinical history and in a cross-examination of the patient during one or more sessions, trying to elucidate the dubious conclusions of the test. In the case of a paranoid schizophrenic, this is not always easy to carry out because of his habitual suspiciousness. But it is sometimes possible to obtain from those interviews a certain number of particulars which help us to have a better understanding of the patient's conflicts. In the present case, on finding the patient at some moment willing to reply to a cross-examination, some of the aspects of his conflicts could possibly be explained; but an overt confession of the patient's homosexual behavior is not to be expected, since the test itself has already shown his intense desire not to have his secret divulged.

2. An indirect proof of the hypothesis of homosexual conflict has been obtained in cases similar to this:

(a) Using the Symonds test and noting how the same types of plot appear in its stories as appeared in those of the TAT. By analyzing the Symonds and the TAT of the same patient, from the point of view of the investigation of his conflicts, almost identical conclusions can be obtained in one test as in the other. This holds true in the case of patients suffering from homosexual tendencies, even when a shock treatment has taken place between both tests.

(b) Using a word association test containing a certain number of words of sexual implication, and especially referring to homosexual problems. For example, the list of Rapaport, given in *Diagnostic Psychological Testing*, I, p. 84, complementing it with some other words that might possibly be related to homosexual behavior. Double-meaning words are especially useful in these tests (in Spanish, for instance, we usually include in those cases the word "pajaro", which means at the same time "a bird" and "an effeminate man").

(c) The use of narcoanalysis and hypnoanalysis may finally be suggested for obtaining an explicit confession from the patient, when it has been unobtainable in his normal state.

H. *Rough Draft Sheet for TAT Final Conclusions*

1. Homosexual conflict: 3BM, 4, 6BM, 7BM, 11, 13MF, 14.

2. Immoral behavior: 3BM (prostitution), 4 (sexual relations with a married man), 6BM (murder), 11 (wicked people), 13MF (sexual intercourse), 14 (robbery, crime).

3. Shame, remorse, guilt feelings: 3BM, 6BM, 11, 13MF.

4. Role of will: 3BM, 7BM; fate: 11, 16.

5. No remedy: 3BM, 7BM, 11, 12M, 16.

6. Fears family may know: 3BM (sister), 6BM (mother), 14 (N hiding).

7. Failure in love: 13MF.

8. Jealousy: 4, 6BM.

9. Vocational difficulties: 4, 12M, 16.

10. No help: 16.

11. Home conflicts: 7BM, 13B.

12. Day dreaming: 1.

13. Tendency to violence: 3BM, 4, 6BM, 14.

## TAT INTERPRETATION

A. *What sure conclusions and what verifiable hypotheses can we deduce from the detailed analysis of the conflicts shown in the stories of the test?*

1. The main trouble of the patient is his homosexual conflict. The basis for this statement has been given above.

2. We are not dealing here with tendencies that have always remained inside the patient's mind, but with tendencies that have determined a homosexual behavior. This can be seen in the story 3BM, where the main subject is the heroine's prostitution acts. It can also be seen in story 4, where sexual relations between the heroine and a man have repeatedly taken place. It appears in story 6BM where the hero has committed a crime. It shows in story 13MF (about consummating sexual relations) and in 14 (about committing a crime). We do not claim, with this, to establish as certain that antinatural copulations have definitely taken place, though that seems exceedingly probable. These stories would be sufficiently explained by the patient's having realized in some way acts of a homosexual kind.

3. The patient considers such acts morally reprehensible and because of them feels shame and remorse. He is "very ashamed" (3BM), considers them "terrifying facts" (6BM), looks upon himself as a "wicked" man (11), and has experienced "a feeling of shame" (13MF).

4. Sometimes the patient thinks he could have solved his problem, if he

had had the will to do so, but at other times feels that his condition is hopeless, having been foreordained by Fate. The idea of having been able to overcome his conflict provided he had had the strength of will appears in story 3BM ("she, at one time, had a chance . . . ") as well as in story 7BM ("it can be cured . . . "). But, on the other hand, in story 11 the heroes save themselves from the first danger because "they must have been predestined to reach their goal," and perhaps will perish later on if that is their "fate." We may also add that in story 16 the heroes, for want of help, "came to their doom." (Is there not here, in the use of the word "doom," a reflection of a general fatalistic concept of life?)

5. The patient thinks that his problems have no remedy now; that it is too late. Things will go from bad to worse. In story 3BM the heroine thinks that it is "too late" to change her way of living. In story 7BM the hero fails to cure himself in the end. In story 11 the heroes are "going deeper into more of a dark place than from where they came from." In story 12M, which may be a story representing some professional failures of the patient, but which may also symbolize his actual disease and his sexual failure, the remedy arrives "too late." And in story 16 the sufferings of the heroes have this end: that "nothing is left except ruins."

6. The patient dreads the revelation of his secret and, above all, the possibility that some of his relatives may get to know it, for he thinks that will severely shock them, in view of their moral principles. In story 3BM the heroine thinks that her immoral way of living has become known throughout the country and suffers in a special way when she thinks how shocked her sister will be for that reason. We may notice that this sister appears in the story as a nun. In story 6BM the hero does not dare tell his mother about the terrible things he has done and uses an indirect way of letting her know of them. Finally, in story 14, this same desire in the patient, of concealing some reprobable act, appears in the efforts made by the central character to hide his crimes.

7. Has the patient experienced any disappointment in love? In story 13MF the patient twice insists that, in the hero's life, there was a girl "he could never get." Further, he notes very emphatically the contrast between that unobtainable girl and the other appearing in the story simply as an instrument of sexual pleasure. The former was "morally a different girl." Does this mean that in the patient's life there has been a disappointment in love? If there had been no definite woman loved by the patient, then this story would have been interpreted in a more general manner, as expressing the patient's feeling of frustration toward the love of women.

8. Has there been jealousy? Is that jealousy related to homosexual relations? In story 4 the man has to leave the heroine for, being married, he

wants to put an end to the affair. Because of that the woman sets fire to the house. And in story 6BM, fundamentally a narrative revealing to us the patient's fear of his crimes becoming known to his family, there occurs in the final phrase, following the examiner's question, a reference to an act of infidelity in relations of a sexual type. Both stories seem to indicate the existence of jealousy feelings in the patient. Is this a normal jealousy about a woman? Or does this mean (as story 4 strongly suggests) that the patient has been sexually interested in some particular man and, because of that, has felt something like jealousy?

9. Has the patient experienced difficulties in making his way economically or professionally? Here we must ask ourselves whether something of the sort has happened, if we take in account the poverty of the heroine in story 4 and, above all, the plot of story 12M. Yet, if there has been nothing in the patient's real life which may correspond to that hypothesis, we may then interpret story 12M as still another reiteration of the sexual failure of the patient and his idea that it is something for which no remedy at all exists.

10. The patient feels that he has not received sufficient help in the great problems of life from those who could have saved him. This appears, highly charged with emotion, in story 16. Nonetheless, it is impossible to state whether this story refers to lack of help in solving the sexual problem or in overcoming other difficulties, such as, for example, that of making one's way in life.

11. The patient has had serious troubles in his home. This has been because either his father or his mother has not dedicated sufficient attention to him, perhaps on account of having abandoned the home, or, on the other hand, because, though looked after in the material sense, he may not have gotten all the loving care he would have been longing for. In story 13B the hero "cannot get much affection from his father who is too busy working in the fields," and thinks that if his mother ceases to love him "it's a hopeless case." Then in story 7BM, the hero's father is pictured as being rather selfish, not only because of the way in which he gives advice to his son, but also of that in which he deals with the son's family later. He pays no attention at all to them until on his deathbed.

12. The patient has sought in day dreams compensation for his misfortunes. In story 1, the child in bed amuses himself by reading a book of adventures instead of studying. Perhaps he is "reading a book without any eyes or knowing what is in the book without reading it."

13. The patient has a strong tendency to violence. This violence may be directed against self or against others. In story 3BM, the heroine commits suicide. In story 4, in order to solve her problems the heroine sets fire to the house. Aggressive characters also appear in stories 6BM and 14; and although "crime" may be only a symbol of sexual misbehavior, it is interesting to

notice how often the patient makes use of concepts of aggression, and how vividly aggressive feelings are depicted by him.

B. *Suggestions for diagnosis.*

Viewing the TAT in search of diagnostic information, we find features suggesting schizophrenia, like the tangled plot of the story of picture 14, or the bizarre idea that the boy is "knowing what is in the book without reading it" (picture 1). Yet the relative coherence of the stories and the originality of some of the plots suggest that we have before us a highly imaginative schizophrenic with a well-preserved front. All these facts fit suitably into the picture of a paranoid schizophrenic.

C. *Hypothetic psychodynamic scheme of the patient's conflicts*

In the Chart of Conflicts, interrogation marks indicate unproved conflicts or purely hypothetical relations among conflicts; large arrows indicate the main conflicts.

CHART OF CONFLICTS

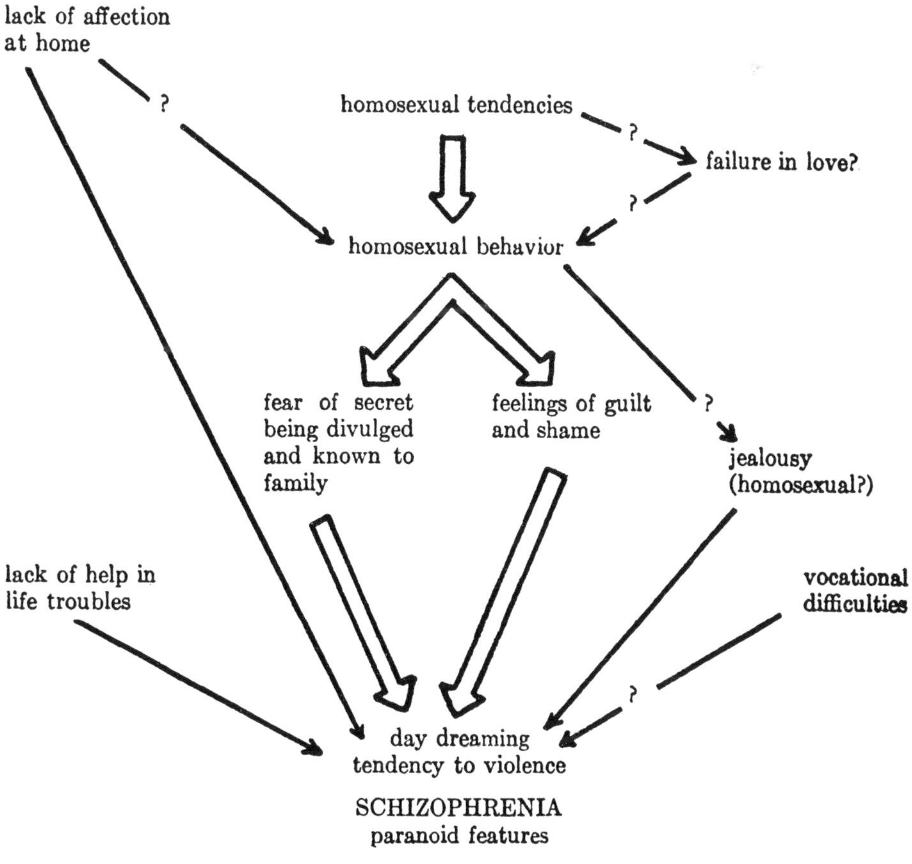

D. *Objectivity of Our Interpretations of the TAT*

One of the criticisms most frequently made of the techniques of interpretation of the TAT employed in the present study is that they lack objectivity. In order to prove that a "symbolic interpretation" does not necessarily mean an interpretation which is arbitrarily subjective, copies of the TAT that had been studied here were given to three other persons by the author of this paper, asking them to make a detailed analysis of the stories. They were: Dr. Carlos Martinez-Arango, co-author of the methods of clinical utilization of the TAT, Dr. Luis M. Cowley and Dr. Santiago Choca, who have worked extensively with the TAT in accordance with our techniques. None of them had any previous knowledge of the present paper or of the conclusions of the others, but all employed the same techniques of interpretation that had been used here. A list of conclusions about the patient's conflicts was separately written by each of the interpreters and then compared with the present paper and with the conclusions of the others.

There was full agreement as to the main conflict of the patient, which was unanimously characterized as: (a) a guilt conflict, (b) of a homosexual nature.

The existence of a jealousy conflict about losing a sexual mate was also unanimously suggested (though some emphasized more than others the possible homosexual character of this relation).

The existence of a more idealized form of love and the vocational difficulties were not explicitly mentioned by all, though were later accepted by everybody as possible sources of conflict.

As to the existence of a home conflict (lack of affection, support, understanding) there was a complete agreement, though admitting that its factual content could not be made perfectly clear without a wider knowledge of the subject's life.

## MAPS TEST WORKING NOTES AND INTERPRETATION

A. *Rough draft sheet for diagnosis.*

1. Livingroom
   - bizarre plot
   - snake (symbolism)
   - "you'll give me. . ." (cryptic statement)
   - introducing ideas not justified by plot
2. Street
   - ghost (in realistic story)
   - figure I-1 standing
3. Bathroom
   - bizarre fantasies
   - placement of figure I-2

4. Dream
   –father poisoned: "didn't have hair"
   –disjointedness of plot elements
   –"things worked out beautifully"
5. Bedroom
   –absurd behavior: denying crime and suicide
   –placement of figure M-12 ("behind bed")
6. Blank
   –bizarre fantasies
   –moving figures
7. Stage
   –bizarre fantasies
   –disjointedness of plot elements
   –cryptic statements
   –unexplained incongruent behavior of characters
   –"life-like" statue
   –moving figures

The items above suggest a schizophrenic disease.

B. *MAPS test signs.*

1. Schizophrenic (minus) signs:
   —four or more average figures per background
   —feet off ground
   —actually moving figures
   —in Livingroom, figure M-5
   —in Dream, figure M-15
   —in any background, figure M-18
   —using a figure as a concept
   ———
   —7
2. Normal (plus) signs:
   + F (female) figure three or more times
   + one figure three or more times
   + interaction with animal
   + interaction with stranger
   + interaction with acquaintance
   + interaction with spouse
   + interaction with parent
   + social violence
   + fatal accident
   + in Bathroom, man cleans up
   ———
   + 10
3. Difference Score: + 3 (See *Diagnosis: Quantitative Viewpoint*, below.)

C. *Analysis of the MAPS test: Conflicts.*

If we had not had at our disposition other stories than those of the MAPS test, we could have applied to the MAPS test exactly the same procedures of interpretation as to the TAT: (A) Are there conflicts? Yes, because there are several stories in which the heroes appear intensely suffering from moral troubles.[2] (B) What sort are they? There is a conflict of guilt (stories 1, 2, 3, 4, 5 and 7?); the patient is a homosexual (stories 1?, 2, 3, 4, 5?, 6, 7?); perhaps some family problem (story 4) and some love problem (story 2) also exist. (C) What other conclusions may we deduce from a minute analysis of the stories? Dread that the homosexual conflict may become known (stories 1, 5 and 6); remorse (story 3); and so on.

But as what we are accustomed to do with the MAPS test, in addition to using it as a diagnostic tool, is to employ it for complementing the study of the patient's conflicts made in the TAT, it will be better in the present paper to start from the conclusions deduced from the TAT in order to see to what extent they can be confirmed in the stories of the MAPS test. In certain other cases such confirmation as this has not been obtained, except in a few stories of the MAPS test, but in this particular case it has been obtained in all of them. Let us therefore proceed to the analysis of the stories one by one in the same order as they appeared in the patient's test.

*Livingroom*

In this story the patient either has identified himself with the figure of the mother or with that of the daughter, or has projected his own feelings into both of them. Whatever he has done, it is clear that the central idea of the story consists of something which has to be concealed. That something is kinship with a deformed person, accompanied by a serpent which is "the symbol of what she really is." Could not this represent the attitude of a sexual pervert wishing to conceal his relations with other men or finding himself rejected by his accomplices, friends or relatives, who no longer want to acknowledge his acquaintanceship in public? This would be, of course, a purely hypothetical interpretation.

The idea that the homosexuality is the fault of fate might perhaps coincide with the attitude of the old woman in the story who insists that it is not her fault that she has such a face.

*Street*

This is a typical story of conflicts arising from a dissolute sexual life. In addition it contains two homosexual features: (a) the first, in itself of little value, of having taken the indeterminate figure I-1 as representing a woman; (b) the second, which constitutes fairly convincing evidence, of having described the girl as a person "quite degraded in character."

In the first part of the story the patient appears to have projected his feelings into the figure of the girl. Towards the end, he appears to have identified himself

[2] Let us repeat even more emphatically than in the TAT that dramatic stories suggest the presence of conflicts but non-dramatic stories do not prove in every case that they do not exist.

rather with the jealous lover. Because of this, the question that we asked in the TAT again comes up: Has there been jealousy of a homosexual type? If nothing of that sort is established as having taken place, it is reasonable to suppose that the patient is a person who has also had sexual experiences with women and has felt jealousy in connection with one of them.

The ghost of a former love hovering over the heroine suggests the hypothesis, which already arose in the TAT, of frustration in a love affair.

*Bathroom*

This story turns on an antinatural wish, that of a person renouncing his own face, that is to say, renouncing what he is naturally. Further, it is a wish that, converted into reality, fills the person who experienced it with anguish and the members of his family with horror. Does not this coincide closely with the homosexual desires of the patient, desires of renouncing what he was naturally, which in a certain sense have been converted into reality through homosexual behavior, leaving him full of deep bitterness? Note also how the narrator on one occasion refers to the heroine as "this thing," that is to say, he considers her to be a neutral subject.

If such is the interpretation of this story, two aspects of the conflict, which came out clearly in the TAT, are to be noted: (a) the sufferings of the members of the patient's family if they get to know his immoral behavior; (b) the irremediable and definite character of his sexual defect, for it is said in the story that the heroine's face "is gone for ever."

*Dream*

The homosexual conflict may appear here: (a) in the "spirit" which "heckled" the heroine's life "by the fact that another man had appeared in the shadows and excited her so much with passion that she was tormented"; (b) in the crime that the heroine feels herself impelled to commit, carried away by this noxious passion.

The absurd phrase stating that the heroine poisoned her father because he had no hair like other fathers, suggests the existence of a conflict of a family type: Does the patient think that his father or mother was not, in some sense, like other fathers or mothers?

There is something of jealousy in this story, as well. Once again the question comes up: What sort of jealousy is it?

*Bedroom*

In this story the principal character: (a) is an abnormal man; (b) has committed a horrid crime. Could not this be a symbol of the patient's sexually abnormal mind and of his sexual crimes? Is there not a sexual flavor in a story about a man killing a young woman who was alone with him in a bedroom?

The only doubt that arises in the story is that of whether the patient has not identified himself rather with the mother than with the man. Yet it does not seem logical to think so, for he does not describe the feelings of the woman faced with the crime, but he does describe the emotional reaction of the man. In other words, this is a "story of crime" and not a "story of having lost a daughter." For indeed the emotional nucleus of the story lies in the criminal conduct of the man, not in the grief of the woman on seeing one dear to her dead.

Should the intepretation proposed above be accurate, what ought to be seen here once more is the patient's desire to hide his evil life and his fear that someone may find out about it.

*Blank*

This is a typical story of people who suffer from homosexual tendencies. Note how the characters of the story observe something in front of them which seems to be coming nearer to them, and that some of them seek it but the others do not. Furthermore what they see is precisely "something evil." It is something which, in short, will ruin them all in one way or another. This "something evil" might reasonably be a symbol for the vice of homosexuality.

Note yet again here the idea of "secret," together with the idea of the hopelessness of the final disaster. In the phrase "some of them are searching for it, some would rather not" perhaps the two main possible attitudes before the homosexual problem should be seen: That of those who do not want to go looking for the vice, and that of those who deliberately want to seek it. Possibly first one attitude and later the other have existed in the patient's life.

*Stage*

This is the most schizophrenic of all the stories, and, because of that, the most difficult to interpret. Nonetheless note the following features which fit into the picture of homosexuality: (a) the patient chooses the "indeterminate" figure I-1 to represent a woman; (b) when the nude woman appears before the audience, she looks "defiant," but speaks "as if from a dream," and the spectators "wonder if it's all real" (is there not a suggestion of a homosexual attitude in this emphasis on the unreal character of a figure possibly representing the normal heterosexual appeal?); (c) the nude woman is later dismembered by a monstrous character; (d) in the last episode of the story, a disaster is the result of the statue's obeying the command of an abnormal creature: the woman without a face (could it not be a symbol of how homosexual behavior caused a disaster in the patient's life?).

D. *Diagnosis: Qualitative Viewpoint*

From a qualitative viewpoint, the MAPS test of the case under consideration presents the following features suggesting a schizophrenic disease:

1. Bizarre plots.

2. The disjointedness of the various elements or episodes of the stories. This is especially noticeable in stories 4 (Dream) and 7 (Stage).

3. The inclusion of symbolic elements in nonsymbolic stories as, for example, the snake, in story 1 (Livingroom) and the unjustified intervention of mythical elements in realistic stories, such as the ghost, in story 2 (Street).

4. The absurd manner of thinking or of reasoning that the narrator attributes to various characters in his stories: for example, when he describes

the heroine in story 4 (Dream) as poisoning her father "because he hadn't hair like other fathers had."

5. The absurd and incoherent behavior of most of the characters in the stories, like that of the man in story 5 (Bedroom) who throws himself out of the window an instant after having been trying to conceal his crime, without any reasonable connection existing between the two attitudes.

6. Cryptic sentences as that used by the old woman in story 1, before leaving.

7. The unreal and bizarre placing of some figures in the pictures. Cases in point are those of the man in the picture of the Bedroom, a figure which the patient insists on our supposing to be behind the bed; or of the figure I-2 in the picture of the Bathroom, a figure which, though the scene is supposed to show a man having a bath, the patient places in front of the bathtub.

The confrontation of these features of schizophrenic type with the richness of the patient's ideas and the striking originality of his stories leads us to suspect strongly that we have before us a paranoid schizophrenia.

### E. *Diagnosis: Quantitative Viewpoint*

If, on the other hand, we use Shneidman's quantitative method, adapting it to a seven-stories test, we can arrive at an analogous result, for in this patient's test we get from the algebraic addition of the "signs" of normality and schizophrenia a difference score of +3, which seems to suggest the existence of schizophrenic disease.

Still we consider that, at the present state of psychology, it is not yet feasible to base a diagnosis only on the quantitative analysis of a test. Because of that we prefer to treat quantitative results as only one of the reasons for or against a particular diagnostic hypothesis, without giving it precedence over the reasons deduced from the qualitative analysis.

### F. *Final Remarks*

Finally, we want to explain why we have, in the qualitative appraisal of the MAPS test and the TAT, deliberately omitted considering the indications which arise from the analysis of the content of the stories in order to concentrate our attention only on their formal elements.

Now, without question, stories about attacks from behind, repugnant crimes, mysterious dangers which cannot be avoided and the like, occur with great frequency in cases of paranoid schizophrenia. But such stories indicate rather the existence of a homosexual conflict in the patient than of paranoid schizophrenia. This is clearly shown by the fact that such stories frequently appear in cases of homosexuals who are not paranoid schizophrenics, but do not, in general show up in tests of those paranoid-schizophrenics whose disease has no connection with homosexual conflicts. The same can be said of confusion as to the sex of the figures appearing in TAT pictures, which, when markedly unreasonable or significantly frequent, may suggest the existence of a homosexual conflict. Nevertheless, this does not mean that "content signs" totally lack diagnostic value. They possess a certain value in those cases where a particular conflict appears with some frequency in persons suffering from a particular disease, as in paranoid schizophrenia, a disease which in many cases, especially in men, is the result of homosexual conflicts. Thus we are not discussing the practical usefulness of such signs, but only the theoretical interpretation which should be given to their use.

In conclusion:

1. We prefer the MAPS test to the TAT as a diagnostic instrument.

2. We consider that, in the present state of science, the qualitative approach to the MAPS test must always be emphasized, without, at the same time disclaiming the usefulness of the quantitative approach.

3. What "content signs" show us directly are the patient's conflicts. Their diagnostic value is only indirect.

# Chapter 15

# JULIAN B. ROTTER AND SHIRLEY JESSOR

Dr. Rotter was born in 1916. He received his Ph.D. degree in Psychology from Indiana University in 1941. Following that, he has been successively Psychologist at Norwich State Hospital, Personnel Consultant and Aviation Psychologist in the United States Army, and, at the present time, Professor of Psychology at The Ohio State University. He has also been a visiting professor at the University of Minnesota. He was an Instructor in the 1950 Post-Doctoral Institute of the APA Division of Clinical and Abnormal Psychology and is Chairman of that committee. Most of his publications are concerned with the measurement of personality, projective tests, and personality theory. He is, at present, an Associate Editor of the *Journal of Applied Psychology* and the *Psychology Service Center Journal.*

Mrs. Jessor was born in 1922. She received the M.A. degree in Psychology from Columbia University in 1946. She is a candidate for the Ph.D. degree in Psychology from Ohio State University in September, 1951. She is an Associate of the American Psychological Association. While at Ohio State University, she has worked as Clinical Psychologist for the Ohio State University Hospital, has been a U. S. Public Health scholar, and has interned at the Bureau of Juvenile Research. In addition, for the past two years, she has been an Assistant Instructor in the Department of Psychology and has taught practicum courses in projective techniques with Dr. Rotter. Her special interests are personality theory, projective techniques, and psychotherapy.

## SELECTED REFERENCES

ROTTER, JULIAN B., Studies in the Use and Validity of the Thematic Apperception Test with Mentally Disordered Patients. I. Methods of Analysis and Clinical Problems. *Character and Personality*, 1940, *9*, 18–34.

——— Thematic Apperception Tests: Suggestions for Administration and Interpretation. *Journal of Personality*, 1946, *15*, 70–92.

## RESUME OF METHOD

THIS CLINICAL METHOD proceeds in five steps: (a) The entire protocol is read for suggestive leads (mood, unusual plots, unique verbalizations, methods of solving problems, and frequency of specific themes) and for the formulation of tentative interpretations and questions to be investigated further; (b) each story is analyzed for basic ideas and structural characteristics and is compared with plot norms; (c) each story is considered as a unit in order to identify the characters, the conflicts, and the relationships, to decide whether the material is wishful, autobiographical, or superficial, and to select hypotheses on the basis of consistency; (d) all the stories are considered as one organized combined unit; and (e) the interpretive hypotheses are integrated in to a final summary under five categories: familial attitudes, social and sexual attitudes, general (educational, vocational, etc.) attitudes, personality characteristics, and etiological implications.

## TAT WORKING NOTES

*Step I—General impressions.*

The method of analysis employed here makes use, ordinarily, of background information, such as the education and vocation of the subject, the age, education, and vocation of siblings and parents, etc. This information helps to define the individual's sub-culture and family constellation and is of aid to the clinician in identifying some of the figures used in the TAT stories and in making a more valid interpretation of the subject's interaction with his meaningful environment. Consequently, the interpretations made in this study will be offered with caution and will be subject to certain limitations due to the lack of background information.

The first step in making a TAT analysis includes a reading of the entire protocol for suggestive leads. Notation is made of mood, unusual plots, unique verbalizations, methods of solving problems, and frequency of specific thema. Alternative hypotheses for the interpretation of the various stories are considered. Questions are raised about interpersonal relationships requiring clarification and about therapeutic implications. The potential answers are dependent on the more detailed analysis to be presented in the following sections.

A first superficial reading of John Doe's protocol suggested the following hypotheses and questions. A check on the validity of these hypotheses will be made on the basis of internal consistency and personality dynamics.

In story 1, John's characterization of the child, sick in bed, may indicate that he utilized illness for gaining affection and protection and for avoiding problem situations. We might guess that John has stepped up his educational level through informal reading beyond high school. The sentence about the "blank eyes" raises the question as to the subject's contact with reality.

In story 3BM, the problem of sex and moral guilt is introduced. Who is the nun in the story? Does John have a sister whom he is describing here? Does he fear revelation of his sexual conflicts and guilt to his family? The nature of the sexual conflict needs further clarification in the other stories. The stabbing which takes place at the end raises the question as to whether S. may be contemplating suicide.

Reiteration of sexual conflict and guilt appears in story 4. Again, death is utilized as a solution for a conflict situation. Are attempted suicide or homicide potential future actions for John?

What is the meaning of the filicide in story 6BM? Is this John's method of alleviating guilt in the story? Reality contact and modes of solving problems are inadequate. Is the prevalent sexual conflict in these stories specifically related to incestuous feelings? Is John's dependency on his mother's approval as contrasted to his other needs for outside relationships creating conflicts? The familiarized use of the theatre as a setting suggests that John or his mother may have vocational affiliations with dramatics.

John appears to consider his own adjustment as precarious in story 7BM. What is his relationship to his father? Does John tend to project blame for his own difficulties on his father? Perhaps John's father is dead, or perhaps the theme of a father's death may be interpreted as an Oedipal wish (related to the preceding story of dependency on the mother).

In 12M, some identification with art and artists is seen. Does John regard himself as strongly dependent?

What is the identity of the "impossible to obtain" girl in story 13MF? Is the subject referring to his mother and/or sister? Have incestuous feelings or actions precipitated the sexual conflict seen throughout these stories?

In the references to affection and rejection in story 13B, we see suggestions of John having undergone psychotherapy at one time. Has he read much about psychological problems? Have relationships with a sibling been a source of conflict for John? Again the importance of the mother is stressed and the solution (wishful?) to the story reinforces a hypothesis of Oedipal wishes.

Story 14 is both violent and aggressive. Is there a danger of the subject committing harm to a frustrating person at some time? Does he require supervision? What is the role of the minister and of religion in general? Is religion one source of satisfaction for John's dependency needs? Is he fearful of authority figures in the role of minister and policeman?

The theme of story 16 again raises the problem of John's poor contact with reality, his inadequate relationships with other people, and his feeling of isolation and withdrawal. Some of the statements about need for communication lead us to ask again as to whether therapy has been a part of his experience. Has John ever hallucinated and reassured himself that "it could all be imagination"?

In summary, the following appear to be important problems and hypotheses to investigate more fully.

Has John engaged in considerable informal intellectual pursuits since High School? Has he ever specifically been engaged in the theatre? Does he view behavior either as good or bad and feel guilty about deviation from somewhat rigid moral standards? What is the nature of the strong sexual conflict which recurs in these stories? Are incestuous feelings or behaviors a source of conflict? John appears to be strongly dependent on his mother. The relationship needs further clarification. Was John ever displaced by a younger sibling with whom he continued to rival? John appears to feel estranged from other people and has difficulty in communicating with them. Does he achieve satisfaction of social acceptance needs through withdrawal and symbolic and irreal behaviors? Has this pattern of withdrawal become so marked as to make him unable to cope with daily problems? John appears to consider himself maladjusted and sees little hope for recovery. Does he have partial insight regarding his conflicts, or is he repeating interpretations made to him in the course of therapy?

Aggressive feelings toward other people are evidenced in these stories. Has some aggressive act precipitated referral? Concern with death and suicide is manifested. Does suicide represent for John a logical outcome of his withdrawal in response to his guilt feelings?

*Steps II, III, and IV (combined).*

Step II: Each story is analyzed for basic trends of repeated ideas and for certain structural characteristics, such as mood, disturbance in thought processes, concern with detail, etc. Reference is made to informal norms of plots for each picture.

Step III: Consideration of the stories as a whole unit. Each story is considered as a possible expression of an important conflict or conflicts or description of relationships as the subject sees them. The examiner is faced with the problem of identifying the characters and deciding whether the material is wishful, autobiographical, or superficial. Selection is made of alternative hypotheses on the basis of their consistency with other stories and their contribution to a unified description of the subject's personality. The hypotheses offered represent those with the highest degree of probability; they are not statements of certainty.

Step IV—*Consideration of the stories as an organized combined unit.*

1. Has illness, as attributed to the central character, been a method utilized by S. for avoiding threatening school and social situations, and as a way of obtaining parental affection and protection. S. characterizes himself as studious and appears to prefer solitary reading to communal activities. Satisfaction is gained through withdrawal, through identification in adventure stories, and conflicts are avoided through illness and sleep. The statement about eyes being blank tends toward the illogical and indicates an unusual concern with details. The reference "he does not fear the chance that his parents will find him," suggests that fear did play a role in the subject's childhood and that he anticipated punishment for not conforming to parental commands.

3BM. The theme of grief, frustration, and suicide is a frequent one for this picture. For John, shame and guilt are sources of grief and sex is a source of conflict. Does he feel guilty because of unacceptable desires or overt acts? In this story, the role of the family as a disapproving agent is again mentioned, only more strongly than in 1. The subject considers punishment for his sins necessary, but is most ashamed of disclosure and recognition on the part of others of secrets about himself. His characterization of the sister as a nun suggests that someone in the family (perhaps his mother or a sister) has imposed on him severe, almost unobtainable, standards of morality. Departure from these standards on his part is equivalent to loss of this familial figure. The suicidal solution suggests that John is inordinately dependent on the approval of his sister or mother, since potential loss of approval leaves him with no other solution but death. Description of the central figure as being familiar with the police and involved in newspaper publicity suggests the possibility that the subject, himself, may have been previously involved with the law and the press. On the other hand, it may be expressive of a wish for punishment by isolation from others and a fear of recognition of his behavior on the part of family and society.

4. Why does the subject mention half-caste? In this story, illicit sexual relationships are punished (as in 3BM). John again describes deviation from his sexual code, for which he desires and accepts punishment. He rejects responsibility in regard to family and child-bearing. The death solution, through arson, suggests that S. is highly conflicted and has few modes of satisfaction, since death appears to be the only alternative. It is an illogical conclusion and reinforces a hypothesis of poor reality contact.

6BM. For the third time, the central character is punished for sexual behavior and aggression. The punishing agent this time is the mother, suggesting that John has been involved in behavior his mother would consider highly unacceptable. Strong guilt for deviating from his mother's standards apparently can be alleviated only by the disapproval of and punishment by his mother. The extremity of the punishment described is illogical as a solution, and suggests a break with reality. The use of a theater scene and the indirect communication of his behavior suggests that the subject fears face-to-face relationships and feels more secure in fantasy and symbolism. The question also arises as to whether acting has been in John's or his mother's repertory.The central character's aggression against an unfaithful girl points up S's heterosexual inadequacy, jealousy, and rigid moral standards. Two major hypotheses are suggested by the aggression and counter-aggression in these last three stories in relationship to sex. The subject may have been involved in aggressive anti-social behavior related to sex—perhaps rape or homicide—and is now suffering intense guilt. Or, the subject may be punishing himself, in fantasy, for impulses, feelings, and attitudes which are highly unacceptable to him. In view of the preponderance of unreal, withdrawing, and fantasy behaviors in the previous stories, the latter hypothesis appears to be more tenable.

7BM. Illness is again mentioned as a theme (see story 1), this time as a problem. A sickness dependent on "will" for cure may be "mental illness," regarding which John has "little hope" for recovery. He equates himself and his father by stating that the father also had this illness as a young man. This may be autobiographical or a projection of blame for his difficulties on his father. The sins of the father are visited upon the children? The father is not seen as a sympathetic figure and S. has a low anticipation of protection or assistance from him. He reacts by rejection of his father. John's concern with the necessity of the father repenting indicates that he feels a strong grievance against this parent figure. Mention of a wife and family to support, coupled with concern about this responsibility, suggest that the subject feels or has felt economic insecurity. Possibly his father has held the purse strings, making the subject unwillingly dependent on him. Perhaps economic insecurity is used as a rationalization against marriage, feared because of inability to achieve a heterosexual adjustment.

11. S. projects his needs and attitudes readily through fantasy and symbolism, although many subjects have difficulty with this picture or give a stereotyped plot. John appears to be of above average intelligence in terms of vocabulary, high level abstractions, and complexity of plot. John's interest in abstractions and concern with rigid moral values of good and evil are most evident here. Guilt is again a theme, indicated by S's identification with "lost souls." Apparently no escape from punishment is considered; "wickedness" leads to greater wickedness. The careful description of the objects in the pictures, as in story 1, suggest a perfectionistic concern with details. Depression, threats from the outside world, and gloom pervade the mood of this story.

12M. Economic insecurity is again seen as a possible problem. Interest in art is manifested. The director, who can offer security, may be the father of 7BM who comes to the hero's aid "too late." He may also represent a therapist and John's pessimistic attitude toward therapy. At the same time, S's need for protection-dependency is depicted as strong in this story.

13MF. Again, shame and guilt are the resultants of sexual relationships. The occurrence of shame when the lights are on suggests the inability of S to face his problems and his tendency to withdraw from the light of discovery. John again rejects promiscuity and appears to have an idealized picture of the girl "he couldn't get." Perhaps this is autobiographical, and he is mourning a lost love object. Perhaps the girl he couldn't get is his mother or sister, with "Oedipal problems" being a source of his guilt. Dichotomizing of good and bad is again observed.

13B. Fear of displacement by a younger child with competition for his mother's love are major themes of this story. John appears to have a low expectancy of affection from his father (as in 7BM). Is the story a wish on S's part for more affection from his mother? Perhaps he was his mother's favorite and perhaps his father bestowed more affection on a younger sibling. John appears, again, to be rejecting his father. In this story he competes with his father, successfully, for his mother's love. The story, together with the previous ones, supports the hypothesis of extreme dependency on his mother.

14. The sequence and plot become confused. Aggression and hostility toward others is revealed. S's need for confession and expiation as well as fear of disclosure of his sins is revealed (as in 3BM). The role of the minister may be related to S's dependency on religion.

16. Withdrawal, in this story, leads to destruction. S. feels his inability to communicate with other people adequately and recognizes this as a major problem contributing to his maladjustment. The possibility of therapy having taken place

at some time is suggested by this partial insight. John suffers from a feeling of lack of understanding on the part of others and has little hope for recovery. He displays partial insight here, or is possibly reiterating interpretation given him.

## TAT INTERPRETATION

*Step V—Integration of interpretative hypotheses into a final summary.*

1. *Familial attitudes.*

In the family constellation, John's mother appears to be most important to him and the person on whom he is dependent for affection, protection, and moral guidance. The standards he has learned from her are rigid and the dichotomy between good and evil is sternly drawn. S is extremely dependent on his mother's approval and loss of her approval is considered tantamount to death or suicide. At present, he appears to be conflicted in that his sex needs and his interpretation of his mother's standards are in opposition. John feels guilty of having violated his mother's moral code and expects and seeks punishment from her to relieve his guilt. Possibly his sexual desires are directed toward his mother or sister, and being reprehensible and unacceptable to him have created guilt and confusion.

John's father appears to be of lesser importance to him and he appears to regard him as potentially unsatisfying to his needs for affection and dependency. There is some suggestion of a tendency to project the blame for his own shortcomings on his father, and perhaps to attribute his present maladjustment to this parent. Perhaps John was dependent on his father economically and rebelled against the potential limitation that this implied. S's reaction to frustration from his father is to reject him and to fantasy repentance on the father's part for his unsatisfactory role. John is unable to disregard his father completely and appears to be competing with him for his mother's affection.

It is not known whether S has any siblings. From several of the stories, we can infer that displacement, whether actual or fantasied, was a threat to him. He probably has a younger sibling and suffered some loss of affection from his mother and father. Competition with siblings, if any exist, probably was in the direction of attempting to achieve and maintain the standards of morality imposed by the mother. Another method probably used by John to reinstate his mother's affection and support was to become sick and helpless.

2. *Social and sexual attitudes.*

There is little evidence of pleasure gained through social activities or relationships with people outside of the immediate family. John appears to be a solitary, withdrawn person who fears social disapproval and censure. He avoids such disapproval by engaging in solitary pursuits. The low degree of striving on his part for social belongingness suggests that, historically, withdrawal has been a long-term pattern for him. It is possible that S was an overprotected and sickly child who gained most of his satisfactions from being home with his mother and reading and daydreaming. Continuation of these satisfying activities may have reduced his opportunity to learn social skills. At present, he apparently feels unable to communicate adequately with others and misses a feeling of understanding and belongingness.

Sex is a major source of conflict for S. The predominant theme for many of these stories revolves about sex, guilt and shame. Sex is considered to be evil for this subject and promiscuity is punished by death and suicide. Two possibilities as to the etiology for the present sex guilt are offered. John may have fantasied sex acts which have been highly unacceptable to him and which have become so disturbing that he is obsessed with guilt and the need for punishment. Or he may have been involved, recently, in an aggressive antisocial act involving rape, homicide, incest, adultery, or homosexuality, which precipitated his referral. This also would lead to extreme guilt, in that it conflicts with his learned sexual attitudes. The first hypothesis seems more likely and is consistent with the interpretation of John as an individual who has little freedom of movement in his attempts to gain affectional need satisfaction and who has adopted a majority of irreal and symbolic behaviors.

John may have experienced rejection from some love object in the past and felt unable to compete with other men. He is concerned with "good" versus "bad" and tends to spurn the promiscuous and yearn for the unobtainable. Whether the unobtainable is a specific person, such as mother, sister, married woman, or girl friend, or whether this refers to his difficulty in obtaining any heterosexual satisfaction, is not entirely clear. There is a strong indication that incestuous conflicts have played an important role for S and have helped to contribute to his present maladjustment.

3. *General attitudes*. (Educational, vocational, religious, economic, etc.)

John is interested in art, literature, and the theatre, sometimes characterized as culturally defined feminine interests. After High School, he probably extended his knowledge informally through reading and studying and he appears to be identified with superior intellectual interests. S is concerned with problems of religion, ethics, and morality. Vocational aspirations are not clear, but he probably would like to be identified with one of the arts. He or his family may have been occupied in the theatre at some time. His actual vocation is undeterminable and there is little evidence of his having achieved vocational success.

John has probably been exposed to economic insecurity at some time. He may have resented economic dependency on his father. Perhaps his own job has been financially unrewarding or he has experienced considerable unemployment.

Religion appears to be a source of comfort to the subject. He seeks a confessor and an expiator.

4. *Description of personality characteristics.*

The subject appears to be of above average intelligence (probably Wechsler I.Q. above 125, verbal I.Q. higher than performance I.Q.). His stories are well constructed, original and fairly complex and indicate some creative and literary ability.

John's concern with explanation of details suggests a perfectionistic approach to problems. His solutions of problems are generally irreal and symbolic and he appears to be in severe conflict in his interpersonal relationships. Withdrawal, aggression against others and himself appear to be his major modes of reaction to frustration.

A major source of conflict lies in the discrepancy between his level of aspiration (especially in regard to morality) and his attainments. He is critical of deviance in himself and others. John considers himself maladjusted and has low hopes for recovery. He sometimes contemplates suicide. The preceding descriptions lead to an over-all impression of an individual who would probably be diagnosed as "schizophrenic."

5. *Summary and etiologic implications.*

Since we do not know whether John's parents are living and whether or not he has any siblings, we cannot be clear as to the present status of S's relationship to them.

John appears to have been an overprotected child who was reared by a dominating mother, toward whom he feels some ambivalence. He may have been displaced by a sibling at some time. There is some evidence in the stories suggesting that S has a sister. Female influences were strong in the home and John appears to have learned feminine interests from his mother and/or sister. He may have been a sickly and weak child. There is a strong possibility that S made use of illness as a way of avoiding threatening social and academic situations and as a way of gaining his mother's affection and protection. This mode of behavior may have been learned early or at the time that a possible sibling entered the familial picture. John's father does not appear to have been as important a source of affection as his mother. S may project some of his present problems on his father. Perhaps the father was an inadequate and weak person in many ways and, at the same time, threatening to John. He does not appear to have achieved an adequate identification with his father or any masculine person in his environment. Rigidity of moral standards appears to have played an important role in the family and S has attempted to conform. S's sex education may have been inadequate.

Such poor relationships with other people are demonstrated in these stories that we are led to suspect that S never adequately learned social skills or achieved meaningful peer relationships. He appears to have incestuous desires toward his mother or toward a sister. This has precipitated intense conflict on his part, since such desires are unacceptable socially and present punishing consequences. Consequently, his relationships with females have been poor, possibly leading to his dichotomizing between "good and bad" girls and restricting sexual relationships mainly to prostitutes. Guilt and retreat have been the resultants of these conflicts. Since he has few realistic modes of gaining satisfaction, John has learned to solve his problems through unrealistic, illogical, symbolic, and avoidant means. He has tended to withdraw from social relationships and to fantasy satisfaction for his dependent and affectional needs. The intensity of his fantasies about aggression and suicide raises the practical problem of the necessity for supervision for S until he has received adequate therapy.

The subject displays partial insight as to his problems of affection and rejection, and as to his need for communication and the danger of withdrawal. Perhaps he has learned to reiterate these things as a function of interpretations made in therapy.

In a therapeutic situation, John may be resistant toward and fearful of an authority figure. But, he has strong dependency needs and is likely to form an intense attachment to the therapist if an adequate relationship is achieved. Because of the subject's tendency to seek symbolic solutions to his problems, it would seem that the early stages of therapy should deal with acceptance and the establishing of a relationship. Probing or interpretations made early in the therapy might serve to threaten John and force him to withdraw and make use of fantasy satisfactions. Since John has learned so few useful and positive modes of dealing with his problems, therapy would probably need to be a long-term learning experience.

## MAPS TEST WORKING NOTES

The same procedure used in analyzing the TAT will be employed here. A major difficulty presents itself in interpreting the MAPS test, in that detailed norms (to supplant the lack of extensive clinical experience with this test) for selection of figures for the various backgrounds and for frequent plots are not available.[1]

*Step I—General impressions.*

An over-all reading of this protocol suggests the following hypotheses to serve as landmarks in making a more detailed interpretation. In addition,

[1] Limited norms of this level are available for various adult populations [21, 49, 52] (*Editor's Note*).

several questions can be raised and some partially answered in making further interpretations.

For the first background (Livingroom), John selects a legendary figure and an animal figure, as well as others. We do not know how usual this is, but his continuing to select a large number of legendary and ambiguous figures suggests a disturbance in social relationships. Does the subject make use of symbolic and irreal methods of obtaining satisfaction?

On the first story, and all the way through, there is evidence of bizarreness, illogical thinking, and dissociation, which raises the question of whether the subject is psychotic and in need of hospitalization.

In story 1, John makes use of the mother and distorts her identity. Hostility is manifested in this story toward the mother and a possible sister. Is John the daughter in this story and is the plot indicative of rejection of the mother? Is concern about the mother's face a function of a professional need, such as in acting, for attractiveness, or is it a symbolic description about the relationship with the mother. What does the fear of old age mean to John?

In story 2 (Street), John again selects legendary figures and the question of withdrawal tendencies is raised. Sexual rejection, infidelity, reprisal, are important problems for the subject. That is something that requires further investigation in the full analysis. Concern with the mother's face is again manifested. It appears that many of his conflicts are related to his mother.

Story 4 (Dream) is extremely illogical and problems of aggression, rivalry, and sex guilt are again posed. Illogicality is seen throughout; e.g.; "father poisoned because he did not have hair like other fathers did." Intrafamilial relationships are disturbed and we wonder about the possibility of incestuous conflicts for S.

In story 5 (Bedroom), sex is portrayed as violent and aggressive, and S. is troubled by guilt feelings for actions or fantasies or both. Rape of the "daughter" again raises the problem of possible incestuous feelings toward a sister.

Concern with insanity is evidenced. Does S make use of irreal behavior as an avoidant mechanism? Is he concerned about his level of adjustment? Does he make use of maladjustment as a rationalization for unacceptable behavior?

The world appears to be a very threatening place in story 6 (Blank), and filled with forces of evil. Is John's concern with ethical problems of good and evil a function of guilt and anticipation of punishment? Is John experiencing a break with reality?

In story 7 (Stage), legendary and ambiguous figures are again selected, reinforcing a hypothesis of withdrawal tendencies. Interest in the theatre is evidenced. Is this autobiographical and related to vocational or avocational interests, or is it symbolic of the role the subject plays? The story is confused and illogical. Concern with facial appearance is again manifested. Generalized hostility and aggression are demonstrated. Does the attribution of magic power to the statue relate to "paranoid" behavior on John's part?

In summary, the first over-all reading of the protocol gives rise to the following leads, problems, and questions.

What is the subject's relationship to his mother and possible sister? Is incest a problem for him? What is the meaning of the excessive concern about faces, loss of faces, etc.? Does the frequent use of legendary figures suggest that withdrawal is a significant pattern of behavior for the subject? What does the utilization of the theatre mean to John? Is John psychotic? Is his contact with reality sufficiently poor to warrant hospitalization? Is there a danger of homicide, sex aggression or suicide?

*Steps II, III, and IV—Individual story hypotheses.*

We wish to emphasize that interpretations are made with considerable caution since we do not know the norms for selection of figures and plots.

A preliminary step can be made to help us in interpreting. What is the relative frequency of the categories of figures selected?

| | | | | | |
|---|---|---|---|---|---|
| M | 7 | 23% | I | 4 | 13% |
| F | 5 | 16% | N | 3 | 10% |
| L | 5 | 16% | A | 2 | 6% |
| S | 4 | 13% | C | 1 | 3% |

Of these, 42 per cent of the figures are men, women, and children from the predominant culture group. The minority group figures, legendary, indefinite, and silhouette figures comprise 55 per cent of the subject's selection. Animal figures are chosen 3 per cent of the time. We do not know what the significance of these figures is for the general population, but selection does appear to be heavily overweighted with "less usual and less everyday" figures.

*Story 1* (Livingroom). The use of the lion for the mother, the snake in the living room and the entrance of the policeman appear to have special significance for the subject. Why is the mother distorted and grotesque? Does making her a lion indicate that John's mother has been dominant and aggressive? Does the inclusion of a snake mean that his mother is sexually tempting to him? Is the subject the daughter in the story, or the "son in a jam" or is he both. Can the daughter be a sister of John's? The subject appears to be rejecting his mother and considering her as ugly and evil. The mother is seen as mistrustful of people—"all snakes don't wear clothes"; i.e., some snakes do? are people? Does the marred face refer to physical disability; is it symbolic of evil, is it related to growing old, which S. and/or his mother find threatening and distasteful? Does John wish to distort his mother so as to make her less sexually attractive to him. Referral to the injury coincident with birth may refer to a feeling of long-term rejection on John's part; i.e., he was instrumental in damaging his mother. Is the snake bite symbolic of sexual aggression on S's part? Is S the snake who is closest to his mother? And finally, rejection of the mother is punished.

Identification appears to shift and change. Our strongest hypotheses are those concerning the mother-son relationship. We have seen evidence that the subject has ambivalent feelings and sex urges toward his mother. He is concerned with her "ugliness and growing old." Perhaps S's mother is deformed in some way or perhaps old age as a detraction to attractiveness interferes with her work (acting?). An alternative hypothesis is that S. seeks to destroy his mother's attractiveness on a fantasy level so that she may be no longer sexually threatening to him. Another alternative is that S. feels strong hostility toward his mother and thus sees her as symbolic of evil; perhaps he is ashamed of her because of real or fantasied transgression on her part.

*Story 2* (Street). The figures selected are legendary, minority group figures or silhouettes. Is this a function of the importance of the problem and the need to push it further away from him by selecting figures removed from his cultural milieu? Is this an indication of S's tendency to fantasize and withdraw from social relationships? "Degraded, but still beautiful." Is this a broad implication that moral deviation does or should lead to loss of attractiveness? Then, perhaps in story 1, the distortion of the mother's features was a function of John's attitude toward her. Perhaps he regarded his mother as degraded for some actions on her part or for being instrumental in precipitating his sexual conflict? Does he fear sexual rejection and infidelity? Does the accidental slaying of the girl represent S's hostility toward some female who has been unfaithful? The aggression is punished and the loss of the loved object leads to suicide. Sex is regarded as degrading in this story. Is the subject punishing himself for illicit sexual urges? Does he project his own inadequacies on females and fear his inability to hold one? Or is this a continuation of the conflict with mother or sister?

*Story 3* (Bathroom). Again, other than usual figures are chosen. The mother theme is repeated. As in story 1, there is concern about the outward change in her appearance. Does John wish to depersonalize his mother so as to make her more accessible? By not permitting her to grow old, does he make her more nearly a girl friend? Does S. make his mother mute and blind so that she cannot observe or criticize his behavior? Does he also make her inaccessible to everyone else but himself?

*Story 4* (Dream). In addition to the male and female, a series of less ordinary figures are chosen. Perhaps, for a dream sequence, this is not unusual. The story is confused and bizarre in many ways. Is John the middle-aged woman? If so, a death wish is evidenced toward the father, hostility toward a sister, and possible homosexual conflict is described. Is John, on the other hand, describing his mother, again? Does he regard her as immoral and evil? Is S. the other man whom the mother seduced? Perhaps S. feels that his mother has betrayed him by being sexually unfaithful to him and/or to his father. Perhaps he is projecting his own incestuous desires onto his mother.

*Story 5* (Bedroom). If John is identifying with the man, he appears to be describing an act of rape and possibly of incest which he fantasied or in which he was involved. If so, he regards himself as demented and, hence, not responsible for his actions. Disclosure of his feelings or acts leads to shame and guilt, followed by suicide as the only solution left to him. S. appears to have strong aggressive feelings toward women and has a need to dominate them. Does he have violent sex desires toward his sister or mother? Does this lead to guilt and self-destruction?

*Story 6* (Blank). John is concerned with abstractions, life and death, and infinity. He regards life as threatening and fears evil and destruction. Is he the young man followed and threatened in an almost paranoid-like fashion? Does he fear old age and loss of power and strength? Is the frightened woman also S? Could it be a sister or girl-friend whose relationship is tinged with evil for him? Does the searching and not searching characterize his ambivalent feelings toward a companion or love object? Is the older woman the mother whose old age makes her less important or less threatening? Is the use of crutches for the young man symbolic of some felt inadequacy on his part; might it specifically be symbolic of his sex urges which he wishes to avoid because of the conflict arising? Evil is punished and the "answer" to all suffering never becomes clear. S. has attempted to conceptualize the nature of his difficulties and has become lost in a maze of symbolism and bizarre abstractions. He is fearful and dependent, but anticipates little comfort in his conflict and suffering.

*Story 7* (Stage). The subject's selection of the stage background coincides with his mention of the theatre and dramatics in the TAT. Is S. or some member of his family connected with the theatre? Or does drama serve as a convenient medium for projecting his difficulties? The indeterminate figure is chosen and described as a girl. Is homosexuality a problem for S? Does he tend to have some feminine identifications? Some concern about role or "origin" of this figure is mentioned. The girl is unclothed. Would John like to exhibit himself? Would he like recognition from a large group? He is concerned about the reality or unreality of his ideas. The old lady is portrayed as aggressive, fiendish, and demented. What is the role of the priest in S's life? Is religion as the source of an ethical code and guilt a source of conflict for S? A girl enters without a face. This is a repetition of previous themes. Ultimate power is invested in the statue who is instrumental in destroying all. Does John feel that people are insincere in their motives and that they have the power to destroy him (last sentence)? And is he the statue who avenges all his frustrations by destroying all the threatening people in his environment?

## MAPS TEST INTERPRETATION

*Step V—Integration of hypotheses into final summary.*

1. *Familial attitudes.* The role of the mother and possibly a sister seems to be extremely important and a source of great conflict for the subject. The role of the father is less clear. There is a strong possibility that marital relationships

were not too satisfactory for his mother and father and that S competed with his father for his mother's love and affection and has felt death wishes toward his father.

S has ambivalent feelings toward his mother and sister. He appears to be sexually attracted to his mother and/or sister and is in conflict because of the cultural ordainments against incestuous behavior. He demonstrates strong aggressive feelings toward this female whom he wishes to dominate. He feels guilty because of those sexual desires and punishes both the love object and himself. S is a dependent person who appears to have been dominated by his mother and who resents potential rivals in a strong and hostile manner. His guilt leads to projection of his own unacceptable desires on the mother with feelings of aggression toward her. His concern about his mother's face and old age is difficult to evaluate. He may be making her faceless in order to depersonalize her and thus make her more accessible as a sex object. He may be desensitizing her so as to avoid blame and censure from her. And the mother, herself, may be dependent on appearance for sustenance—actress, prostitute, etc., and so be concerned, herself, about the effects of the aging process. Perhaps, like Dorian Gray, John is fearful of having the effects of his behavior show in his face and so removes all such effects. S may be somewhat ashamed of his mother, culturally, and rejecting of her way of life.

2. *Social and sexual attitudes.*

In all of the stories, poor interaction is seen between the central figure and the other characters. Relationships are marked by aggression, hostility, domination, suspicion, and lack of warmth. John views other people as threatening and expects and anticipates punishment and destruction from them. He would like to be powerful and be able to dominate them. He apparently anticipates little satisfaction in social relationships and tends to achieve satisfaction for his needs for affection, domination, recognition, and dependency on a symbolic level. He may have worked in theatrical groups and gained some recognition in that fashion, but it is doubtful that he achieved a good working relationship with his peers. S's withdrawal is abnormal.

John appears to fantasize sex experiences with members of his family—mother or sister or both—and is in a state of conflict because of the unacceptability of such behavior. Perhaps he has actually engaged in such behavior. S sees sex as degrading, evil, and something that should be punished. Perhaps he has had rigid training about sex and overreacts to what might be casual to others. In John's fantasies, he sees himself as strong, dominating and violently aggressive. He may have fantasied rape or actually have been involved in an aggressive act. He tends to project blame for wishes or behaviors on the evil of other people.

3. *General attitudes.*

John appears to have had informal education beyond High School and probably has done a lot of reading, theatre-going, etc. Possibly he was identified with the theatre at one time or some member of his family was.

Religious identification is not clear, but perhaps, at one time, S was dependent on religion (Catholicism?) and has, by virtue of his training, found most of his present desires conflicting, untenable, and productive of guilt.

Broad social, political, or economic attitudes are not given voice in this protocol, since the greater part of it is concerned with immediate interpersonal and sexual problems.

4. *General personality characteristics.*

S is a person of above average intelligence, who has gained many satisfactions from reading and the theatre, especially the lurid, the melodramatic and the sexually complicated. He has learned to be interested in things which are often characterized as feminine, such as the theatre, personal attractiveness. He is a rather dependent person, possibly overprotected by his mother and without a close identification with his father. He has been frustrated by the social unacceptability of many of his desires and takes refuge in fantasy and withdrawal. His fantasies revolve about aggression and counter-aggression, violent sexual activities, broad and bizarre abstractions about the nature of good and evil, and concern about punishment, which he anticipates for almost anything he does. He is mistrustful of others and projects his own attitudes on them. The kinds of behaviors he manifests would probably lead to a diagnosis of "schizophrenic," possibly "paranoid schizophrenic."

5. *Summary and etiologic implications*

S appears to have come from a home where his mother played the most dominant and significant role. He is deeply attached to his mother and she (perhaps also a sister) is his major source of love and protection. He has learned to feel a strong sexual attraction to his mother and has been unable to generalize his sexual feelings to other women. He is in conflict between his desire to be closer to his mother and his feeling about the unacceptability of such behavior. Since he has no alternative sources of love and affection, and since he anticipates punishment for sexual intercourse with his mother, he has withdrawn into fantasy and visualizes satisfactions of a violent and aggressive nature in which he gains satisfaction for his need for domination and for affection. The cultural pressures to be manly have set up a conflict and since he has no available behaviors for demonstrating his masculinity he fantasies aggression toward females. Part of this aggression appears to be a function of ambivalent feelings toward his mother and his need to punish her for setting up intolerable conflicts for him.

To defend himself, John tends to project his own unacceptable feelings on others and sees the world as threatening and evil. Because of his aggressive fantasies against others and himself and his low anticipation of acceptance and satisfaction, there is a strong possibility that S might become dangerous to himself and others. This suggests the need for hospitalization, supervision, or protection at home while being treated on an out-patient basis. Therapy for John would be difficult, since he has so few socially acceptable behaviors in his repertoire. These new behaviors would have to be provided so that he might find acceptable ways of satisfying his needs for love and affection, dependency, recognition, and domination. He also needs help in developing a goal of independence and for generalizing his dependency on his mother toward more socially mature objects and relationships. S may also be in need of sex education and reorientation of his sexual attitudes. His learned attitudes of dichotomizing good and evil will provide another difficulty in therapy.

# Chapter 16

# HELEN D. SARGENT

Dr. Sargent was born in 1904. She received the M.A. degree in 1934 and the Ph.D. degree in 1944 from Northwestern University. Before going to the Winter V.A. Hospital in Topeka as Chief Clinical Psychologist and Associate Professor of Clinical Psychology at the University of Kansas, she taught at Northwestern University, where she was also Assistant Director of the Psychological Clinic, from 1932 to 1943, and consultant to the Family Service of Evanston, the Evanston public schools, and the Northshore Health Resort. She is a Diplomate in Clinical Psychology of the American Board of Examiners in Professional Psychology and a Fellow in the American Psychological Association. She is best known for her critical review of projective methods which appeared in the *Psychological Bulletin* in 1945 and for her monograph, "An Experimental Application of Projective Principles to a Paper and Pencil Personality Test." At present she is at work on a revision of the Insight Test and a manual for its use which will appear in book form.

## SELECTED REFERENCES

*A. Sargent Insight Test Scoring Method*

SARGENT, HELEN, An Experimental Application of Projective Principles to a Paper and Pencil Personality Test. *Psychological Monographs*, 1944, *57*, No. 265, 1–57.

———, Projective Techniques: Their Origins, Theory and Application in Personality Research. *Psychological Bulletin*, 1945, *5*, 257–293.

———, *The Insight Test: Manual for Administration and Scoring.* (To be published.)

*B. Cox-Sargent TAT Normative Scoring Method*

COX, BEVERLY, AND SARGENT, HELEN, TAT Responses of Emotionally Disturbed and Emotionally Stable Children: Clinical Judgment versus Normative Data. *Journal of Projective Techniques*, 1950, *14*, 61–74.

## RESUME OF METHODS

### A. SARGENT INSIGHT TEST SCORING METHOD

THIS METHOD was originally developed for scoring written responses to the author's "Insight Test." Affects (A) are scored under twelve categories (pleasure, aggression, etc.), and three expressive modes (action, manifest and latent feeling expression)[1]; Defense Activities (D) are scored under three categories (evaluations, elaborations, and qualifications). Maladjustment (M) scores, based on the use of first person pronouns, irrelevant feeling expressions

[1] The classification of modes of feeling expression was not found applicable to the thematic material, but is important in the analysis of responses to the Insight Test, for which the scoring was designed.

and "subjectivism," are also obtained. The A/D ratio and the A-D-A/D pattern are evaluated and interpreted in terms of established norms, together with qualitative interpretation of content.

### B. Cox-Sargent TAT Normative Scoring Method

This scoring system is designed as a research tool for analyzing the normative aspects of responses to individual TAT pictures. It uses the following main categories: feelings (frustration, anxiety, etc.); heroes (man, girl, etc.); needs (security, conformity, etc.); threats (guilt, death, etc.); actions to meet need or evade threat (negative, evasive, etc.); and outcomes (success, failure, etc.).

## TAT WORKING NOTES: SARGENT INSIGHT TEST SCORING METHOD

*TAT Story No. 1.*

1. [This child is $^{(6)\ E1}$ *sick in bed*.] [He $^{E1}$ *has been given sheet music* to study,] but $^{Q}$ instead of the music, [he $^{E1}$ *has come across a novel*] that $^{(7)}$ *interests him more than the music*. It is [$^{Q}$ *probably*] an [$^{E1}$ *adventure story*.] He evidently $^{(10)}$ *does not fear* the chance that [his $^{E1}$ parents will find him thusly occupied] as he $^{(7)}$ *seems quite at ease*. He seems to be quite [a $^{E1}$ studious type] and perhaps $^{(10)}$ *regrets* missing school, but he seems $^{(7)}$ *quite occupied with the adventure* in the story. [$^{M\text{-}Ir.}$ Adventure has something to do with ocean or water.] He is $^{(6)}$ *not too happy*, though $^{(11)}$ *not too sad*. His $^{E1}$ *eyes are somewhat blank*—coincidence of ($^{M\text{-}Sj}$ reading a book without any eyes) or ($^{M\text{-}Sj}$ knowing what is in the book without reading it.) He $^{(5)}$ *disregards the music* and [$^{E1}$ *falls asleep reading the book*.]

*Comment:* Much conflict; anxiety avoidance with intrusion of psychotic ideation unsuccessfully evaded. Probably a decompensated obsessive-compulsive. Schizophrenic process in evidence. Guilt feelings may overwhelm the patient and he may become suicidal. Panicky fear of engulfment. Feelings of depersonalization not unlikely. Still superficially oriented. Able to follow instructions.

*Sargent Insight Test Scoring Summary Sheet*

| | |
|---|---|
| I. *Affect (A) Scores* | |
| A. *Sit. Apr.* | |
| 1. Frustration | 0 |
| 2. Facilitation | 0 |
| B. *Sit. Reaction* | |
| 3. Aggression | 0 |
| 4. Passivity | 0 |
| 5. Evasion | 1 |

| | |
|---|---|
| C. *Mood* | |
| 6. Depression | 2 |
| 7. Pleasure | 3 |
| D. *Relationship* | |
| 8. Positive attitude | 0 |
| 9. Negative attitude | 0 |
| E. *Stress* | |
| 10. Anxiety | 2 |
| 11. Conflict | 1 |
| 12. Rationalization | 0 |
| Total | 9 |
| II. *Ego-activity (E) Scores* | |
| 1. Evaluations | 0 |
| 2. Elaborations | 8 |
| 3. Qualifications | 2 |
| Total | 10 |
| III. *Maladjustment (M) Scores* | |
| 1. Pronouns in first person; irrelevant feeling | 1 |
| 2. Subjectivism | 2 |
| Total | 3 |
| IV. *Tabulations* | |
| A. Number of armatures answered | 1 |
| B. Total M | 3 |
| C. $\frac{\text{Raw A Score}}{\text{N}}$ | 9 |
| D. Converted[2] A score | 77 |
| E. $\frac{\text{Raw D Score}}{\text{N}}$ | 10 |
| F. Converted[3] D score | 94 |
| G. A/D Quotient | 81 |

*Summary:* The *Affect* score (A) and the *Defense activity* score (D) are both excessively high, A falling at plus two sigma and D at plus three sigma. The *AD* ratio is low, falling at minus one sigma (which is the mean for a group of veteran out-patients at a community clinic). The A-D-A/D pattern is thus H-H-LA, which has been found characteristic in obsessive compulsive disorders and in the overideational type of paranoid psychotic. Three *M* scores (*maladjustment indicators*) appear in two Sj and one Ir *subjectivism* scores. The range of feeling expression is fairly wide but lacking in spontaneity and sometimes inappropriate. Emphasis is upon avoidance and evasion of pervasive guilt with accompanying confusion. On the basis of the quantitative analysis, the patient may be best classified as a decompensating obsessive-compulsive neurotic in whom schizophrenic pathology is in process.

Qualitative analysis of this short sample suggests at least the possibility

[2, 3] Conversion to standard scores by means of tables to be published in *Manual.*

that the avoidance of anxiety and the effort to repress guilt are so unsuccessful as to give way to overwhelming panic at times, to a degree which may lead the patient to become suicidal. Feelings of depersonalization are not unlikely and/or delusions of mystical power (e.g., "blank eyes," "knowing what is in the book without reading it"). Awareness of illness is present (e.g., the child is "sick"). In spite of imminent ego breakdown, already in process, a portion of the defense structure is intact and the patient is probably not disoriented or entirely out of contact. Over-alertness, twisted detail and distant inference suggest paranoid ideation.

*Note:* The above interpretation is based on analysis of the first TAT story only. The writer chose the alternative (offered by the editor) of working from a single story rather than with the entire protocol, since the doubtful applicability of the Insight scoring method seemed not to justify detailed categorical analysis of the larger sample. It should be noted also that the quantitative scoring method utilized must be interpreted with caution when used with TAT or Insight tests administered orally, because of the differences between oral and written style which may be introduced. (Research on this question is now in progress.) Both A and D scores are apt to be elevated in oral protocols, although this is not always the case. This record contains much more *Elaboration* than is ordinarily found even in oral records, and suggests gross distortion of reality in terms of inner need which may reach psychotic proportions. In spite of the correction needed for the absolute levels of A and D scores, the significance of the ratio appears to hold in oral material.

## TAT WORKING NOTES: COX-SARGENT NORMATIVE APPROACH[4]

*TAT Story No. 1.*

A. Feeling categories:
- *2a.* Unhappiness; misery; grief; loneliness. (Where "2" is *depression*).
- *3d.* Enjoyment; interest. (Where "3" is *pleasure*).
- *4c.* Resistance; opposition. (Where "4" is *negative attitudes*).
- *6d.* Fear; worry; dread. (Where "6" is *anxiety and conflict*).

B. Hero categories:
- 3. Boy

C. Need categories:
- *2b.* Avoidance of death, illness and catastrophe. (Where "2" is *security*).

D. Threat categories:
- Intra-psychic threats.
- *1c.* Self-recrimination; consciousness of moral shortcomings. (Where "1" is *guilt*).

E. Action categories:
- 3. Evasive action.

F. Outcome categories:
- *3c.* Ending is asocial. (Where "3" is *modified success*).

[4] *Editor's note:* This section on the Cox-Sargent normative approach was written by Dr. Sargent.

*Comment*: Strong anxiety handled by avoidance and denial. Need unsatisfied: threats remain. Threats are intra-psychic, not outside. Vague spector haunts him. Water is important. Strong dependent, regressive needs. Breaking ego.

*Summary*: The dominant *need* in this story falls in the category "security" (security against psychic disaster) and the dominant *threat* is the underlying guilt and confusion with which the subject copes by evasive *action*. The final *outcome* solves the *need* and overcomes the *threat* only by escape. It should be noted that the threats to this individual are intra-psychic rather than external. It is the introjected parent figure which he "does not fear"—the fear showing through in this over-determined denial. Interpretively, water, symbolic of regression and deep dependent needs, suggests fear of engulfment associated with the dangerous encroachment of unsuccessfully repressed id impulses.

*Note*: The above scoring system is not designed for use with individual records but as a research tool for analyzing the normative aspects of response to the individual TAT pictures. It adds little except a schematic representation of the more obvious features of a TAT story.

*Over-all Summary*: On the basis of the story analyzed, plus a cursory perusal of the remainder of the record, it is believed that a diagnosis of paranoid schizophrenia, with advancing thought disorder but with preservation of affect and strong depressive coloring, is justified. There is, on the other hand, especially in the MAPS test, the suggestion of an hysterical, histrionic component which is not inconsistent with heavy reliance in the TAT on evasive defenses. One can feel quite certain that delusions are manifest clinically.

# Chapter 17

# PERCIVAL M. SYMONDS

Dr. Symonds was born in 1893 and has been Professor of Education at Teachers College, Columbia University, since 1924. A graduate of Harvard College of the class of 1915, he received his Ph.D. degree from Columbia University in 1923. For two years he was Professor of Education and Psychology at the University of Hawaii. He has been a member of the American Psychological Association since 1923, and is a Diplomate in Clinical Psychology of the American Board of Examiners in Professional Psychology. During World War II, he was senior staff psychologist in area S of the Office of Strategic Services. His main interest is in dynamic psychology and its applications to child guidance, mental hygiene and personality theory. At present he is carrying on extensive research in the counseling of teachers and in studying the relation of teaching personality to teaching effectiveness. He is the author of the following books: *Measurement in Secondary Education, Ability Standards for Standardized Achievement Tests in the High School, The Nature of Conduct, Tests and Interest Questionnaires in the Guidance of High School Boys, Diagnosing Personality and Conduct, Mental Hygiene of the School Child, Psychological Diagnosis in Social Adjustment, Measurement of the Personality Adjustments of High School Pupils, Education and the Psychology of Thinking, The Psychology of Parent-Child Relationships, The Dynamics of Home Adjustment, Dynamic Psychology, Adolescent Fantasy, Dynamics of Parent-Child Relationships, The Ego and the Self*. He is on the editorial boards of the *Journal of Educational Psychology, Journal of Educational Research, Psychological Monographs,* and *Personality Symposia*. He was President of the Educational Division of the American Psychological Association in 1947–1948, and at present is President of the New York Society of Clinical Psychologists.

## SELECTED REFERENCES


SYMONDS, PERCIVAL M., Criteria for the Selection of Pictures for the Investigation of Adolescent Phantasies. *Journal of Abnormal and Social Psychology*, 1939, *34*, 271–274.

———, *Symonds Picture-Story Test*. New York: Bureau of Publications, Teachers College, Columbia University, 1948. 20 plates; manual (20 pp.)

———, *Adolescent Fantasy*. New York: Columbia University Press, 1949. Pp. xii, 397.


## RESUME OF METHOD

THE GOAL of this method is "to get a picture of the dynamic structure of an individual's adjustment." It utilizes the impressions received from careful readings of the protocol as a whole, rather than from the separate stories. The data extracted from the stories are classified largely in terms of *themes* (aggression, love, punishment, anxiety, defenses, moral standards, conflicts, guilt, depression, forms of sublimation, etc.) and *relationships* (to parents, siblings, teachers, etc.). The final write-up attempts to synthesize the themes of primary importance and to indicate the dynamic relationships among them.

## TAT WORKING NOTES

In terms of technique, in general, I do not try to draw conclusions from separate stories even though different TAT pictures are supposed to draw out certain types of responses. Usually my plan is to read through the stories, carefully of course, and to give attention to the psychological themes that each contains. As I go through them, I am noting repetitions of themes. I find it difficult to keep these themes in mind and when I have finished reading through a set of stories it is my custom to start reading them through again in reverse order. Even then I do not attempt to force an interpretation but set them aside over a twenty-four hour period and read them again. Gradually, thematic material will take structure and certain of the themes begin to stand out as having primary importance and the dynamic relation between them begins to take some organization.

Sometimes I use the device of jotting down separate themes on small slips, together with the number of the story in which the theme appeared. These slips can then be sorted, classified and arranged in order to bring out the organization of the themes.

My goal is to attempt to get a picture of the dynamic structure of an individual's adjustments which tend to divorce themselves from the stories themselves and to take an entirely different organization.

## TAT INTERPRETATION

The principal theme expressed in this record is that of sexual aggression (4, 6BM, 11, 14). The aggression may result in murder (6BM), or total destruction (16). The aggression may have a revenge motive (14). The sexual fantasies of this subject have the dual nature of sacred and profane love (13MF) as described by Freud. On the one hand, themes of prostitution are introduced, while on the other hand, relationships toward a mother figure on a tender basis are included. Themes of illicit sexual relationships are given (3BM, 4, 13MF). There is guilt and punishment for the aggression (3BM, 16). However, this guilt is handled by self-punishment (3BM, 14), and by themes of suicide (3BM). Guilt is also handled in other ways by self-pity (12M), by poverty (4, 12M, 13B) and by reparation, repentance and confession (7BM, 14). The reaction toward sex is shame (3BM). Behind this principal theme of self-aggression are feelings of rejection (13B), of seduction (13MF), of being hungry (12M), of sibling rivalry (3BM and 13B). There is also an indication that there was fear of parents in connection with wrongdoing (1). Further reactions to the feeling of rejection and the attempt to meet this need by sexual aggression are found in themes of running away and separation (7BM, 11, 13B, 16) and in themes of depression (1, 7BM, 13MF). On the other hand, a cyclic tendency is indicated and the depression may easily be turned into feelings of elation when the subject feels that he is needed and as a result of receiving credit for excellence (12M, 13B). There is a tendency to rationalize (14) and to ascribe his difficulties to fate (11).

I should judge that the subject was a rather severely disturbed person, an individual who was severely repressed and found ways of taking care of deep-seated guilt feelings; what I am not able to tell from the stories is what his symptoms in real life are, what methods of defense he uses, or which ones of the many trends revealed by the stories are those which he expresses in his actual personality and behavior.[1]

[1] Dr. Symonds indicates that his "interpretation refers only to trends within the individual in the shape of drives, wishes, impulses and the like, and no implication is made with regard to how these trends may be expressed in the overt personality." Further, he indicates, in relation to blind interpretation of TAT and MAPS test protocols in general, his "point of view is that blind interpretation of projective materials is at best only hypothetical and that the value of projective materials is enhanced when they can be interpreted in the light of case history data. In my judgment, the more case history data are available the more significant and meaningful the projective material will be. With only sex, age, and marital status given, an interpretation is bound to be extremely tentative and I would hesitate to make a report on TAT material in an actual clinical situation with no more information about the subject. . . ."

# Chapter 18

# RALPH K. WHITE

Dr. White was born in 1907. He received the Ph.D. degree in Psychology from Stanford University in 1937. He is an Associate Member of the American Psychological Association. He has taught at Wesleyan University and Cornell University. From 1937 to 1939, at the State University of Iowa, he worked with Ronald Lippitt under Kurt Lewin on "experiments in autocracy and democracy" in small children's groups; with Lippitt he is now completing a book on these experiments. Since 1939 his interest has been primarily in the field of public opinion (with a focus on the psychological aspects of war and nationalism), and in the development of research methods in this field. The method of content-analysis which he calls "value analysis" is applicable to the public opinion type of data as well as to the personality-study type of data. A methodologic manual describing the method, and discussing also the general problems and pit-falls of content-analysis is now in press. Between 1947 and 1951 he worked for the Central Intelligence Agency, and is now Chief of the Analysis Section of the Program Evaluation Branch of the Voice of America.

## SELECTED REFERENCES

WHITE, RALPH K., Value-Analysis: A Quantitative Method for Describing Qualitative Data. *Journal of Social Psychology*, 1944, *19*, 351–358.

———, Black Boy: A Value-Analysis. *Journal of Abnormal and Social Psychology*, 1947, *42*, 440–461.

———, Verbal Data and "Self Evident" Values. *Personality—Symposium No. 1*, 1950, 35–44.

———, *Value Analysis: The Nature and Use of the Method*. New York: Society for the Psychological Study of Social Issues, 1951.

## RESUME OF METHOD

IN THE "value analysis" method, the manifest content is rewritten in terms of fifty value words which represent motivating forces. In addition, the notations indicate whose point of view is considered, so as to shed light on the story teller's identification, and also indicate the terms in which the characters are described, in order to get at the story teller's "social perception." The data are treated quantitatively by tallying. A frustration-satisfaction ratio is obtained from the frequencies of the positive and negative values. The over-all interpretation "depends on the clinical insight and disciplined imagination of the analyst."

## TAT AND MAPS TEST WORKING NOTES

*Step One: Marginal Notations Describing the Manifest Content.*

The first step in any value-analysis is to put appropriate symbols in the left-hand (or right-hand) margin. These symbols are designed to reproduce as completely as possible, but with a maximum of compactness, the manifest content of the material, and to be immediately translatable into sentences which reproduce schematically the essential thoughts of the original material.

Like Murray's terminology for describing "needs," the terms and symbols involved in this process are designed to represent the motivating forces which are apparent on the manifest level. And, in addition, they represent, more fully than Murray's symbols do, two additional aspects of the data: (1) *Whose point of view is being considered?* This is necessary in order to give an empirically-based answer to the problems of identification or role-playing. (2) *In what terms does the person describe the various actors in his drama?* This is necessary in order to give an adequately differentiated picture of the person's "social perception"—how he tends to perceive the various types of persons in his environment: mother-figures, father-figures, women, foreigners, etc. For this purpose value-analysis provides a terminology which permits classification of such "standards of judgment" as (in the two stories analyzed below) studiousness, truthfulness, and personal appearance.

*Symbols Needed*

| | | | | | |
|---|---|---|---|---|---|
| b | boy | ( | wants, experiences | He | Health |
| m | man | ' | no, not | N | New Experience |
| w | woman | ° | having | Ex | Excitement |
| mo | mother | - | leading to | T | Tolerance; nonhostility |
| a | animal | | | P | Practicality, possibility |
| | | Ap | Appearance (good) | S | Physical Safety |
| Cn | Concealment | M | Morality | | |
| Se | Emotional Security | Ag | Aggression (desired) | Sy | Symbol |
| Ha | Happiness | E | Economic Value | Bi | Bizarre or disorganized |
| K | Knowledge | Tr | Truthfulness | | response |
| W | Work | Lo | Family-Love | | |
| Re | Rest | | | | |

It should be noted that all of the above "values" are in the positive form; they mean that something is wanted or positively valued. To form their opposites the apostrophe (') is used; it always means frustration or negative evaluation. For instance; 'He (No Health) means illness; 'K (No Knowledge) means ignorance; 'Ap (No Appearance) means ugliness; 'S (No Safety) means physical danger or aggression, negatively evaluated.

In personal descriptions, the person-symbol is followed immediately by the value-symbol if the evaluation is positive. For instance, to represent the statement "he seems to be quite a studious type," the symbols used are bW, which means "boy is a (hard) Worker." If evaluation is negative, the apostrophe is inserted between person-symbol and value-symbol. For instance, to represent "this terrible-looking woman . . . her mother," the symbols used are mo'Ap, which means "mother does not have (a good) Appearance."

*First Story in John Doe's TAT Record*

| | Marginal Notations | Translation of Marginal Notations |
|---|---|---|
| This child is sick in bed. | 'He | No Health |
| He has come across a novel that interests him. | °N | Having New Experience. |
| It is probably an adventure story. | °Ex | Having Excitement. |
| He evidently does not fear the chance that his parents will find him thusly occupied . . . | °Cn-°T | Having Concealment which leads to having the Tolerance or nonhostility of others. |
| . . . as he seems quite at ease. | °Se | Having Emotional Security. |
| He seems to be quite a studious . . . | bW | Boy is a (hard) Worker. |
| . . . and perhaps regrets missing school . . . | 'K | No Knowledge; not getting Knowledge. |
| . . . but he seems quite occupied with the adventure in the story. | °Ex | Having Excitement; major theme in story. |
| Adventure has something to do with ocean or water. | [Sy | Probably significant symbol; calls for special treatment. (A clue to the meaning of "Excitement.") |
| He is not too happy, though not too sad. | 'Ha+°Ha | No Happiness, plus having Happiness. |
| His eyes are somewhat blank—coincidence of reading a book without any eyes or knowing what is in the book without | [Sy? | Possibly a symbol. |
| reading it. | [Bi | Bizarre and probably highly significant response. |
| He falls asleep reading the book. | °Re | Having Rest. |

*Notes:*

1. The nonviolent and mildly pleasant character of this story contrasts markedly with nearly all the others. John is not yet warmed up; he isn't letting himself go.

2. The gratuitous introduction of "ocean or water" suggests that it has a very special importance to John—especially since after making this association he retreats into a statement of emotional neutrality, then "blankness," and finally sleep, all of which contrast strikingly with the "adventure" idea with which he started. (Immensity and vagueness, which may be related to "ocean or water" in his mind, also appear later in the record: the "great plain," which appears twice, the "dark place" in story 11, the vagueness and immensity of "fate.")

3. The central role of Excitement in this story may be related to the violently exciting character of nearly all the other stories. This suggests that Excitement as such may play an important part in his emotional economy. Possibly it is a self-distracting device—a way of distracting his own attention from repressed material, which thus constitutes one of the mechanisms of re-

pression. There is no reason, however, to think that he overtly seeks excitement; this story suggests that he is capable of combining violently melodramatic fantasy with complete overt passivity (a sick child, safe in bed, slipping off to sleep in spite of reading an "adventure" story).

4. "His eyes are blank . . . without any eyes." Absence of eyes (or face) is also the main theme of MAPS 3. More significant, perhaps, is the idea of "knowing what is in the book without reading it." John's preoccupation with hidden meanings, and with things not being what they seem, comes out in many other of his stories, such as 6BM, where a son conveys a message of murder to his mother through a play in which she acts, and the climactic MAPS 7 in which a statue turns out to be the supporter of a building and the source of wholly irrational mass destruction. There is also a confusion of fantasy with reality which takes bizarre forms, such as the statement that the settlement which is now in ruins "could all be imagination." And he speaks in a matter-of-fact way about "telepathic touch with the outside world." It seems likely that he has fantasies of possessing supernatural perceptive powers, and that he has imagined—with almost the vividness of reality—that he himself could "know what is in a book without reading it."

*Notes on Method:*

1. Since there is only one person in this picture, the problem of "whose point of view is being considered" does not come up, and special notation for dealing with it is unnecessary.

2. The differentiation between New Experience and Excitement does not follow necessarily from the connotations of the terms themselves. Here, as in many other instances, reliable use of the value-analysis technique requires careful study of and adherence to the definitions of the value-concepts in the manual of directions (or to other definitions which are equally clear and explicit). For instance, the definition of New Experience in this manual includes "reading of fiction," so that John's reference to "a novel" clearly calls for this term. Excitement is defined as "A higher intensity of interest or 'new experience'; intensity of feeling considered as an end in itself; thrills, adventure; . . . horror stories . . ." John's use of the word "adventure" makes this definition clearly applicable, and his extreme predilection for horror stories also supports the use of the word as here defined.

3. After a story has been read through, the analyst makes a selection of one or more symbol-combinations which seem to represent the "major theme" or themes in that story, and he encircles this symbol-combination. In this case °Ex was encircled.

4. The single square bracket, [, is used for any inference or interpretation by the analyst which does not paraphrase the actual content of the material.

*First Story in John Doe's MAPS Record*

| | Marginal Notations | Translation of Marginal Notations |
|---|---|---|
| This housewife goes to the door and sees this terrible-looking woman, and recognizes it as her mother. | w(mo'Ap | Woman experiences mother (who) does not have (good) Appearance. |
| The woman is being followed by a snake, which is the symbol of what she really is, I suppose. | mo'M<br>mo = a<br>[Sy | Mother is not Moral; (i.e., she is evil); mother is animal (snake). (A symbol) |
| Her husband is very indignant . . . | m(Ag mo | Man wants Aggression against mother. |
| . . . at having the old woman come to the door . . . | m(Cn'Ap | Man wants to Conceal (his mother-in-law's) lack of (good) Appearance. |
| and also the daughter is very indignant . . . | w(Ag mo | Woman wants Aggression against mother. |
| . . . because she had told her mother never to come and let the neighbors see her. | w(Cn'Ap | Woman wants to Conceal (her mother's) lack of (good) Appearance. |
| But the mother tells her that I had— she had . . . | [i = mo | I equals mother. (A slip which perhaps indicates identification.) |
| . . . come because she wants some money to help her son out of a jam. | mo(E so | Mother wants Economic Value for her son. |
| | moG so | Mother is Generous to her son. |
| The daughter asked her why she insisted on having that awful-looking snake following her. | w(Cn'Ap | Woman wants to Conceal (the snake's) lack of (good) Appearance. |
| The mother said 'He' the only one I can trust because all snakes don't wear clothes.' | [Bi<br>[Sy | Bizarre response probably related to symbolic meaning of snake. |
| The daughter turns on the officer and says 'I have never seen this woman before.' | w(Cn'Ap | Woman wants to Conceal (mother's) lack of Appearance. |
| | w'T,'Tr | Woman is not Tolerant (i.e., she is hostile), and not Truthful. |
| The mother, of course, is brokenhearted. | mo(w'T | Mother experiences woman's non-Tolerance (hostility). |
| She says, 'I can't help it if my face is this way.— | mo(Ap = 'P | Mother feels that (good) Appearance is not Possible. |
| It all happened the day you were born. When they were taking me to the hospital there was an accident and I received both you and a terrible face.' | mo(w = 'S,<br>'Ap | Mother feels that woman equals physical non-Safety (injury) and lack of Appearance (for herself). |
| The daughter takes out her handbag and says, 'Here's five dollars, beggar. | w(Ag mo | Woman wants Aggression against mother. |
| Now, officer, see that she goes.' | w'T | Woman is not Tolerant (i.e., she is hostile). |

| | Marginal Notations | Translation of Marginal Notations |
|---|---|---|
| As the old lady leaves she turns and says, 'Before I am through you'll give me more than money.' | mo(Ag w | Mother wants Aggression against woman. |
| . . . The daughter replies, 'Perhaps I've seen her but I would not want to admit it.' | w(Cn'Ap | Woman wants to Conceal (her mother's) lack of Appearance. |
| The husband . . . says, 'I hope I don't have to look forward to the day when you'll get that old and look like that.' | m(w Ap | Man wants woman (to have) Appearance. |
| Quite an argument ensues. | m'T | Man is not Tolerant. |
| | w'T | Woman is not Tolerant. |
| The snake slithers in and bites them both. | a'S | Animal is not 'Safe' (i.e., it causes injury). |
| As the wife is dying she says, 'At least you won't have to see me when I get old.' | w('S-Se'Ap | Woman feels that non-Safety (death) leads to Security from lack of (good) Appearance. |
| They both collapse. | w,m('S | Woman and man experience non-Safety (death). |
| | [a(Ag w,m | Animal wants Aggression against man and woman. (An inference, implying some degree of identification with the snake—i.e., the old woman.) |

*Notes:*

1. There is here an extraordinary diversity of viewpoints; John takes the viewpoint of the woman nine times, the "terrible-looking" mother five times (with a slip of the tongue which lends some added weight to this identification), and the man four times. If it is legitimate to infer that the snake is equivalent to the old woman, and that its biting of the man and woman represents the mother's revenge on both of them for treating her so badly, then we can say that John also identifies with the snake.

2. The value "Appearance" seems to have a meaning in the context of this record which is quite different from its meaning in ordinary everyday judgments of "good-looking" or "unattractive." John does not pay much attention to the appearance of most of the actors in his stories (whose looks vary within the normal range), but in this story, where the mother's hideous face lies quite outside the normal range, he seizes on it and builds the whole story around it. This suggests that for him it has a symbolic meaning; it is perhaps equivalent to Absolute Evil, or something of the sort. (And insofar as he identifies with the mother, this suggests a conviction—on some level of consciousness—that there is Absolute Evil in himself.) This interpretation is reinforced by the fact that he associated the woman with a snake ("the symbol of what she really is") immediately after calling her "terrible-looking."

3. If the snake is also a male sexual symbol, John's associating of it with the old woman adds still greater confusion to a confusion of sex roles which was already great enough. Here, as in most of the other stories, he takes the viewpoint of a woman at least as readily as that of a man.

4. This story is typical of most of the others in the extraordinary amount of aggression and hostility which it depicts. There is little except hostility between child and parent or between man and woman. This suggests that there is a great deal of hostility—probably conscious, but perhaps not overtly expressed—in John himself. His relationship to his mother, for instance, probably contained a good deal of hostility on both sides.

5. The importance of Concealment in this and other stories—covering up evil rather than combating it—is consistent with the hypothesis that John's life is full of deception of others, if not also self-deception. It is consistent also with his tendency to see hidden meanings, and especially hidden evil meanings, in his environment. The chances are that he projects his own deceptiveness (as well as his own hostilities and "evil" sexual impulses) into many of the actual persons in his environment, and continually suspects them of concealing evil designs toward him.

In other words, the whole picture looks like that of a thoroughly paranoid personality structure, with bizarre thought-trends which suggest actual psychosis. Even delusions of grandeur are present, if we are correct in inferring that he has fantasies of possessing supernatural perceptive powers. The statue story suggests too that (insofar as he identifies with the statue) he has fantasies of supernatural power to hurt and destroy others. On the other hand, the many illogical elements in this and other stories suggest that his delusions are not well systematized; the picture is more like paranoid schizophrenia than like "true paranoia."

6. Although this story, unlike several of the others, does not contain anything which has been labelled as Aggression-against-self (Ag s), it does resemble the explicit self-aggression stories in that the central characters end up dead. The central character here is the woman, and at the end she "collapses."

*Notes on Method:*

1. In this case there appeared to be three major themes, each of which called for encircling the corresponding symbols: the woman's revulsion from and desire to conceal the appearance of her mother; her consequent hostility to her mother; and although this is an inference—the old woman's retaliatory hostility, expressed in the end through her equivalent, the snake.

2. At eight points in this record, personal descriptions have been presented by marginal notations: mother is not Moral (mo'M), mother is Generous to her son (moG so), woman is hostile or not Tolerant (w'T), etc. None of these

is made explicit by John himself, and there is some real doubt as to whether they are even implicit. He may not be thinking that the woman is too hostile to her mother, even when he puts into her mouth the cruel remark, "Here's five dollars, beggar." But an ordinary person probably would be making such implicit judgments, and since we are here illustrating a method, it seemed better to represent in full the type of notation which would ordinarily be applicable.

3. Here again the value-symbols chosen may at times seem not to represent precisely the content of the material. For instance, the word Aggression may seem rather strong for representing the word "indignant." This is quite consistent, however, with the definition of Aggression in the manual of directions. It is there defined as "The goal which is implied when feelings of anger or hostility are admitted . . ." Since indignation is a mild form of anger, the term "indignation" clearly comes within the broad meaning-area which is represented by our term Aggression.

An effort was made to define each term as nearly as possible in accordance with common usage. Some slight departures from common usage were necessitated, however, by the need to cover, with only fifty value-words, the extremely variegated picture of goals and standards of judgment which human behavior presents, even within our own culture. Several terms had to be stretched somewhat in order to cover meaning-areas broader than those which they would normally include.

4. The reinterpretation of the meaning of John's emphasis on Appearance is an illustration of the gestalt-like character of any meaningful value-analysis. The meaning of any single element within the total picture often needs to be reinterpreted in the light of its relationship to the total picture. The "values" themselves are not entities, each with an immutable meaning, but are simply verbal counters, the meaning of which in a given instance has to be inferred partly from the specific things to which the label has been applied and partly from inferences based on other knowledge about the individual. Perhaps even more than the Rorschach test, an autobiography or set of TAT stories evaluated by value-analysis is a matter of relationships rather than of additive totals as such.

Another illustration of the same thing is the interpretation put on the final Aggression by the snake. This can be interpreted as a wish-fulfillment of John himself only on the basis of two further assumptions derived from other parts of the record: the assumption that the mother and the snake are largely equivalent (mo = a), and the further assumption that John identifies to some extent with the mother. The latter is based on several things, including the five instances of "taking the mother's viewpoint," the slip of the tongue ("I had—she had . . ."), the highly unsympathetic picture of the daughter (which in a normal person would suggest identification with the mother whom the daughter was treating so heartlessly), John's readiness in other stories to see things from the viewpoint of a woman, etc.

*Step Two: Tabulation.*

Tabulation ordinarily involves the following steps:

1. A tallying of relative frequencies of each *value*, on a chart which contains the symbol for each of the fifty values. For instance, the totals for all stories in both tests in this case show that the five most emphasized values are Aggression (30 emphasis-units), Safety—including its opposites, danger and death (21 units), Concealment (16), Emotional Security—including its opposite, non-physical fear or anxiety (14), and Sex (12). Norms for both tests would be necessary, of course, in order to make even a first tentative judgment as to how significant these totals are.

The "emphasis-unit," in this tabulation, calls for definition. In ordinary verbal data, not divided into "stories," a single unemphasized value-judgment counts as one emphasis-unit, and an emphasized (encircled) value-judgment counts as three units. In stories of this type it is suggested that a somewhat greater weight be given to the "major themes." In the above calculation, for instance, each major theme was counted as four emphasis-units. (In the tabulation, a major theme was recorded as a very small circle, and an ordinary nonencircled value-symbol was recorded as a dot.)

Since the occurrence of a value-symbol in each of two stories seems more significant than its occurrence twice in one story, it is also suggested that a value-symbol which occurs two or three times in a given story should be recorded only once in the tabulation. On the other hand if it occurs four or more times, this seems to warrant giving it a weight equivalent to that of a major theme—i.e., tabulating it as a circle instead of a dot, and counting it as four emphasis-units. This means that just two degrees of emphasis are recognized: strong emphasis (represented by a small circle in the tabulation, and counted as four units, and weak emphasis (represented by a dot in the tabulation, and counted as one unit). This method simplifies the tabulation considerably, and it has the added advantage that the combined total of dots and circles represents directly the number of stories in which a given value-symbol occurs at all.

2. A tallying of the frequency of frustration (') and of satisfaction (°)—again in terms of emphasis-units. This gives the frustration-satisfaction ratio, which in the case of John Doe was extremely high: 10.9.

3. A tallying of the frequency of various "points of view." For instance, the cases in which John took a man's point of view (where more than one possibility presented itself) totalled 42 emphasis-units; the corresponding

figure for a young woman's point of view was 24, and for a mother's or older woman's point of view, 15. The combination of the two latter figures is 39, which is almost equal to the figure of 42 for a man's point of view. Norms are necessary, of course, to determine how this differs from the mean of a normal population. On the face of it, it looks like an exceptionally high proportion of feminine identification.

4. A tallying of the frequency of various evaluative descriptions of different types of persons. For instance, John's most frequent description of women is that they are sexually impure, and all but three of his descriptions of women are unfavorable. His most frequent description of men is that they are physically aggressive or dangerous, and all but two of his descriptions of men also are unfavorable.

## TAT AND MAPS TEST INTERPRETATIONS

*Step Three: Over-All Interpretation.*

There are no rules for step three; everything depends on the clinical insight and disciplined imagination of the analyst, as he goes over and tries to integrate not only all the material (projective and nonprojective) which he has value-analyzed, but also all other available data about the individual in question.

Some of the over-all interpretation has already been suggested in the "notes" to the detailed analysis of two stories, and it will now be evident how some of the numerical totals fit into that interpretation. For instance: (1) The large totals for Aggression and Safety support the generalization that John is preoccupied with physical violence, and also—since fantasies of physical violence are one of the most exciting types of fantasy—that Excitement may be for him a form of distraction or escape from what he does not want to contemplate. (2) The large total for Concealment is congruent with the hypothesis that he tends to see hidden meanings everywhere, and to suspect others of harboring, and concealing, the "evil" impulses which he himself has. (3) The high total for Sex—if it is high relative to others who take the same tests—and also his tendency to see sexual impurity in women are consistent with the hypothesis that the snake in MAPS 1 was in fact a sexual symbol, and that much of the "evil" with which he is preoccupied is sexual in character. (4) The readiness to take the viewpoint of a woman, and also the impartial way in which he characterizes both men and women as evil, suggest confusion as to his own sex role. (In a different personality the same equality of numerical totals might suggest a healthy and realistic type of understanding of the opposite sex. In John, however, the tendency to see evil everywhere is in itself a sufficient sign that he is very far from realism, and probably actually psychotic. A wealth of qualitative observations, including the high frequency of bizarre associations, also supports the hypothesis of pathology. It is highly probable, therefore, that the equality of sex-totals does represent confusion of sex-roles rather than genuine understanding.) (5) The presence of delusions of grandeur, which would round out the picture of a thoroughly paranoid personality, is not directly indicated by any of the numerical totals; but there are the fantasies of supernatural perceptive powers and supernatural power to hurt and destroy others. (6) The very high frustration-satisfaction ratio is difficult to interpret. Certainly it cannot be taken at its face value, because I, for one, got the impression that he killed off his characters with a sort of gay abandon, and that he was thoroughly enjoying even his most gruesome and frightening fantasies. And this purely subjective impression gains some support from his own positive evaluation of Excitement (he called it "adventure") in the first TAT story. If the high F/S ratio were combined with evidence of guilt feelings—which are virtually absent in John's stories—it might suggest depression; but as it is, there is no reason whatever to infer depression. The high F/S ratio suggests, rather, that he craves strong psychological medicine to keep him from thinking about something which he prefers not to think about. John does not seem to be unhappy; he seems to derive great satisfaction from his own psychotic trends. (If this inference is correct, the prognosis is of course very unfavorable.)

Other inferences which might be drawn are definitely more speculative in character. For instance, one might speculate that the homosexual element in his "confusion of sex roles" is the chief repressed element in his makeup (he tells no stories with overt homosexual content), and that this is what all the melodrama serves to keep out of his conscious mind. If this is correct, it would suggest that his paranoid trends are rooted in the classic Freudian mechanism: "I love him; he loves me; he hates me." This might be the vaguely seen Evil which figures so largely, especially in MAPS 6 ("I don't know. Just what they couldn't see, but they knew it was there because they could almost see it.").

Or one might speculate that the vaguely-seen Evil is a repressed sexual component in a pathologically developed relationship to his mother. There are, in fact, at least three hints of positive attachment to a mother-figure: the sick and safe child in TAT 1 who does not fear parental disapproval, the old woman in MAPS 1 who wants money to help her son out of a jam, and especially the boy in TAT 13B who helps his mother in childbirth and has her "thank God that she has a son like him." This is the one story with a really happy ending. A complete Oedipal relationship is also suggested by its final sentence, "He had really done more than his father in doing this." Moreover, his decision that he "would never leave home" suggests a clinging to an infantile type of son-mother relationship. His ability to identify with a mother figure, as in MAPS 1, may or may not support the same interpretation. But, at the same time, he tends strongly to see all women as evil, notably the mother-figure in MAPS 1, which would be consistent with the hypothesis of a strong ambivalence in his attitude toward his mother, and also with the hypothesis of an inability to contemplate a sexual component in his attachment to her.

Or, finally, one might speculate, along less specifically Freudian lines, that the vaguely-seen Evil is a homicidal impulse. This interpretation would be supported, perhaps, by his tendency to see men as physically violent, and it is certainly supported by the general preponderance of Aggression and Safety (including its opposites, injury and death) in the record as a whole. Self-destructive fantasies are also conspicuous, and there might be various possible relationships between the homicidal and the suicidal elements in his makeup.

These three interpretations are not, of course, mutually exclusive. They might all be true, and dynamically related to each other. All of them, however, are speculative, and should definitely not be put on the same level of probability as the more direct inferences which preceded them.

# Part III

# ADDITIONAL TEST DATA

# Chapter 19

# RORSCHACH TEST

## Interpreted by
## BRUNO KLOPFER

Dr. Klopfer was born in 1900. He received the Ph.D. degree in Psychology from the University of Munich in 1922. He is a Diplomate in Clinical Psychology of the American Board of Examiners in Professional Psychology. He has taught at Columbia University Teachers College, CCNY, Claremont College, and UCLA. Since 1946 he has been at UCLA, where he is now Associate Clinical Professor of Psychology and Consultant in Clinical Psychology to the Veterans Administration. His work is largely in the fields of projective techniques and psychotherapy. He is the author of the book, *The Rorschach Technique*. He has done psychotherapy with children for the past thirty years and with adults for the past seventeen years, using primarily a Jungian orientation. He has been Director of the Rorschach Institute and is now Chairman of the Advisory Board of the Society for Projective Techniques. For the last fifteen years he has been Editor of the *Rorschach Research Exchange*, now the *Journal of Projective Techniques*. See Bibliography [34].

## RORSCHACH RESPONSES

### Card I

4. . . . 165

1. Looks like two witches with a cow in the middle. Pulling the horns. Brain is split. They are kicking him. Hurting him. Pulling him apart. Naturally they are cloaked in black. Is indistinct. Can see the foot on each side of the witch. Might have heads turned in opposite directions like seeing if are being followed. They are doing wrong. Which way to go. Indecision. Pulling in opposite directions. The cow is facing this way. His eye looks like he knows what is going on.

1. (Points out all the parts)
(Eye?) One eye right here.
(How much included?)
The whole thing.

### Card II

5. . . . 175

1. This looks like two clowns. In an accident, blood on their feet, or fighting each other. Daggers in their hands. Kneeling. Sort of look like ghosts. Showing their teeth at each

1. (Points out all of the parts)

(Ghost?) Sort of bones here.
(Teeth?) Right here.

other. Arms together, each have a knife. Something sticking out of their backs. Their back feet look like claws or paws. The things they are holding the daggers with look like hooves. Wearing red under the black robes. Have gotten each other in a number of places. Arguing because they are so much alike. Trying to kill each other. There is nothing one has accomplished that the other hasn't.

(Gotten each other?) Stabbed, blood here and here.

## Card III

5. . . . 181

1. They look like both have hooves, picking over bones of a skeleton. Look like cannibals. Are pulling apart. Either men or women. Looks like something ready to hit them in head on both sides. Flame or fire. Eyes in the side of the head. Not looking at each other, I suppose. Look like have snouts or something like a dog. Top of heads look like they would hurt if the things hit them because looks kind of weak.

1. (Men or women?) Like women up here because have breasts. More like women.
(Something ready to hit them?) Perhaps swinging ready to hit them. Looks like hot burning coal, something hot.
(Snout?) This sort of a little thing on the end.
(Weak head?) Sort of split here, not shadowed so deeply. And little notches here.

2. Looks like a bow tie in the center.

2. (What reminds?) These things in the center look like the way it was tied.
(Would it look like a bow tie if it were black?) Perhaps more so.

## Card IV

3. . . . 170

1. This looks like a bear or something. Cross between a bear or a crab. Claw on each side. A squid underneath. You know, a sea animal. Two feet almost the shape of human feet. Looks like crushing the thing under it.

1. This more like a bear skin rug laid flat out when I look at it. This looks like claws. (What reminds?) Furry, soft or furry. (Squid?) If only had tentacles would look like one. (Feet?) Here, more human than bear's claws. (Crushing?) Looks like on top of it. Now more like a monster to me than a bear. Eyebrows, eyes, nose.

2. Looks like an x-ray of chest or spine. The whole thing.

2. (What reminds?) The coloring of it. The different hollow places. Spine. Here sort of shape of chest plate.

3. Like a rug or something.

3. Bear rug (As described in 1)

4. Almost see the face of a man in there. Eyes, long nose, arms outstretched. Some-

4. (Something behind?) This squid or whatever it is. Looks like head split open.

thing behind him. All hairy. Top of head comes to two points.

Something sticking out of there (Hair?) Hair all over here.

When look at it like this (hand over half) one side sleeping peacefully, one side wrinkling forehead.

Card V

4. . . . 190

1. Looks like a bat with legs on each side, almost human without foot.

1. I'll change. More like a man with helmet, cape, no feet, boots. Legs hiding behind.

2. Could be a butterfly.

2. (What reminds?) The feelers here.

3. Looks like two teeth pulled out. Not same on each side.

3. (What reminds?) Sort of like two teeth. The shape. [Upper middle d]

4. Looks like some dead animal skinned and laid out.

4. (Skin or animal?) Fur, the skin. Fur side up.

5. Or a man standing up with big cloak outstretched. Looks like his head split if is a man. Ears stick out. Wearing boots. Hiding something behind the cloak. A dead animal maybe from the legs.

5. (Points out details)

Card VI

28. . . . 166

Can I turn it any way?

1. Well . . . this looks like a snake head or something. Some kind of an animal with two big black eyes. Wings on top. A long shaft going up here. Separates the snake.

1. This looks like a snake. Wings don't belong. Butterfly behind. (Shaft?) Center thing here. Separates it into two. [Upper outer d]

2. Two small birds perched on something looking up at the head.

2. These right here. [Light gray on both sides of top center d]

3. Looks like a butterfly hiding behind this thing because of the feelers and wings. Can't make anything out of this though.

3. Here and here.

Looks like another rug, spread out skin. Looks furry too.

Card VII

7. . . . 160

1. Well, this looks like the lower part of a human being, I guess, with variations. Same upside down.

1. (Parts?) Legs, lower part.

2. This way, two colored children, feather in hair, animal body with tail. Looks like going to kiss.

2. Like getting ready to kiss. (Feather?) Sitting on back of head. Position, I guess.

3. Looks like could be two faces in the feathers up on top.

3. Even shading on cheeks looks natural. Round eye, dot in center. [Tiny detail at very top]

4. About a hundred little profiles on the sides. All different shapes. That about covers that one.

4. (Points out several)

## Card VIII

7. . . . 163

1. Looks like. . . . Well I don't know animals very well. Looks like two beavers trying to. . . . Not beavers. Don't know.

1. (Trying to what?) To get this thing apart, I guess.

2. Connected to this bat.

2. (What reminds of bat?) Little claws here to hang on. Big blank. Two little front paws. A lot of points on the wings like bats have. [Top gray D]

3. Corset in the middle.

3. Ribbing. Looks like made out of elastic or something.

4. Something dropped down the middle like a knife.

4. (Knife?) Here, this piece. This is a stain of some kind. [Middle of dark gray stripes]

5. Someone's backbone. All connected, very slimly.

5. (Bone?) This in here.

6. This thing in the middle looks like the head of a monster. Funny eyes.

6. Eyes, nose, mouth.

7. Looks like a little boy's suit of clothes. Coat, pants, arms empty, just hanging there.

7. (What reminds?) Short pants. Way cut, opening here. Boy hurt, bloody, stained. Linen. (Why?) Sort of texture of the thing. Pants velvet. Linen first.

## Card IX

4. . . . 188

1. These look like two witches fighting with claws out, they have machine guns trying to get each other. Long toe nails hanging on something.

1. Here, pointing at each other. (Points out details)

2. Two people trying to pull the witches apart so they won't get at each other. Looks like both have long hair. Looks like men from another world. Looks like a skeleton they are trying to pull apart. Looks like a backbone in the middle.

2. Looks like pleading with them. (Kind of people?) Horrible green people. Head, nose. (What reminded of a skeleton?) Mostly these two holes here. Some places in the human body have holes like that.

3. Turned up like this looks like an old woman with an apron on.

3. Women are fat. Waist line. Apron strings sticking out here. Like scrubbing the floor.

4. On the bottom, a head on each side with long tooth hanging out. Like a prehistoric man or something.

4. This is the bust. (Prehistoric?) Blunt profile. Shape of head.

Card X

8. . . . 252

| | |
|---|---|
| 1. This is really something. Looks like two things or something . . . anteaters trying to get in a bird with their snout. | 1. Not the whole animal. (Bird?) Cooked bird, roasted chicken. |
| 2. A tooth. | 2. (Reminds?) Shape and everything. [Center portion of inner blue] |
| 3. Crabs on both sides. | 3. (Reminds?) Claws. |
| 4. On top two things fighting over a bone or something. | 4. (What?) Just things. More like animals. |
| 5. Down here, two dogs . . . poodles. | 5. (Why poodles?) Shape of the head and body. The way you see drawings of poodles sitting. |
| 6. Birds, more birds. | 6. Birds like canaries. Mostly by color. Long feather in tail. |
| 7. These up here getting ready to jump off. Both have knives in their hands. One horn. | 7. Animals, I guess. Goats. |
| 8. Worms trying to eat this one's eyes out. | 8. (What reminds of worms?) Worm, long and shapeless, no head. |
| 9. This looks like a moose here. | 9. Antlers. Just the head and three-fourths of the body. |

## RORSCHACH INTERPRETATION

THE MOST striking and surprising element foı Rorschach analysis in this case is the contrast between the superficial impression given by the quantitative data, on the one hand and the serious impression given by the sequence and content analysis on the other. There are only two parts where the quantitative picture yields any indication of serious imbalance: one is on the location distribution, where six of the seven unusual details are on the last three cards (which certainly are less inclined to yield unusual details than the first seven cards); and the other imbalance is that the clear picture of the "burned child" constellation—of the tendency to withdraw from emotional challenges to a safe distance—is counteracted by a slight but present tendency for CF to outweigh FC.

With regard to the content, the overwhelming preoccupation with extreme aggressive thoughts and concepts speaks for itself, and it permeates the record through all ten cards. This happens usually only in the case of acting-out individuals. The whole constellation of the record, however, and the extreme care in regard to the specification and organization of these aggressive concepts again contradicts the impression of acting-out, so that one gets the feeling that there is an acting-out in fantasy which is cut just short of acting-out in reality.

The second general impression from the content analysis is the extreme inadequacy of emotional response to his very strange concepts. In fact, one has the feeling that he has no emotional response. This again, however, is not accompanied by the usual indications of blunted affect. There is a variety of signs of discomfort and of disturbability which usually are associated with strong ego defensiveness, but they are spotty and inconsistent. The fact that they are present, though, would again indicate the same tendency that he very often goes to the brink of an acting-out situation and stops right there. One way in which this discomfort is expressed is by a very strangely naive projection of ambivalent or perplexed feelings into the characters which he creates, like in Card I where he says the witches are doing wrong, they have indecision, they are pulling in opposite directions. One has the feeling that he has found a way to act out psychodramatically in his fantasy instead of doing it in reality to other human beings. On the other hand, what his characters do is rather hair-raising.

A third thread going through the content of the record is the repeating of terms of split heads, split brains, and the visualization of the instruments which produced the splits. It would be naive to assume that any time someone sees a split head or a split brain in a record that this could be associated with the existence of a personality split, especially on Card I where the top d is often referred to as a split head by individuals without any psychotic tendencies. His way of using it, however, is certainly most conspicuous.

A fourth repetitive theme is the existence of teeth, which quite generally can be accepted as representations of the animalic form of aggression. He actually contributes quite a bit of strength to this hypothesis in the strangely naive and elaborate way in which he uses this concept. In Card II, the two clowns showing their teeth at each other, each having a knife to back the teeth up, and their teeth look like claws; they are holding daggers with something that looks like hoofs, but they are still clowns. Another repetitive theme in the record is this extreme unconcern about the fabulatory relationship of the various specifications of his concept that could not have any realistic co-existence; this can be considered as the fifth characteristic of the content of this record. He seems neither to have the kind of wry humor which gifted normal or neurotic people show in forming fabulatory concepts, nor does he seem to be in any way disturbed or perplexed about clowns having hoofs and holding knives with their hoofs, having at the same time black robes, etc. This lack of feeling in his fabulatory efforts is most extremely expressed in Card IV, where he has a cross between a bear and a crab and a squid underneath and the human feet crushing the thing under them. (Card IV also establishes for the first time the fact that his shading disturbance is more profound and deep than his color disturbance. He wavers and oscillates between the expression of his need for affection, great anxiety about his need for affection, and a tendency to avoid affective involvement altogether.)

A sixth factor is that his aggression very often takes the form of a chain reaction. For example, in Card III, the cannibals are pulling something apart and something else is ready to hit them. The same thing is repeated in Card IX. In Card III, following this chain reaction of aggressions, there appears, by contrast, the very peaceful bow-tie added without any emotional expression.

The seventh characteristic of the content is quite pronounced. Throughout the record there are clear indications of an existing homosexual panic. The overt paranoid references of people looking around, not being able to face each other, the indecision about the sex of the figures in Card III without any feeling of the necessity to solve it, but most clearly, the response to the top of Card VI, the big black eyes and the long shaft that separates the snake, all seem to be associated with a paranoid reaction to sexual problems. The fact that the response to Card VI, which is an obviously disturbed response, does not keep him from seeing the two birds looking up at the head and the butterfly behind it, indicates that this is an unconscious rather than conscious disturbance. There are sufficient other indications of the basically homosexual fixation to re-enforce this part of the diagnosis, especially the constant mixture of animal and human characteristics, and the corset and clothing response in Card VIII. The great number of destructive aggressive responses like the anteaters trying to get in a bird, or the worms trying to eat the eyes out, both in Card X, add the necessary anal sadistic flavor to the fixation picture. Also, the relationships between his more or less human figures are almost invariably destructive, as the indications of the teeth and knives mentioned above.

In over-all clinical terms, the picture can best be described as that of an individual who is on the brink of a psychotic reaction; more correctly, as a latent psychosis, since this brink condition would seem to have prevailed now for quite some time. The strange development of his fantasy catharsis would be one possible explanation of how someone can teeter on the brink of a psychotic break as long as he seems to have been able to do so. Also, his very superior intellectual capacity has a good deal to do with that, but his intellectual capacity is, however, mostly engrossed in feeding this strange fantasy life.

He is not an incipient psychotic because this implies a temporary state. One could better call his disturbance a latent psychosis, since it goes on and is likely to go on for some time in this way. One can, depending on what one prefers, call him near psychotic or call him a latent psychotic. The latter is the better term, judging from the personality organization. He is not a schizoid personality, because for that he has too many disturbance factors. He is not blunted enough in his affect for a pure schizoid personality and yet he does not have enough ego strength to overcome his brink position, so the very fact that he is not schizoid enough nails him to the position in which he is. What one finds here is sufficient fragments of ego defensiveness to keep him in this precarious position, but not enough to make him really accessible for successful psychotherapy—to pull him back. Also, the fact that he accumulates all the signs of his disturbance in the last three cards would indicate that even if he teeter-totters for a long time, he is more likely to break than not to break in the long run.

The outstanding characteristic about him, then, is this brink position, added to it the ever present pressure of the homosexual panic, added to that his extremely perverse fantasy life and his inability to establish any real emotional relationships to other people. This would be the best way of summarizing his psychological characteristics.

# Chapter 20

# WECHSLER-BELLEVUE SCALE

## Interpreted by

## HELEN KITZINGER

Mrs. Kitzinger was born in 1901. She received the M.A. degree in Psychology from Columbia University in 1931. She is a Diplomate in Clinical Psychology of the American Board of Examiners in Professional Psychology. She has been Psychologist at the Bellevue Psychiatric Hospital, the New York City Board of Education, and the New York City Bureau of Child Guidance. Her work is largely in the field of psychodiagnosis, especially mental testing. At present she is Clinical Psychologist, Veterans Administration Neuropsychiatric Hospital, Los Angeles, and Lecturer at the University of Southern California. See Bibliography [32].

## WECHSLER-BELLEVUE INTELLIGENCE SCALE—FORM II

### SUMMARY

| *Test* | *Raw Score* | *Weighted Score* |
|---|---|---|
| INFORMATION | 21 | 11 |
| COMPREHENSION | 12 | 10 |
| DIGIT SPAN | 15 | 14 |
| ARITHMETIC | 18 | 12 |
| SIMILARITIES | 16 | 12 |
| VOCABULARY | 37½ | 15 |
| | | |
| P. ARRANGEMENT | 16 | 13 |
| P. COMPLETION | 10 | 10 |
| BLOCK DESIGN | 38 | 15 |
| OBJECT ASSEMBLY | 23 | 13 |
| DIGIT SYMBOL | 92 | 17 |
| | *Weighted Score* | *I.Q.* |
| VERBAL SCALE | 62 (+2) | 120 |
| PERFORM. SCALE | 68 | 126 |
| FULL SCALE | 130 (+2) | 125 |

### DETERIORATION

| *"Hold" Tests* | *Score* | *"Don't Hold" Tests* | *Score* |
|---|---|---|---|
| INFORMATION | 11 | DIGIT SPAN | 14 |
| VOCABULARY | 15 | ARITHMETIC | 12 |
| P. COMPLETION | 10 | BLOCK DESIGN | 15 |
| OBJECT ASSEMBLY | 13 | DIGIT SYMBOL | 17 |
| SUM | 49 | SUM | 58 |

% OF LOSS (Deterioration)

"Hold" (49) minus "Don't Hold" (58) divided by "Hold" = −.18
Correction for age, 1.0 % of loss, −19

1. INFORMATION (Sits on edge of chair very straight).

| | | |
|---|---|---|
| 3 | A, B, C, D, E, F | |
| 1 | 1. Days | Seven |
| 1 | 2. Water—Boil | Put it over the fire |
| 1 | 3. Things—Dozen | Twelve |
| 1 | 4. Seasons—Year | Winter, summer, autumn, spring |
| 1 | 5. C.O.D. | Collect on delivery |
| 1 | 6. Color—rubies | Red |
| 1 | 7. Fourth—July | Independence |
| 1 | 8. Chile | South America |
| 1 | 9. Pounds—ton | Two thousand |
| 1 | 10. Romeo—Juliet | Shakespeare |
| 1 | 11. Sun—set | West |
| 1 | 12. Stomach | Takes care of your food by digesting it. |
| 1 | 13. American—man | I'd say five feet, eight inches, I suppose |
| 1 | 14. Capitol—Greece | Athens |
| – | 15. Oil—float | Heavier than water. Oh, because it's not dilutable or soluble. Doesn't jell with water. |
| – | 16. Labor day | September 11th, I think |
| 1 | 17. Turpentine | Sap of tree |
| 1 | 18. N. Y.—Chicago | Nine hundred miles |
| – | 19. Rayon | Cotton. Spun cotton |
| – | 20. Harrow | Foxes of harrow. Oh, it's a hole in the ground or a ditch. |
| 1 | 21. Hieroglyphic | Ancient Egyptian writing on the wall. Prehistoric. |
| – | 22. Impeach | To have arrested or investigate them for political reasons. |
| – | 23. Lien | Time. A certain time they're allowed or something like that. |
| – | 24. Ghengis Khan | A Hindu Chief, I believe. A warlord |
| 1 | 25. Paradise Lost | Milton |
| – | 26. Barometer | Tells rise or fall of different endeavors. Get results by it |
| – | 27. Prime number | One of the main numbers. One of the pivotal numbers or something |
| 21 | | |

2. COMPREHENSION (Crosses and uncrosses legs several times. Plays with shoe laces)

| | | |
|---|---|---|
| 2 | 1. Book (Watch) | Report it and pay the fine. Try to find it. |
| 1 | 2. House—Brick | Bricks fit together better and it's warmer |
| 2 | 3. Train | Flag them down |
| 1 | 4. Charity—beggar | Give to charity. They're supposed to see that it's distributed evenly, which I don't believe is so. You don't have to put the last phrase down (laughs) |

| | | |
|---|---|---|
| 2 | 5. Friend | See if I can get it. Have to be a good friend (laughs) |
| – | 6. Criminals | Because guilty of a criminal offense, supposed to be. |
| 1 | 7. Civil Service | Because, I suppose, certain requirements to be filled. (Q) So they can investigate the person because it's Civil Service and government work. Same thing with other employees. Require different things. |
| 2 | 8. Citizen | So he'll have plenty of time to change his mind or the government will. Investigation. |
| 1 | 9. Cotton—cloth | Because—that's a silly question. Because it makes inexpensive material. Something to wear. Keeps people in work. A big industry. Probably could enlarge on that. That's all. |
| – | 10. Promise | Because it shows your character |
| 12 | | |

3. DIGITS FORWARD

| | |
|---|---|
| + | 3, 8, 6 |
| + | 3, 4, 1, 7 |
| + | 8, 4, 2, 3, 9 |
| + | 3, 8, 9, 1, 7, 4 |
| + | 5, 1, 7, 4, 2, 3, 8 |
| 16549763 Fooey | 1, 6, 4, 5, 9, 7, 6, 3 |
| 29761534 | 2, 9, 7, 6, 3, 1, 5, 4 |
| 583812689 I'll take a guess | 5, 3, 8, 7, 1, 2, 4, 6, 9 |
| 426917385 I don't know | 4, 2, 6, 9, 1, 7, 8, 3, 5 |
| 7 | |

DIGITS BACKWARD

| | |
|---|---|
| + | 2, 5 |
| + | 5, 7, 4 |
| + | 7, 2, 9, 6 |
| + | 4, 1, 6, 2, 7 |
| + | 1, 6, 5, 2, 9, 8 |
| + | 8, 5, 9, 2, 3, 4, 2 |
| + | 6, 9, 1, 6, 3, 2, 5, 8 |
| 8 | |

("You've got my hands wringing wet from that. You're a slave driver.")

4. ARITHMETIC (Taps fingers on table. Plays with pencils on table.)

| *Score* | | | *Time* | *Answer* | *Score* | | | *Time* | *Answer* |
|---|---|---|---|---|---|---|---|---|---|
| 1 | 1. | (15″) | 2 | 6 | 2 | 6. | (60″) | 4 | 10 |
| 2 | 2. | (15″) | 4 | 7 | 4 | 7. | (60″) | 2 | 40 |
| 2 | 3. | (15″) | 2 | 21 | 3 | 8. | (120″) | 8 | 55 |
| 2 | 4. | (30″) | 3 | 14 | — | 9. | (120″) | 39 | 33 |
| 2 | 5. | (30″) | 4 | 9 | — | 10. | (120″) | 24 | 27 |
| | | | | | 18 | I just can't concentrate. My mind's a blank. I just can't think. | | | |

5. SIMILARITIES (Looks at Examiner when question is given, then looks away when answering. Gazes out of window occasionally.)

| | | |
|---|---|---|
| 2 | 1. Plum—Peach | Both have seeds and they're both fruit |
| 2 | 2. Beer—wine | Both beverages. Both have alcohol and both are intoxicating and I don't like either one of them |
| 2 | 3. Cat—mouse | They're animals. One's a rodent and they both have a dislike for each other |
| 2 | 4. Piano—violin | Both musical instruments |
| 1 | 5. Paper—coal | Can burn both of them |
| 1 | 6. Pound—yard | Both measurements |
| 2 | 7. Scissors—pan | Both made out of metal |
| 1 | 8. Mountain—lake | Both, you know, nature. Of nature's bounty or however you want to say (laughs) |
| 2 | 9. First—last | Both extremes |
| – | 10. Salt—water | Minerals |
| 1 | 11. Liberty—justice | They go together because both man's rights |
| – | 12. 49—121 | Both numbers. Why should they be alike? Let me think a minute. I don't know. Could you tell me now? It's too late. |
| — | | |
| 16 | | |

5A. VOCABULARY (Sits back in chair. Leans back; hands behind head.)

| | | |
|---|---|---|
| 1 | 1. Bicycle | |
| 1 | 2. Knife | |
| 1 | 3. Hat | |
| 1 | 4. Apple | |
| 1 | 5. Donkey | |
| 1 | 6. Box | |
| 1 | 7. Bad | |
| 1 | 8. Umbrella | |
| 1 | 9. Brave | |
| 1 | 10. Nuisance | |
| 1 | 11. Diamond | |
| 1 | 12. Letter | |
| 1 | 13. Join | |
| 1 | 14. Fur | |
| 1 | 15. Cushion | Seat |
| 1 | 16. Nail | Implement to join usually two pieces of wood together |
| 1 | 17. Gamble | To bet |
| 1 | 18. Spade | A shovel. Small shovel |
| 1 | 19. Shilling | English coin |
| 1 | 20. Fable | A fantasy. A story that comes to us usually from long ago and usually a fantasy. |
| 1 | 21. Sword | A long piece of metal used in dueling. In old days used it in combat. |
| 1 | 22. Nonsense | Foolishness. Something not pertaining to reality. |
| 1 | 23. Hero | A man who does something heroic—of valor |
| 1 | 24. Nitroglycerine | Powerful mineral. Blasting powder, I suppose |

| | | |
|---|---|---|
| 1 | 25. Microscope | Instrument by which—that has a microscopic glass in it by which can see various minute things |
| – | 26. Espionage | Sabotage. Usually pertains to spying or the work of a traitor |
| 1 | 27. Stanza | Usually a verse in a poem |
| 1 | 28. Seclude | To hide away |
| 1 | 29. Spangle | Ornament. Glittering ornament. |
| 1 | 30. Belfry | What I have bats in (laughs). Steeple in a church that usually has chimes in it and bats |
| 1 | 31. Recede | To back away or retreat |
| 1 | 32. Affliction | Something wrought on a person such as illness or handicap of some kind |
| – | 33. Ballast | Overflow or excess, I believe |
| 1 | 34. Catacomb | Underground tombs. Network of dungeons or rooms underground |
| 1 | 35. Imminent | In the near future. Can't escape it. Definitely going to happen |
| ½ | 36. Mantis | I believe that's the name of a bug. |
| 1 | 37. Hara-kiri | It's connected with committing suicide. Japanese |
| 1 | 38. Vesper | Usually evening prayers |
| 1 | 39. Aseptic | I'll say something sterilized or clean. You think I'm thinking of antiseptic |
| – | 40. Chattel | Could be a substitute. I know I'm entirely wrong but that's all I'll say. Won't get any deeper |
| – | 41. Dilatory | To go around or enlarge |
| – | 42. Amanuensis | Don't know |
| – | 43. Moiety | Don't know |
| 1 | 44. Flout | Means to make something of something when someone's present. To cast aspersions or something |
| – | 45. Traduce | Intrude |
| 37½ | | |

6. PICTURE ARRANGEMENT (Works quickly. Uses both hands. Sits straight in chair; leans forward slightly. Picks up pictures to hand back to Examiner until asked to leave them. Looks at last three a little while before moving any of them.)

| *Score* | | | *Time* | *Order* | *Patient's Comments* |
|---|---|---|---|---|---|
| 2 | 1. Farmer | (45″) | 7 | QRST | Planting corn. Watching it grow here. Picking corn and it's sent to market. That's a corny story (laughs). (Points to each as he tells story.) |
| 2 | 2. Burglar | (45″) | 12 | THUG | Opening window. Climbing in. Looking over loot. Being caught in act. |
| 2 | 3. Picnic | (45″) | 14 | EFGH | Dog's following. About ready to get chicken. Gets chicken. They get to picnic and find nothing there. |

| Score | | | Time | Order | Patient's Comments |
|---|---|---|---|---|---|
| 2 | 4. Sleeper | (75") | 11 | EPRCY | He's still in bed. Shuts off alarm clock. Wife bawling him out because late. Runs to work and when gets to work falls asleep. |
| 3 | 5. Gardener | (60") | 33 | FISHER | Hoeing in garden. Wife's watching him. See's a worm. Makes him think of fishing. Gets out tackle. Walks down road and sits on bank fishing. |
| 2 | 6. King | (60") | 20 | IHJKL | He meets officer here. Starts walking down road. Takes off hat. Reaches in hat and pulls out food. |
| 3 | 7. Rain | (75") | 59 | MASTER | How could he get the umbrella up there? She wants him to take umbrella. He doesn't want to. She follows to window. Feels rain. Gets caught in rain and next time takes umbrella. |
| — | | | | | |
| 16 | | | | | |

7. PICTURE COMPLETION

| | | |
|---|---|---|
| 1 | 1. Mouth | Mouth |
| 1 | 2. Whiskers | Whiskers |
| 1 | 3. Door hinge | Hinge |
| – | 4. Screw | The pin |
| 1 | 5. Spur | This little thing up here |
| 1 | 6. Spade | One spade |
| 1 | 7. Buttonholes | Buttonholes |
| 1 | 8. Fin | Fins |
| – | 9. Antennae | Nothing missing on that one |
| – | 10. Mercury | Does it go higher? Can't see anything missing. Probably one of these little digits here. |
| – | 11. Hatband | Seam or brim of hat. Part of lip but that's the way it's drawn. Buttonhole on coat |
| 1 | 12. Spokes | Ribs up here |
| – | 13. Cleft | This isn't the same hoof here (Points) and of course only one eye but it could be turned other way |
| 1 | 14. Shadow | I wouldn't say anything. Oh, the shadows under the tree |
| 1 | 15. Eyebrow | Eyebrows |
| — | | |
| 10 | | |

8. BLOCKS (Works very quickly. Blocks not fitted together well. Says, "Through" each time rather loudly and looks at Examiner.)

| *Score* | | | *Time* | *AC.* |
|---|---|---|---|---|
| 2 | DEM. | | 3 | + |
| 5 | 1. | (75″) | 8 | + |
| 3 | 2. | (75″) | 20 | + |
| 6 | 3. | (75″) | 9 | + |
| 4 | 4. | (75″) | 13 | + |
| 6 | 5. | (150″) | 21 | + |
| 6 | 6. | (150″) | 38 | + |
| 6 | 7. | (150″) | 41 | + |
| — | | | | |
| 38 | | | | |

9. OBJECT ASSEMBLY

| *Score* | | | *Time* | *Place* | *Patient's Comments* |
|---|---|---|---|---|---|
| 9 | 1. Horse | (3′) | 15 | + | That's a horse. |
| 6 | 2. Face | (3′) | 124 | + | It's a face. Are you sure this makes something. What can this be? That must be hair. |
| 8 | 3. Auto | (3′) | 59 | + | That's an automobile. |
| — | | | | | |
| 23 | | | | | |

10. DIGIT SYBOL

Number right: 92. (Finished all but last item).

## WECHSLER-BELLEVUE SCALE INTERPRETATION

THE *quantitative* results of the Wechsler-Bellevue test reveal the following: The patient is of superior intellectual ability. The discrepancy between verbal and performance abilities is not a significant one. Although there is a seven point weighted score variability among all subtests, the significance of this can be greatly discounted when it is noted that 10 (considered average for each subtest) is his *lowest* weighted score.

The tests ordinarily used to measure impairment ("Hold" vs. "Don't Hold") reveal trends directly contrary to a loss in mental abilities. The weighted scores are 18 per cent higher for the "Don't Hold" tests than for the "Hold". This fact plus an extremely high Digit Symbol score, and the patient's ability to repeat eight digits reversed as contrasted with seven forward, introduce the possibility that an obsessive compulsive character structure should be investigated. All the foregoing statements point to the impression that the patient, at the time of testing, was not actively psychotic or intellectually incapacitated. Anxiety may also be ruled out as a major disruptive factor in his functioning, judging by his good abilities in Arithmetic and in Digit Span.

Superficiality of interests and loosely integrated knowledge are suggested by the patient's weighted score in Information falling below his Vocabulary level. A general loosening process or impaired judgment is indicated by relatively lower scores on Comprehension (10) and Picture Completion (10), with considerable unevenness on responses within these tests in contrast to his high functioning on Vocabulary (15). There is the additional suspicion that there may be the beginning of a loss of reality contact. He falls down on those tasks which involve making or relying upon his own decisions and judgments, particularly as they may pertain to his functioning within his own environment.

The patient's performance scores indicate that his functioning in the visual motor areas is practically unimpaired. High Block Design (15) reflects his superior intellectual level. His unusually good powers of concentration and unimpaired learning ability are shown in the Digit Symbol in which he attains his highest weighted score (17).

*Qualitative* analysis of the test reveals the following impressions concerning this patient's underlying character structure:

Mild confusion and impairment in judgment which may be indicative of a breakdown in ego organization is suggested by the general unevenness in functioning within the subtests—failures on some easy items and successes on more difficult ones. This becomes particularly severe in Picture Completion, where the 4th item (Screw)—see test protocol—was missed, as were the 9th, 10th, 11th and 13th items. However, the 12th, 14th and 15th, which are particularly difficult, were passed.

No disorganization is evident in Comprehension responses although he expresses knowledge of, and his own rejection of, some conventional precepts (Charity). He tends to indulge in some inappropriate affect, laughing defensively where he feels threatened or inadequate; he uses a "superior" approach, intellectualizing and belittling a question (Cotton) to which he can give merely an adequate "1" response; he then proceeds to elaborate on this borderline response, completely losing sight of the original question.

His thinking as exemplified in Comprehension, Information, Similarities and Vocabulary is uncritical and loose, tending toward the over-ideational. He uses strong defenses against loss of ego functioning by making many wrong and inappropriate guesses rather than by admitting that he does not know an answer, by "sophisticated intellectualizing," pretentiousness of speech, and irrelevant elaborations (*Oil float on water*). Confusion and contaminatory thinking in Information (*Harrow*), affect-laden reasoning, clang associations and self references in Similarities and Vocabulary all point to a generalized loosening in reasoning and thinking. Examples of these include *Cat-mouse* in Similarities, Vocabulary definitions of *Belfry*, *Ballast*, *Nonsense*. This latter response may give a clue as to his own awareness and concern that he may be losing contact with reality. In addition to the foregoing, an inappropriate response in Picture Completion (#10 *Mercury*) and references to details not expected to be present (#13 "only one eye") all point to the possibility of the beginning of a break of a schizophrenic type.

His uncertainty and his frequent requests for reassurance point to his dependency and to his wish to conform to what is expected of him.

His attainment on Digit Span and Arithmetic indicate the good attention and concentration of which he is capable. He showed no evidence of distractibility, but almost compulsively felt that he must succeed (his comment: "You are a slave driver"); he gave speedy and accurate responses to Arithmetic problems, giving evidence of good abstractive abilities and failing only the last two. These successes, as well as Digit Symbol on which he gives an outstanding performance, represent well-defined unthreatening routine tasks; little opportunity is afforded on these for him to use his own judgment and discrimination.

Although he attains a good score in Object Assembly, receiving extra time credits for the horse and auto, it is worth noting that he has difficulty with the face. He finally succeeds in getting this together within the time limit but gets no extra credit for time. He takes more than twice as long as he did in putting together the automobile, which is considered the most difficult item. His comments strengthen the assumption that the human face may be anxiety-provoking to him. His concern as to what the face is and his singling out "hair" rather than any of the facial features for comment suggest the difficulties he may encounter in making comfortable associations involving interpersonal relationships. This is further borne out in the Picture Arrangement test. In spite of a good total score, indicating perhaps his awareness of social situations which do not involve him personally or emotionally, his outstanding characteristic is his breakdown in anticipatory functions. In his story telling of each picture he used the pictures concretely with minimal interpretation. Even those which he is able to place in correct order show the meagreness and concreteness of his interpretations.

In final summary, this is a person whose defensive systems are of an obsessive compulsive character—intellectualization, overdetailed verbalizations and pretentiousness. There seems to be a gradual breaking of these defenses in a process characterized mainly by impaired judgment, disorganization, and peculiarities in thinking. Thus, at the time of testing, his diagnosis may be said to be that of an incipient schizophrenic, or of a person who is compulsively building strong defenses in order to avoid a further break.

# Chapter 21

# THE MINNESOTA MULTIPHASIC PERSONALITY INVENTORY

## Interpreted by

## HARRY GRAYSON

Dr. Grayson was born in 1911. He received the Ph.D. degree in Psychology from Columbia University in 1940. He has Diplomate status in Clinical Psychology from the American Board of Examiners in Professional Psychology and is a Fellow in the American Psychological Association. He has been at CCNY as Instructor and Research Consultant. During World War II he was a Psychological Officer in the Adjutant General's Department. Since 1946, he has been Chief Clinical Psychologist, V.A. Neuropsychiatric Hospital, Los Angeles, and is now also Instructor at the UCLA University Extension. His work is largely in the fields of personality diagnosis and clinical research. He has published several articles in the professional journals. See Bibliography [22].

THIS PROFILE may, with a good deal of confidence, be considered as a valid representation (F within limits) of a seriously disturbed patient (unusually elevated profile), who has a tremendous amount of anxiety and depression (D), with sad, worrisome feelings of inadequacy (high D, Pt). The patient is self-depreciative (low L, low K) and lacking in self-assurance to the point of being a "compulsive doubter" (high ?). He has attempted to resolve his anxiety through hypochondriacal displacement (high Hs) and obsessive-compulsive mechanisms (high Pt) but these have been unsuccessful, with the result that the overwhelming anxiety has cracked his weak ego structure (high Sc). In addition, the patient has a considerable degree of hostility directed both against self (high Pd) and others (high Pa). The strong feelings of anxiety and depression (D) combined with introverted and extraverted aggression (Pd, Pa), in an individual who possesses insufficient ego control (Sc) to inhibit his tendency to act out impulses (Ma) add up to an explosive picture which presents strong possibilities of suicidal and homicidal behavior. Diagnostically, the patient may be classified as incipient paranoid schizophrenia.

# The Minnesota Multiphasic Personality Inventory

Starke R. Hathaway and J. Charnley McKinley

DOE, JOHN Male Age 25 Single Scorer's Initials

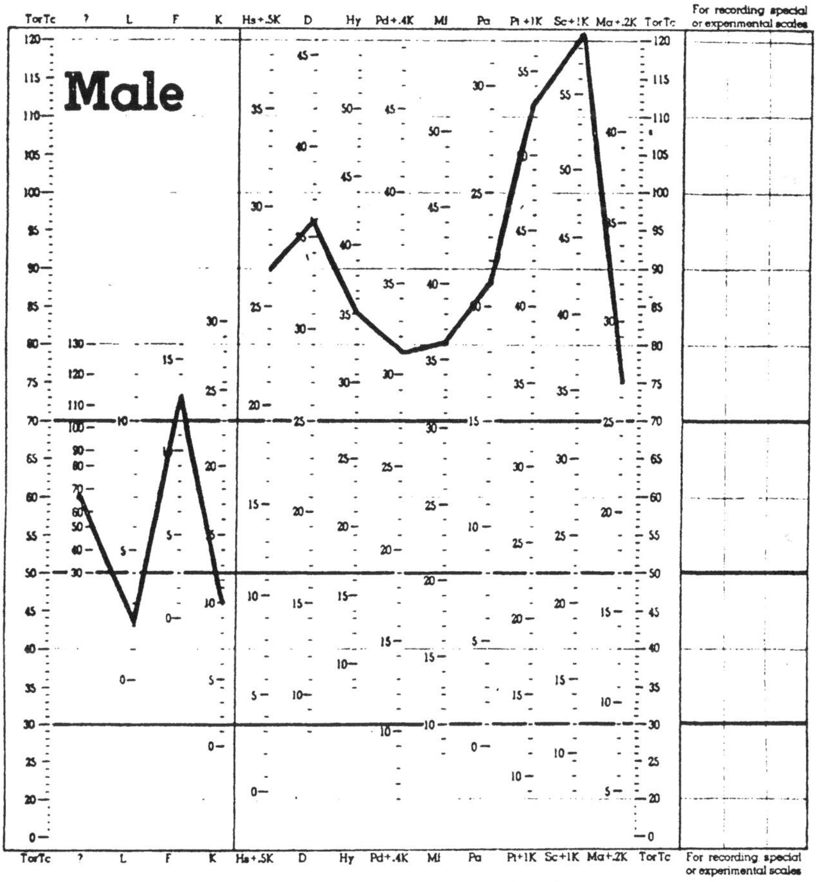


| | ? | L | F | K | Hs+.5K | D | Hy | Pd+.4K | Mf | Pa | Pt+1K | Sc+1K | Ma+.2K |
|---|---|---|---|---|---|---|---|---|---|---|---|---|---|
| Raw Score | 68 | 2 | 13 | 10 | 22 | 36 | 35 | 27 | 36 | 21 | 43 | 49 | 25 |
| K to be added | | | | | 5 | | | 4 | | | 10 | 10 | 2 |
| Raw Score with K | | | | | 27 | | | 31 | | | 53 | 59 | 27 |

# Chapter 22

# DRAW A PERSON

## Interpreted by

## KAREN MACHOVER

Mrs. Machover was born in 1902. She received the M.A. degree in Psychology from New York University in 1930 and has done post-graduate study at Columbia University. She has Diplomate status in Clinical Psychology from the American Board of Examiners in Professional Psychology. For more than twenty years, she has been with the New York City Department of Hospitals. Currently, she is Assistant to the Chief of the Psychology Department of the Kings County Psychiatric Hospital, Brooklyn, New York. She is also Clinical Associate of the State of New York College of Medicine and teaches at the New School for Social Research and the Graduate School of Brooklyn College. She has done extensive work in the investigation of personality through the drawing of the human figure. She has collaborated with the U.S. Navy Project on personality and perception (under the direction of Dr. Herman A. Witkin) and a study of adolescent and young adult girls (under the direction of Lawrence K. Frank). She is an Associate Editor of the *Journal of Projective Techniques* and Editorial Chairman of the journal, *Case Reports in Clinical Psychology*. See Bibliography [37].

THE DRAWINGS[1] confront us primarily with a severe obsessive-compulsive (perfection, symmetry, detailing, introversive features) neurosis in a young man of high average to superior intelligence (excellent proportions, detailing, integration, good perspective, and variety of line treatment).

Several features in the drawing raise the problem of loosening of defenses to a serious degree. To estimate the real meaning would require knowledge of the succession of the drawings, procedure of the examination, and identification by the patient of questionable parts of the drawings. The most serious of these "soft spots" is the question of whether the patient gave title and age designation to the drawings without examiner prompting. This generally constitutes a lapse in propriety that is seen mainly in paranoids, hypomanics, clear manics, or impulse disorders (excluding children). The second of these questionable areas is the intention of the tie treatment of the male, and the neck treatment of both drawings. Was a collar intended, or are the lines serving to widen the neck? The uncertainty and fragmentation around this most important sexually symbolic and control area may be the clues to beginning disorganization which overstep the boundaries of a neurosis.

[1] In reproduction here, both drawings are reduced by about one-third from the original size.

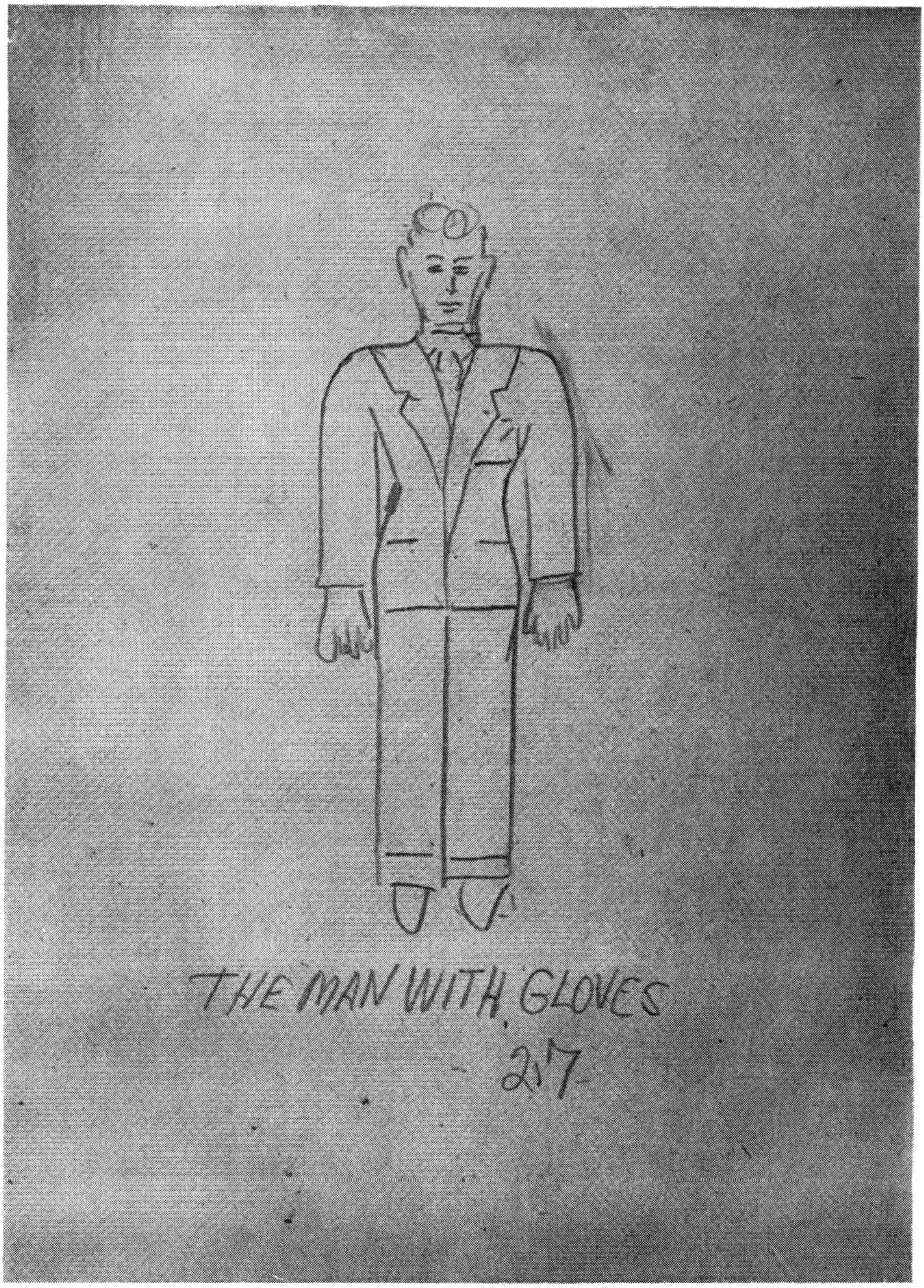
THE MAN WITH GLOVES
- 27

THE
SHORT WOMAN
35

Setting aside diagnostic considerations, we find certain traits dominating the record. Egocentricity is marked by middle placement, display themes, self-absorbtion, and meager differential between male and female figures. Combined with this egocentricity is a narcissistic love for his body (careful modelling and front view display), and an interest in power and brawn (overbroadened shoulders, erased in conflict) on the one hand, while on the other, the drawings are replete with features of a passive and effeminate nature. Facial features are effete, the figures are posing, the clothing of the male is dandyish, hips of the male are large and bulging, his heels are emphasized, the trousers appear like a skirt divided in half, and emphasis and treatment of lapels are effeminate in manner. Other feminine details are given in the open oval treatment of the head, the pompadour, curly coiffeur, and the sort of horizontal tie arrangement. The fervor and consistency with which the patient offers these self-display features, and the compulsive setting in which they appear, would suggest that the patient's homosexuality is acted out.

The extremely high waistline adds evidence to the inference that the patient's sexual problems are immediate and pressing. Oral sensuality is pronounced in both the male and female figures, but in the male, it is flavored with cruelty and sadistic impulses. Again, it may be considered that the patient's sexual and social behavior is punctuated with this sadism, since the compulsively swollen hands must be gloved. Other compulsive features are the perfectionist strivings, the precise placement, male-female size relationships, the meticulous clothing, and the "measured" proportions. The power needs expressed in the overbroadened shoulders, and the open arm-body connections give further support to the impression of accumulating and uncontrollable compulsions. Fortunately, the impulse-laden arms are at their sides now. In the plunging and excited neckline of the female, the wide horizontal flair of her uncertain hemline, and in the eyes that shut out guilty seeing, (Does the patient have eye symptoms?) we see projected strong voyeuristic appetites, particularly favorable to the soil of immature psychosexual development which he shows. Masturbatory guilt, manifested in the hidden hands of the female, and swollen and conflicted hands of the male, round out the sexual picture.

Insecurity, seen in the detached feet, tension in the "holding on" line of the male, rigidity of postural model, wariness of the male eyes, and incorporation of ears in the head contour, suggest a degree of paranoid sensitivity and tension which must be converted into a host of somatic symptoms (persistent midline emphasis, active fragmentation and anxiety in the drawing of the female). The patient is losing courage. In his tension and holding on, he is unable to meet, or complete, any of his problems (lines do not join although they are executed with dogged intention in the male). The control area, the neck, is particularly desperate in its confusion and lack of definitiveness. The head contour, which in many respects constitutes the signature for the self, is given some solidity in the female, but in the male, it is broken and patched up. The chin is given a determined squaring in a wave of decisiveness. Eyes no longer look out at the world, but are in the female, self-absorbed and sad; and in the male, guarded and suspicious. Is it competitiveness with the male and frustration with the female?

The female is presumably older than the male figure, and despite the glamour touches, has the drooping breasts of a mother-figure. She is saddled with the "shortness" (shortness of what?) that the patient rejects. Her head is relatively larger in authority, brains, and social dominance. The arms behind her back and self-absorbed expression, make her glamour and softness unavailable to the patient. She succeeds only in arousing great anxiety (line, less completion defenses) in him. The overclothing of the male and pocket detailing suggest that material deprivation may have added further insult to the obvious affectional deprivation (pockets, breasts) shown. This is further added to feelings of weakness, inferiority, and passivity—a pattern of defeat which clashes with the patient's need for perfection, achievement, and social prestige. The emptiness of the hair suggests some struggle for emancipation from the feminine and dependent ties. Much of the patient's sado-masochistic development and confusion of sexual identification appears to stem from an unresolved Oedipal situation, fanned by a rejecting mother. Emotional growth has been stunted and relationships toward people are necessarily guarded, distant, and tense, resulting in extreme loneliness in his narcissistic isolation. The self-doubting, ambivalence, and activity of the struggle add a note of depressiveness.

# Chapter 23

# BENDER-GESTALT DRAWINGS

Interpreted by

MAX L. HUTT

Max L. Hutt is Associate Professor of Psychology at the University of Michigan. He obtained his undergraduate training at C.C.N.Y. and his doctoral training at Columbia University. He is a Diplomate in Clinical Psychology. For a number of years he was head of the Educational Clinic at C.C.N.Y. and later was Director of the Child Consultation Service. During World War II he served in a variety of capacities and, for a time, was Chief of the Clinical Psychology Branch, Surgeon General's Office. He has taught at C.C.N.Y., Columbia University and the University of Michigan. His work has been in the field of clinical psychology with major interests in projective theory and technique, and in therapy and therapeutic research. He had been President of the Psychologists' League, a member of the council of the American Psychological Association, and is currently Chairman of the committee on psychotherapy of the Clinical Division of the A.P.A. See Bibliography [28].

It shall not be our purpose to discuss the types of qualifications one must bear in mind in discussing this record—qualifications arising from a situation in which the interpreter is in ignorance of such things as the nature of the setting in which this examination was administered; the sequence of tests and/or therapy preceding the test; the nature of the interpersonal relations between examiner and examinee; the precise method of test administration; and the like. This interpreter has the following data at his disposal: the test record (photographic reproductions) and some very brief notes on methods of work (both of which are included with this record of interpretation); these limited identification data: age, 25 years; sex, male; marital status, single; education, high school; handedness, left; no gross physical limitations.[1]

Our first "general" inspection of the test protocol reveals the following: the drawings[2] are arranged in "correct" sequence from "A," the introductory design, to "8," the last design, and the subject "lines" his drawings up along the left margin until he has reached the bottom of the sheet, then proceeds

[1] Dr. Hutt indicated that he needed information about John Doe's education, handedness, and gross physical limitations. These data were given to him before he did his interpretation of John Doe's Bender-Gestalt drawings.

[2] In reproduction here, the drawings are reduced by about one-third from the original size.

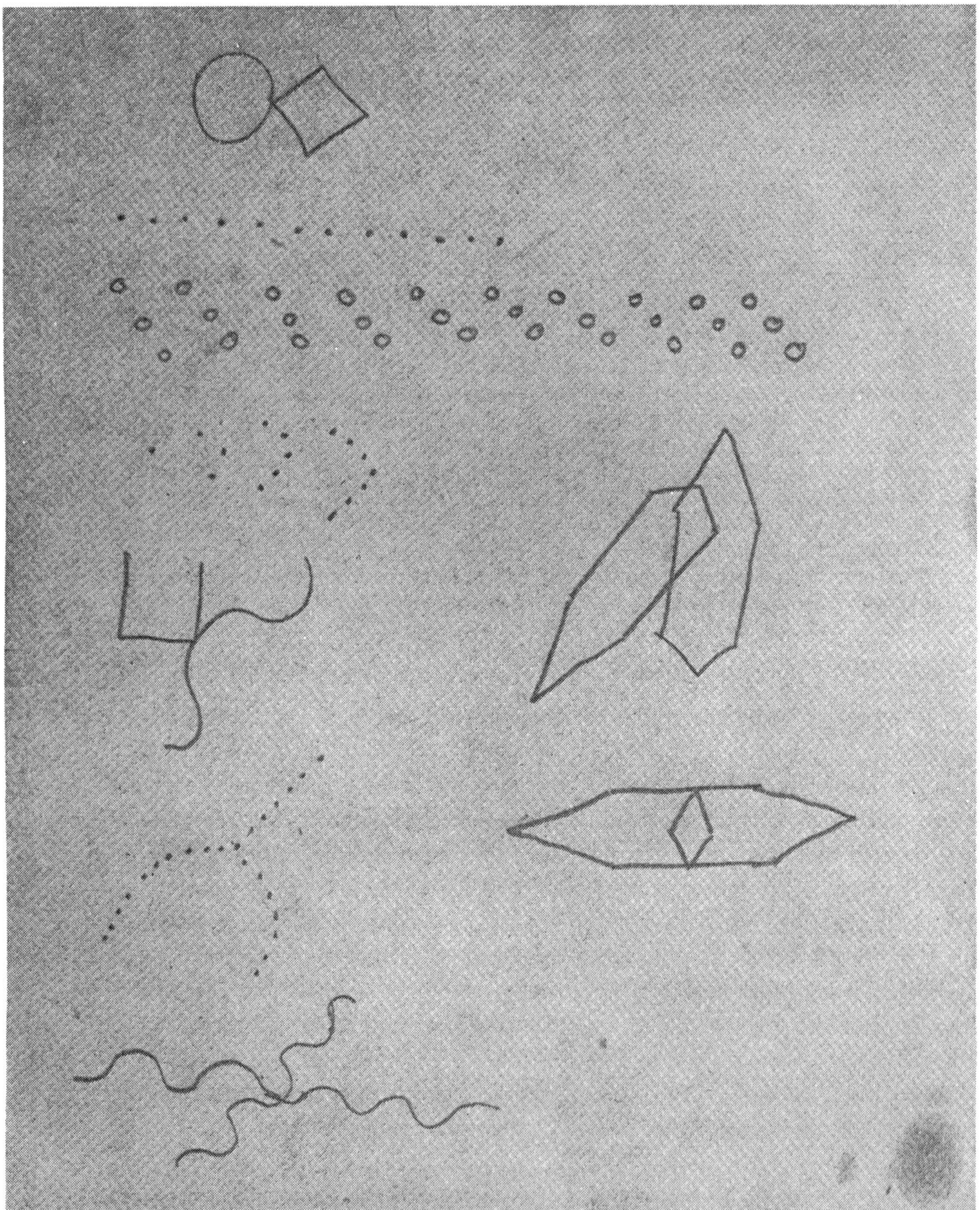

by "completing the available space," introducing design "7" to the right of and under design "2", and follows this, again in sequence and in the vertical plane, with the last design. We note further that design "A" is attempted in a locus slightly to the right of the next six designs which follow it. Our first hunches then are: this individual has strong orderly, i.e., compulsive needs, tending towards a sort of compulsive ritual, but tries to deny them (the aberrant position of "A" plus the examiner's comment on this design, "Draws fast, without hesitation"), and he is oppressed with some (probably) generalized feelings of anxiety and (more specifically) personal inadequacy (clings to the left margin and is "constrained" to use all of the space available to him on this one sheet). We raise the question for consideration, at once, "How strong and from what source is this anxiety and what is his defense?" We can speculate, from his use of space, that he attempts in some way to "bind" his anxiety, i.e., he cannot tolerate it for long or in large amounts, and that one of the features of this young adult's functioning is the need of control. Taken together, the compulsivity, the "binding" of anxiety and the need of control offer the first general inference: the super-ego is very strict.

Permit us to interrupt the formal analysis at this point to review some features of our method of interpretation, since what we have attempted to demonstrate thus far is characteristic of our approach to the analysis of this test. We examined two main features of the test record: spatial arrangement (sequence) and use of the total space area. We correlated extreme orderliness of sequence with compulsivity in functioning (based on the normative findings from our clinical samples from young adults) and the fairly extreme use of the margin with anxiety (again a normative clinical finding). These are considered *tentative* formulations at this point, to be confirmed, modified or rejected in the light of our subsequent analysis. We also noted that the "locus" of figure "A" was slightly deviant from the others (in the use of the margin), considered the examiner's comment regarding subject's haste in drawing, and offered the implication: "but tries to deny them," i.e., his needs for control. Next, utilizing our *general knowledge* of pathology (or better, personality dynamics) we tried to speculate concerning the meaning of these clinical manifestations and offered the *inference:* "the super-ego is very strict". This in microcosm is our method of analyzing traits, needs, defenses, symptoms and function. The test is a sample of the nonverbal, perceptual-motor behavior of the individual. As such it has intrinsic validity as a behavioral representation of the subject's adaptation at the moment. We utilize our normative data as *cues to interpretation* for this particular sample of this particular individual. Some of the cues may appear to be contradictory; others may supplement and confirm each other. The clinical task is to make meaning not only of the cues, but their inter-relationships, and based on the frame of reference for all humans from a similar population (i.e., the personality dynamics of young, American, ostensibly white, high school graduate, adults, in this case) to predict the underlying kind of personality which could be responsible for this total production.

Returning now to the test record, we examine figure "A" more carefully. The size is slightly smaller than the original. The horizontal axis of the figure is rotated slightly in a clock-wise direction. These suggest: fear (self-critical attitude) and depressive reaction, respectively. Both figures are of proportionate size (no specific, exaggerated reaction to either male or female sex symbol), but perhaps, the moderate rotation of the horizontal axis of the total figure is due to a specific reaction (dread of, hostility towards or lack of identification with, the male parent or surrogate). The latter possibility, or a derivative of it, is supported by the difficulty in "joining" the two figures (exaggerated, redrawn, overemphasized junction of the figures). This point is the more likely to be significant in view of the subject's speed in drawing, and in view of the apparently impulsive, concave sides of the square.

Figure "1," the twelve dots, is also drawn fast, with "no checking back on number of dots," the examiner notes. The number of dots is correct (confirms S's need for exactness, i.e., his compulsive trend), but the line of dots is wavy, the dots are filled in, and they are somewhat uneven in size and intensity. Here again, we find the apparent dilemma proposed above: S is compulsive but attempts to deny it. For a person who arranges his drawings on the page so methodically this "carelessness" in the alignment and size of the dots is striking. Perhaps he perceives the task of figure "1" as too simple for him to require careful effort. His tendency towards "haste" on all of the drawings suggests: impulsivity *or* a derogatory attitude toward the test *or* inner tension which is flowing over. The fact that the dots are *heavily* (and unevenly) *filled in* suggests that it is the last alternative which fits best. General, tentative inference: high aspiration level in a tense individual unable to accept simple experiences as nonchallenging. It is also worth noting that the dots tend to follow a downward trend: depressive reaction.

Figure "2," the ten diagonal columns of circles, offers further evidence of the marked variability which begins to appear to be characteristic of this "S." The examiner notes, "Checks number of rows (i.e., columns) about two-thirds through." We note that the angles of the columns of dots differ, becoming more obtuse (from the vertical) with a correction towards the end. The whole figure is exaggerated in the lateral plane. Together, these findings suggest a strong need to relate to people, but difficulty in establishing such relationships. The orientation of the first column is correct, so the variation in "angulation" is not a simple perceptual difficulty. "S" gets the number of columns correct, but varies *both* angulation and spacing. We have evidence, then, for the presence of considerable internal tension with an attempt at denial of its existence. How can we explain the apparent contradiction of the need for order and control with the speed and variability of performance? His compulsive defenses do not function effectively enough. In addition to the postulation of his impulsivity, we must add some mechanism which permits him to react so emotionally, i.e., so violently. This is especially necessary in view of "collision tendency" (figures "1" and "2"). We therefore think of "acting out," a mechanism in which ego controls are cut off (cease to function temporarily) and regressive impulsivity breaks through. If this is indeed the case, we can argue that super-ego demands can be side-stepped, guilt is temporarily overcome only to return in increasing intensity once the ego is later able to survey the transgression. This would thereby satisfy S's masochistic needs (to expiate his guilt) and thus serve a doubly useful purpose. Another possibility, which we should like to consider, is that of psychotic episodes, but the evidence for this in the record is lacking (There is no indication of a full-fledged psychotic process in the record), so we abandon this for the more parsimonious explanation already given.

Figure "3" is elongated laterally, a further indication of S's attempt to relate to others. The dissociation of the parts of the "arrowhead" supports the possibility of the "acting out" mechanism offered above. The downward orientation of the figure again suggests depressive reaction. The correct number of dots and the intensity of the dots indicate: orderliness (i.e., compulsive trend) and inner tension. The gestalt is accurate, although, again, in the segment consisting of five dots, the "post-mark" of impulsivity is revealed. The increase in the horizontal dimension of the figure is accompanied by a *decrease* in the vertical dimension; is S fearful of authority figures?

In figure "4," "S" has increased the vertical sides of the open square; (There are no notes by the examiner); this is deduced from the "breaks" occurring in both vertical lines. S's reaction to authority figures can now be inferred more completely: he is hostile to such figures, unable to express this hostility directly, and reacts either symbolically or impulsively. In line with the "acting out" hypothesis, the former is more likely. The curved portion of this figure is enlarged, flattened out in the middle and reveals an impulsive flourish at the upper end. Now we may speculate that S's major identification is with a female figure, but she is perceived as more masculine (i.e., dominant, aggressive) than feminine and is reacted to openly with antagonism. It is interesting that the upper portion of the curved figure extends well above its position on the stimulus card, and is at least as high up as the vertical lines. Here we may conjecture that S's mother (or surrogate) was stronger psychologically than his father, or at least seemed so to S, and that S would like to use his mother (or women) to defy his father (or men).

The depressive coloring in S's attempt at figure "5" is striking (clock-wise orientation of the total figure). He has difficulty with the projecting line of dots, attaching it about mid-way on the circumference of the "semi-circle" of dots, although it is off-center on the stimulus. Despite this, other features of the drawing are *precisely* accurate: the number of dots in the "semi-circle," the number of dots in the projection, and the position between the 7th and 8th dot of the circumference for the point of union. Here is, indeed, compulsive attention to detail, despite which, the figure in toto is distorted. If we accept the premise that this figure "stands for" the mother surrogate, we may then infer that S's vehemence against this symbol can be, and is, expressed in an open-structured figure, while he cannot so distort it in the simpler, more conventional symbolism of figure "1." Again this would support the premise of a symbolic acting out of S's conflict with his mother (and with women) although conventionally he is deferent, obedient, and conformist.

Figure "6," the sinusoidal curves, taxes S to the utmost. Affect is strong (amplitude of curves), but is expressed unevenly (uneven wave lengths). Marked difficulty occurs at the crossing. (E's notes support this.) The excessive loop at the top of the vertical curve plus the fact that this curve was drawn first, from the top down, express S's suppressed hostility to male, parental symbols. The gestalt is accurate, but the difficulty with this figure is apparent in the drawing. One would expect this S to show some apathy in his typical behavior, but react on occasion with outbursts, probably of a sexual—or better, sexual–symbolic character.

On figure "7," the right hand figure is rotated slightly in a clock-wise direction and all of the joinings show "closure difficulty." There is an exaggeration of the lower section of the left-hand figure. The gestalt is accurate. We infer: depressive reactions; difficulty in maintaining inter-personal relations; feelings of sexual inadequacy (possibly feelings of impotence).

The same closure difficulty is noted on figure "8," on which E says, "Draws small inside diamond first, then encloses." The figure is increased in size laterally and the ends are exaggerated. Inferences: difficulty in inter-personal relations; major identification with female figures; sexual impotency (or fear thereof).

One final observation: the spacing between successive figures is constricted. This fits in with our conception of S as essentially anal in fixation and generally suppressive of conscious hostility feelings.

From all of the above, we may attempt to etch out the personality as it functions on this psychological task, and offer some predictions, to be considered in the light of other data.

We would suspect that this individual tries to give the impression of a sophisticated, but conforming individual. He has unusually high aspirations, but feels limited and inadequate, although ordinarily denying this to others and attempting to deny it to himself. He is subject to marked inner turmoil, but attempts to conceal this, too, from others and himself. His ambition and drive towards achievement, and in general his compulsive controls offer some compensation; but they are not enough. He suffers from melancholy and intense feelings of frustration. He finds it increasingly difficult to work effectively. At the root of his difficulty lies an identification with a dominant, and to him, unrewarding mother-figure, towards whom he reacts with some hostility, but towards whom he is very attracted sexually. For some reason (the record is not indicative) he is also fearful (and unable to express it) towards the father-figure. We may speculate that the father is perceived as strong but ineffectual in relation to the mother (for some reason) and that S has guilt over his attraction to the mother who is objective, strong, just, but unobtainable. With this nucleus in this type of oedipal conflict as a base, S's development was attended by deep guilt reactions stirred by a strict super-ego development. A relatively strong ego enabled him to move along foı a time until late adolescent and young adult situational factors decreased the effectiveness of ego functions—at least for a time. It is suggested that then either Don Juan behavior or symbolic acting out occurred (possibly both), and guilt increased until the prevalent masochistic pattern was re-established. One would suspect that depressive reactions, possibly suicidal preoccupation, began as the cycle became tighter and as the vocational-occupational sublimations became less effective with decreased efficiency in total functioning. The Don Juan hypothesis is in line with the speculation that S tried to act out his needs for masculine competence in the face of increasing feelings of sexual inadequacy and guilt. The anchorage of good, intense relations with peers is lacking although wished for.

Superficially this young man may give the impression of control and fair effectiveness. If our speculations concerning the nature of his difficulties are substantially correct, we may also suggest that he will be able to make very effective use of analytically-oriented therapy, providing this is both intensive and fairly extensive.

# Part IV

# BEHAVIORAL DATA

# Chapter 24

# PSYCHIATRIC CASE HISTORY ABSTRACT

## V.A. NEUROPSYCHIATRIC HOSPITAL

The case history abstract was compiled by Dr. William L. Unger, who was also John Doe's psychotherapist in the neuropsychiatric hospital. He was born in 1920. He received the B.S. degree in 1943 and the M.D. degree in 1946 from Marquette University. He is a Fellow in the American Medical Association and a member of the American Psychiatric Association. At present he is a staff Psychiatrist at the V.A. Neuropsychiatric Hospital, Los Angeles. His present activities include doing group psychotherapy with mental hospital patients, using a psychoanalytic orientation.

PRESENT COMPLAINT: Patient is a 25 year old white single male who entered voluntarily with the following symptoms: Insomnia, palpitation, night sweats, trembling when people observe him, and feelings of inadequacy. He states his difficulties began about six months after being in the Navy. He was in the medical corps and was a corpsman in the "psycho unit," later stationed on a hospital ship. Since his discharge, he has been unable to maintain a job because of the above symptoms. He dreads people watching him. His concentration is quite poor and this has become more intense within recent weeks. He is in good contact.

*Family History:* His father, a pharmacist by profession, was 60 years old at the time of his death from tuberculosis. The patient says that he did not have very close contact with his father because of the tuberculous condition. At the time of his father's death, the patient cried for 8 hours and says that he regrets that he had not been been able to put his arms around his father. The patient was 12 years old at the time of the father's death. The father is described as being moderate tempered, cool, and aloof.

The mother, age 63, is in good health. She is generous with people. She is emotional and demonstrative. It was necessary for her to work while the husband was still living. She is, at present, living in an apartment which she shares with the patient. A sister of the mother also lives in the same apartment, but at one time, neither spoke to each other for a period of five years. She is described by the patient as being solicitous and sympathetic, yet, she has frequently told the patient, "I never want to tell you what to do." When the patient goes out with friends, the only thing he talks about is his mother.

He speaks of how beautiful and how wonderful she is, and calls her up many times during the evening while he is out.

*Siblings:* A brother, age 41, has a history of many attempts at running away from home. He has been married twice and frequently has been found drunk by the patient. This brother frequently had altercations with the father while he was alive and the patient felt sorry for the antagonism caused by this brother. He is opinionated, but "wrong 99 per cent of the time."

Another brother is eighteen months older than the patient. This brother was closer to the patient all through their school years, but the patient says that this brother always wanted his own way, wanted to be the leader. He is now married, has three children, and has a responsible job. He was described as having a genuine interest in the welfare of the patient.

*Personal History:* As a child, the patient bit his nails and sucked his thumbs. He describes himself as being quite meticulous as far as habits were concerned and liked to keep things in order. He was always jealous of his toys and was afraid of wearing them out. He had enuresis until the age of 12. As a child, he frequently dreamed of being chased and not being able to run away. He was usually caught and would wake up frightened. At the age of 7, the patient was in an automobile accident in which the mother, father and the eldest brother were seriously hurt. The patient was not seriously injured. At the age of 8, he was accosted by a man he describes as a "degenerate," who attempted to kidnap him. This had a profound effect on him and he frequently thought of this traumatic experience. As a child, the patient was frightened by the eldest brother who would grimace and make peculiar noises outside the bedroom window of the two younger boys. He was always afraid of the dark and did not like to be left alone.

*Military History:* Patient enlisted in 1943 and was discharged in 1946 with a diagnosis of psychoneurosis, severe. While in the service he befriended another corpsman with whom he spent a major part of his service. One incident that the patient relates took place while riding cross-country on a hospital train. They had gotten off the train for a stretch during a ten minute stop-over and he urged his friend to look at some souvenirs being displayed on the station platform. The train began to pull out and as the patient was able to run faster than his friend, he had gotten on the train, but the friend slipped and fell beneath the wheels of the railroad car. The patient says he did not go to the aid of his friend but sat down in a chair and prayed that his friend was not killed. He overheard from spectators at the scene of the accident, that his friend's leg was injured. He later learned that an amputation was necessary and he visited this friend in the hospital. He says that he did not feel guilty any longer but felt badly for some time the after accident occurred.

He relates another incident that occurred at a camp. While out on maneuvers, a group of men were injured in a training accident. The patient felt that more should have been done for them than what the medical staff was already doing. He left the scene in disgust and returned to his bunk to remain there for the rest of the day. From that time on he felt that he was frequently criticized for his lack of interest in his work.

*Schooling:* During his school years he always received good grades and A's for effort. His memory was remarkable and he memorized an entire play in three days while in high school. At the age of 15, he wrote a short story which dealt with a young man who decided to become a priest. The hero had led a carefree life and had come from a wealthy family. His mother objected to his entering the seminary and for that reason, the hero postponed his desire. A short time later, the hero was killed and the mother felt great remorse because she did not allow the hero to become a priest. The patient states that he very seriously considered entering the seminary at one time, and that essentially was the story of his life.

*Social History:* The patient states that he has the desire to meet people, but cannot stand to have them look into his face because he believes that people will think he is strange. He preferred elderly people because he says "they will understand my condition." At the age of 20, he went with a girl of the same age but never had the intention of proposing marriage. He had sexual relations with the girl and believes that she was the source of his present luetic infection. He states that he had frequent sexual contact with pickups while in the service, but never felt gratification.

*Present Illness:* The patient relates a recent incident wherein he went to a motion picture theater in the afternoon of a week day when the house was relatively empty. He decided to visit the washroom before going to his seat and walked upstairs to the men's room. However, when he wished to take his seat, he could not walk down the stairs because he would have to face the manager, several ushers and the popcorn girl as he descended. He remained upstairs in the wash room for five hours and descended only when he was able to walk behind an old man. He also states that he frequently waits for people to gather at the corner where he wishes to board a bus because he cannot get into a bus alone. He admits compulsive behavior in that he frequently counts steps, blocks in the linoleum, and squares in the ceiling. He says that the hair on the nape of his neck bothers him and he frequently shaves his back.

*Mental Examination:* The patient is always very tense and evades giving history of his luetic infection. He states that he feels relieved now that the interviewer knows his condition and is anxious to have treatment for it. He has been preoccupied with pains in his chest, and believed something was wrong with his heart. He was greatly relieved when he was told that the electrocardiogram was negative. He receives interpretations willingly and states that he is anxious to make an adjustment. He feels that he owes his mother support, but is anxious to make a life for himself. He has good insight and is well oriented in all spheres. He denies any hallucinations. On the ward, he is described by his ward physician as being rather facetious and playful and enjoys occupational therapy.

# Chapter 25

# COURSE IN NEUROPSYCHIATRIC HOSPITAL

THE FOLLOWING notes are taken, verbatim, from the patient's "Clinical Folder," maintained while he was in the neuropsychiatric hospital. They are presented in order to give a picture of how this patient appeared to various professional personnel at different times. The dates of other events, such as the psychological testing, the initiation and termination of insulin coma therapy, etc. have been inserted. Attention is directed to the various diagnostic labels given this patient during his relatively short hospitalization. Actual dates, doctor's initials, and other possibly identifying data have been changed, but the relative chronology of events has been preserved.

*1. January 24, 1947 Admission Interview, Dr. V.*

Age 24. White male, voluntarily entered with following symptoms: insomnia, palpitation, trembling when people observe him, dysorexia, feelings of inadequacy, night sweats, feelings of weakness. He states his difficulties began about six months after entering the Service. He was Corpsman in "Psycho" Units, then stationed on Hospital ship. He has been unable to keep a job because of these above symptoms. He dreads people watching him. His concentration is quite poor and this has become more acute within recent weeks. Is in good contact.

Tentative diagnosis: Psychoneurosis, anxiety type, acute and severe.

*2. January 25, 1947. Admission Staff. Dr. M.*

Patient enters room rather tense and tremulous but later loosens up. States he has insomnia and perspires freely at night. He would rather be seclusive but is not asocial. He is unable to adjust himself in a gainful occupation and to apply himself, and entertains guilt feelings and will avoid people on the street. He denies any hallucinations or delusions. Affect appropriate; correctly oriented. Insight and judgment adequate.

Diagnosis: Psychoneurosis, anxiety severe.

*3. January 29, 1947. Ward Psychiatrist. Dr. V.*

Patient still anxious and tense in group and while on ward. Tremors of anxiety occur periodically. Patient is still tense while attending group psychotherapy, although improved. Verbalizes freely, but not wholly accessible. Patient states he has been used to bathing two or three times a day and shaving twice daily—"Tries to keep as clean as he can." Visits with mother for short periods and becomes tense in her presence.

This all tends to create an impression that the present condition may be due to homosexual panic.

*4. February 8, 1947. Psychiatric Consultant. Dr. I.*

Diagnosis lies between obsessive-compulsive neurosis, anxiety-hysteria and schizophrenia. Most likely appears to be obsessive-compulsive.

*5. April 13, 1947. Ward Psychiatrist. Dr. H.*

Patient expresses considerable anxiety and feels that he could not get along well on outside. Expresses ideas of insecurity. Would like individual psychotherapy.

Impression: Psychoneurosis, anxiety type.

*6. June 10, 1947. Ward Psychiatrist. Dr. H.*

Patient was presented to Psychiatric Consultant. At present there is some question of early schizophrenic reaction and severe obsessive-compulsive neurosis. Patient has become somewhat upset and confused in past several days.

*7. June 15, 1947. Psychological Testing.*

The following psychological tests were administered: Rorschach Test, Wechsler-Bellevue—Form II, and Bender-Gestalt.

*8. June 16, 1947. Ward Psychiatrist. Dr. G.*

Patient seems superficially to be in good condition and is getting impatient with hospitalization. Doctors who have worked with him feel that he is an incipient schizophrenic.

*9. June 19, 1947. Psychological Testing.*

The following psychological test was administered: Make A Picture Story test.

*10. July 20, 1947. Insulin Coma Therapy.*

Patient started on ICT

*11. July 27, 1947. Insulin Coma Therapy.*

Patient had first insulin coma at fifth treatment.

*12. August 9, 1947. Insulin Coma Therapy.*

ICT was terminated after six comas.

*13. August 10, 1947. Record of insulin treatment:*

a. Admission date: January 24, 1947
b. Diagnosis (final): Psychoneurosis, anxiety type, acute and severe
c. Date treatment started: June 20, 1947
d. Number insulin days: eleven
e. Number insulin hours: 25 hours, 15 minutes
f. Number hours unconscious: 6 hours, 45 minutes
g. Number shocks: six
h. Basal ganglia reached: 4 hours, 30 minutes
i. Midbrain reached: 2 hours, 15 minutes
j. Premedullary: none
k. Medullary: none
l. Shock dose: minimum, 300 units; maximum, 400 units; average, 316 units
m. Total amount of insulin used: 2,720 units
n. Date terminated: August 9, 1947
o. Reason for termination: nonpsychotic diagnosis

*14. August 11, 1947. Psychological Testing*

The following psychological tests were administered: Thematic Apperception Test, Minnesota Multiphasic Personality Inventory, and Draw-A-Person.

*15. August 12, 1947. Ward Psychiatrist. Dr. B.*

Mother states that patient was seclusive and highly irritable on return home from Service. He sat around the house all day but was never delusional. He was always a "mother's boy." Most of his friends were "older men with money." Both older brothers were "very nervous." Patient states he began worrying about his appearance during Service, gradually withdrew from social contacts, often felt that surrounding objects "looked different." Has an abnormal fear that people watch him because he looks odd.

Impression: Early dementia praecox, paranoid

*16. August 13, 1947. Psychological Test Report.*

Psychologist reports that the over-all impression is that of a schizoid personality subjected to strong emotional conflicts and attempting to adjust on an obsessive-compulsive level in order to prevent a schizophrenic break.

*17. August 17, 1947. Ward Psychiatrist. Dr. S.*

This patient presents a complex clinical picture. It has been considered a psychosis by some and a psychoneurosis by others. At a review of the psychological test data, felt patient to be nonpsychotic and insulin coma therapy was therefore discontinued August 9, 1947. Patient transferred to an open ward where he will receive psychotherapy.

*18. September 18, 1947. Hospital Disposition.*

Discharge diagnosis: Anxiety reaction.

# Chapter 26

# PSYCHIATRIC NOTES FROM THE NEURO-PSYCHIATRIC HOSPITAL

The therapist was Dr. William L. Unger. See biographical note to Psychiatric Case History Abstract, page 237.

THE FOLLOWING are excerpts of psychiatric interviews with John Doe during the time he was receiving insulin coma therapy (ICT). The therapist saw the patient for interviews twice a week, immediately following his (daily) insulin treatment. The notes are verbatim, but they represent only a part of the content of each of the sessions.

1. *July 24, 1947*. (This was the fourth day of ICT. The patient had not yet reached coma level. This interview was at 11:00 A.M., one-half hour after the termination of ICT for that day. The patient's face bore a look of marked apprehension. The therapist began by inquiring as to what made him feel upset.)

Today I've felt like killing myself. I've thought of jumping out of the window. I feel as though I'm liable to do anything. I don't want to go on pass over the week-end with my mother anymore. I went home and felt like killing her. I couldn't sleep all the time I was home. I had a feeling she was standing over me with a knife. (Long pause.) I couldn't take it at home, so I went over to a friend's house to visit. While I was there I got so mad at myself I picked up a table lamp and smashed it. Nobody said anything, but I felt ashamed. Oh doctor, I hate myself. I hate everything about me. I hate myself for being homosexual. I don't want to grovel in the dirt. I don't know what to do. If I run away I have nowhere to go. (Patient stood up, glared at the therapist and paced the floor). If I do wait for things to come about, I still won't be happy. By things, I mean a job, wife, home and a family. If I could commit suicide without inflicting pain, I wouldn't hesitate to do it, now. Everybody gets on my nerves. One thing though, I've learned to call you "Doc" and I couldn't when I came here. Really, I can't see that psychotherapy is helping me; I feel like I want to quit.

2. (Second day that patient had been in coma while in ICT. The patient describes his feelings toward the physician attending the insulin patients in the following excerpt.)

I had the feeling that Dr. L. was God. It seemed as though some evil forces controlled me and I was atoning for all the sins of man. I know I was yelling when I told Dr. L. that I believe in God. They were starving me and keeping me thirsty; it was a wonder that I stood up under it.

3. Doc, I don't feel much like talking today. It's no use, I feel terrible—and it's worse at night when I'm alone. But that's a funny thing—sometimes I like being alone. Sometimes I used to hide behind the newspaper and wish Mother would leave me alone. I never liked the dark, and hated to go to bed. When I was small my older brother used to sneak out of his bedroom window and climb over the porch and stand outside my window and make all kinds of noises and ugly faces at me; and I always hated him because of that and Mother would yell at him to stop, but he wouldn't. She could never make him mind her.

I have a feeling like I'm being punished, because I deserve it. If someone got to know me, they wouldn't like me because I'm homosexual. I get tired of things so easily. I couldn't make a go of marriage. I'd be selfish, like I was with my toys and the way I looked back at my heels to see if they were wearing out. I never liked to have other kids play with my toys because they'd wear them out or break them. I would be tired of a woman who is used for sex and just homemaking. (*Long pause.*)

Mother kisses me in public and that's something I can't stand. She deliberately does it when we're away from home and I try to shove her away. She doesn't hesitate to tell other people what a good mother she is, and how much she does for me. I guess I really hate and have hated her for a long time. I remember when I was eleven, I saw a man kiss her, this man used to come to our house ever so often. But when I saw that, I thought she was making a fool of herself. I wanted mother to love me. Before that time I had a wonderful feeling for Mother, but it's a different feeling now. We used to have happy times together. That was when my mother and older brother and I used to go to shows. We were very poor. My father was in the hospital with tuberculosis, and we had to scrimp and save.

4. I left the hospital on Friday with a week-end pass. I went home. I couldn't relax. I felt my face get hot when anyone looked at me. But, that night I sat up and played cards until one o'clock.

Saturday I took a long walk. I saw a man selling papers at a corner stand. I was afraid of him. It reminded me of the time when I was twelve and went for a newspaper. The newspaper man talked to me for a long time and then put his hand down here. I got scared and ran home all the way. When I got home Mother asked me what was the matter, but I couldn't tell her. She tried to get it out of me, but I still couldn't say it, so she slapped me.

On my way back to the hospital there was a woman who got on the bus and sat down next to me. She must have been about fifty years old. Her umbrella was right next to my leg and it kept touching me. I was so angry I felt like strangling her or braining her. I got nervous, my face got red and my heart started to pound. I disliked her as soon as I knew she was going to sit next to me, and she sat so close to me. It upset me very much.

I'm scared to go out with a girl now; I just don't feel I can hold together. She'll see that I'm shaky and ask what's wrong.

When I was thirteen I went collecting clothes-hangers for a drive on at school. One place I went there was a married woman in a nightgown who came to the door. She told me to come in while she got a couple of hangers. Then she sat down next to me and put her arms around me. I kept thinking that her husband would walk in. Sex frightened me then; it still does, because it seems so seductive, I guess.

(The following is a fragment of the previous night's dream.)

I was in a car and we were crossing a bridge. I saw a woman in a black satin dress standing at the end of the bridge. For some reason I think she was waiting for a policeman to come out of the station near the bridge. She looked bad to me. I was about four or five years old in the dream.

Mother used to wear black as her good clothes. She thought she would look better in black because she wasn't a girl any longer. Now she dresses like she was sixteen years old and I think it's silly or foolish. I hate to be seen anywhere with her. People say to her that she looks so young to have sons who are grown up.

5. I remember when I was seven we were in a traffic accident. My mother, dad and brother were in the hospital. But I wasn't hurt, so I stayed with another family. I had to sleep with the girl who worked for them. She was quite bold, but pleasant. When we'd go to sleep, she'd put her arms around me. It was a wonderful feeling I had toward her; I felt very close to her. I recall enjoyable days when she and I would go out together and pick berries. She was wonderful and I think I would have done anything on this earth for her. I felt very bad when Mother came to get me. I hated to leave that place—I don't remember the people she worked for. I would rather have stayed there than gone back to my family. Really I wanted this girl more than I wanted Mother. I actually wished that my father and brother would die and then maybe I wouldn't have to go back with Mother.

6. I always felt disgusted with my brother. No matter what we did, we'd always argue. He always was the leader and I could never be; I hated him for that. I never wanted to be seen with him. I felt ashamed of him. He was dark and had thick bushy hair. He had a wide nose—this, I think was the thing I hated about him most of all. He used to bite his lips and it used to aggravate me. To me, he always appeared sloppy and needed a bath. But I knew he was clean. I used to have to sleep in the same bed with him and

dreaded going to bed with him because he was dirty. He got along pretty well with other kids—always had friends. I used to wonder why kids preferred to play with him and not me. I would go crazy with jealousy if Mother bought him something and nothing for me. If he even so much as looked at my toys, I felt like batting his brains out.

I always wanted a dog and finally we got one. But the dog liked him. The dog bit me on the finger—that was like the end of the world for me.

7. When I was a small boy, I liked to play with dolls and bits of ribbons. My mother used to give me all her old jewelry to play with. My father would get angry about this and made me stop and then he'd fight with Mother on account of it. She got me a buggy and doll dresses. I enjoyed playing and got along with girls better than I did with boys. I never liked active sports.

I used to wet my pants and even wet the bed until I was twelve or thirteen. Mother would come in during the night to see if I did wet. I could have kept from doing it, but I knew that Mother would come anyway. She would be mad at me sometimes for it, but never hit me.

Mother thought that maybe my bladder was weak. She took me to a doctor and he massaged my prostate. I only had to go once to him. I remember he was nice to me and gave me some foreign stamps.

Something else happened about that same time. Mother took me to a doctor because I had some trouble with my eyes. The doctor said I had some rare eye disease and I'd be blind by the time I was seventeen. My eyes were tested and some glasses were made, but I never picked them up. Mother never did anything about my eyes after that. I used to try to feel thankful if I could get by until I was seventeen. But nothing happened and then I gave myself until I'd be twenty-one.

8. (On this day patient related the following dream). I was going downhill in a car and couldn't stop it. The brakes were screeching and I was steering around dangerous curves. Next, I found myself at the top of the hill again, but this time it was at night and there was a woman dressed in a chiffon negligee driving. We were going over the same route and the brakes screeched. We went down one stretch of road that was particularly steep but got down safely. I didn't wake up. She was a girl who knew what she was doing. She just seemed to appear from out of the night dressed in a negligee. She seemed friendly to me and the negligee was appropriate. But in a way she was unfriendly. She was just there and made no bones about taking the wheel. I especially noticed her hand reaching out to the gearshift. To me the meaning of the dream is that I lack something in myself because the first time I rode alone it was worse. I need somebody to show me. Her attire excited me.

She reminded me of a big WAVE I knew in the Navy. She worked on the same ward in the hospital with me. She followed me everywhere, she would never let me out of her sight. I disliked her when she was near, yet I wanted her when she was away. She was a homely girl, at least I thought so. I wanted to marry her. She would be a good cook and not unfaithful to me. I used to assign her to the worst jobs and she'd do them and never complain. She liked me no matter what I did to her. One day I said, "Step into the broom closet a moment." I locked her in for four hours. It was a relief.

She wrote to her family about me. She showed me letters from them; they were glad because anyone that she picked out would be a good husband. I've thought about her a lot. She didn't have a good figure, but I could get away with anything with her. I felt superior to her. I used to break dates with her and she'd take it. Her girlfriend told me I treated her terrible. Used to tell me I ought to be nice to her or leave her alone. I feel sorry for the way I treated her. I'd get in touch with her if I could and probably would marry her. I looked forward to stringing her along. She was transferred from camp. She was willing to desert the Navy to stay with me. Then, when she left I was lost.

9. (ICT had been terminated prior to this session.)

I feel terrible today. This morning I felt like I was falling out of bed. Now, I feel like I was hit over the head. I had a dream but I can remember just parts of it. The outstanding part was seeing two hands playing a piano. Then it seemed like the hands started to reach out for me. The room we were in was very small and dark. I felt frightened. I was afraid the hands would harm me—they might touch me. I'm thinking now that I'm afraid of the fellow in the bed next to mine. (Reference is to another patient who sleeps next to John Doe.) Seems like he was in the dream somewhere. I felt afraid like that when my oldest brother made faces at me while I was in bed. My throat feels like it's up in my mouth. I have to cough to clear my throat. I remember having a lump in my throat when I was about nine years old. My parents used to quarrel. I would side with my mother. I guess I really blame my father for being sick. But I knew mother wanted sympathy. She always complained that her sisters were jealous of her because she was prettier. My mother's brother drinks a lot. I guess he's an alcoholic, but he's a successful businessman. Her other brother is well-to-do also, but very tight. I think he would help Mother if she asked him.

I didn't get along with my brother. I never liked his features. He reminds me of Dad. He's dark, has a big nose and always wants to be the leader. Besides, he was Dad's favorite.

If only Mother had been a different type. I wish she'd let her hair grow natural and not try to color it. I wish she wouldn't drink. One time she got me so mad when she was drunk, I had to hit her. She had a black eye for a week. If she'd only be content and not always talk about wanting to go places.

She thinks she's thirty-five years old and ought to be escorted around like a young girl.

If only Dad had died sooner and she would have remarried. I think she would have been better off. There was a man about fifty who was interested in her. He would have been like a father to her and could handle her. I can't. Mother is not an easy person to get along with.

(At this point, the therapist was transferred to another Service and, because seeing the patient was not administratively feasible, therapy was discontinued.)

# Chapter 27

# PSYCHOTHERAPY NOTES FROM MENTAL HYGIENE CLINIC

John Doe's psychotherapist at the V.A. Mental Hygiene Clinic was Miss Lillian P. Kaplan. Miss Kaplan received a Master of Social Work degree from the Graduate School of Social Work, University of Southern California in 1941. She was a social worker at a children's agency and in public welfare. During World War II, she was a psychiatric case worker for the American Red Cross and was assigned to neuropsychiatric sections in Army hospitals, where she participated in diagnostic evaluations and in individual and group psychotherapy. She has been at the Veterans Administration Mental Hygiene Clinic, Los Angeles, since 1946. In addition to her individual and group psychotherapy with veterans, she supervises social work therapists in the Clinic and is a student training supervisor for psychiatric social work students at the School of Social Welfare at UCLA. She is co-author of articles on individual and individual-group therapy. She is a member of the American Orthopsychiatric Association and an active member of the American Association of Psychiatric Social Workers. At present, she is vice-chairman of the Southern California branch of this latter organization.

THESE NOTES are from the Veterans Administration Mental Hygiene Clinic, where John Doe went for out-patient treatment following his discharge from the hospital.

## INITIAL INTERVIEW, September 22, 1947

When I went to the Reception Room to get the patient I found him pacing back and forth in the hallway, a tall, slender, somewhat athletic looking fellow with black hair and grey eyes. He was quite tense during the interview, shifted frequently in the chair, looked out the window, frequently crossed and uncrossed his legs, and spoke rather rapidly. Early in the interview the patient was very hostile and indicated a lot of resistance about treatment. I therefore spent considerable time discussing this with him. He became noticeably more relaxed at the point that I talked with him about the interrelationship of physical symptoms and emotions.

Patient was discharged from the V.A. Hospital after eight months' hospitalization. Even though the personnel at the hospital encouraged the patient to remain for further treatment, he decided not to stay because he didn't feel that the treatment was really helpful. He was given insulin at the Hospital—he had a reaction to this; he was unconscious until the following day. He said that he also had individual therapy with five different doctors. He felt that the hospital aggravated his condition—he frequently blew up at everything—

for example, the food. I wondered why he went to the hospital; there was then some discussion of his symptoms. He indicated that he is very indecisive about things. He wants to go to school, yet he feels that he'll make a failure of this if he does go to school. He can't concentrate, is restless, can't sit still, he wants to be alone, yet he's not happy. When he's alone, he's tearful, feels like he's going to blow up, feels angry towards people. He then commented that he also has this feeling about his mother. His heart goes fast, his legs shake. At times he gets nervous because he thinks people are looking at him. That was somewhat his feeling about coming here. He gets nervous when he comes downtown, goes to the grocery, etc. He feels like he's constantly trembling. For example, he will be on the street, he begins trembling (physical trembling), he'll stand in a doorway because he's ashamed that people might see him in this condition. He felt that these symptoms began three months after he was in the Service. It was then that he got nervous and was sent to a psychiatrist. He said that just previous to this an incident had happened which was related to the nervousness, but he apparently found it difficult to discuss this until later in the interview. When he came out of Service people were constantly telling him that he was nervous, and this upset him. Before Service, people always said that nothing upset him and he was able to work, meet people, and was very comfortable. Since he had brought out some feelings of resistance about coming to the clinic, I picked those up, and wondered what his feelings were about coming to the clinic. He replied by saying that he wanted help, and that's why he came. This was said with a great deal of hidden hostility. He then said, "People kill me by saying 'don't be nervous, and that doesn't help.' " I wondered whether he felt that treatment would consist of someone telling him what to do. He replied rather ambivalently he wasn't sure; he then said that one doctor in service had told him there was nothing that he should be nervous about, and he didn't think that kind of an approach was very helpful. I then talked with him a little bit about the treatment and the role of therapist. In reply to this he brought out some further symptoms. He said he gets tense in every situation; even when he's alone he can't relax. Sometimes he feels he would like to step in front of a car and end it all. Yet, he doesn't want to die. He then brought out some anxiety about "Catholic people being punished for that." I said that I could see that living was pretty hard for him. He said, "Yeah—I hate myself, I don't feel adequate, I would like to go to school to study business administration, I don't feel that I can do this because I'm too nervous." I said that I could see that maybe he wasn't ready to go to school, and that being nervous and tense does take a lot of energy, and maybe he doesn't have enough energy left for the other things that he would like to plan for himself.

Patient entered the Service in 1943, and was a medical corpsman. There was some verbalization of hostility about his responsibility in the Service. He felt that the patients made him worse—in fact, at times he felt that he was more emotionally disturbed than the patients he was escorting to a hospital. He told how he would come back from one trip from escorting a patient somewhere, and ten minutes after his return he was sent somewhere else. Sometimes "I would have a bad time with a patient and have to sit up with him all night." At this point of the interview he was able to tell me about the incident in Service which was related to his seeing a psychiatrist for the first time. "I practically had a black-out at that time. It wasn't serious, just humiliating." Patient then told that the company was drilling on parade ground. He was called out in front of the group, and was made a spectacle of. This had been done several times previously. This particular time patient blew up. During the following week, he "was in a rage." I said apparently he felt that he couldn't express his anger about the situation. Patient then brought out feelings about "not being able to express myself in the Service." It was during that time that his head began hurting him. He then said that he also developed a pain in his chest and heart. While at the V.A. Hospital he had all kinds of tests, an EKG, EEG, x-rays, etc., but all these were negative. Yet he "still has pains." He then commented, "I'm not a psychosomatic mental case." He then brought out some feeling about imaginary pain. I discussed this in detail with him. I gave him examples of how being emotionally upset can manifest itself physically. As we discussed this it was apparent that the patient became more accepting of it, and he said, "It's never been explained to me that way—now it makes more sense."

For one year prior to going into Service he worked at a millinery shop, as a clerk. Before that he worked at a drug store. He began working there when he was 17, and he remained with the latter company for four years. I said it sounded as if he had done a good job in view of his promotion to assistant managership. Patient said that was true, and then added that he wasn't nervous at that time. I asked about the circumstances of his leaving there, and he then told me that he was waiting on one of the employees to whom he gave a discount for some merchandise he was buying. The manager corrected him for this, saying he shouldn't have done it. Patient said he would continue doing it, and thereupon quit. He was asked to stay on, but he refused to do so. When he left for Service, he was told that he could return and that they would work with him so he could be advanced. When patient returned from Service, he did go back there and saw one of the owners, but he was so extremely upset and nervous that he left during the interview, and is "now ashamed to return." After he came back from Service, he worked for two months in a men's furnishing store and became quite nervous doing this work and quit his job. He then commented that there were so many things about himself that he couldn't understand—for example, he's constantly writing himself notes. He never consults them. Also, sudden noises bother him.

Patient says that he quit school in the 10th grade. While in the hospital he took some tests and received credit for high school work. He says he quit school because he wanted to go to work. In fact, while he was going through high school he was working part-time. He liked school, his grades were pretty good, and he always got "A" for effort. He took an academic course. He got along fine in high school. He was president of his class, was well-liked, but now he has the feeling that nobody likes him and he likes no one. He would like to have friends, but he isn't able to do anything about it.

Patient's father, who was a pharmacist, died after an illness of ten years, during which time he had TB. His mother worked. She is not working now. If patient goes to school his mother will of necessity have to work at least part-time. At this time he commented that he doesn't worry about money, and he never did. Patient has two older married brothers.

At the end of the interview patient said that the thing he wanted to hear me say is that he will get well. I said that I could understand his wishing this kind of a guarantee about his getting well, but the thing I could say to him was that we had helped others who perhaps had similar symptoms to his and maybe we could help him too. When I said this his eyes filled with tears, and he commented, "I dislike myself, I'm not a man." At the end of the interview I explained to the patient that we would get in touch with him about treatment. He then indicated that even though he was planning to go to school, he could work out his plans so that he could come in for an afternoon appointment.

*Brief Summary:* Patient gives the impression of being a rather immature, dependent, very anxious, somewhat narcissistic person. He just left the V.A. Hospital, where he was hospitalized for eight months, and his feeling about it was that it was not too helpful. He seemed resistant to treatment. However, I was able to work through some of this with him, and by the end of the interview I believe that he felt more positively about treatment. It is my impression that patient has difficulty handling his feelings about dependency, hostility, aggression and authority.

## SECOND INTERVIEW, October 7, 1947

Since this patient has been seen at intake both he and his mother had called numerous times in order to arrange for an appointment for an interview. It was finally arranged for me to see him and when they came in he arrived about one-half hour early and seemed very agitated. He walked in my office, sat down and said that he seems to become more and more nervous and excitable. Everything bothers him, he is trembling both physically and mentally. It has been the same since he has been out of the hospital. Maybe he was a little worse since he has been out. He has had eight months of psychotherapy and insulin and nothing has helped him. Because he can't concentrate he can't read a page. It seems that he looks at the same place and finds that the scenery changes. It seems as if it is twitching in his mind. He loses trace of the thoughts, and he blocks. He talked about the various doctors he had seen in the hospital. He finally said that he had seen so many people that he was confused and this together with being confused inside was not of help to him. Everything in general bothers him. Patient then went on to describe some of the feelings. People look at him all the time and he feels guilty as if he had done something. He again told the story of going to a movie and not being able to go out until he could walk in back of a man who would hide him. He talked of his physical difficulties and was not quite sure that all of the examinations were really negative. He is tired all the time, feels like a rag. He is afraid of people, doesn't like anyone, won't trust anyone, and doesn't think anyone is worth while. It seems that every time there is some motive behind it all, and no one means anything that they say. He is suspicious of people and yet he is afraid of showing his nervousness toward them. Whenever he is with people his legs wobble. When someone is around there is a pressure and he can't think.

Patient talked about his experiences in the hospital. At night he would feel that the fellows sleeping next to him would harm him. Now he is afraid that his mother will do something to him. The same thing had been true in the Service when he felt that some of the men would do something to him. Many times he has been afraid that his mother would harm him and he knows this is silly. During all of this patient stammered and stuttered and slapped his legs.

He talked about the Service, the difficulty there and finally his hospitalization there. He feels that he changed completely while he was in Service. He was a person who never expressed any feeling. He did very well economically and now he is a failure in everything. He hates people to look at him and if I didn't look at him he would feel safer.

He then talked about the time before he was hospitalized. He was nervous and he and his mother went to a resort. She thought that he ought to go to the hospital but he never believed anyone would help him. It got so bad that his brother finally took him to the hospital.

Patient again talked about seeing the same scene which changed frequently. He talked about insulin shock and the horror of coming out of it. He felt worse after that than before. He recalled that coming out of them he had the feeling that he was dead with his eyes open. He couldn't focus. Then he saw someone in front of him. It looked like God and he had to make up for all his sins, so he yelled and struck out at random. He believed in God then but now he doesn't know if he did. When he finally came to it was the doctor. In his own mind the patient doesn't believe that he is a good person. He can't pray anymore.

Patient then talked about being staffed at the hospital in front of an audience of fifty or sixty people. They talked over his whole case. He finally accepted coming to the clinic. When the appointment was not made readily and quickly for him he felt very anxious but now that he is coming to treatment he feels much better. He thinks he feels better with women and that they understand him more. Perhaps he can be helped better. He was glad of a female therapist. Patient said he had a lot of psychology tests and had psychodrama too. The thing that he hates more than anything else are the ink blots. He daydreams constantly, and always daydreams of someone else or being someplace. Somehow the ink blot test frightened him in that respect.

The patient then told me that he had a habit of writing notes of all the conversations he had. He puts these notes in his pocket and keeps them for a long time and later he throws them away. It seems that he can forget the things when he writes them down. It seems as if he writes a load off of his mind.

Patient was so upset and agitated that I suggested that he come in to see me twice a week for the time being.

(I conferred with the two psychiatrists who had known the patient at the hospital. They both felt that he would be a good therapeutic bet and felt that the insulin shock was unnecessary in this situation. They seemed to think that this was a psychoneurotic patient with obsessive-compulsive symptoms.)

## THIRD INTERVIEW, October 9, 1947

Patient came in today and immediately launched into a discussion. Like the previous interview he smoked one cigarette after another, lighting the new cigarette with the old. He said that he had decided that he might have to move away from his mother because he can't stand being interrupted. He'd rather be off by himself because he is so irritable. For instance, sitting in the room it seems to change and everything is different. As he talked on and on he finally came out with the feeling that he was afraid of being hostile and acting out his aggressiveness to his mother. "What would happen if I took a knife to my mother or to anybody. I am afraid of harm coming to me from other people and I might do likewise to them."

The patient wants to be alone. He is so fearful of his ideas, which make him feel powerful and it is wrong to feel that way. He doesn't know if he wants to have that much power. He is also afraid that his fear of what he can do won't hold him back. He talked of having worked out plans like a problem in arithmetic for killing his mother. There is something in him that makes him feel that that is not as bad a thought as he should think it is. He knows that he avoids crowds, going out, etc., because he is afraid of throwing something. I asked for examples and he said he did once and the example was that he threw an ashtray against the floor. Another example was that he was going out one night and didn't know which of two sport coats to choose; consequently, he tore the one at hand to pieces. Also, it seemed that there were several times in the hospital when he wanted to rave and rant. He would have broken anything or hit anyone. He has a great desire to destroy and the only reason he doesn't do it is that he is afraid he will go too far. Again he recalled nothing of what he had discussed with the therapists in the hospital.

He again brought up the idea that he feels exceptional because he has destructive thoughts, mostly. For instance, he is always tearing something, a newspaper, or a match cover. He carried a book or some keys in his hand as a defense. He is afraid of himself.

The patient then went into a long discussion about the fact that he feels like two people. Often when he is alone he doesn't know which person he is. It seems that there is one person telling him to do one thing which is good and another person telling him to do the opposite, which could be evil. He is compelled to do the things which either side tells him to do. He cannot help it. It seems that he has to accept it. He has had this feeling for a long time, even before the hospital. He has never explained it before or put it into words. He then drew a picture in the air showing himself in the middle and the good side on one side and bad side on the other. One side whispers one thing and the other says the opposite. He is in conflict. Sometimes it seems so real that it's as if there were really two people inside of him. He wants to be strong but he knows he isn't. He knows that he doesn't have much time to live and he is sure that in three years he will be dead. Therefore, it is like killing time. With this in mind, what is the sense of living and trying to keep impulses in. The break will come anyway so why not give in. But the better side of himself keeps him from doing the things just for the time being.

Patient talked a little bit about the fact that he doesn't fully believe that he is 100 per cent physically well, although proof has been given to him. He doesn't believe in religion anymore, but he has never found a real spiritual leader and maybe he is mixed up.

He talked of wanting to be a priest at one time and then felt he wasn't really good enough. Now he is glad that he didn't become one because he would be committing a sin if he did become a priest in a hypocritical way. He was an alter boy for a long time and very much impressed. He recalled that during adolescence he was in church one day and it seemed as if the statue of a saint moved. This meant that she was giving approval. When he was in high school a priest thought it would be a good idea but he finally decided that he wasn't good enough. Last Sunday he went to church with his aunt and saw something which he couldn't quite discuss with his aunt. He was looking at the statue of Jesus Christ. The more he looked at the statue the more aware he became that the blood from the heart was real and it seemed as if Christ was moving his hands toward him. It made him feel very strange. It looked as if this were not a statue but a real human being and he was very frightened.

Following this the patient again talked about his destructive thoughts and the fact that God knew what he was thinking and that he was very distressed about that. I said he had destructive ideas to people and particularly toward his mother. He said that he hated himself, he was no good, he wanted to find peace of mind. There is always the fear of a knife in the back of his head. Whenever the phone rings it is bad news, everything seems to have a sinister meaning. Everyone seems to laugh at him. He feels and hears it. Sometimes it is not real words but the way people look. At school the patient is restless, he feels like he's lost but he is trying desperately to hang on.

During this interview and the one previously the patient smoked one cigarette after another, talked continuously, moved around in his chair considerably but did not get up and walk around as he had in the first interview.

The impression I gained during the interview was that he was obviously suffering from obsessive ideas in relation to destruction. On the other hand, I was concerned about the possible hallucinatory experiences and his description of himself as a divided person. The impression I gained was that this was much more of a paranoid schizophrenic process than was evidenced in the intake interview or in the report from the hospital. In my consultation with the two psychiatrists, both of whom had seen him at the V.A. Hospital, the feeling was that this was more of a severe psychoneurotic.

## CONSULTATION, October 13, 1947

Conference with Assistant Chief Psychiatrist: The case to date was reviewed as was the material in the record from the V.A. Hospital. It was felt that to transfer this case would be very traumatic and that I should continue with this man since it seemed that some kind of a relationship is in the process of being established. It was also felt that this case should be supervised by a psychiatrist. The patient seemed to present a severe obsessional picture and could be considered as a borderline psychotic. Therapeutic procedure at this time would be to listen and give the patient reassuring interpretations. It may be possible to relieve some of the anxiety. Constant and careful check should be made for signs of acting out. At such times hospitalization should be considered. It might be helpful for the patient to have a relationship with an understanding person who will help him find sense to these things and ideas that are bothering him. Interpretation should be more along the line that these things are not so terrible and also to generalize much of this for him. It is quite obvious that this patient is fearful of domination by the mother.

## FOURTH INTERVIEW, October 13, 1947

In this interview the patient was somewhat calmer. He looked a little better and smoked only three cigarettes.

Interview was started by discussion of his feeling in class. It seems that occasionally he has the feeling of rocking back and forth as if it were a terrific earthquake. It frightens him considerably. This has happened several times both in the hospital and out of the hospital. He talked of having some "awful feelings" whenever he seems to feel a change of surroundings. He has had some suicidal impulses which came along with depression. Patient said that he was disturbed in class today and then thinking back he recalled that he had wanted to ask a question and was afraid of doing it because the teacher looked right at him. He sits in back of the class because he doesn't want anyone to look at him, particularly when he begins to shake and feels upset. He talked of having pains in his head and feeling that the top of his head is stuffed. He is always tired out, he is afraid to sleep and it seems as if he feels he can't close his eyes. We talked a little bit about physical reactions and I gave him a very simple interpretation of psychosomatic theory.

Patient again talked about not being able to relax and not getting anything out of life and feeling that he just can't learn. In the hospital the doctor told him that he would be better if he thought of someone else instead of himself and the patient didn't like it. He recalled telling the therapist so in group therapy. He finds that many things depress him. He is easily influenced by appearance of objects and people scare him. He is always fearful of the dark. Somehow it is related to evil spirits being there. He is afraid that somebody may jump out on him from behind a tree. He then related the story that at the age of seven while walking in the park just back of his mother and brother a man did pull him through a clump of trees but he screamed and yelled and was able to get help both from his mother and a policeman. He was told never to talk to strangers and he has always been afraid of someone murdering him. When he was about four he used to go to town frequently in an automobile. They would pass a bridge. A woman in black used to stand on the bridge. He was fascinated by her and would always look for her. In fact he still sees her and often looks at women to see if they in some way look like her. He never asked his parents about her and it seemed to be a mystery. It didn't seem real. Somehow it often seemed as if she was part of the idea that a devil could take any form. He recalled that as a child he was told that a devil lived in a certain church. He didn't believe it because in his religion devils can't live in church. However, he had always got the feeling that church meant protection and when anyone asked him where he lived he would always say, "In church," and it was safe there. He talked considerably about the feeling of security in the church and the feeling that he always had of harm possibly coming to him.

He has never really loved anyone or liked anyone, not even his mother. He knows that his mother will really not hurt him yet he has this fear. He has a fear that the mother will knife him in the back. Then he is also afraid that he might use the knife on her. He is fearful of losing control. His mother plays on his sympathy by saying, "After all I have done for you," and this builds up the hatred.

He has never forgotten the fact that at age eight he had his eyes examined and the doctor said he had a rare disease and would someday be blind. Other than checking this further his mother refused to take him to any doctor. Now he knows that this is not true but his eyes still bother him, he still can't read. He still carries with him the feeling that maybe he will go blind. He talked about his father who had TB. He resented the fact that in his early childhood he couldn't go near him or touch him, because he was ill. Everything had to be sterilized. He recalled that he couldn't even sit in a chair that his father sat in. With a good deal of feeling he told about the fact that he was not allowed to go to the funeral of his father or to see him during the last week of his life. He used to blame his father for everything but now doesn't do so. He dislikes his mother because she is a weak person and allows everyone to run over her; by this he means his relatives after the father's death. The patient talked about his mother wanting to be called beautiful. He hates to tell her that she wasn't and isn't that beautiful. He recalls that he was always ashamed of having no father. He was always fearful of bringing any friends home. He envied people who could. He used to think if only he had another father or mother. He hated his older brother too. Somehow he always goes back to a period when they used to play games and his brother wanted to be the commanding officer while the patient was supposed to be a private. He can't stand to be near him. Although the brother is 18 months older, the patient feels as if he is 20 years older. His brother tries to be nice to him but the patient can't accept this.

He talked again about his resentment towards his mother and brother, both trying to dominate him, watching him, etc.

There was a thing that had bothered the patient for some time. He is always afraid of his shoes wearing out. In fact, for a period of two years, after each step he would turn around and look to see if the heels wore off. This was true as a youngster. If anyone gave him anything or if he bought anything he would ask if it would wear out. If it did he didn't want it. If he were given gifts if he found that they were strong and would not wear out he would hang onto them and get rid of all the other things. Patient said that he got relief out of talking. During this time I did give him assurance and very simple interpretations, or else tried to make a few connections on a simple level for him. He accepted this eagerly and it was difficult to close this interview.

## FIFTH INTERVIEW, October 16, 1947

The patient said that he wanted to see a doctor again because his arm was still numb from the shots that he had had. When I asked which arm he didn't know. He then went on to tell me that he had a dream the previous night. Previously he used to dream considerably but it was usually the exact repetition of what happened during the day. Now his dreams are a little different. They are repetitive dreams, usually about hands. It seems as if hands mean a lot to him. This is also significant in the last dream. He was dreaming that he was lying in bed. There was someone by the side of the bed. Something said to him, "If you don't get out you will be hurt." Then something came in and he heard it. He imagined that it was hands. He also felt that if he could use his hands he could push the chair away and then things won't bother him any more. But he had a hard time pushing the chair. Hands then came reaching for him but instead they came for the chair and saved him from things.

Last night he had a dream that he was on a sailing trip around the world. There were lots of people on the boat. As the boat got ready to dock, everybody would get off but he couldn't. The people that were taken off were greeted with open arms but somehow he wasn't allowed to get off the boat. The boat stopped at twenty places and something happened each time where he was not allowed to get off the boat. He was pretty discouraged yet he was pretty happy too to be left alone. I didn't go into any interpretation of it and the patient told me that he thought it meant that he was not at home at any place and that he didn't seem to fit in. No one seemed to like him. He wanted people to greet him and to meet him but it didn't turn out that way. I then asked him if the boat had any special meaning to him and he said that it did. It meant drifting around, no stability. It seemed as if it were like his mind, moving from one place to another. He then went on to say, too, that he never thinks of people but of their hands because they could do harm, they could choke, stick a knife in one's back, etc.

Whenever he gets angry he is afraid of expressing his anger. What happens is that he pounds on something and tears come to his eyes. He has looked at his hands whenever he thinks of doing away with his mother. Probably he won't do anything but he doesn't like those thoughts.

When the patient was six years old there was an automobile accident in which everybody was hurt but the patient. He stayed with a family during that period and was very happy. In fact, he was rather disappointed, it seemed, that everybody was alive. He enjoyed his situation then. It seems as if he is never satisfied with what happens.

Another thing that occurred to him was that he always wanted to be somebody else. His mind was transparent. His mind was like millions of buildings, each one with thoughts of their own and he doesn't know what is going on.

He doesn't like himself. He never did and still doesn't. He thinks he is a funny person. He doesn't like himself because he has wild irrational thoughts. If you have thoughts of killing you can't be much good. Yet he never gives anyone the opportunity to like him. He is afraid they won't. We went into a brief discussion in which I said to him that from the little I knew of him it seemed that people did like him. He had told me that the doctors at the hospital were nice to him. Apparently, they did like him. He said that whenever anyone is nice to him he looks for an ulterior motive. In discussion he finally said that he wondered how his mother could like him so much. He had all of these hostile thoughts toward her. He again talked of his feelings at the time his father died and how he cried for eight straight hours. He felt guilty over some of his ideas in reference to his father. From this the patient went on to talk about the way he had always felt left out, not part of anything, not part of his family. He has ideas that people can look through him. He imagines he is someone else, he daydreams considerably.

## SIXTH INTERVIEW, October 20, 1947

Patient said that he was pretty nervous although he felt rather quiet over the week-end. He was at his brother's house on Sunday and he was somewhat disturbed. To see someone happy makes him feel terrible. His brother has everything he wants. He is so lucky and the patient has nothing. His brother is happily married, has three children and this is a source of envy for the patient.

Patient talked again about being tired lately, and we discussed fatigue in relation to emotional disturbance. He then told me that he had a dream over the week-end. He was in a field and there were a lot of people there walking ahead of him. When they got to the end of the field they seemed to drop with fright. That scared him, too, but when he got there everything was all right. From this he began talking about the fact that he was always afraid. He had a chance for a ride to the clinic this afternoon and he refused it. He doesn't want people to know him.

Patient then talked about wanting to leave home if he only had the money. He wanted me to give him some advice and I said it might be well for us to discuss this somewhat.

He pointed out that while he would like to be completely alone he knew that he would be lonely, but practically it would be a good idea because he would be so close to school. Then as he talked of it he said that he could only afford a room in a house and here again there would be other people in the house. He would like to separate himself from his mother but then where else could he go. Patient then talked about his difficulty in eating in a restaurant. He doesn't like people to look at him, even the waitress. He always hides behind a newspaper. He often stands outside and waits for the right moment to go in. At home it doesn't bother him. He eats too much.

He told me that when he and his mother sit at the table he can't look her in the eye. I tried to help him to relate this to his feelings towards her. Patient then told me that in the Service he went with a WAVE for several months. She was very unattractive and he liked her a lot. He used to keep her guessing. For instance, he would promise to take her out and then not show up. He couldn't go on a dance floor with her because he was ashamed of her. Yet when he was with her alone he felt perfectly at ease. She was unsophisticated, ordinary. She liked him a lot. He even asked her to marry him and then dropped her, when she said she would. The reason he did ask her to marry him was because he felt that if she promised him the other fellows would leave her alone. He talked of being thrown off balance by women and he told me that some women do make him feel inferior. For instance, there was a girl he knew who worked for an author. He called her and then couldn't see her because he felt that he wouldn't come up to her expectations. He described her as a very attractive girl, well-groomed although a little too heavy. She was very sure of herself and seemed to have a lot of friends. As he discussed her it seemed to me that in many ways he was describing his own mother, too, although I did not point it up at this time. He said that there seemed to be no happy medium with women, either they do everything for you or they expect you to do everything for them.

He has seldom gone with girls. He then told me that he had met a girl at the USO once. She was wearing a red suit and somehow he liked to dance with her and felt comfortable with her. That night he asked her to marry him. She replied in the affirmative. After he left her she sent him a bracelet which he now wears. However, he never replied to her correspondence.

Patient said that he has wanted marriage but then is afraid of it, too, because of the kind of husband he would make. Perhaps if he would want to be alone he would feel like strangling his wife. Then again what girl would like him. The hour ended and this time the patient left without too much hesitation.

## SEVENTH INTERVIEW, October 23, 1947

Patient came in today and began the interview by describing one of the rocking spells. As before, it was involved with some problem at school. This was also in relation to some pains in the head that he had had.

Patient talked about his capability to use his imagination both as a relief and escape yet he feels himself incapable at school. He told of trying to write short stories, had written quite a few, none of which were published. They were mostly about death and suicide. He repeated again the story that he had written about a fellow who wanted to become a priest and didn't. When he died he regretted it. His mother was to blame for his not being a priest. He had also written a book in longhand which involved a girl in love going with a fellow who was going insane. The priest did not wish them to get married but they did. In all of this he finds that he puts himself in the characters. In this book it was a suicide and a homicide. In writing he feels that he can make people change and this gives him some satisfaction.

Patient talked about feeling that he wasn't real and sometimes sitting in a room, seeing people there but also having the feeling that they were not real. When he gets depressed he has the feeling of unreality. It seems at times as if he were a shell walking around. At such times he wonders if it is all worthwhile. His whole life is a game to him. God placed him here so that he could move him around. Everything is predestined so what's the use of going through the motions. He had never done anything to get glory or peace, etc. I gave the patient a good deal of assurance that he was a good person in spite of what he may think of himself. Perhaps much of his feeling about himself which he can't accept is the very thing that we may be able to work through here. He talked about not feeling good towards people, having a bad temper, etc. He always tried to take the easy way out. I gave him some more assurance and pointed out that people had emotions, that it was sometimes necessary to express them, and that we all sought the easy way out. This was done to point out to him that many of his reactions were not so abnormal, but that his feelings about them were causing his difficulties.

The patient then talked about his mother who was good to him but he wanted to flee from her. Before going in Service he lived alone, was employed at a millinery shop and had a dog that he cared for more than any human being. He didn't go anywhere, just stayed home in his free time and talked to the dog.

Patient then brought out some feelings about an uncle who helped to support the family after the father's hospitalization. His uncle was an alcoholic and used to hide the liquor in the patient's home. This uncle's wife would not allow him to have liquor. Now whenever the patient sees anyone drunk he can't control his temper. He would hit people for it, even his mother. Whenever his mother has a little too much liquor he hits her and there were several times when he had knocked her down. It makes him feel awful but he can't seem to control his anger. His mother drinks very seldom but when she does and gets drunk he will even go as far as threatening to kill her. At one time he even gave her a black eye. He often has a hard time to keep from strangling her.

He was at his brother's house a few days ago and his brother had a few too many. This bothered him too. Drunks are repulsive to him. Perhaps it is recalling his hatred for his uncle. He hated the fact that his mother was submissive to him. He hated the fact that the whole family had to be a slave to him and be fearful of him or else he would not aid in the support of the family. He told of an instance where the family and the uncle were riding in the car. They had a pet dog with them. The uncle threw the dog out of the car and killed him. Patient then expressed hostility to his older brother who ran away from home. This same brother used to scare him all the time.

Although the patient seemed calmer today he told me that he was worried about his health. He still feels that he has a limited time to live.

## EIGHTH INTERVIEW, November 7, 1947

I had not heard from the patient for a few weeks and was unable to get in touch with him. He came in at the usual time today and looked more disturbed and upset than I had ever seen him before. He told me that he had moved away from home and he had to go back tonight because he had no money. He was despondent, depressed and fatigued. Living in a room did not help him because he felt the same way there that he did at home. He felt that there was nothing anyone could do. He had no energy left. There was some talk of feeling suicidal. He felt guilty over not calling me. He really wanted to come but somehow could not get here. He was unable to study or concentrate at school and there was nothing to look forward to.

Since he had seen me he had three repetitive dreams which were very similar in that they all had the idea of being a priest. Each time there was a man at the desk who gave him $5.00 and said that he could take it. He was sent to a place by a cliff which looked like a monastery. It was near an ocean. There were windows there and he felt happy. All he could think of was what would have happened if he did not have the $5.00, and would not have been qualified. It seemed everybody thought he must have been a good fellow or else he would not be a priest. Then a bird flew in before the close of the dream. The bird perched himself on the shelf in front of him. The windows were tightly closed. There was a wind outside and he wondered how the bird got in. I did very little with this dream, both because I felt that this patient was very close to a psychosis if not already schizophrenic and also because he continued on telling me about how difficult things were for him. I assured him of my interest in him. He told me again about feeling suicidal and I wondered if he had considered the possibility of hospitalization. He said he knew this, but somehow he did not dare to go through the admissions procedure. I also asked him why he couldn't call me during this period of being so upset and he said he was afraid. He was afraid that I would be mad at him, that I would be too busy and possibly not think of him. I again told him that I was interested, that I was sorry that he couldn't call on me and suggested to him that in the event that he ever feels that way he could call me and that I would give him my personal telephone number.

Patient then told me about having feelings of depersonalization while in the park the other day. He told me about dreading to go home and then said he really had to tell me the whole truth. He started off by saying that he was angry at his mother and that he often gets so angry that he gets near hitting her. This time he took his pension check and left. She always opens his mail. He resents it but he has never had the courage to tell her that he resented it. He has been going around in circles, living in a room did not help much and finally he told the incident behind the whole thing. It seems the patient came home one day and found his mother drunk. He beat her up to the point where she had a black eye. He hated her so much that when she gets drunk it gives him the opportunity and the excuse to really act out. He confronted her with the idea that it was either him or liquor. He told her he was going to leave and she cried and begged him not to. He did leave, came home several days later to get clothing and she begged him again to stay. Now the patient feels confused. Should he return home or should he stay away. He wants to be home. He does not want to be home. He is depressed. There was a good deal of circular thinking in this. He also told me about not being able to eat in a restaurant. He feels like a criminal, like he had done something wrong. And then he said that his mother was not his real problem. She was just one of those things.

In all of this I kept assuring him of my interest in him and he told me that he does want warm friendship yet he runs away from it. He is embarrassed constantly that people might find out about him. He feels inferior. He told me of going on the other side of the street in order to avoid people.

In all of this I again suggested the possibility of hospitalization but he refused. I gave him an appointment for Monday, gave him my telephone again and told him that perhaps we might discuss further what can be done in this situation. He told me again of dreading to go home and I suggested that I would phone his mother if he wanted me to. This appealed to him. He started to go out of the room and I suggested that he come back. I told him that what I was going to tell his mother was something that he should hear, I had no secrets from him. He wondered if his mother would come in to the clinic and I said that she could but I would prefer she see another worker as my relationship to him was his and I didn't want to have him feel in any way that I had any secrets about him with his mother. This had a great effect upon this patient. I did try to call his mother several times during the interview but she was not at home. We ended the interview by continuation of talking about hospitalization, the fact that it may often be helpful to him if he feels depressed and very upset. Patient promised to come in on Monday.

NOTE, November 10, 1947

Patient did not come in.

NOTE, November 11, 1947

I telephoned the patient's home and talked to his mother. She did not seem too concerned about her son and felt that if he would get married his problems would be solved. She seemed to have little insight into his condition. He did return home after the last interview with me. I asked her to have him telephone me.

NOTE, November 13, 1947

To date, the patient has not telephoned.

CONSULTATION, November 14, 1947

Conference was held with Assistant Chief Psychiatrist and Chief Psychologist: Clinical information and psychological test information were discussed. It was felt that this was a very disturbed person who could probably be considered a paranoid schizophrenic, who has very little control of himself and could possibly become very impulsive in his behavior, and act out in either a homicidal or suicidal way. It was felt that he should be hospitalized, even if it meant persuading him. This man did not present enough obvious overt symptoms that could be used in commitment. From what we knew of the mother, she probably would not commit him.

CLOSING NOTES, December 30, 1947

Several attempts had been made to contact the patient, but to date he has not returned to the Clinic. Case therefore closed December 30, 1947. Patient was seen for eight interviews. Several conferences were held with the psychiatrists who had known the patient at the hospital, in addition to conferences with Assistant Chief Psychiatrist and Chief Psychologist at the Clinic. In the interviews he talked freely about himself, ventilated considerable feeling about his mother, hospitalization, etc. He gave much case history material and had a tenuous relationship with the therapist. No ego alien interpretations were made as it was felt that this patient was too disturbed. The material obtained seemed to indicate more and more clearly that his defenses were crumbling and that he was either close to a psychotic break or actually psychotic. Case is closed. Patient failed to come in. Unimproved. Diagnosis: Schizophrenic reaction, paranoid type.

NOTE, April 25, 1949

The patient came into the Reception Room and said he wanted to come back to the clinic for treatment. The receptionist explained the usual procedure and told him it would take approximately ten days. He said this was all right. He never returned.

## SUMMARY EVALUATION OF JOHN DOE BY MENTAL HYGIENE CLINIC PSYCHOTHERAPIST

The patient, a 25 year old single man, is a tall, slender, young man, who gives the impression of boyishness. He seemed suspicious, indecisive and unable to relax. There seemed to be considerable effeminate mannerisms in his behavior. He showed his anxiety by smoking considerably, moving about in his chair, and speaking constantly. The history of this patient indicated that this is a person who had never been able to make secure object relationships. One got the impression that his mother had been a very seductive, oversolicitous, overprotective, inconsistent person. Apparently, she had always been conscious of her appearance, acted as if she were younger than her actual age, and, in general, seemed to be a very narcissistic and controlling person. The patient reacted with violence to her use of alcohol. He considered her to be a very nagging, complaining person, who frequently irritated him. He described instances where his hostile impulses were so great that he was unable to control himself and thus had blackened her eyes and threatened to kill her. He talked also of wishing to strangle her. He recalled his resentment towards his mother for her keeping him away from his father with whom he wanted to have a close relationship. The patient felt that his mother's dependency on her family for support, since the father's death, had been one of the reasons why he had undergone insecurity and disturbance. This was particularly true, he said, in the way she required the patient to cater to her family in order not to alienate them. The father seems to be a hazy person in the patient's life. The patient resented his father's tuberculosis and death as well as his mother's prohibitions in permitting any kind of relationship. He recalled the way in which everything had to be sterilized. He could not even sit on father's chair. With much feeling he also talked of not being allowed to go to the funeral of his father. He used to blame his father for everything that had happened to him since but now does not do it any more. He was ashamed of having no father and would envy people who had fathers. From this, it seemed quite obvious that this patient lacked male identification and that he not only had hostility toward the father-person, of whom he was deprived, but also felt that his mother kept him from having a father.

Patient has two older brothers with whom there seems to be no close relationship except in terms of rivalry and resentment. Patient talked of the way in which his brothers would scare him, tell him ghost stories, and tease him. The oldest brother is apparently an alcoholic, whereas the second brother seems to have made the best adjustment of the three.

The patient's childhood, from his own description, seems to be a turbulent one. Apparently he was very fearful and withdrawn from early childhood. He was always meticulous in his clothing and was unwilling to share anything with others. Somehow, religion seemed to play a great part in his life and apparently a source of security to him was Catholicism. He was drawn toward religion and toward priesthood because he felt that he would receive protection and security there. At an early age he wrote a story and an autobiography which revealed his loneliness and his hope that Catholicism and priesthood would be the way out. In adolescence, although extremely religious he was too guilty to consider entering the priesthood. Obviously, some of this guilt is in relation to his sexual drives, masturbation, and probably also in relation to incestuous feelings that he must have had toward his seductive mother. There seems to be considerable guilt in relation to his own hostility. He has established some defenses against this through obsessions but these defenses are cracking and he fears that his hostile impulses might become so great that he would be unable to control them. It is probably quite true that this man's reality world has never been too kind to him, that it is hostile to him and that he fears he cannot control his reactions to it.

Prior to his going into the Service, the patient was able to hold a job, although it was quite obvious that he had difficulty with authoritative figures and was very sensitive to other people's opinions of him. Military service for him was a very difficult experience, especially having to live with so many people. It was a very traumatic affair for him when his buddy was run over by a train. It was in Service, too, that the patient must have had considerable homosexual panic since he was constantly with men. He told of a relationship with a WAVE who was unattractive and at the same time a girl whom he used to test constantly. The patient has considerable fear of women and has the feeling that they are somehow superior to him. He also told of an attraction to a girl with bleached hair, very well groomed, and apparently somewhat theatrical. In this description one got the feeling that perhaps the patient was also describing his own mother and that this kind of girl was also an incestuous relationship for him.

The patient seemed obsessed with thoughts about death, homicide, and suicide, and apparently these thoughts have been with him even before adolescence. Since Service, the patient has had numerous fears, which actually seem to be fears of his own impulses. There was depersonalization, many ideas of reference, and a considerable amount of hostile fantasies. It is felt that this patient is a paranoid schizophrenic who is still able to maintain control over his hostile and destructive impulses, although this control is very tenuous. He is suspicious of any relationship, male or female. His use of obsessive ideas and compulsive actions has gradually broken down so that one now sees remnants of them. As long as he can live a withdrawn and sheltered life perhaps he can continue to function outside of a hospital; however, in the face of frustration he may become an active psychotic with homicidal and suicidal impulses.

# Chapter 28

# PSYCHIATRIC FOLLOW-UP INTERVIEW

The psychiatric follow-up interview was held approximately twenty-eight months after the psychological testing at the neuropsychiatric hospital and twenty-five months after the last psychotherapeutic session at the mental hygiene clinic. The follow-up interview was conducted by Dr. Samuel Futterman. Dr. Futterman was born in 1909. He received the B.A. degree from CCNY in 1930 and the M.D. degree from the University of Geneva (Switzerland) in 1935. He is a Diplomate of the American Board of Neurology and Psychiatry. He is at present Chief Psychiatrist, Veterans Administration Mental Hygiene Clinic, Los Angeles, California. He is a member of the American Psychoanalytic Association, Los Angeles Psychoanalytic Association, American Psychiatric Association, and American Orthopsychiatric Association. He is a Visiting Professor at the Graduate School of Social Work, University of Southern California, and has been a contributor to various journals in psychiatry and social work.

THIS PATIENT was seen for a period of about one and a half hours following a letter which was sent to him, by the Chief Psychiatrist of the V.A. Mental Hygiene Clinic, as follows:

> "In reviewing your case, it was noticed that you have been a patient at this clinic and had been interested in continuing. For some reason that is not too clear, which we feel might be due to the fact that there has been a change of address, you did not continue at this clinic. It would be appreciated if you could come in for an interview with me [date], at 2:00 P.M., at which time we can discuss any future plans you might have, either of continuing or of other arrangements. If this time is not suitable, please call me and another time will be arranged. I also would appreciate it if you could drop me a note confirming this time."

Patient was a few minutes ahead of time on his appointment. This was the first time that I had seen the patient, but I had read through roughly his entire case folder, as well as all the psychological test reports.

Patient immediately impresses one by the open tension that he shows. He sits at the edge of his chair, the lines on his face seem tight, and there is a general restlessness about his whole person. The interview had to be interrupted at one time because of a flood of tears that might ensue because of the increasing tension. The interview was carried on by both general and specific questions on my part. He was told that the reason for this interview was to see how he was coming along as we had not heard from him in several months. We knew also that he had moved in the interim and wondered whether that was the reason we had not heard from him.

He stated that he had moved in with his mother up into a lonely canyon home, which was quite isolated and where he could best feel alone. He had been living with his mother for some time in this fashion. He has a large dog at this home whom he feels is the only being that he can really feel close to. He has continued to go to a business school and just manages to get by in his studies. He thinks he will become some kind of an accountant.

He says that he is just scared all the time. He is frightened about all people. He is afraid that he is being constantly watched. At school he does not want to take a front seat for fear that others are staring at him. He moved to the back of the room. In restaurants, he buys a newspaper before going in and hides his face behind the newspaper so others will not see him. He feels this more with people hc does not know, although the feeling is still there with people he does know. He wants to go out with the girls but is afraid that if he did go out with them they would find out about him and they would tell other people and he could not face either the girls or the other people the next day. He is never specific as to what they will find out or why he is afraid of people staring at him. It is indefinable. He avoids taking the street that passes the mental hospital in which he was placed, even though it means going about one-half mile out of his way.

He feels that the psychiatrists treated him well; they did it more as a duty. They were not really interested in him. They were kind; they gave him time, but somehow they lacked a real liking for him.

The reason why he could not come back to the clinic for treatment was because he might be assigned to one of the psychiatrists who made him wait at the hospital and he knows that he likes the psychiatrist but because he made him wait, he would have to blow up at him.

He has many somatic complaints which could be related to any organ if the examiner would mention it. Spontaneously he mentioned tension in the back of his head, pain in his stomach, a loss of energy in his arms.

He mentioned about the statue of Jesus Christ and the Sacred Heart. He described how the blood from the heart was real and that the hands of Christ were moving toward him. He still wants to be a priest to know other people's secrets instead of their knowing his own.

It is interesting to note that the aggressive feelings toward the mother are suppressed at this time, compared with evaluation two years previously.

He has the feeling that he knows that he is sitting in a chair talking with me, but if he did not know that, he would doubt that it was himself here talking. He wonders whether the examiner can understand this. This occurs at many times during the day. He has to sort of tell himself that it is his real self that is there. He is afraid to walk in the streets because of the crowds. They might do something to him. He might do something to them. Therefore, he tends to go walking in the country. He is afraid of what he might do. He does not know what it is. He is afraid of the dark.

His relationship with his mother is one in which he feels now he is getting along quite well with her. He says that she lived a pretty rough life before and drank a good deal. This is no longer the case. He can talk a bit to her but never about what's inside of him. Yet, he can never state to anyone, even to himself, what is inside of him. It is something indefinable about to break loose and he just knows that he has to hold it back. He talked about being humiliated in Service by having to drill alone in front of his company.

He doesn't see his brother anymore. He cannot blame his father for anything. Things just were that way. He would like to get help but does not really wish to come to the clinic because of the fear of being assigned to this one psychiatrist that kept him waiting, and the fact that the clinic is in a crowded section. He would like to see a psychiatrist who was not in a crowded neighborhood. He wonders whether anyone could help him. He knows that he is all wrong inside. He is constantly apprehensive during the day. He goes to the bathroom to urinate twenty to thirty times a day.

No real auditory or visual hallucinations could be obtained. Depersonalization is present. There are vague ideas of reference, as indicated above. There were no organic processes in evidence from a psychiatric or neurologic point of view.

Clinically, this is a case of schizophrenia, paranoid form, with almost preconscious self-destructive or outward destructive tendencies. The outward world is hostile and he himself feels that he must react to it by his hostility, but so far has not really acted out on it.

# Part V

# SYNTHESIS AND SUMMARY

# Chapter 29

# SYNTHESIS OF TAT-MAPS TEST COMPARISONS

EACH OF THE TAT contributors, in addition to his interpretation of John Doe's TAT and MAPS test protocol, compared the two tests by indicating the extent to which his TAT method was applicable to the MAPS test and by formulating general comparisons between the two tests. This chapter is devoted to these TAT-MAPS test comparisons. It is divided into two main sections: (I) the verbatim comments comparing the TAT and MAPS test; and (II) a discussion of all the various points of view indicated in the comments. The general purpose of this chapter is broader than that of merely presenting *a priori* comparisons between two thematic tests; it is, rather, to stimulate individuals to work experimentally on the broad problem implicit in this particular inter-test comparison; viz., what effects do various degrees of structurization in the stimulus material have upon the resultant thematic fantasy productions. Scientific meaning can be given to the different functions of these two (and other) tests only through properly designed experimental research.

## VERBATIM COMMENTS

*Magda Arnold*

1. The TAT forces the patient to take a stand even to people he does not want to be concerned with; hence, in the TAT (in this case) we get the father figure in a much more prominent position.

2. Because the TAT provides samples of real people while the MAPS offers a choice of fantastic *or* real figures, any disturbance in the patient's thinking will have a much better chance of being detected in the MAPS. In the present set, the MAPS gives a much clearer indication of a schizophrenic disturbance than the TAT. On the other hand, the TAT forces the patient to pay attention to the real situation in which he finds himself. Especially in the sequential analysis it can be noted that the patient talks about his own illness, the attitudes of those around him, his growing difficulty of contact with others and his conviction that now nothing can be done to help him anymore. In the MAPS, there is a much more abstract picture of life as the patient sees it and a justification of his own illness, together with the same conviction that there is no way out.

3. In the present series, only eleven pictures of the TAT were given; if the complete set had been given, I would expect that the TAT would have provided enough additional material to reconstruct the same attitudes to life betrayed in the MAPS. At the same time, I do concede that the MAPS produced such a picture on the basis of only seven test cards.

4. Our preference for the one or other test will be determined, I think, by the value we put on clinical events in the life of the patient, on his relationships with actual people. For any genetically-oriented psychologist, therefore, there may be a slight advantage in using the TAT. But if our main emphasis is to get at the present attitude of the patient, to let ourselves be led by the people he himself sees as important in his universe, then the MAPS test no doubt is preferable.

*Betty Aron*

Although the technique presented here was originally designed for the TAT, as is demonstrated here, it can readily be applied to MAPS test protocols. Consideration will need to be given to comparison of the two tests with regard to pull of picture stimuli before the differences in results obtained from these tests can be evaluated. The experience of the writer with the MAPS test is too limited to attempt to compare it with the TAT. However, in the case presented here, the two tests elicit differences in story content that may be worth subjecting to speculation. Themas of aggression and destruction, and others deprecating women, appear in stories of both tests, but, whereas these themas virtually compose the entire story content of the MAPS test, in the TAT other themas (of expressions of dependency needs) also appear. It may be that in allowing the patient greater choice of subject matter, the MAPS test brings into focus that material which is most representative of the patient's world of fantasy, and in this way lends itself better than does the TAT to analysis of formal aspects intended to indicate the way in which the patient approaches a situation. On the other hand, by forcing the patient to deal with many different kinds of picture stimuli, perhaps the TAT also taps fantasy material which the patient does not ordinarily express and which may throw a great deal of light on deeper personality dynamics involved.

*Leopold Bellak*

I feel that the method I use for the TAT can be used with advantage for the MAPS. For that purpose, my category of "Figures introduced" would have to be adapted to the MAPS (also "Objects introduced", possibly) while "Objects omitted" might not be useful. The rest, I would think, can stand as is. Both tests are apperceptive: "A method of investigating personality by studying the dynamic meaningfulness of the individual differences of perception of standard stimuli" (and by studying the recurrent themes—patterns of individual interpretation).

The implication is, that I believe structural and formal analysis is not as advantageous as content analysis for either of the two tests. While the MAPS has greater flexibility and potential richness, it loses by the same token some economy and validity as well as repeat reliability pertaining to the more standard stimuli of the TAT.

It seems to me that the two tests in this case show clearly the comparability and the practically identical dynamic material derived from them.

*Leonard Eron*

It is doubtful whether my kind of analysis could be applicable to the MAPS test. The present check list and scales, utilized for specific pictures of the TAT are, of course, not appropriate. New ones would have to be empirically derived in the same manner; however, since the MAPS test is so much less structured than the TAT and the number of possibilities of kinds of responses is so great, it is not likely that comprehensive scales and check lists could easily be organized. The MAPS test, it seems, is much more a projective test than the TAT, since responses to the latter are more clearly determined by the stimulus pictures themselves. A more or less rigid framework could not be applicable because the number of possible combinations is great and therefore the number of possible situations and themas unlimited. I tried to apply my TAT check lists to the MAPS protocol to see if anything at all could be gotten from it that way which might corroborate what was obtained on the TAT. However, it soon became evident that I was missing very much by trying to fit the MAPS stories into that framework.

*Reuben Fine*

Except for figure choice, the MAPS test can be handled in exactly the same manner as the TAT. The psychograms of the two tests lend themselves to some interesting comparisons.

The total number of feelings in the MAPS is 45, or a mean of 6.42 per story, which is very close to the mean of 6.81 for the TAT. The average number of interpersonal relationships, however, is 4.43 per story in the MAPS, as contrasted with 3.36 in the TAT.

In the individual categories, we find less affection, frustration, superiority and wishful thinking in the MAPS, but more externalized hostility and more pathologic indicators. One might say that there is acting out of bizarre fantasy in the MAPS which is often only hinted at in the TAT. Every story in the MAPS is obviously bizarre, while only four of the eleven TAT stories were so labelled.

In the MAPS, hostility is externalized in every story where it occurs. Further, the direction of hostility, now yields significant results: it is primarily women who are killed by others, while in the two cases where suicide occurs, the story relates to a man who has done harm to a woman, and then kills himself. The externalization of hostility is usually found in individuals who live out their aggression in fantasy, but who have so much near the surface that there are occasional violent outbursts; the same conclusion arose from the TAT.

Apart from the parts mentioned above, which are supplementary rather than contradictory, there is a striking similarity between the psychograms for the MAPS and the TAT. In a previous study (the dissertation), the writer obtained an analogous result.

The differences and similarities between the subject's TAT and MAPS can be summarized as follows. In essence, the structure revealed is the same in both. In the MAPS the pathology comes out more clearly—every story is bizarre. Further, the MAPS seems to bring out primarily the fantasy defenses, especially the confused identification and the wish to take revenge on the mother, which were not so apparent in the TAT. It is as though in the TAT he were telling what had happened to him, while in the MAPS he is revealing in fantasies what he would like to see happen.

Not enough material has been accumulated to support an adequate comparison between the TAT and MAPS. There is of course little doubt that in competent hands the two will yield similar pictures of the personality; that is true, by and large, of all the projective techniques. But there are also differences. The main one which appears in the present study is that the TAT tends to give more a picture of what the patient thinks has happened to him in the course of his lifetime while the MAPS has more of the fantasy defenses. In the writer's experience, this is more or less true in general. It accounts for the fact that subjects find the MAPS a more pleasant test —there are few people who would not rather dream than face reality. It also implies that the usefulness of the two tests will vary with the clinical picture, an important point which also applies as well to other techniques. There are patients, e.g., who give much in the TAT and little in the Rorschach, and vice versa. As far as the type of patient with whom the MAPS test would be more useful is concerned, and the one for whom the TAT is more appropriate, more information must be accumulated. If the above hypothesis is correct, it would follow that the patient with a conventionalized fantasy life, who tells movie or comic-book stories on the MAPS, would reveal somewhat more of himself in the TAT, while the one with unusual fantasies would give more in the MAPS, but this is a theoretical deduction which remains to be explored.

*Arthur Hartman*

Most of the main trends which characterized the subjects's response to the TAT were also revealed in the MAPS test .... Although the MAPS test record gives a first impression of greater thematic richness, the actual quantitative scoring on the two tests yields practically identical averages per picture and also for the total responses.[1]

From the results obtained in would appear that a method of category analysis is as applicable to the MAPS test as to the TAT. It is quite likely that the personality correlates of given types or characteristics of response are similar for both tests and possibly, more generally, for a wide range of thematic materials. These, however, are judgments which need to be empirically tested.

*Robert R. Holt*

I believe that the kind of clinical analysis that I use in approaching a TAT story is in almost all respects applicable to stories told in the MAPS test, or in a Story-Completion test, or any similar kind of approach. A great deal depends on a kind of sequence analysis, which treats the material as if it were free associations, and tries to get at the latent meaning. The analysis of verbalization, which is a cornerstone of all psychological testing in my estimation, is of course possible in any test which yields freely verbalized material. As far as the analysis of content is concerned, a great deal of the kind of content analysis that one does in the TAT can be carried over directly to MAPS stories, although I feel a good deal more uncertain about the interpretation since I have no experience with the MAPS test and have no personal

[1]This paragraph is repeated from the section on the MAPS test in Chapter 9 (*Editor's note.*)

norms, nor are there any thematic norms available. If such norms, giving popular stories for each background, popular apperceptions of each figure and each background figure, were available, it would do a good deal to overcome this difficulty and to make it possible to approach the analysis of MAPS stories almost identically with TAT stories.

The same comments apply to formal analysis of the MAPS stories. Although some features, such as verbalization, general story structure and coherence, stereotypy of sentiments, and the like are not specific to any particular cards nor to any particular test, there are quite a number of things which I look for in TAT stories and feel uncertain about in the MAPS test. Perceptual distortions are one obvious thing; when they are really gross one has the feeling that they can be taken at face value, but a great deal of apperceptive normative material would be necessary in order to evaluate most perceptual distortions. One thing the MAPS test lacks that the TAT does have is pictures which in themselves are traumatic and which allow no escape from facing a situation which arouses anxiety. I am thinking of cards such as 15 and 13BM, the reactions to which, compared with other less traumatic cards, are important indications to me of emotional control and ability to maintain intellectual efficiency under the impact of emotional trauma. I suppose that if the examiner wanted to use the MAPS test in that way, he could, by making up his own constellations of figures on backgrounds and confronting the subjects with them, but that's not the case in the method of administration used with John Doe. With a subject like this, there is little question about the originality (and its pathological derivation) of most of his stories, but with many other subjects, that would again be a matter where norms would be necessary. A formal variable like sensitivity to the mood of the picture is dependent on having definitely structured pictures, though it is not a particularly important one.

On the whole, then, I would say that if I had enough experience with the MAPS test or if adequate norms were available, or preferably if both these conditions could be met, most of what I draw on in analyzing TAT stories could be applied just as well to the MAPS test. There are a few respects in which having definitely structured pictures with the correspondingly greater structure in the examiner's expectations of what to look for and what would be important had advantages over the greater unstructuredness of the MAPS test; but I am sure that there are other respects in which the MAPS test has its own advantages.

I found it interesting to compare the two sets of stories on a number of counts. First, the MAPS stories were on the whole longer and richer in a way, yet I did not feel that I could get as much out of them as I could out of the TAT stories. This feeling is probably a compound of prejudice, greater familiarity with the TAT, and possibly some reality, as well as the fact that of course I had analyzed the TAT before I went over the MAPS stories. But I have the impression that for this particular patient, the MAPS test played in a little too well with some of his own pathological acting out tendencies. It was very easy for him to be as he usually is, histrionic, more so in the MAPS test than in the TAT. Consequently we saw him at his worst, in a way; it may be that this test was best designed to bring out schizophrenic material for this kind of patient. I am sure that the active participation and manipulation in which the patient engages helps him produce more material very often. I just had the feeling that for this patient there was not a great deal of essentially new content in much of his long dramatic stories, but a repetition of the same themes simply spelled out in greater detail and served up with a more dramatic flourish. Using a variety of structured pictures, one can force the patient to deal with a variety of problems, preselected by you as areas you wish to explore. In doing so, you may of course neglect to go into areas which the patient himself would choose and which are most directly important for him; in such a case, the MAPS test would be better. I have the feeling, though, that it enables him a little bit too much to go down the line of his own preoccupations, recreating pretty much the same thing over and over again, rather than giving you your money's worth, so to speak, for each additional card you use. This is just a speculation on the basis of one case, of course.

*Walther Joel and David Shapiro*

In comparing the two tests we shall limit ourselves to the following question: How much does each reveal about the modes of ego-functioning of the subject?

First let us state an important limitation of this comparison. We do not know whether both tests were administered by the same or different examiners. We believe, however, that the personality of the examiner has its effect upon the kind of projective material produced and that this effect is particularly important in an examination of the social functioning of the ego. The reader should keep this limitation in mind.

Our interpretation was primarily derived from an examination of the symbolized interaction between subject and story material, and among the story characters themselves. It follows that a story with little interaction such as is the case with the TAT story analyzed here would lend itself less to this type of analysis. More important, however, than the difference in the *amount* of interaction available in the two stories is the fact that the flexibility of the MAPS test permitted the subject to develop a much greater variety of situations and identifications and thereby to display more completely the range of ego adaptations of which he was capable. Yet it can be seen in the interpretive conclusions that the TAT story, in spite of presenting less interaction, gives us the essential core of the subject's ego functioning.

*Seymour Klebanoff*

With respect to the data in this case, I find that my schema was just as appropriate to the MAPS test material as it was to the TAT, for which it was developed. No appreciable difference in applicability was noted. However, the results of the profiles on the TAT and MAPS test show certain basic similarities, but also some differences. One might suspect that possibly differences in the very structure of the two techniques explain the obtained differences; differences in the stimulus situations or differences in the manner of administration of the two tests conceivably could account for the observed discrepancy; and lack of reliability of this scoring schema might contribute to the differences in profiles upon the two tests.

*Sheldon Korchin*

I have never worked with the MAPS test before but I am most impressed from this experience with its possibilities. I do not think we should have the slightest hesitancy in applying any method found fruitful with the TAT directly to the MAPS test. The only reservation I would have is in terms of what differences might be directly attributable to the stimulus-given of the test materials themselves. We have certain expectations in analyzing the TAT about what type of story can be told to each card and what the "popular response" is. And one step in analysis is to compare the obtained story to this expectation. This is of course less possible in the MAPS test.

As has been stated, the MAPS test productions are more fantastic, less realistic and, we may suppose, more closely related to the subject's schizophrenic ideation than are the stories told to the TAT pictures. This is probably due to the differences in the stimulus materials of the two techniques—the less structured MAPS test situations allowing more direct "projection" of inner needs and fantasy, while the somewhat more structured TAT pictures exerted some reality constraint. It is notable, in this connection, that the subject gives stories comparable to those elicited by the MAPS test on cards 11 and 16 of the TAT. These are, or course, the least well defined and structured of the TAT series presented.

*Jose Lasaga*

Both tests can be used as diagnostic instruments and for investigating the psychodynamic mechanisms of a subject's conflicts.

But the MAPS test is better than the TAT for diagnosis: (a) because there are more elements capable of being analyzed (manner of putting the figures on the table, pictures without figures, selection of figures, placing of figures in the pictures, movements of the figures and so on); (b) because the pictures of the TAT give a solid zone of contact with reality to the subject, so that he may build up on it a fairly reasonable story, but as such a base is lacking in the MAPS test, the psychotic subject easily loses himself amid the chaotic and unreal thoughts of his disturbed mind. This is the reason why it so frequently happens that certain psychotics who have made relatively acceptable stories in the TAT, when faced with the MAPS test completely reveal their mental disorganization. Hence we consider the MAPS test one of the most powerful diagnostic tests produced up to now, especially for differential diagnoses between psychotic and psychoneurotic disturbances. We have had in our experience some cases in which the Rorschach test left us in doubt, but in which the MAPS test proved clearly the existence of a psychotic process, such as an incipient schizophrenia or psychotic depression. Sometimes a single story of the MAPS test sufficiently established with almost absolute certainty a diagnosis of psychosis.

The TAT, on the other hand, is much superior to the MAPS test as an instrument for investigating the mental conflicts of a subject. In the first place because the very disorganization of the patient's mind in the MAPS test sometimes produces less understandable stories. In the second place, and this is the principal reason, because in very many cases patients construct in the MAPS test a certain number of stories lacking passion and dramatic quality. Such stories are often useless for investigating conflicts. And this happens even with some subjects who have told in the TAT a long series of stories overflowing with passion which clearly revealed their internal conflicts. Yet, in the MAPS test, they had made only a few stories of emotional character in which, of course, some traces of their conflicts might be detected.

Perhaps the explanation of this phenomenon can be found in the mechanism of producing the leading idea of a story, which is completely different in the MAPS test from that in the TAT. In this latter, the steps of this process are the following: (a) perception of a picture in which the subject frequently discovers sad countenances or dramatic gestures; (b) tendency to think of something sad or something dramatic; (c) tendency of his own conflicts, in a more or less conscious way, to come into the subject's mind; (d) expression of these conflicts in literal form (if there is no repression and if fully conscious) or in symbolic form (if the repression or the wish to conceal makes the subject, willingly in some cases, unconsciously in most of them, tend to avoid the remembrance of his conflict).

On the contrary, in the MAPS test the process of creation of a story frequently shows the following steps: (a) perception of a picture, which does not represent any event in human life, but a landscape, a view of an interior, etc.; (b) tendency to seek some character doing something which goes well with the picture, and which may be in many cases an unimportant act of daily life or, at least, an event on which the great problems of life do not turn. This possibility of not having, of necessity, to seek a dramatic plot often allows patients who are victims of intense mental troubles to elude, in the greater part of the stories of the MAPS test, expressing them in a literal or symbolic form.

Examples: (a) In picture 3GF of the TAT a patient sees a woman weeping and tends to think of the reasons which can cause a woman to weep in that way. This then stirs up his own conflicts which may appear in literal form, should the patient be fully conscious of them and not want to conceal them. If, on the contrary, forces of repressive character (which perhaps are acting in a totally unconscious form) exist in his mind, the patient will not speak of his own conflict literally. He will think of other conflicts which, although different from his own, will have a certain analogy with them. In such a case he will produce a response of "symbolic" character. Though this will not openly reveal the patient's secrets, it may give us a significant clue to them. (b) In the picture of the MAPS test entitled "Bathroom," on the other hand, patients may happen to reason this way: "This is a bathroom, so I must put here a person having a bath," and thus his whole story is reduced to a description of that act.

For these reasons, a TAT in which stories depicting situations of conflict do not anywhere appear may suggest to us the absence of intense mental conflicts in the patient who has made the test. But the same affirmation cannot be made if in the MAPS test of a given subject no stories of conflictive character appear.

*Julian Rotter and Shirley Jessor*

1. *Clinical findings.* The major findings for the two tests are similar. Some of the tendencies observed on the TAT appear to be more exaggerated in the MAPS

test protocol. We do not know what is normal for responses for the MAPS test. Is more fluidity and more illogicality to be expected, as evidenced in the protocol? We wonder if the subject appeared more disturbed than on the TAT because of the greater freedom of selection, or if the time at which the test was administered was an important factor. What was the time interval between the administration of the TAT and MAPS test? Did responding to the TAT facilitate greater freedom on the next test?

2. *Application of the method of interpreting TAT to the MAPS test.* In general, the same method used for interpreting the TAT seemed to be applicable to the MAPS tests, but, as on the TAT, more knowledge of plot norms (formal and informal) than is now available is needed to make an adequate interpretation. An additional variable, concerning which normative data are needed, is found in the MAPS test, in terms of the characters chosen for the various backgrounds. The problem of the kinds of figures selected appears to be a more significant one in the MAPS test than in the TAT, since there is a greater opportunity for wide variability in selection.

*Helen Sargent*

Neither the Cox-Sargent Normative TAT Method or the Sargent Insight Scoring System are appropriate for the MAPS story, since neither system provides a means for handling the freer elaboration and the amount of introduced content which the structure of this test elicits. The same principles of content analysis appropriate to any projective material apply, but very formal scores lose meaning, with one exception. One of the most significant "M" (maladjustment) scores on the Insight Test is the PP, or first person pronoun. In the MAPS story this intrudes at a significant point and is quickly changed to "she." Some critical reality testing remains in this patient, but this slip underlines the conclusion already reached that he is controlling with great difficulty the upsurge of psychotic fantasy.

The content of the MAPS story, however, supports the conclusions from the TAT, and adds additional clues to dynamics in the open hostility toward parent figures, with concomitant anxiety and guilt clearly evident. Psychotic symbolization (e.g., the snake and the woman) points to a homoerotic component with deep aggressive wishes against women. The psychosis suggested in the TAT appears even more frankly in the fantasies elicited by the MAPS. The latter test brings out preconscious material of deeper dynamic significance than the TAT, which, in conjunction with clinical and history material, should prove very illuminating. Without the latter. it is felt that interpretation is risky.

*Percival Symonds*

I have not had experience with the MAPS material but assume that it would be very similar to the TAT material. Actually it is clear to me that the nature of the MAPS test makes it yield material at a deeper fantasy level than the TAT, although I am not sure that I have been able to indicate this in my interpretations.

*Ralph White*

It seems to me that the two tests serve essentially the same function; I would have drawn pretty much the same inferences, and actually did obtain pretty much the same statistical results, from both of them. The TAT probably has the advantage (although it is perhaps only a temporary one) of having better established norms and a richer background of clinical data on which to base inferences. On the other hand, the greater flexibility of the MAPS test, in allowing the subject to choose his own actors, seems to make the result more purely a result of inner fantasy-trends and less a matter of "picture-pull" than in the case of the TAT. This probably means that in a given amount of time there is a larger (and hence more reliable) body of evidence obtained which bears directly on personality dynamics. I found this to be particularly useful in obtaining evidence on "whose viewpoint the person tends to take"—i.e., on the problem of identification. The TAT gave relatively little usable data on this problem because of the number of pictures in which the subject had no choice, or only a limited choice, as to the kind of person he could identify with.

## DISCUSSION

The comments made by the contributors comparing the TAT and the MAPS test may be divided into two types: (a) those relating to the applicability of methods originally designed for the TAT to use with the MAPS test; and (b) those relating to comparisons of the MAPS test with the TAT as to nature of stimulus material and as to the results obtained. In this section an attempt is made to summarize these comments.

### Applicability of the TAT Methods to the MAPS Test

Of the sixteen methods of TAT analysis, thirteen are said to be applicable to the MAPS test. Of these thirteen, eight authors (Aron, Bellak, Fine, Hartman, Holt, Klebanoff, Korchin, Rotter-Jessor) state so explicitly, one of these (Bellak) recommends some adaptation, while four, who agree as to applicability, also express a desire for test norms (Aron, Holt, Korchin, Rotter-Jessor). The other five (Arnold, Joel and Shapiro, Lasaga, Symonds, White) imply applicability without discussing it as a problem. Of this latter group, all but one (Symonds) apply their methods with equal intensity to both tests. Only three of the sixteen TAT methods are said not to be applicable to the MAPS test, according to statements by their authors (Eron, Sargent, Cox-Sargent), and this is so chiefly because these methods are based on norms derived from TAT material.

### Comparisons of the Nature of the Stimulus Material and of the Results Obtained

A. *Similarities*

Some of the contributors refer to the similarities in the nature of the two tests and in the results obtained. Specifically, a synthesis of the various analyses reveal the following:

1. *Similarities between the two tests*

*a.* Both the TAT and the MAPS test are apperceptive tests. Bellak especially makes the point in indicating that both tests study "the dynamic meaningfulness of the individual differences of perception of standard stimuli."

2. *Similarities in results*

*a.* Major clinical findings in both tests are in substantial agreement. Rotter and Jessor, as well as Hartman, indicate this point of view. In addition, Rotter and Jessor feel that "some of the tendencies observed on the TAT appear to be more exaggerated on the MAPS test protocol."

*b.* The personality structure revealed by both tests is similar. Klebanoff notes certain basic similarities in the personality profiles he obtained for each test. Again, Fine, using a different scoring system also reports a striking similarity between psychograms for the two tests, and, in addition, points out that the analysis of each test reveals a fundamentally identical personality structure. Joel and Shapiro also remark that both the TAT and the MAPS test analyses give the essential core of the subject's ego functioning.

B. *Differences*

1. *Differences between the stimulus materials of the two tests*

*a.* Most of the contributors remark on the fact that the TAT material is more structured than the MAPS test material.

2. *Differences in results*

*a.* The TAT, as compared with the MAPS test, has a greater degree of structure which forces the subject to face certain situations so that the responses are more stimulus-determined. This is cited by a number of contributors: Arnold, Aron, Eron, Holt, Korchin, Lasaga, and White. Specifically, the differences in results are as follows:

(i) The more structured TAT pictures exert some reality constraint to produce more realistic and reasonable stories more closely related to the real situation, to the subject's actual past, and to events that have really happened to him. Fine cites as evidence in support of this that every one of John Doe's MAPS test stories, but only four of his TAT stories, are bizarre. Korchin believes that TAT cards 11 and 16, which are the least structured of the TAT pictures, produce stories more similar to the MAPS test stimuli than do the other TAT cards.

(ii) The TAT taps fantasy material which would not ordinarily be expressed by the subject and which may throw light on deeper personality dynamics, whereas the MAPS test brings into focus material more representative of the subject's general fantasy life. Aron believes this is done by forcing the subject to deal with many different kinds of stimuli.

(iii) Similar to Aron's point, above, is Holt's statement that the TAT enables the clinician to pre-select the areas that the clinician is interested in exploring, and Arnold's feeling that "the TAT forces the patient to take a stand even to people he does not want to be concerned with" and to pay attention to more-or-less real situations and relationships with more-or-less actual people. For this reason, Arnold also believes that for a genetically oriented clinician—one who was interested in the clinical events in the life of the patient —"there may be a slight advantage in using the TAT."

(iv) The TAT is said to be superior to the MAPS test for investigating mental conflict (this is Lasaga's point of view) because the TAT, more than the MAPS test, forces the subject to tell stories involving "passion and dramatic quality." This is explained by Lasaga on the basis of the differences in the mechanisms involved in producing the stories in the two test situations.

*b.* The MAPS test, generally thought by the contributors as being less structured than the TAT, apparently allows the subject greater freedom of response and thus permits opportunities in which more aspects of the subject's personality can be detected. Some of the specific differences mentioned are as follows:

(i) In respect to the stories themselves, the stories given to the MAPS test materials, as compared with those given to the TAT, are said by Holt to be more dramatic and histrionic (cf. Lasaga, above) and more abstract and fantastic in nature (Arnold, Fine, Korchin). Also, inasmuch as the MAPS test materials leave the subject free to repeat themes, choose or avoid situations, and select "real" or fantastic figures, the MAPS test stories have more concern with specific themes (or defenses against specific themes) which are important for the subject.

(ii) The MAPS test is said to have some unique diagnostic features. Fine indicates that on the MAPS test the subject is more apt to lose himself in his own unreal thoughts so that whatever pathology is present seems to come out more clearly. Along the same line, both Arnold and Korchin feel that there are more direct projections of inner needs on the MAPS test than on the TAT.

(iii) In contrast to Aron's feeling—2(a)(ii), above—are the points of view of Sargent that the MAPS test may bring out preconscious material of deeper dynamic significance and of Symonds that the MAPS test yields material at a deeper fantasy level than does the TAT.

(iv) Joel and Shapiro and White feel that there is more opportunity for the subject to demonstrate a greater variety of identification on the MAPS test. It is further believed by Joel and Shapiro that the MAPS test enables the subject to display more completely the range of ego adaptations of which he is capable.

3. *Different uses of the tests*

These comparisons lead to an examination of the possible differences in the uses of the two tests. The MAPS test is said to lend itself better to the analysis of formal aspects, such as the way the subject approaches a situation

(Aron), and, because of the greater variety of situations, is said to enable the subject to display more completely the range of ego adaptations of which he is capable (Joel and Shapiro). The TAT is said to have an advantage for the genetically oriented clinician, while the MAPS test is held preferable for getting at present attitudes and at attitudes toward people the subject sees as important in his universe (Arnold). The TAT is said to be superior for investigating mental conflict, and the MAPS test for detecting disturbances in thinking (Arnold) and for diagnosis, especially for differential diagnosis between psychotic and neurotic disturbances (Lasaga).

4. *Reasons for the differences*

Concerning the *reasons* for these differences in the test productions there are two main points of view which seem to emerge.

*a.* According to some, the more structured TAT pictures exert some reality constraint and produce more realistic and reasonable stories which are more closely related to the real situation, to the subject's actual past, and to what really happened to him; while the less structured MAPS test materials allow more direct "projection" of inner needs and fantasies and therefore produce stories of a more abstract and fantastic nature which reflect the subject's attitude in the present and tell what he would like to have happen (Arnold, Fine, Korchin).

*b.* According to others, and in contrast to this view which emphasizes reality *vs.* fantasy, there are explanations of the differences between the two tests in terms of different kinds or different levels of fantasy. It is felt that the greater choice of subject matter in the MAPS test brings into focus material most representative of the subject's fantasy, while the TAT, by forcing the subject to deal with many different kinds of picture stimuli, taps fantasy material which would not ordinarily be expressed by the subject and which may throw light on deeper personality dynamics (Aron). Others believe that the MAPS test brings out preconscious material of deeper dynamic significance (Sargent) and that it yields material at a deeper fantasy level than the TAT (Symonds). It has also been pointed out that the MAPS test material leaves the subject free to repeat the same theme over and over again in his stories—a theme that may be an important (or defensive) one for him—while the TAT enables the clinician to preselect areas that *he* wants to explore (Holt). The TAT forces the subject to take a stand even toward people he does not want to be concerned with and to pay attention to more-or-less real situations and to relationships with more-or-less actual people, while the MAPS test permits the subject not to choose, and thus to avoid, distasteful situations and allows him the choice of real or *fanastic* figures. This latter is said to be better for detecting disturbances in thinking (Arnold). Another difference between the two tests is that relating to the problem of identification, i.e., whose viewpoint the subject tends to take. On this issue, there is said to be a limited choice of persons with whom the subject can identify in the TAT (White) and the possibility of greater variety of identifications in the MAPS test (Joel-Shapiro).

## Need for Experimental Researches

Many issues and hypotheses in the fields of perception and projection have been both stated and implied in the above comparisons of the two tests. The need for *experimental* investigation of these should be apparent to the scientifically oriented reader.

# Chapter 30

# SYNTHESIS OF THEMATIC TEST METHODS

In this chapter, some kind of summing-up and synthesizing will be attempted. This will be done in two sections: the first is devoted to a series of qualitative synopses of all the methods of TAT interpretation represented in this volume; and the second presents some tabulations which resulted from reducing the contributors' interpretations of John Doe's TAT to separate, discrete items of personality description.

## SYNOPSES OF APPROACHES

It is the purpose of this section to bring together and to synthesize the different approaches to thematic test analysis represented in the previous chapters. Although it is recognized that each of these makes a unique contribution to thematic test interpretation, it should be stated that the intention here is not to emphasize the diversity of approaches but rather to attempt to encompass them in terms of general overviews. It should also be mentioned that the material dealt with in this section—as contrasted to the second section of this chapter—is not the *outcome* of the approaches but rather the approaches themselves.

Four kinds of overviews of the methods contributed to this volume will be presented. These will be in terms of the different *purposes* or uses for which methods are intended; in terms of the manifold *elements* which they seek out for analysis and interpretation; in terms of the actual work *procedures;* and in terms of the main *emphases*. These four types of consideration of the TAT methods will be presented, seriatim, in the remainder of this section.

### Uses to Which Thematic Test Analysis Is Put

Thematic material may be analyzed for the immediate benefit of the person tested. In this case, the findings aid directly in his diagnosis and treatment. This function of thematic test analysis is referred to here as the "clinical" or "service" use. Thematic material may also be analyzed for the purpose of testing hypotheses about an infinite number of psychological problems, for purposes of "science" or research. Thus the oft discussed dual role played by clinical psychology finds expression in the dual function to which thematic tests are put: service in the clinical setting and research for the enrichment of psychological science.

Of the approaches to thematic test analysis illustrated in this volume, three were developed for research purposes only and are, according to their authors, not intended for clinical use (Aron, Cox-Sargent, Klebanoff).

Another seven methods were originally developed for research purposes but later adapted by their authors or others for clinical use, so that they now can serve both functions. (Eron, Fine, Hartman, Joel and Shapiro, Korchin, Sargent, White).

The remaining six approaches are designed exclusively for clinical use (Arnold, Bellak, Holt, Lasaga, Rotter-Jessor, Symonds). Some of these (Arnold, Bellak) are also intended for training in thematic test analysis for clinical purposes.

## Elements Used as a Basis for Analysis and Interpretation

Taken as a whole, the various approaches to thematic test analysis illustrated in this volume utilize an impressive number of different elements or aspects of the thematic material. These can be divided into aspects of the *story* and aspects of the *characters*.

### 1. *Story Aspects*

*Relation of story to stimulus material.* Some TAT interpreters (Bellak, Eron, Holt) observe the way in which the story distorts the physical properties of the TAT pictures, for example, by adding or omitting objects or persons or by distorting their commonly perceived nature.

*Form.* Since the subject is instructed to make up a story containing antecedents, present events and an ending, any deviation from this task is noteworthy (Eron). Other formal aspects of the story which are considered in some of the approaches are its length (Fine) and vocabulary used (Fine, Hartman, Holt). Cohesiveness (Fine, Holt, Lasaga), peculiar verbalization (Holt, Rotter-Jessor), bizarre ideas (Lasaga), the degree to which a plot is unusual or unstructured (Bellak, Fine, Holt, Rotter-Jessor), the use of first person pronoun and of subjectivisms (Sargent)—all these are employed, primarily to detect characteristics of the subject's thinking. The levels of the story, such as description, behavior, wish, mood, etc., are of interest also (Korchin). The emotional tone or mood of the story is also noted (Eron, Rotter-Jessor). Finally, the material is classified as autobiographical (Eron, Rotter-Jessor), wishful, superficial (Rotter-Jessor), symbolic, or unreal (Eron).

*Content.* In the individual story, some authors (Arnold, Bellak, Holt, Korchin, Lasaga) look for the main theme, others for more than one theme, such as all themes of disequilibrium or equilibrium (Eron) in each story. Sequence of events is studied (Aron) as well as sequence of personal interaction (Joel and Shapiro). Attention is also paid to methods of solving problems (Rotter-Jessor), solutions (Klebanoff), and to outcomes (Aron, Bellak, Eron, Fine, Hartman, Holt, Korchin, Cox-Sargent).

The stories are also taken together as a whole in order to make a sequence analysis (Arnold, Rotter-Jessor), to study the frequency of specific themes (Klebanoff, Rotter-Jessor), or to investigate themes and interpersonal relations and to discover the dynamic relationships among themes of primary importance (Symonds).

2. *Aspects of the Characters*

Many elements used for analysis are related to the story characters. The terms in which the characters are described are noted (White). The affects, feelings, or moods of the characters are analyzed (Arnold, Aron, Fine, Sargent, Cox-Sargent), including irrelevant feelings (Sargent), aesthetic, paranoid, guilt, narcissistic, sadistic, and inferiority feelings (Hartman). Their needs, press, and threats are examined (Aron, Holt, Cox-Sargent) as well as their values or motivating forces (White). Their actions (Arnold, Lasaga, Cox-Sargent) and conflicts (Bellak, Lasaga), interpersonal feelings and relations (Arnold, Fine, Hartman, Joel and Shapiro, Rotter-Jessor) and specifically their attitudes toward parents or authority (Bellak, Holt) are studied. Punishment, attribution or blame and patterns of need gratification (Bellak) are used, and attention is paid to defenses, such as fantasy and denial (Aron). Inhibition of aggression or sex (Bellak), and flight from expressing or facing interpersonal feelings (Joel and Shapiro), are also used.

While most of these aspects are considered for all the characters in the story, some authors place emphasis on the main hero (Bellak, Holt, Korchin, Cox-Sargent). In this case the main hero's age, sex, and other characteristics are noted.

## Work Methods

Considerable diversity is reported by the various contributors as to the actual manner of working. The following synopsis of work methods presents a highly over-simplified picture of the procedures generally followed.

1. *The First Step*

Some experts begin by reading and rereading the stories and making notes as they go along, either jotting down impressions and associations (Holt), getting suggestive leads for hypotheses (Rotter-Jessor), or indicating on separate slips of paper the main themes and the numbers of stories in which these themes appear (Symonds). Others first write a synopsis for each story (Arnold, Lasaga) or write semi-organized notes according to an outline (Korchin). There are also scoring systems (Aron, Cox-Sargent, Eron, Hartman, Joel and Shapiro, Sargent, White), methods involving the use of check lists (Bellak, Fine, Klebanoff) and rating scales (Hartman).

2. *Subsequent Steps*

Depending on the nature of the material obtained by the first step, further analysis may be qualitative or quantitative. Qualitative analysis proceeds in several ways. The stories are restated in terms of situations, attitudes, and sequence (Arnold); they are analyzed on descriptive, interpretative, diagnostic, symbolic, and elaborative levels (Bellak); they are studied with respect to such areas as social relationships, work, sex and love, and defenses (Korchin); the sequence of interaction is examined to obtain evidence for functioning modes of the ego (Joel and Shapiro); sequence of events is analyzed to understand personality dynamics (Aron); hypotheses are tested and verified through comparison of stories and themes (Holt, Lasaga, Rotter-Jessor); and the main themes are sorted, classified, and arranged (Symonds).

In quantitative methods, the data obtained in the first step in form of psychograms (Fine), profiles (Klebanoff), ratings (Eron, Hartman), ratios (Sargent, White), patterns (Sargent), and scorings (Aron, Cox-Sargent) are studied and compared with norms. It should be mentioned in this connection that a number of authors quantify the frequency (Fine, Klebanoff, Sargent, Cox-Sargent, White) or the intensity (Aron, Bellak, Hartman) of their variables, or both (Eron).

Some of the contributors take a stand against quantification because they believe that the conditions under which certain feelings arise (Arnold) or the manner in which the characters cope with the conditions (Joel and Shapiro) are more important than the amount.

The final step for most methods consists in the more or less organized integration of the findings into a general personality description of the subject who gave the test protocol (Arnold, Bellak, Fine, Holt, Korchin, Lasaga, Rotter-Jessor, Symonds, White), or specifically a picture of the subject's ego functioning (Joel and Shapiro). There are those who base their final personality interpretation on deviation of the subject's "scores" from the "norms" for his group (Aron, Cox-Sargent, Eron, Hartman, Klebanoff, Sargent). In large measure, these two final forms of the personality report parallel the two major purposes or uses of test interpretation—clinical and research—discussed above.

## Main Emphasis

Although we were keenly aware that any over-all classification of the methods of thematic test analysis would immediately fall heir to many shortcomings, we felt that we were somewhat obligated to make this attempt. We ourselves recognized some faults of our proposed scheme: that we have somewhat arbitrarily categorized our contributors; and that the categories themselves are overlapping. Nevertheless, we developed a classification scheme of the major types of thematic test interpretation, in terms of the primary emphasis of the method. All the methods were subsumed under one of five categories: normative, hero-oriented, intuitive, interpersonal, and perceptual. These are discussed below.

1. *The Normative Approach to Thematic Test Analysis.* The normative techniques are those which aim at quantifying thematic test interpretation. They are typically tabular and statistical in nature. The basic operation is one of comparing the tabulations derived from the test protocol of the subject under study with the normative data for similar (or different) groups of subjects. The general purpose of such techniques is more often personality research than psychodiagnostic service. Four TAT contributors to this volume are identified primarily with the normative approach (Cox-Sargent, Eron, Hartman, Klebanoff). For two others (Rotter-Jessor, Sargent), it is a secondary characteristic of their methods, their primary emphasis being in some other area.

2. *The Hero-Oriented Approach to Thematic Test Analysis.* It is quite understandable that many interpreters of thematic test material would concentrate on the chief protagonists in the stories—this is the essence of the hero-oriented, need-press, or story character analysis method—inasmuch as historically it is the most important TAT method. These approaches emphasize the *story* hero—his needs and pressures upon him and his defenses (Aron); his feelings and interactions (Fine); his characteristics and his relations to other story characters (Korchin); and his affects and ego activities (Sargent). Other methods, whose primary emphasis is in some other area, have secondary emphasis on the hero-oriented approach (Arnold, Bellak, Cox-Sargent, Eron, Klebanoff, Lasaga, Symonds, White).

3. *The Intuitive Approach to Thematic Test Analysis.* The intuitive approach, based on psychoanalytic theory, is the most unstructured of the approaches to the analysis of thematic tests. It uses the insightful empathy of the interpreter; it is a kind of free association of the clinician's unconscious against the back-board of the test protocol. To say that it is "subjective" is not to criticize it (or distinguish it from any of the other approaches), but merely to describe it. Five contributors to this volume seem to use this approach primarily (Bellak, Holt, Lasaga, Rotter-Jessor, Symonds). Perhaps all the others use it as a secondary technique.

4. *The Interpersonal Approach to Thematic Test Analysis.* The interpersonal approach has three proponents for its use as a primary technique. In one variation, the interpersonal situations of the characters are analyzed (Arnold); in another method (Joel and Shapiro), the attention is focused on directed

interpersonal feelings—hostility, warmth, and flight—both among the story characters and on the part of the subject toward the characters; and, in the third variation, the subject's "social perception" of his story characters and their interaction with one another are the central aspects of the analysis (White). The interpersonal approach is a kind of psychodramatic variation, in which the interactions of the *dramatis personae* of the thematic drama hold the center of the stage, so to speak, for the interpreter.

5. *The Perceptual Approach to Thematic Test Analysis.* The perceptual approach has to do with the so-called "formal" aspects of the subject's production, such as his distortions of the visual stimulus of the test materials, his idiosyncratic use of language, his peculiarities of thought or logic, or his loose or queer twists within the story itself. No one of the contributors is identified with this technique as his primary mode of approach, although several use it as a secondary technique in some of its aspects (Bellak, Eron, Fine, Hartman, Holt, Lasaga, Rotter-Jessor, Sargent).

## TABULATIONS

The preceding section of this chapter presents a resume of the methods used by the various contributors to analyze thematic test material. This section considers not the techniques but the results of some tabulations of discrete items of personality description. These items resulted from translating the contributors' interpretations of John Doe's test and behavioral data into separate units of personality description.

The problem of comparing a number of qualitative evaluations about the same subject is one that the psychologist faces constantly. He may have to decide whether a social worker's report, a psychiatrist's report, and a psychological test report agree in their respective descriptions of a patient. He finds, in general, that the reports are not directly comparable inasmuch as each one focuses on different areas of personality description and evolves from different sets of objective clues and is done within the frameworks of a different set of concepts—not to mention their differences in length.[1] All the reports may be "true" (i.e., meaningful and useful), yet none of them may say the same thing about the subject. Even with the reports herein considered, where the same objective data—John Doe's TAT and MAPS test protocols—were presented to all fifteen experts, each contributor approached the task with certain theoretical biases and with certain preconceived ideas as to what was most important in describing John Doe's personality.

Two possible modes of investigation are present in such a situation: one might study the actual agreement in what predictions are made about the

[1] The interpretations of John Doe's TAT submitted by the fifteen contributors ranged in length from four typewritten pages to over forty typewritten pages.

subject; or, as a second alternative, one might study the more formal aspects of the report, i.e., the extent of agreement as to what *areas* of personality are deemed most important in describing the subject. In this volume we have selected the second alternative for the following reasons: the complete open-ended nature of a clinical report precludes for the most part any quantitative study of the extent of agreement in what is said about the subject except by rather involved statistical procedures which, although they are being undertaken, are beyond the scope of this volume (see footnote, page 303); and, secondly, it was believed that the areas of discussion within the reports would best reflect the actual differential value of the several analytical processes for evaluating thematic material. (For example, if a majority of a particular expert's statements in his report are devoted to John Doe's interpersonal relations and none to John Doe's intellectual status, we would conclude that that expert's method of TAT analysis is more efficient in determining interpersonal relations than intellectual status. The protest might be made, with some justification, that the expert could have made statements about intellectual status if he had considered this a useful area of personality description for the subject. We believe, however, that the method of analysis devised by an expert will extract what he considers important and what he feels thematic material can reveal and that these elements will then appear in his report. While it is true that on another test protocol the areas of discussion might be different for the same expert, this possibility is also true for all the other contributors and if, for John Doe, they are able to discuss areas that this one expert does not, then presumably their methods are more efficient in evaluating those other areas.)

The method decided upon for determining the differential area emphases among the various contributors was one of reducing each report to a series of meaningful statements and then categorizing each statement under one of various descriptive headings. Accordingly, each report on John Doe was rewritten as a series of discrete statements of personality description. Each statement is one that might be considered a separate factual or descriptive item about John Doe. Certain sentences in a report became a number of statements rather than just one; e.g., "Self centered and aloof, he is incapable of giving any kind of love to another and of expecting love from anyone else," became the following statements: (1) "He is self centered." (2) "He is aloof." (3) "He is incapable of giving any kind of love to another." (4) "He is incapable of expecting love from anyone else." In this manner, the reports of the fifteen TAT contributors, the five supplementary test contributors, the summary evaluation of the Mental Hygiene Clinic therapist, and the psychiatrist's follow-up interview were made into a series of separate statements about John Doe. It must be realized that such a procedure destroys the *gestalten* of integrated reports in that certain information—or, more accurately, certain attitudes—about the subject are no longer communicated from the writer to the reader. This kind of loss is unavoidable at the present time if other than qualitative comparisons are made.

All of the reports were made into separate items by a single coder (K.B.L.), after a period of initial training and practice.[2] In this manner 802 items were secured from the sixteen TAT reports. The supplementary test reports (Rorschach, Wechsler-Bellevue, Draw A Person, Bender Gestalt, and Minnesota Multiphasic Personality Inventory) were also coded; these reports yielded 239 items. Some aspects of the behavioral data—the therapist's resume of John Doe from the Mental Hygiene Clinic psychotherapy sessions and the psychiatric follow-up interview—were also coded and they yielded 91 and 78 items, respectively. The total number of items was 1210.

The second step in the tabulation of the items consisted of eliminating certain of each contributor's items. These eliminated items were characterized as either "Test Description" or as "Duplicates." In the first of these categories fell those items which, in the opinion of the two judges, were not about John Doe but were about the test protocols, e.g., "There are themes of suicide present in the record." or "In his stories, women are presented as either completely good or completely bad." (This last item can be contrasted with an item about John Doe which reads: "He sees women as either good or evil.") In the second category were those items which duplicated previous similar statements by that contributor. (This occurred mainly because a contributor would make a statement about John Doe in the body of his report and then repeat that same statement in his summary evaluation of John Doe.) The two coders examined each apparently duplicating item in its context and decided whether or not it was intended to imply something different than in its preceding use. If not, it was eliminated. This process of eliminating test description items and duplicate items reduced the total number of items, 1210, by 7 per cent (85 items) to 1125 items.

The next phase in the tabulation consisted of placing each item into a class within a category set. The establishing of this category set posed one of the major methodologic problems of the entire analysis. The first temptation was to take one school of personality description, e.g., the psychoanalytic, and to use its formulations as the basis for classifying all the items. A brief reflection, however, was enough to indicate that this would be unsatisfactory. Each

[2] Check coding by a second individual (E.S.S.) of four of the sixteen reports selected at random indicated no appreciable difference in the number of items abstracted. The total number of items abstracted from the four reports by the first coder was 167, and by the second coder was 162. There was thus approximately 97 per cent agreement between the two coders.

contributor wrote within the frames of reference of his own personality theory and it seemed impractical to force statements into a descriptive system which the statements did not represent. The necessity of making the translation of terminology and nomenclature was an additional deterrent.

The category set which was finally developed grew out of the reports themselves. It reflects all the methods used by all the contributors for the analysis of thematic material. There are eighteen different categories which cover all the different statements made about John Doe. However, inasmuch as no single integrated theory of personality or personality system was used, the set was not unidimensional. Some categories can readily be considered as being subcategories of other more general ones, but, because the purpose of developing this category set was primarily descriptive, this did not pose a great methodologic problem. It should be pointed out that this set of categories is not intended to represent dimensions of personality; it is, rather, the enumeration of the categories under which items of personality description in TAT reports can be subsumed and it is thus a "TAT Interpretation Areas Outline"; i.e., it indicates the areas within TAT *reports* under which TAT interpretive *statements* may be subsumed. The eighteen categories finally established, together with representative items for each category, are presented in Table I. (The significance of the summary statement for each category is discussed later in this section.)

The actual categorizing of each item was a joint procedure by two individuals (E.S.S. and K.B.L.). Certain items were unavoidably ambiguous, but reference to the context in which they appeared indicated, in most cases, what the appropriate category should be.[3]

The results of this categorizing are shown in Table II. This table presents the percentages of statements made about John Doe in each of the eighteen categories by the fifteen TAT interpreters, the five additional test interpreters, the Mental Hygiene Clinic therapist, and the psychiatrist who did the follow-up interview. Only the eleven TAT contributors whose reports yielded twenty or more statements of personality description are represented in the Table. The "mean per cent" column represents the mean percentage for these eleven reports. Because of the unreliability of the percentages, no attempt was

[3] As a check upon the reliability of the categorizing, 100 items were recategorized after a period of two months by the same judges. All but nine items were categorized as they had been previously. Reference to the figures published by Guetzkow [23] gives the least value that p—the probability that an item has been consistently categorized—might take 99 times out of 100 as .90; i.e., the probability that an item has been "incorrectly" categorized would be as high as .10 only one time in 100. Such a reliability figure must be considered merely as indicative rather than as a rigorous expression of the actual consistency of categorizing, since memory factors may play a significant part in determining it.

TABLE I

1. PRESSURES, FORCES, PRESS (0.2%)

*Sample items:* "He is pressed by the outside world."
"Elements are agencies of disaster."
"Fate is an agency of disaster."

*Summary impression:* Abstract aspects of the environment, such as fate and the elements, press heavily upon him.

2. MOTIVATIONS, GOALS, DRIVES (4%)

*Sample items:* "There is a desperate but hopeless yearning for love."
"One dominant drive is for security."
"He is interested in literature."

*Summary impression:* He wants love from, and a dependent relationship upon, his parents, which he never gets; he settles for such substitutes as fantasied fame and prestige. Love is conceived of in infantile terms.

3. OUTLOOKS, ATTITUDES, BELIEFS (8%)

*Sample items:* "He seems fatalistically resigned to a rejecting world."
"He is very much aware of economic differences among people."
"He has an ingrained hopeless pessimism."

*Summary impression:* He perceives the world as hostile and rejecting. He has a pessimistic outlook in general. He is sensitive to class and economic differences.

4. FRUSTRATIONS, CONFLICTS, FEARS (5%)

*Sample items:* "His principal conflict is in the sexual area."
"His problems are expressed in symbolic form."
"He fears social disapproval and censure."

*Summary impression:* There are deep intense conflicts around sexuality—voyeurism, exhibitionism, incest, and homosexuality—and around aggression. Conflicts are expressed symbolically and they markedly disrupt his everyday life patterns.

5. AFFECTS, FEELINGS, EMOTIONS

A. GENERAL—OTHER THAN HOSTILITY (10%)

*Sample items:* "His feeling expression is sometimes inappropriate."
"He feels depressed."
"There is no reason whatever to infer depression."

*Summary impression:* There are guilt and shame over sexuality and aggression; fear that fantasies and conflicts will become known; considerable depression, anxiety, and feeling of being rejected.

B. HOSTILITY FEELINGS (3%)

*Sample items:* "He has an enormous amount of hostility."
"His aggressive impulses are both externally and internally directed."
"He may not be notably aggressive in his overt behavior."

*Summary impression:* There are very strong hostility feelings, unacceptable to him, which are rarely expressed overtly. The direction of hostility is both external and internal.

6. SEXUAL THOUGHT AND BEHAVIOR (9%)

*Sample items:* "He may have had a number of transitory sexual affairs."
"He has never had a stable heterosexual relationship."
"He has had homosexual contacts more out of desperation than out of desire."

*Summary impression:* He has never had a stable heterosexual relationship, inasmuch as this represents incest to him. There is considerable confusion as to his own sex role. There are strong latent homosexual trends. There are also voyeuristic-exhibitionistic conflicts and masturbation guilt. Most of his sexual behavior and fantasy is unacceptable to him.

7. PSYCHOSEXUAL LEVEL AND DEVELOPMENT (0.2%)

*Sample items:* "Definite immaturity in psychosexual development."
"This case demonstrates a complete Oedipal relationship."
"His Oedipal problems are entirely unresolved."

*Summary impression:* Immature psychosexual development; Oedipal relationships unresolved.

8. SUPER-EGO, VALUES, EGO IDEAL (2%)

*Sample items:* "His ego ideal was delayed in development."
"He has a poorly internalized super-ego."
"He has been unable to form a personally meaningful, integrated set of values."

*Summary impression:* His super-ego and ego ideal are delayed in development and incompletely formed. There is lack of interiorization of parental and cultural values. He has been unable to form a personally meaningful set of values directing him toward positive goals.

9. SELF CONTROL, EGO STRENGTH, EGO CAPACITY (2%)

*Sample items:* "Ego breakdown is already in process."
"Suspicious self control."
"A number of factors may be noted which are indicative of ego strength."

*Summary impression:* There are certain areas of functioning where ego strength is apparent, but ego breakdown is already in process.

10. SELF CONCEPT, INSIGHT INTO SELF (2%)

*Sample items:* "He conceives of himself as ill."
"He himself has little hope for his recovery."
"He shows some degree of insight."

*Summary impression:* He considers himself sick and helpless. Generally, there is very little insight in relation to his problems regarding affectional needs.

11. PERSONALITY DEFENSES AND MECHANISMS (12%)

*Sample items:* "The primary defenses to his conflicts have been withdrawal and fantasy."
"Patently paranoid form of projective mechanism."
"Obsessive defenses."

*Summary impression:* He uses a variety of defensive mechanisms with few useful modes of gaining satisfactions. The primary emphasis is on the use of projection and withdrawal. (He handles anxiety by avoidance, denial and use of illness; he reacts to frustration by withdrawal, by aggression against others, and by aggression against himself; he reacts to frustration from his father by rejecting the father and by a fantasy repentance on his father's part; he tends to project his own problems and shortcomings onto his father; he reacts to his fear of his parents with an overly determined denial of the fear; he copes with guilt and confusion by evasion and self-punishment; he originally handled his hostility by reaction formation; his defense against sexual conflicts is withdrawal; his defenses against incestuous impulses are retreat and guilt; and his defense against his oral and passive cravings is reaction formation.)

12. REALITY CONTACT, ORIENTATION (3%)

*Sample items:* "There is distortion of perceptual contact with reality."
"He has a lessening of the ability to distinguish fantasy from reality."
"He is still superficially oriented."

*Summary impression:* There is considerable distortion of reality with signs of confusion and disorientation.

13. INTERPERSONAL AND OBJECT RELATIONS

A. GENERAL—OTHER THAN WITH PARENTS (3%)

*Sample items:* "He lacks positive interpersonal relationships."
"Sibling rivalry conflict."
"He has a dichotomous conception of women as either good or bad."

*Summary impression:* There is no clear pattern of identification with either sex. He has never had adequate relationships with other people. There is considerable sibling rivalry. He sees women as either "good" or "evil."

B. ATTITUDES TOWARD/FROM PARENTS (9%)

*Sample items:* "His father does not appear to be as important a source of affection as his mother."
"He sees the father as an inadequate person."
"The mother is pictured as distant."

*Summary impression:* He did not identify adequately with either parent, but more with the mother than with the father. His parents rejected him. *Re* mother: he feared the mother, but was strongly attracted to her; mother was the more important figure in his life than the father and also the more frustrating parent. *Re* father: father is seen as sick and inadequate; the father offered no protection for him against the mother.

14. QUALITY OF PERCEPTION, FANTASY, LANGUAGE AND THOUGHT (5%)

*Sample items:* "His fantasy life is not well organized."
"He often lapses into autistic use of language."
"There is a pathologic loosening of orderly thought processes."

*Summary impression:* There are pathologic thought processes and autistic and contaminated thinking. There is rich fantasy material but it is loosely organized. There is good but somewhat pretentious vocabulary with some impairment of his ability to communicate.

15. INTELLECT AND ABILITIES (2%)

*Sample items:* "At least bright normal intelligence."
"His comprehension is little affected."
"Some creative and literary ability."

*Summary impression:* Basic intellectual functions are little affected, although there are some deviant intellectual processes. He has many unrealized potentialities. His intelligence level is bright normal to superior, but with some lowering of actual efficiency due to emotional disturbances.

16. SYMPTOMS, DIAGNOSES, AND ETIOLOGY (15%)

*Sample items:* "In early stages of paranoid schizophrenia."
"He presents many psychosomatic symptoms."
"The main etiologic factor in this case is an extremely hostile, domineering mother."

*Summary impression:* The diagnosis is schizophrenic or near-schizophrenic reaction, paranoid type, of relatively brief duration. He is a withdrawn individual with delusions, hallucinations, and ideas of reference. He probably acts out his conflicts. He presents some hypochondriacal complaints and possibly shows extreme mood shifts. Of the nine TAT interpreters who made specific diagnostic statements, one called him a decompensating obsessive-compulsive neurotic with a schizophrenic process, one called him psychotic, two labelled him schizophrenic, four indicated he was a paranoid schizophrenic, and one stated that he was schizophrenic with potential paranoid and hebephrenic coloring.

17. PROGNOSES AND PREDICTIONS, TREATMENT (4%)

*Sample items:* "His depression is so powerful that suicide is a possibility that must be considered."
"The psychotherapy prognosis for him is only fair."
"Without therapy, he will become a chronic psychotic."

*Summary impression:* There is a definite suicidal risk and some possibility of homicidal acts. Without therapy, he is likely to become a chronic psychotic. Psychotherapy would be a long-term, difficult process.

18. POSTDICTIONS

A. Factual Biographical Data (2%)

*Sample items:* "Quite likely he is a member of some minority group (Negro?)"
"He probably has had some college training, but no degree."
"He probably has a younger sibling."

*Summary impression:* He has probably had protracted childhood illnesses. He has a vocational history characterized by lack of occupational success. He has had some college training. He had siblings.

B. Psychological Biographical Data (1%)

*Sample items:* "He was an overprotected child."
"As a child he gained much of his satisfactions from reading and daydreaming."
"Religion appears to have provided a source of comfort to him."

*Summary impression:* He was an overprotected child. He made early use of fantasy escapes such as reading and daydreaming and of religion.

TABLE II

| Category | Bellak | Cox-Sargent | Fine | Hartman | Holt | Korchin | Lasaga | Rotter | Sargent | Symonds | White | Mean per cent | Rorschach | Draw a person | MMPI | Wechsler-Bellevue | Bender-Gestalt | Therapist | Follow-up |
|---|---|---|---|---|---|---|---|---|---|---|---|---|---|---|---|---|---|---|---|
| 1. Pressures; forces; press | 00 | 00 | 00 | 00 | 00 | 1 | 00 | 00 | 00 | 00 | 00 | .5 | 00 | 2 | 00 | 00 | 00 | 00 | 00 |
| 2. Motivations; goals; drives | 00 | 17 | 2 | 3 | 7 | 1 | 3 | 10 | 00 | 00 | 4 | 4 | 5 | 19 | 00 | 6 | 11 | 00 | 9 |
| 3. Outlooks; attitudes; beliefs | 2 | 00 | 3 | 3 | 7 | 13 | 29 | 4 | 3 | 11 | 7 | 8 | 00 | 00 | 00 | 2 | 3 | 3 | 5 |
| 4. Frustrations; conflicts; fears | 5 | 10 | 5 | 12 | 2 | 13 | 5 | 4 | 3 | 00 | 00 | 5 | 00 | 5 | 00 | 00 | 1 | 2 | 5 |
| 5. Affects; feelings; emotions: | | | | | | | | | | | | | | | | | | | |
| a. General, other than hostility | 9 | 22 | 9 | 1 | 4 | 3 | 16 | 4 | 21 | 14 | 7 | 10 | 15 | 12 | 12 | 6 | 3 | 5 | 3 |
| b. Hostility feelings | 2 | 00 | 5 | 6 | 4 | 8 | 00 | 1 | 00 | 4 | 7 | 3 | 6 | 00 | 12 | 2 | 2 | 4 | 00 |
| 6. Sexual thought and behavior | 16 | 00 | 8 | 7 | 10 | 15 | 16 | 6 | 00 | 7 | 14 | 9 | 7 | 9 | 00 | 00 | 5 | 3 | 00 |
| 7. Psychosexual level and development | 2 | 00 | 00 | 1 | 00 | 00 | 00 | 00 | 00 | 00 | 4 | 1 | 5 | 9 | 00 | 00 | 1 | 00 | 00 |
| 8. Super-ego; values; ego ideal | 00 | 00 | 00 | 00 | 5 | 6 | 3 | 3 | 00 | 00 | 00 | 2 | 00 | 00 | 00 | 00 | 1 | 00 | 00 |
| 9. Self-control; ego capacity | 00 | 5 | 5 | 1 | 3 | 00 | 00 | 00 | 3 | 00 | 00 | 2 | 7 | 00 | 13 | 2 | 3 | 3 | 00 |
| 10. Self-concept; insight into self | 7 | 00 | 00 | 2 | 3 | 2 | 00 | 5 | 00 | 00 | 00 | 2 | 00 | 9 | 17 | 4 | 1 | 1 | 00 |
| 11. Personality defenses and mechanisms | 00 | 26 | 9 | 3 | 6 | 4 | 3 | 17 | 12 | 39 | 9 | 12 | 7 | 2 | 13 | 21 | 16 | 2 | 00 |
| 12. Reality contact; orientation | 00 | 00 | 2 | 00 | 2 | 00 | 00 | 00 | 21 | 00 | 4 | 3 | 00 | 00 | 00 | 2 | 00 | 00 | 00 |
| 13. Interpersonal and object relations: | | | | | | | | | | | | | | | | | | | |
| a. General, other than parents | 5 | 00 | 8 | 3 | 5 | 3 | 00 | 6 | 00 | 4 | 00 | 3 | 5 | 7 | 00 | 4 | 11 | 10 | 9 |
| b. Toward/from parents | 26 | 00 | 8 | 6 | 5 | 22 | 3 | 11 | 00 | 7 | 14 | 9 | 00 | 2 | 00 | 00 | 11 | 13 | 4 |
| 14. Perception; fantasy; language; thought | 7 | 10 | 7 | 6 | 9 | 00 | 00 | 2 | 6 | 00 | 9 | 5 | 12 | 00 | 00 | 15 | 00 | 00 | 00 |
| 15. Intellect and abilities | 00 | 00 | 3 | 11 | 2 | 00 | 00 | 3 | 00 | 00 | 00 | 2 | 3 | 2 | 00 | 23 | 00 | 00 | 00 |
| 16. Symptoms; diagnoses; etiology | 12 | 10 | 24 | 30 | 19 | 8 | 11 | 6 | 24 | 14 | 9 | 14.5 | 23 | 22 | 25 | 13 | 27 | 18 | 48 |
| 17. Prognoses and predictions; treatment | 7 | 00 | 2 | 4 | 3 | 1 | 00 | 6 | 6 | 00 | 12 | 4 | 5 | 00 | 8 | 00 | 3 | 2 | 1 |
| 18. Postdictions: | | | | | | | | | | | | | | | | | | | |
| a. Factual biographical data | 00 | 00 | 00 | 1 | 4 | 00 | 11 | 6 | 00 | 00 | 00 | 2 | 00 | 00 | 00 | 00 | 1 | 12 | 13 |
| b. Psychological biographical data | 00 | 00 | 00 | 00 | 00 | 00 | 00 | 6 | 00 | 00 | 00 | 1 | 00 | 00 | 00 | 00 | 00 | 21 | 3 |

made to evaluate the values in the table rigorously, but rather the figures were examined in terms of the general trends indicated by their rank order.

Upon examining the "mean per cent" column for the TAT contributors it is apparent—as would be expected—that the largest proportion of the statements is in the category "symptoms; diagnoses; etiology" (14.5 per cent). The same situation is true of the Rorschach, Draw A Person, Minnesota Multiphasic Personality Inventory, and Bender-Gestalt, all of which, like the TAT, are diagnostic personality tests. With the Wechsler-Bellevue, on the other hand, again as might be expected, the greatest proportion of statements made are concerned with the intellectual functioning of the subject (23 per cent). The psychiatric follow-up interview, as in the case of most of the tests, apparently was primarily a diagnostic instrument with almost half the items falling in this category (48 per cent). The Mental Hygiene Clinic psychotherapist's summary evaluation report, however, showed the heaviest concentration of items in the category of life data, "postdictions" (33 per cent), possibly reflecting the major orientation of the social worker therapist.

Following in order after the heaviest emphasis on symptoms and diagnoses, the second-order emphasis for the TAT interpretations appears to be about equally divided among "affects; feelings; emotions" (13 per cent); "personality defenses and mechanisms" (12 per cent); and "interpersonal and object relations" (12 per cent). In the last named category, emphasis is laid largely on the child-parent relationships and interactions (9 per cent). To a certain extent the same pattern occurs in the supplementary test reports, although variation among the individual test interpreters is apparent. It seems possible that this pattern represents a general psychological bias as to what information is most useful in test reports or as to what information the tests are best able to report about.

The third most heavily weighted areas concern the areas of "sexual thought and behavior" (9 per cent) and "outlooks; attitudes; beliefs" (8 per cent). Beyond this point, the percentages are too small to permit meaningful differentiating statements to be made. The same situation exists in respect to the individual percentages for each contributor.

The interested reader may wish to examine Table II for the relative areas of concentration of the individual contributors. While a sample of one case does not permit clear-cut conclusions, it does permit the formulation of interesting hypotheses as to the reasons for the different types of information elicited by the different interpretive techniques.

A qualitative examination of the reports with a view to discerning their agreement with one another and, more importantly, their agreement with the behavioral data, was made. All that was done was what any reader of this volume can do; i.e., we read all the material and came to some general conclusions. Our over-all impression was that the reports show a high degree of correspondence with one another in their description of John Doe and that they correlate quite well with the behavioral data. The "summary impression" paragraphs for each of the eighteen areas of interpretation in Table I represent our composite summaries of all the statements made about John Doe in each of these categories. They are, in effect, the modal views of John Doe in terms of the topics by which he was delineated.

No attempt will be made to present either the exact extents of agreement or disagreement of the test interpretations with each other or their exact relationships with the behavioral data. A statistical treatment of the results is beyond the scope of the present volume, which is primarily that of presenting an integrated set of descriptive data.[4]

[4] The richness of the clinical data contained in this volume and the responsibilities for rigorous statistical inquiry are recognized by the authors. Although a full-scale statistical treatment of the data does not fit in with the purposes of this book and is thus not presented herein, it is important to state that statistical treatment of these data, using as the primary method of analysis the inverted factor technique (Q-technique) devised by W. S. Stephenson [53], is being prepared for separate publication. This will involve judgments by the TAT contributors and the supplementary test contributors made on the basis of test data only; judgments by eminent psychotherapists made on the basis of behavioral data only; and judgments by eminent academic psychologists and bright paranoid schizophrenics made on the basis of either test data or behavioral data.

# Chapter 31

# SUMMARY

THIS FINAL chapter consists of a summary of what we have done (as presented in this volume) and some of our general reactions to the combined efforts of all the contributors.

This book presents the results of a research which was primarily an investigation of two psychological tests, the Thematic Apperception Test (TAT) and the Make A Picture Story (MAPS) test. (Other tests were also included in the study: the Rorschach test, the Wechsler-Bellevue Scale, the Bender-Gestalt figures, the Draw A Person test, and the Minnesota Multiphasic Personality Inventory.) The procedure was to send the verbatim TAT and MAPS test stories for one person, called John Doe, to each clinical psychologist who had published, in the psychological literature, his own method for interpreting the TAT. We asked each thematic test expert to interpret John Doe's TAT and MAPS test records for us. We also asked him to submit his working notes and procedures as well as his final write-up. The only information given these experts about John Doe was that he was male, age 25, and single. Fifteen of the TAT experts so contacted responded with sixteen "blind" interpretations of John Doe's TAT and MAPS test protocols. Thus we had a thematic test roundtable on this one case. The TAT contributors were Magda Arnold, Betty Aron, Leopold Bellak, Leonard Eron, Reuben Fine, Arthur Hartman, Robert R. Holt, Walther Joel and David Shapiro, Seymour Klebanoff, Sheldon Korchin, Jose Lasaga, Julian Rotter and Shirley Jessor, Helen Sargent, Percival Symonds, and Ralph K. White.

Five other psychological tests, supplementary to this study, were submitted for interpretation, each to one expert. These test protocols and test interpretations also appear in this volume. The tests, and the interpreter for each, are: Rorschach test, Bruno Klopfer; Bender-Gestalt, Max Hutt; Draw-A-Person, Karen Machover; Wechsler-Bellevue Scale, Helen Kitzinger; and Minnesota Multiphasic Personality Inventory, Harry Grayson.

Although the TAT and supplementary test interpreters knew only John Doe's sex (male), age (25), and marital status (single),[1] genuine behavioral data were present. These behavioral data are presented in this volume for the reader to see what the "facts" about John Doe are. The behavioral data are about a real person—only minor changes have been made to maintain his anonymity

[1] Plus amount of formal education, included on the MAPS Figure Location Sheet; plus additional information in two instances previously noted.

and contain the following sections: (a) an abstract of John Doe's case history, compiled at the neuropsychiatric hospital where he was a patient by the psychiatrist in charge of his case; (b) notes from John Doe's "Clinical Folder" at the neuropsychiatric hospital, including the notations of the ward psychiatrists, consultant psychiatrists, and nurses; (c) notes from the psychotherapy sessions given to John Doe by a psychiatrist at the neuropsychiatric hospital; (d) notes from the psychotherapy sessions given to John Doe by a psychiatric social worker therapist at the out-patient mental hygiene clinic, where he went after his discharge from the hospital; and (e) the report of a psychiatric follow-up interview held with John Doe by the chief psychiatrist of the mental hygiene clinic approximately two and one-half years after all the preceding.

The TAT interpreters were also asked to compare, in any way they wished, the TAT and the MAPS test, with particular reference to the applicability of their method of handling the TAT to the MAPS test. The data from the comparison of the two tests, reported in Chapter 29, indicated that, according to the comments of thirteen of the sixteen contributors, their methods, although originally designed for use with the TAT, are applicable directly or with slight modification to the MAPS test, although the desirability of norms was stressed by some. A number of similarities between both tests were pointed out: both are apperceptive tests, the major clinical findings agree, and the personality structure revealed by both is very similar. The most generally agreed upon difference in the test materials is the greater structuredness in the stimulus material of the TAT. The effect of the difference in the degree of structuredness is described by some as the production of more realistic material with the TAT and more fantasy-like material with the MAPS test. Others find a difference in the kind or level of the fantasy produced. No general agreement exists as to whether the TAT or the MAPS test taps "deeper" personality levels. Advantages and disadvantages of either test were mentioned by a number of contributors. The need for investigating these questions experimentally was indicated.

The sixteen TAT contributions were subjected to *a priori* analysis and are discussed (in Chapter 30) in terms of our regrouping of them under purposes, elements of analysis, work procedures, and main emphases. These four modes of approaching TAT interpretations were further outlined as follows:

I. Purposes. The primary purpose of a method is either clinical (Arnold, Bellak, Holt, Lasaga, Rotter, Symonds), or research (Aron, Cox-Sargent, Klebanoff), or both (Eron, Fine, Hartman, Joel and Shapiro, Korchin, Sargent, White).

II. Elements of Analysis. These elements were divided into either aspects of the story, such as length, vocabulary, content, etc., or aspects of the characters, such as feelings, motivations, attitudes, psychological defenses, etc.

The various TAT interpreters emphasizing these different aspects were identified.

III. Work Procedures. The various initial steps of analysis and interpretation, such as reading and rereading, making synopses, using scoring systems or check lists, etc., and the various subsequent steps, such as restatement, analysis on different "levels," examination of the character interaction, using profiles or psychograms, etc., were indicated and the proponents of each were enumerated.

IV. Main Emphasis. A comprehensive outline of TAT methods was suggested to include the following (overlapping) categories:

(a) *Normative;* tabular; research. (Primarily Cox-Sargent, Eron, Hartman, Klebanoff; secondarily Rotter, Sargent.)

(b) *Hero-oriented;* need-press; story character analysis. (Primarily Aron, Fine, Korchin, Sargent; secondarily Arnold, Bellak, Cox-Sargent, Eron, Klebanoff, Lasaga, Symonds, White.)

(c) *Intuitive;* psychoanalytic; clinical. (Primarily Bellak, Holt, Lasaga, Rotter, Symonds.)

(d) *Interpersonal;* psychodramatic. (Primarily Arnold, Joel and Shapiro, White.)

(e) *Perceptual;* distortions of story, language, thought, or stimulus material. (Secondarily Bellak, Eron, Fine, Hartman, Holt, Lasaga, Rotter, Sargent.)

Although this volume presents primarily the qualitative aspects of the test interpretation data, some tabulations (basic to the future statistical treatment of the results) are presented. The sixteen TAT interpretations, which ranged in length from four typewritten pages to over forty typewritten pages, were reduced to separate, discrete items of personality description. This process yielded 802 distinct items of personality description. Each of these 802 items was subsumed under one of eighteen categories in a "TAT Interpretation Areas Outline," which was developed for this purpose. The largest percentages of items were in the categories of (a) symptoms, diagnoses, and etiology, 15 per cent; (b) personality defenses and personality mechanisms, 12 per cent; (c) affects, feelings, and emotions, 13 per cent; (d) interpersonal and object relations, especially relationships with parents, 12 per cent; and (e) attitudes, outlooks, and beliefs, 8 per cent. An over-all summary statement of the personality description items deduced from all the TAT interpretations was made for each of the eighteen report areas.

The plans for the future statistical treatment of the data were mentioned. These plans include the use of Stephenson's technique of inverse factor analysis (Q-technique) in our effort to determine some of the fundamental factors which are operative in the analysis of thematic tests.

Some sort of reaction to all this effort is now perhaps permissible. What are, in retrospect, the main impressions from the various contributions to this clinical roundtable on John Doe? After viewing all the parts of the data—the sixteen "blind" interpretations of the TAT, the five separate supplementary test interpretations, the behavioral data, the psychiatric follow-up, and the compilation of results—singly and in relation to each other, we feel that there are at least two rather striking impressions that merit elaboration:

(1) In the first place, the amount of agreement of the TAT and supplementary test interpreters with each other, and, more importantly, with the behavioral data seems to be remarkable. Although this is primarily a qualitative impression based largely on simply reading the reports (to be checked by the statistical treatment of the data), the general impression is that most of the interpretive arrows were not only on the correct target but many were even near the bullseye. Perusal of the test interpretations and then the behavioral data seems to demonstrate that undeniably there is something to the clinical interpretation of projective test results. What that "something" is, how it works, how it is developed, and how it can be fostered are all questions to be answered in the future, but—and this is the heartening part for clinical psychologists—the several contributions to the single case of John Doe seem to have demonstrated its existence.

(2) The other outstanding impression is an equally favorable one: it is the spirit of scientific research evidenced in the willingness of the many workers in this field to participate in this study. This was more than a gracious giving of excellent effort and valuable time; it was the courage to stand up and be counted—a willingness to take a position, right or wrong, and to run the risk of public scrutiny. One of the contributors expressed this sentiment to us in this manner:

> "You, no doubt, are getting a great deal of insight out of the varied interpretations of the same set of stories, and for us, the interpreters, the results will no doubt be an occasion for considerable heart-searching. However, an effort such as this is necessary if we are going to have any assurance that what we do is any more than produce projective material ourselves. And while I cannot help but hope that I may not be too far wrong in my interpretations, I hope that as a scientist I shall have enough humility to admit it if I am."

One cannot but conclude that so long as these spirits of objective inquiry and personal humility prevail, the future development of clinical psychology —science and service—is secure.

# BIBLIOGRAPHY


1. ARNOLD, MAGDA B., A Demonstration Analysis of the Thematic Apperception Test in a Clinical Setting, *Journal of Abnormal and Social Psychology*, 1949, *44*, 97–111.
2. ARON, BETTY, *A Manual for Analysis of the Thematic Apperception Test*. Berkeley, California: Willis E. Berg, 1949.
3. ———, The Thematic Apperception Test in the Study of Prejudiced and Unprejudiced Individuals—in ADORNO, T., FRENKEL-BRUNSWIK, E., LEVINSON, D. J., AND SANFORD, R. N., *The Authoritarian Personality*. New York: Harpers, 1950.
4. BACH, GEORGE R., Dramatic Play Therapy with Adult Groups, *Journal of Psychology*, 1950, *29*, 225–246.
5. BELL, JOHN E., *Projective Techniques*. New York: Longmans, Green and Company, 1948.
6. BELLAK, LEOPOLD, The Concept of Projection; an Experimental Investigation and Study of the Concept, *Psychiatry*, 1944, *7*, 353–370.
7. ———, *A Guide to the Interpretation of the Thematic Apperception Test*. New York: Psychological Corporation, 1948.
8. ———, *Bellak TAT Blank: for Recording and Analyzing Thematic Apperception Test Stories*. New York: Psychological Corporation, 1947.
9. ———, The Clinical Use of the Thematic Apperception Test—in ABT, L., AND BELLAK, L. (eds.) *Projective Psychology*. New York: Knopf and Company, 1950.
10. CONANT, JAMES C., A Comparison of Thematic Fantasy Among Normals, Neurotics, and Schizophrenics. Unpublished Ph.D. Dissertation, University of Southern California, 1950.
11. COX, BEVERLY, AND SARGENT, HELEN, TAT Responses of Emotionally Disturbed and Emotionally Stable Children: Clinical Judgment versus Normative Data, *Journal of Projective Techniques*, 1950, *14*, 61–74.
12. ERON, LEONARD D., Frequencies of Themes and Identifications in the Stories of Schizophrenic Patients and Non-hospitalized College Students, *Journal of Consulting Psychology*, 1948, *12*, 387–395.
13. ———, AND HAKE, D. T., Psychometric Approach to the Evaluation of the Thematic Apperception Test—in ZUBIN, J., AND YOUNG, K. M., *Manual of Projective Techniques*. Madison: College Typing Company, 1948.
14. ———, A Normative Study of the Thematic Apperception Test, *Psychological Monographs*, 1950, *64*, No. 11.
15. ———, TERRY, D., AND CALLAHAN, R., The Use of Rating Scales for Emotional Tone of Thematic Apperception Test Stories, *Journal of Consulting Psychology*, 1950, *14*, 473–478.
16. FANTEL, ERNEST, AND SHNEIDMAN, EDWIN S., Psychodrama and the MAPS Test, *Rorschach Research Exchange and Journal of Projective Techniques*, 1947, *11*, 42–67.
17. ———, Report on Psychodramatic Therapy, *Group Psychotherapy*, 1950, *3*, 55–58.
18. FARBEROW, NORMAN, Personality Patterns of Suicidal Mental Hospital Patients, *Genetic Psychology Monographs*, 1950, *42*, 3–79.
19. FINE, REUBEN, The Personality of the Asthmatic Child. Unpublished Ph.D. Dissertation, University of Southern California, 1948.
20. ———, *Manual for Scoring Scheme for Verbal Projective Techniques (TAT, MAPS, Stories and the Like)*. Washington, D. C.: Veterans Administration, 1948. Mimeographed.

21. GOLDENBERG, HERBERT C., A Resume of Some Make-A-Picture-Story (MAPS) Test Results, *Journal of Projective Techniques*, 1951, *15*, 79–86.
22. GRAYSON, HARRY M., *Psychological Admissions Testing Program and Manual*. Los Angeles: V. A. Center, Neuropsychiatric Hospital, 1950. Pp. 19–26.
23. GUETZKOW, HAROLD, Unitizing and Categorizing Problems in Coding Qualitative Data, *Journal of Clinical Psychology*, 1950, *6*, 47–58.
24. HARTMAN, ARTHUR, An Experimental Examination of the Thematic Apperception Technique in Clinical Diagnosis, *Psychological Monographs*, 1949, *63*, 1–48.
25. HOLT, ROBERT R. (ed.), *The TAT Newsletter*. Topeka, Kansas: Menninger Foundation. Vol. *1*, No. 1, October 1946, through Vol. *2*, No. 4, June 1949. Mimeographed.
26. ——— (ed.), The TAT Newsletter, in *Rorschach Research Exchange and Journal of Projective Techniques*, 1949, *13*, No. 2, et seq.
27. ———, The Thematic Apperception Test—in ANDERSON, H., AND ANDERSON, G., *Introduction to Projective Techniques*. New York: Prentice Hall, 1951.
28. HUTT, MAX L., The Use of Projective Techniques of Personality Measurement in Army Medical Installations, *Journal of Clinical Psychology*, 1945, *1*, 134–140.
29. JOEL, WALTHER, The Use of the Make A Picture Story (MAPS) Test with Disturbed Adolescents, *Rorschach Research Exchange and Journal of Projective Techniques*, 1948, *12*, 1–10.
30. ———, AND SHAPIRO, DAVID, A Genotypical Approach to the Analysis of Personal Interaction, *Journal of Psychology*, 1949, *28*, 9–17.
31. ———, The Interpersonal Equation in Projective Methods, *Rorschach Research Exchange and Journal of Projective Techniques*, 1949, *13*, 479–482.
32. KITZINGER, HELEN, AND BLUMBERG, EUGENE, Supplementary Guide for Administering and Scoring the Wechsler-Bellevue Intelligence Scale (Form I), *Psychological Monographs*, 1951, *65*, 1–20.
33. KLEBANOFF, SEYMOUR G., Personality Factors in Symptomatic Chronic Alcoholism as Indicated by the Thematic Apperception Test, *Journal of Consulting Psychology*, 1947, *11*, 111–119.
34. KLOPFER, BRUNO, AND KELLEY, DOUGLAS G., *The Rorschach Technique*. New York: World Book Company, 1942.
35. LASAGA Y TRAVIESO, JOSE I., AND MARTINEZ-ARANGO, CARLOS, Some Suggestions Concerning the Administration and Interpretation of the Thematic Apperception Test, *Journal of Psychology*, 1946, *22*, 117–163.
36. ———, AND ———, Four Detailed Examples of How Mental Conflicts of Psychoneurotic and Psychotic Patients May be Discovered by Means of the Thematic Apperception Test, *Journal of Psychology*, 1948, *26*, 299–345.
37. MACHOVER, KAREN, *Personality Projection in the Drawing of the Human Figure*. Springfield: C. C. Thomas, 1949.
38. MAYMAN, MARTIN, Review of the Literature on the Thematic Apperception Test—in RAPAPORT, DAVID, *Diagnostic Psychological Testing*. Chicago: The Year Book Publishers, 1946. Volume II.
39. MURRAY, HENRY A., *Explorations in Personality*. New York: Oxford University Press, 1938.
40. ———, *Thematic Apperception Test Manual*. Cambridge: Harvard University Press, 1943.
41. RAPAPORT, DAVID, *Diagnostic Psychological Testing*. Chicago: The Year Book Publishers, 1946. Volume II.
42. RITTER, A. M., AND ERON, LEONARD D., The Use of the Thematic Apperception Test

to Differentiate Normal from Abnormal Groups, *Journal of Abnormal and Social Psychology* (in press).

43. ROTTER, JULIAN B., Studies in the Use and Validity of the Thematic Apperception Test with Mentally Disordered Patients. I. Methods of Analysis and Clinical Problems, *Character and Personality*, 1940, *9*, 18–34.
44. ———, Thematic Apperception Tests: Suggestions for Administration and Interpretation, *Journal of Personality*, 1946, *15*, 70–92.
45. SARGENT, HELEN, An Experimental Application of Projective Principles to a Paper and Pencil Personality Test, *Psychological Monographs*, 1944, *57*, No. 265, 1–57.
46. ———, Projective Techniques: Their Origins, Theory and Application in Personality Research, *Psychological Bulletin*, 1945, *5*, 257–293.
47. ———, *The Insight Test.* Manual for Administration and Scoring. (To be published).
48. SHAPIRO, DAVID, A Study of the Influence of the Social Field on Individual Behavior, *Genetic Psychology Monographs*, 1950, *42*, 161–230.
49. SHNEIDMAN, EDWIN S., Schizophrenia and the MAPS Test, *Genetic Psychology Monographs*, 1948, *38*, 145–223.
50. ———, *The Make A Picture Story Test.* New York: The Psychological Corporation, 1949.
51. ———, Some Comparisons Among the Four Picture Test, Thematic Apperception Test, and Make A Picture Story Test, *Rorschach Research Exchange and Journal of Projective Techniques*, 1949, *13*, 150–154.
52. ———, A MAPS Test Manual, *Projective Techniques Monographs*, 1951, *1*, No. 2 (in press).
53. STEPHENSON, WILLIAM, Statistical Approach to Typology: The Study of Trait Universes, *Journal of Clinical Psychology*, 1950, *6*, 26–38.
54. SYMONDS, PERCIVAL M., Criteria for the Selection of Pictures for the Investigation of Adolescent Phantasies, *Journal of Abnormal and Social Psychology*, 1939, *34*, 271–274.
55. ———, *Symonds Picture-Story Test.* New York: Bureau of Publications, Teachers College, Columbia University, 1948. 20 plates; manual (20 pp.)
56. ———, *Adolescent Fantasy.* New York: Columbia University Press, 1949.
57. TOMKINS, SILVAN S., (with the collaboration of Elizabeth J. Tomkins). *The Thematic Apperception Test: the Theory and Technique of Interpretation.* New York: Grune & Stratton, 1947.
58. WALKER, ROBERT G., A Comparison of Clinical Manifestations of Hostility with Rorschach and MAPS Test Performances. Unpublished Ph.D. Dissertation, University of Southern California, 1950.
59. WHITE, RALPH K., Value-Analysis: A Quantitative Method for Describing Qualitative Data, *Journal of Social Psychology*, 1944, *19*, 351–358.
60. ———, Black Boy: A Value-Analysis, *Journal of Abnormal and Social Psychology*, 1947, *42*, 440–461.
61. ———, Verbal Data and "Self Evident" Values, *Personality—Symposium No. 1*, 1950, 35–44.
62. ———, *Value Analysis: The Nature and Use of the Method.* New York: Society for the Psychological Study of Social Issues, 1951.
63. WHITE, ROBERT W., Interpretation of Imaginative Productions—in HUNT, J. McV. (ed.), *Personality and the Behavior Disorders.* New York: Ronald Press Company, 1944. Volume I, pp. 214–251.

# NAME INDEX

(Page numbers in *italics* indicate content written by an individual; other page numbers indicate references to an individual.)

# SUBJECT INDEX

Printed in Dunstable, United Kingdom

7892227c-0f46-4a2c-98f9-b5cee1581e11R01